GIRL GANGS, BIKER BOYS, AND REAL COOL CATS

GIRL GANGS, BIKER BOYS,

CONTRIBUTORS:

ROBERT BAKER

JOE BLEVINS

JAMES COCKINGTON

BRIAN COFFEY

JAMES DOIG

DAVID JAMES FOSTER

MATTHEW ASPREY GEAR

MOLLY GRATTAN

BRIAN GREENE

JOHN HARRISON

STEWART HOME

DAVE KIERSH

IAIN McINTYRE

AUSTIN MATTHEWS

ANDREW NETTE

J. F. NORRIS

BILL OSGERBY

DAVID RIFE

MIKE STAX

NICOLAS TREDELL

ALWYN W. TURNER

CLINTON WALKER

AND REAL COOL CATS

Pulp Fiction and Youth Culture, 1950 to 1980

edited by

IAIN McINTYRE

and

ANDREW NETTE

with a foreword by

PETER DOYLE

In memory of Graeme Flanagan

Girl Gangs, Biker Boys, and Real Cool Cats: Pulp Fiction and Youth Culture, 1950 to 1980
Edited by Iain McIntyre and Andrew Nette

PM Press
PO Box 23912
Oakland, CA 94623
www.pmpress.org

Cover design by Steve Connell/Transgraphic Services and John Yates | www.stealworks.com
Design and layout by Steve Connell/Transgraphic Services
Indexing by Simon Strong

ISBN: 978-1-62963-438-8
Library of Congress Control Number: 2017942910

10 9 8 7 6 5 4 3 2 1

Printed in the USA by the Employee Owners of Thomson-Shore in Dexter, Michigan.
www.thomsonshore.com

CONTENTS

FOREWORD
Through Beatnik Eyes

Consider the masses of stuff, quickly and cheaply written, drawn, edited, laid out, run off in printing houses, shipped, unpacked and lined up in shops and newsstands, alongside masses of stuff almost exactly the same, all of it taking part in a vast Darwinian competition to catch some punter's eye, and remove a little spare change from said punter's pocket. Some of it will be sold, maybe even in large numbers, but more often in modest numbers (which isn't too much of a problem since production costs are low) and dog-eared copies will end up in lunchrooms or barracks or dormitories, or wedged behind downpipes in factory toilets, or stacked in back sheds. Some may go straight to the dump, unread. Maybe it was put together in an atmosphere of high-minded artistic ambition, or it may have been regarded even by its own makers as junk. Regardless, the huge bulk of low-culture product will drop out of sight almost immediately. Live fast, die young, as the saying goes.

But there are some good-looking corpses. Over the past half century, maybe since the ascent of rock and roll, people have come to particularly value certain items recovered from the bogs of culture. Low-down, dirty, utterly disposable jukebox music from half a century ago is in much greater circulation and held in infinitely higher esteem now than it ever was then. Mid-20th-century book and magazine art, in its day often regarded as slightly shameful, even crypto-pornographic, is highly prized and traded, and continues to inform both contemporary high art and everyday design. B-grade film and various forms of extreme kitsch from the past continue to come to the notice of the alert retro hawks and are carefully fed back into the cultural mainstreams.

Low paperback fiction has seen one of the most successful rehabilitation jobs. *Some* material which in its day received little notice from cultural gatekeepers and commentators has steadily worked its way up the prestige ladder. Crime fiction of the early to mid 20th century is the obvious case, and since Quentin Tarantino borrowed the term 'pulp fiction' everyone, even your high school English teacher, pretty well gets the principle that gems may come from trash. There are no prizes to be won by declaring now that last century's pulp—crime, supernatural, science fiction, romance, cheesecake and fantasy—sometimes turns out to be amazingly awesome.

The pleasures of pulp are complex and contradictory. If you start digging you *might* find unexpected literary finesse—plenty of people who later graduated to high—or middle-brow respectability paid the bills back then by writing serviceable pulps. And there were plenty who never graduated, but whose work ranks high on modern literary criteria: balance, flow, economy, freshness of image and language. Natural writerly grace and all that stuff.

You might find earlier versions of the punk aesthetic—the textual equivalent of harder, faster, louder, badder and crazier. Pulp regularly managed to be way more out there, because no one was paying all that much attention. There wasn't time to sand down the sharp edges. And that was trash lit's natural default territory: out there.

Or you might find laid bare the mostly unspoken fears, desires, dreams and nightmares of the time. Doubly, trebly so when it comes to sex and sexuality. Pulp as cultural Freudian slip, loony bulletins from the collective id. Maybe not so loony.

Or you might say to hell with that and just go with the flow, enjoying pulp for its couldn't-give-that-much-of-a-shit attitude. There's deep dark perverse mad, and then there's fun, bracing, energizing mad. There's the sort of mad that the author or artist is complicit in, and there's the naive unselfconscious, weird, obsessive, maybe on-the-spectrum, medication-all-wrong mad, the kind the artist denies, disavows, or else seems to be entirely unaware of.

Anyway, let's agree, pulp is good. Or can be. And it seems so far to have proven inexhaustible. New titles and genres no one much knew about keep turning up. Old paperbacks are offered for sale on eBay. Hitherto unknown gems and minor treasures keep surfacing in hip reprints.

But that doesn't happen by accident. The word 'curator' gets a lot of bogus circulation these days, often used to glorify some chancer who happens to glance at a bit of culture for longer than a nanosecond or happens to post a comment somewhere. It also connotes the bow-tie-wearing professional arts ponce, smugly appropriating the culture which until just last week they were way too good for. Once it's

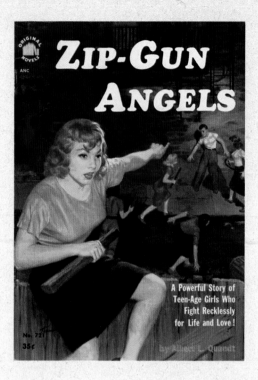

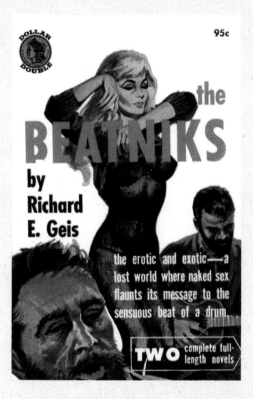

Zip-Gun Angels (Original Novels, 1952)
The Beatniks (Dollar Book Company, 1962)

cool, they want a piece. A big piece. In fact, they want to take it over.

But the fakes are forever obliged to wait until the moment is right, when *all* the dogs are barking, when they can sense that there's a strategic advantage in getting on board. They're best at bestowing the mantle of respectability on nice, clean, fully appraised and certified, thoroughly rehabilitated, parlour-ready trash. They're never going to unearth anything new.

And to be fair, it's not that easy to spot the diamonds in the rough. Most of us need a gentle eye-opening pointer now and then in order to see the value. And some of the time the 'value' is really just a surfeit of pure, exemplary, transcendent crappiness. The Ed Wood Jr. factor. (Ed Wood, we shouldn't be surprised to learn, is to be found in this book with a piece of ageless über-schlock, *Devil Girls*). It takes a lot of work and a lot of time spent combing through junk shops, flea markets or the stacks of public library stacks. It's gruelling. You can find yourself soon hating everything. It's called trash for a reason. More scarily, a kind of rapture of the deep can set in, and you start loving everything. Finding virtue *everywhere*.

Doing the footwork, spotting and coming to terms with the stuff is hard graft. The authors of this volume have paid their dues. They've haunted the junk shops and flea markets, combed through the ratty cardboard boxes, smelled the mildew, inhaled the dust. They've turned a fresh and fearless eye to the unambiguously collectible, blue-ribbon 50s and 60s pulps, and then turned that same awareness to later material, from the 1970s, and have identified a surprisingly durable pulp tradition, which we can refer to as 'tribe pulp', a tradition which to my knowledge hasn't been really named till now, certainly not as clearly and cogently as here.

It's an old story now that successions of youth subcultures, each more bad-mannered and unruly than the one before, provided one of the most durable panic refrains of postwar public life in the west. Ad hoc alliances of tabloid journalists, social workers and media commentators eagerly identified and sensationalised each emerging type. In the late 1940s, early 1950s it was juvenile delinquents, of course. Then came beatniks. And bikers. Gays and lesbians. Hard-dope fiends. Later on, hippies and countercultural types, mods, rockers, surfers, skinheads, youthful revolutionaries. Trippers, potheads and ravers. Rock musicians and groupies. Nearly always the subculture was characterised as a kind of cultish, freemason-like quasi-conspiracy or secret society. The tabloid exposés were sometimes written in a bogus ethnographic style, by pipe-smoking, civilised blokes in horn-rimmed glasses, who maybe listened to Dave Brubeck in their own time, turning a not so friendly eye to the newest weird *other* to appear on the cultural landscape. Often the group in question was represented in faux anthropological terms as a kind of tribe, obviously. With secret rituals, which most likely involved something sexy and forbidden.

So, that's a promising set of circumstances for the low-end fiction factories of the day: there's anxiety (*shallow* anxiety, probably, but still . . .) mixed with genuine curiosity, mixed with sexual frisson. With an element of secrecy. The cheap paperback industry knew how to come up with appropriate product.

Tribe pulps in the 1950s typically depicted the *other*. The people on the train to work who read about lesbians or artists or ghetto dope fiends mostly weren't themselves of those groups, and the separation of domains was core to the cheap kicks that the books delivered. But during the golden age of tribe pulps, the tribes themselves went from being strange often relatively remote 'movements' to global mass cultures. By the early 1970s the countercultures were changing the entire moral configuration of western society.

It's easy to picture the old-school, 1950s and 60s–era type of pulp writer: a World War Two veteran, maybe, or a middle-aged literary lady, or a journalist or low-on-the-totem pole copy writer or schoolteacher, chasing a few extra bucks, turning their gaze to some upstart, déclassé youth craze or other. No surprise if their default position was one of disdain or prurient but shallow curiosity. But by the 1970s that same pulp author might actually *be* a pot smoker or tripper, or a surfer or a hippie. Maybe of non-mainstream sexual orientation, and not interested in keeping that a secret. Or a New Left–sympathising, anti–law and order, pro–social change person. Or a gun-toting survivalist. Or a professional hack strung out on Benzedrine. While that might help the authenticity, it could compromise the prurience and lofty disdain.

The result is a mixed-up, deeply ambiguous, sometimes complex, dare I say nuanced, body of work. The players, both the authors and their fictional characters often defy easy categorisation. And what happens when a piece of plainly inauthentic fiction ends up being widely read by and influencing the very subculture it so spuriously depicts? And what happens when publishers, realising that the market has shifted, start

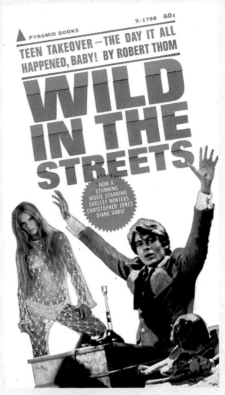

Wild in the Streets (Pyramid Books, 1968)
The Wow Factor (Gold Medal, 1970)

blending genres? What's not to like in principle about a surfer private-eye yarn, or a stoner spy?

So the attention in the essays herein moves easily from plot to characterization, to author biography, to company history, to the eternal verities of scabrous and crapulent publishing, to shrewd rumination about the morphing of genre, to light-touch reflection about the lurching social change of which these very pulps are a minor epiphenomenon. And one of pulp's special gifts is the melding of prose and visuality: the cover art, book design qualities, the various ways of setting up blurbs and strap lines, the colour philosophies—pulps absolutely had to keep breaking new ground, design-wise, in order to simply survive, and this book offers a generous feast of visual delights.

Last thing to note: for all the insight and knowledge here, the contributors to this volume approach the Literature of the People with an admirably light touch. That's good. Okay, over to you. Dig it, cats.

PETER DOYLE

The War Babies (Bantam, 1968)
Tex (Fontana, 1981)

SAVAGE STREETS AND SECRET SWINGERS
The Longed-for World of Pulp Fiction and Youth Culture

Girl Gangs, Biker Boys, and Real Cool Cats chronicles three decades of public anxiety, fear and fascination in the United States, Britain and Australia around the concept of out-of-control youth, and the rapacious genius of pulp publishers in exploiting it to sell books. The period examined is the 1950s to the end of the 70s, a time in which the postwar boom in mass-market paperbacks collided with rising concerns about the impact of growing economic affluence, rapidly shifting social mores and urbanisation, particularly on the young.

Delinquent youth gangs, beatniks, hippies—every attempt by young people to celebrate their youth—resulted in hysterical tabloid headlines that fed popular fears and fascinations, all eagerly mined by the purveyors of youthsploitation fiction and fed back to the masses in cheap paperback form. This continued until the mid 70s, when pulp publishing began to wane, the victim of loosening censorship laws and changes in consumption that saw pulp replaced by film and television as the main vehicles of adult escapism for the masses.

Only recently has the mass-market pulp novel acquired the status of ersatz art object and sought after retro collectible. Originally designed as a cheap form of disposable entertainment, pulp paperbacks were shipped in the millions to members of the armed forces during World War Two. These servicemen and women returned home after the end of hostilities wanting more.

The newfound fascination with the outré nature of pulp relates mainly to their covers. Designed to help them stand out among their competitors on newsstands, the lurid painted covers of the 1950s and early 60s and the fly-on-the-wall photographs that began to replace them from the mid-60s onwards, certainly make the books marvellous cultural artefacts.

But the covers are only one aspect. As Susan Stryker writes in her book, *Queer Pulp: Perverted Passions from the Golden Age of the Paperback* (2001), pulp fiction "functioned as a vast cultural unconscious. Deposited there were fantasies of fulfilment as well as desperate yearnings, petty betrayals, unrequited passions, and unreasoning violence that troubled the margins of the longed-for world."

The emotions aroused in mainstream society by youth subcultures have always been varied and contradictory. So it was in the years after World War Two. Age-old fears about the reckless energy of the young, the potential threat they posed to adult authority, structures and traditions, as well as physical life and limb, went into overdrive as the post war economic boom delivered young people an unprecedented level of disposable income and mobility.

Of course, lingering under the surface of the impulse to control the young was an intense curiosity about their activities. Pulp allowed readers to indulge this, if only for 150 or so pages. It allowed the average working stiff to smoke reefer in an after-hours jazz club, take part in an LSD-fuelled love-in, or wield a bike chain with fiendish abandon in a Benzedrine-soaked back alley gang rumble.

Pulp fiction, as with much of 1950s society in these three countries, was, officially at least, very much a white man's world. This applied to those doing the writing as well as the visions of society they projected. Depictions of anyone outside of the mythical mainstream, be it by choice or by birth, tended towards the stereotypical and negative. Female characters ran usually to type in echoing the goddess/whore dichotomy, with the occasional man-eating psycho or vicious girl gang thrown in as a terrifying yet titillating alternative. The level of sexual violence sometimes meted out in novels can be disturbing to the modern reader.

Within this framework a handful of writers, including those from diverse backgrounds, peppered their work with liberal and subversive themes. Some pulp novels, most particularly those dealing with lesbian and gay themes, also provided a rare lifeline for women and men lacking any other connection to seemingly distant alternatives and enclaves. During the 1960s and 1970s much pulp fiction would retain its conservative nature, but the radical changes wrought by the period opened the field to themes and authors that had previously been largely excluded.

Most of the authors covered in this book started writing pulp to make a dollar. Many had ambitions to transition to more commercially successful literary endeavours. Only a few made it. The rest either moved on to other jobs or, grudgingly or otherwise, accepted the life of a pulp hack, toiling under assumed names and taking whatever assignment was handed to them. Research mostly composed of the latest tabloid newspaper story or a conversation in the writer's local bar. Even so, much of their work is infused with a rough, undeniable cultural authenticity. They had to write so fast to pay the rent, feed families or finance less wholesome needs, that they threw every experience, the chunks of daily reality often missed by more mainstream literary writing, into their work.

Some of the writers had a genuine connection to the youth subcultures they wrote about. Harlan Ellison changed his name and joined the Brooklyn gang, 'The Barons', even supposedly acting as their war counsellor for a period, to research his 1958 novel, *Rumble* (re-released in 2008 as *Web of the City*). Hal Ellson worked as a recreational therapist in a New York City hospital in the 1950s, where he had daily contact with the disturbed adolescents that would feature in many of his novels. Malcolm Braly, who wrote perhaps the best pulp novel dealing with the early-60s American West Coast beat scene, *Shake Him Till He Rattles* (1963), spent 17 of his first 40 years in jail and had firsthand experience of the criminal milieu, policing and drug scene. Sharon Rudahl's erotic tale *Acid Temple Ball* (1969) is keenly informed by her participation in the counterculture of the late 60s.

This book doesn't provide a detailed historical overview of youth subcultures in the United States, Britain and Australia in the three decades after World War Two. Indeed, terms like 'movement' or 'subculture' are used more as convenient shorthand than to suggest the existence of any cohesive and articulate forces. Youth culture, then as now, is a complex road map of attitudes and rituals, appropriated and interpreted from numerous sources and cross-referenced by factors such as class, race and gender.

That said, since this book is divided into seven roughly chronological sections, a brief overview of some of the key youth subcultures touched on in each will be useful in helping the reader to navigate it.

In the beginning were the juvenile delinquents or 'JDs'. These teenage American gangs emerged from impoverished urban areas to engage in initiation rites and wage territorial battles before joining the military, settling into adult responsibilities or moving on to serious crime. Initially localised in style, male JDs came to be stereotyped as leather jacket-wearing rock-and-rollers with slicked-back hair, often combed into a 'duck's ass' at the back. Irving Shulman's gritty 1947 novel *The Amboy Dukes* was among the earliest postwar pulp novels to showcase this emerging subculture and opened the floodgates for a torrent of pulp about the heavily sensationalised misdeeds of youth gangs. These books influenced and were in turn inspired by public concerns about escalating juvenile delinquency, a mood graphically captured by the 1955 non-fiction bestseller, *1,000,000 Delinquents*, which declared rising juvenile crime a national epidemic that threatened the preservation of the American way of life. As an aside, *1,000,000 Delinquents* was also an early example of another rich subgenre of pulp that would feed off youth for the next three decades, but which this book does not deal with, the heavily sensationalist 'investigation' of pressing social issues dressed up as hard-hitting non-fiction sociological inquiry.

Youth delinquency was also the subject of major debate in 50s Britain and Australia. In Britain, the major focus of attention was teddy boys or 'teds'. Teddy boys originated in London in the 50s and were distinguished, as were so many youth tribes, by their fashion aesthetic, wearing clothing similar to that favoured by dandies during the Edwardian period, mixed with a dash of style taken from American zoot suit gangs and, later, rock-and-rollers. Gangs of teddy boys engaged in violent, sometimes racially motivated clashes throughout the 50s, as depicted in numerous books, including Ernest Ryman's *Teddy Boy* (1958).

The Australian variant, known as 'bodgies', from the local slang for something fake or of poor quality, aroused similar public order concerns. Based on a six-month study of 15 young men and women in Australia and New Zealand, Auckland psychologist A.E. Manning's *The Bodgie: A Study in Abnormal Psychology* (1958), typically concluded that young people who identified as bodgies and widgies were juvenile delinquents who needed psychiatric treatment.

Young females were active in juvenile delinquent gangs in all three countries. They were known as 'judies' in Britain and 'widgies' in Australia. Female delinquency provided rich pickings for pulp publishers, particularly the inference that young females' proximity to gang activities somehow imbued them with a freer sexual morality and a penchant for violence.

While juvenile delinquent gangs continued to nourish pulp fiction well into the 60s, publishers were soon on the lookout for the next big thing to move paperbacks. They found it in rise of the so-called Beat Generation in the late 1950s. The underlying sensibility of the American beats, to the degree any existed, was an artistic and jazz-fuelled rebellion against the conformity and paranoia of suburban life in 50s Cold War America. This took a back seat in most pulp to more sensationalist aspects of beat culture, especially drug use and sexual experimentation, and soon a slew of books set in coffee-houses, folk dens and art colonies emerged. As was the case with JDs, the allure of beat women, their semi-masculine dress sense and affectations combined with their supposed sexual promiscuity, was a key thematic strand of much of the beat pulp produced during this time.

As depicted in books like Colin Wilson's *Adrift in Soho* (1961), Britain's equivalents of the beats were less hedonistic and more intellectual. The description 'beat' was loosely applied in 60s Australian pulp fiction to any young person who didn't have a full time job, experimented with drugs, hung around in dimly lit espresso bars and listened to jazz. Australia also had its own genuine variation, a loose Sydney-based grouping known as the Push. The Push shared their British and American counterparts abhorrence of middle-class values, especially regarding careers and full-time paid employment, but were less oriented towards art and music and more explicitly libertarian. They opposed censorship, monogamy and formal political activism.

By the mid-60s, beat became hip and pulp was given fresh material to work with: drug use (including LSD and other psychedelic substances), free love, communal living, happenings and campus protest. Everyone was fighting the man. Everyone was high. Or so it seemed in the world of pulp hacks.

The tendrils of the hippie counterculture reached deep into the mainstream and pulp followed. Typically most presented a jaded and excessive take on social and political radicalism, but there were also genuine attempts to create countercultural private investigators (Brad Lang's Crockett series featuring a long-haired, hip detective who takes on the cases the police can't solve, is one example examined in this book) and spies (Adam Diment's character, Philip McAlpine, to name one of many).

The darker side of hippie culture became apparent in the late 60s, most clearly symbolised by the killing spree embarked on by Charles Manson and his 'Family' (of which the Tate/Libianca killings in August 1969 were only the most prominent). The capture

The Trip (Midwood, 1968)
The Teddy-Boy Mystery (Sexton Blake Library, 1955)

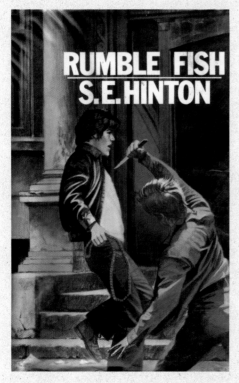

Turn Me On! (Bantam, 1972)
Rumble Fish (Gollancz, 1976)

and subsequent high-profile trial of Manson and his followers resulted in a slew of books in which members of 'straight society' were menaced by murderous hippie cults and their deranged messianic leaders.

The 1970s in Britain witnessed a fragmentation of youth culture, a process that mirrored the country's political, social and economic turbulence in the lead-up to the election of the Conservative government of Margaret Thatcher in 1979. Keen to appeal to a younger readership, Britain's foremost pulp publisher, New English Library (NEL), produced a stream of 'youthsploitation' novels, a large proportion of which were written by one man, Richard Allen. Allen was a pseudonym for James Moffat, a right-wing alcoholic pulp hack who was 48 years old in 1970, the year his first and most successful NEL title, *Skinhead*, hit the shelves featuring the exploits of a vicious thug called Joe Hawkins.

Skinheads evolved out of another working-class British youth movement, 'mods'. Short for 'modernists', so called because early proponents liked to listen to modern jazz, mods also had a taste for amphetamines, fashionable suits and motor scooters. As the subculture evolved it became increasingly associated with R&B and soul music, and by the mid-60s it had gone thoroughly mainstream, generating its own offshoots in Australia. Many of its proponents later joined the rising psychedelic scene or followed their subcultural forebears in settling down to raise a family.

The skinhead scene's roots can be found among those mods who, rejecting the frippery of the counterculture, were drawn to the musical and fashion tastes of their black neighbours, mainly smartly dressed ska and rocksteady loving West Indian 'rude boys', in the suburbs of south London during the late 60s. Maintaining the sharp style of mod, while adding the essential Doc Martens and braces, the subculture became primarily known for its trademark haircut and aggressive outlook. The fusion of white working class and black culture among early skinheads is significant given the subsequent co-option of some so-called boot boys by the racist National Front and British Movement during the 70s and 80s.

By all accounts, Moffat knew next to nothing about Britain's diffuse youth culture and did not even particularly like young people. His main research for *Skinhead* allegedly consisted of driving to London's East End, going into a pub and talking to a gang of drunken skinheads. Despite this, the book sold over a million copies and was even celebrated by many young skins as an accurate depiction of their culture. "I thought whoever wrote this book must be a skinhead himself, must be involved in football violence . . . because the way he wrote it was just like real life," a former skin told a 1996 BBC TV documentary.

Skinhead became the first of 18 NEL youthsploitation novels by Moffat. In addition to sequels featuring Hawkins, Moffat also tackled emerging subcultural trends such as 'suedeheads' (an offshoot of skinhead culture whose members grew their hair longer and dressed more suavely), female suedeheads (called 'sorts'), and 'smoothies' (skinhead types who wore their hair shoulder length and wore smart but casual clothes) as well as glam, mods and punks.

The 70s also saw US publishers try to appeal to a younger market. While traditional pulp fare continued, a new type of popular novel, the realistic teen book, also emerged. The counterculture may have been on its last legs, but in its wake open season was declared on a number of issues previously seen as taboo for young readers. Writers such as Kin Platt, Marijane Meaker, S.E. Hinton and Frank Bonham, all examined in this book, saw an opening for a new kind of novel, gritty but more character focused, which put a different slant on topics such as sex, drugs and gang violence, as well as investigating new issues, including parental neglect, poverty, unwanted pregnancies and suicide. These books were early examples of the now ubiquitous and popular subgenre of books known as 'Young Adult' fiction.

Two other groups feature in this book, both of which cut across national boundaries and the spectrum of youth tribes. The first is musicians. Wild youth has always needed a soundtrack, whether it was rock and roll for JD gangs and bodgies, jazz for the beats and bohemians, psychedelic rock for hippies or ska for skinheads. What you listened to identified your tribe, who was with you and, just as importantly, who you were against. The people who made the music were stars, be it at a local level or internationally. But there was a murkier side to their success that pulp publishers were happy to exploit: drug use, groupies, inter-band feuds and exploitation at the hands of unscrupulous agents and promoters.

The second group is motorcycle gangs. Pulp is about speed, both in the way it was written and its narrative pace and plots, and nothing is faster or more dangerous and difficult to control than young people on two wheels. Bikers in the US had various origins, one of which was the working-class teenage gangs

of the 50s who took to the road. The popularity of such motorcycle gangs grew in parallel with the phenomenal success of Stanley Kramer's The Wild One (1953), which fixed the sullen leather-clad image of Marlon Brando firmly in the mind of many a wannabe motorcycle enthusiast.

Hunter S. Thompson's 1966 book, Hell's Angels: The Strange and Terrible Saga of the Outlaw Motorcycle Gangs, not only launched his writing career but helped make biker gangs a major domestic law-and-order threat in the public's imagination. This status was further entrenched at the Altamont Free Concert in December 1969, when Hells Angels, employed as bouncers, killed an audience member. The mid-to-late-60s breed of bikers were typified by long hair, filthy clothes and chopped-out Harleys. Sharing the bacchanalian tastes of the counterculture in terms of illicit drugs and a rejection of mainstream society's mores, contemporary bikers nevertheless represented a different kind of outlaw, one that was far more criminal, misogynistic and quixotically patriotic.

Most biker-themed pulp fiction published in the US and Australia (where motorcycle gangs were known as 'bikies') followed a similar trajectory: a gang of vicious motorcycle thugs menace selected members of mainstream society, particularly females, often in a small, rural town. Carnage inevitably follows. As was the case with pulp's depiction of women in earlier subculture books, the vicious female biker gang was a key trope.

Motorcycle gangs first started in Britain in the 50s and followed a similar trajectory to the US. Known as 'rockers', 'ton-up boys' and 'leather boys' they were initially heavily influenced by US biker culture, especially in their adopted 'uniform': jeans, leather jackets, heavy boots and pompadour hairstyles. By the early to mid-60s their mortal enemies were the mods, with whom they fought a series of well-publicised beachside clashes. In the late 1960s and early 1970s the UK scene followed the US with Harley riding local chapters of the Hells Angels and Outlaws representing the new wave. Bikers became another mainstay of the books produced by NEL in the 70s. The better among these combined extreme sex and violence with a more sophisticated dystopian edge, such as outlandishly themed biker gangs engaged in occult rituals and authoritarian government crackdowns.

Not every title included in this book meets the strict definition of pulp, but we're not going to get caught up in hair-splitting. Purists will say 'pulp publishing' only applies to the cheap fiction magazines printed on low-cost groundwood paper in the 1920s and 1930s, titles like *Argosy*, *Black Mask*, *Amazing Stories* and *Dime Detective*.

The broad parameters we have applied to the novels encompassed here are that they were ephemeral, included fast writing and editing, were produced cheaply for mass-market audiences and contained sensationalist and popular themes. The transitory nature of these books can be seen in the physical nature of the product—the cheap printing, the poor binding—as well as in a literary sense, as books that for the most part have not been deemed to be part of our literary heritage (there are many problems with how mainstream critics define 'literature', but that is an argument for another day).

The definition of pulp becomes even more blurred in the context of the 60s and early 70s, a time when publishers embraced subjects relating to countercultural and radical politics, and the distinction between 'high' and 'low' culture began to fragment. Mainstream or aspiring mainstream literary writers often explored counterculture themes in their writing, but these books were generally issued by small or less prestigious publishers or in pulp paperback. This was either because no one else would touch them or because the author needed the money and thought that getting their book out by any means was better than the manuscript languishing in a drawer.

For all its faults, pulp's focus on action, immediacy and excitement makes the work of its ablest exponents captivating, not to mention fun. After all, where else but a pulp novel are you going to read about sadistic bikers getting their comeuppance by being chewed alive by sewer-dwelling alligators, or meet a surfing detective who's really a secret agent for the CIA? And while much of its treatment is negative, pulp publishing represents the principal, if not the sole, repository of fiction writing about youth subcultures—and, in the case of NEL's youthsploitation books, the only writing that was actually read by those it claimed to depict.

As previously mentioned, much of what has been published in recent decades about pulp fiction has focused on the arresting covers created by imaginative artists, often working from only a title, if any information at all. This book includes numerous examples of these while also going inside the covers to provide, via reviews, analyses, histories and interviews, insights into the text therein. *Girl Gangs, Biker Boys, and Real Cool Cats* is neither a definitive guide to the fiction of the era nor a collector's checklist of rare and valuable titles. Instead, we have sought to investigate, uncover and celebrate those novels and authors whose stories were highly influential, original or otherwise intriguing.

Many of the covers presented here are extremely rare and now hard to come by. In addition to the editors' own collections, the images in this volume were supplied by various pulp enthusiasts and paperback collectors, all of whom we are grateful to. The details listed for each cover refer to the edition pictured, which may not necessarily be the first published edition.

Some of the covers are worn, but this reflects the fact that these objects, bundles of cheaply bound coarse paper and simple card covers, were never designed to last. Yet, as the creases, stains, doodles and (sometimes multiple) price markings attest, they have lived long lives. Their condition tells the hidden story of their journey from the initial point at which they first appeared on a shelf or spinner rack, the myriad of owners they've had since, and the places they were later found, many of which, like the publishing houses that produced them, no longer exist.

ANDREW NETTE and IAIN McINTYRE

GIRL GANGS, BIKER BOYS, AND REAL COOL CATS

Pulp Fiction's Juvenile Delinquents

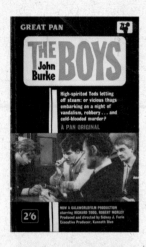

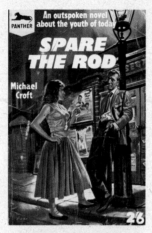

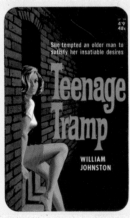

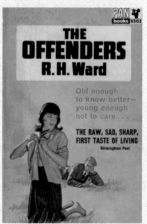

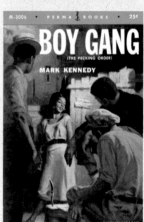

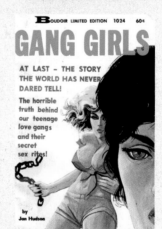

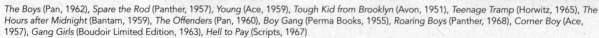

The Boys (Pan, 1962), *Spare the Rod* (Panther, 1957), *Young* (Ace, 1959), *Tough Kid from Brooklyn* (Avon, 1951), *Teenage Tramp* (Horwitz, 1965), *The Hours after Midnight* (Bantam, 1959), *The Offenders* (Pan, 1960), *Boy Gang* (Perma Books, 1955), *Roaring Boys* (Panther, 1968), *Corner Boy* (Ace, 1957), *Gang Girls* (Boudoir Limited Edition, 1963), *Hell to Pay* (Scripts, 1967)

Violent Streets
(Signet, 1959)

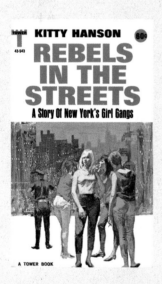

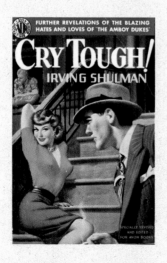

High School Confidential (Avon, 1958)

Juvenile Delinquents (Avon, 1955)

Cry Tough! (Pocket Books, 1950)

Rebels in the Streets (Midwood Tower, 1965)

THE PULP DELINQUENTS
The Teenage Crime Wave and 1950s Pulp Fiction

Lurking alongside the usual crop of romance novels and historical fiction, American literary successes of 1947 included a tough tale of delinquent rebellion—*The Amboy Dukes*. Written by New York native Irving Shulman, the book chronicles the grim, violent (and invariably short) lives of teenage street gangs in east Brooklyn's Brownsville neighbourhood. Set in the summer of 1944, the book recounts the exploits of 16-year-old Frank Goldfarb and his titular gang of Jewish hoodlums. Shulman gives full play to the Amboy Dukes' gritty lifestyle of sex, violence and crime; but also has a sharp eye for the gang's aura of effortless cool:

> The boys stood around on Saturday nights, ready for action. Between the ages of fifteen and twenty-two, they stood on the corners and discussed the deadly gossip of rackets: whores, guys who were cut up, and the dough you could make from one sweet job . . . The bunches spoiled for a fight, and their technique was swift and murderous: a kick in the ankle, a hook to the groin, a clout behind the ear—then some well-placed kicks in the kidneys and head, and the victim was ready for the ambulance . . . They wore open-collared sports shirts or white, blue or brown buttoned down oxford shirts, and their ties were tied neatly in broad knots. Nonchalantly they swung long key chains that hung from a right or left belt loop, and the keys spun in continuous enlarging and contracting circles. The boys sported duck-tail haircuts: long, shaggy, and clipped to form a point at the backs of their heads. Their slick vaselined hair shone in the reflections of light.

A hit with readers, *The Amboy Dukes* quickly went to a series of editions, notching up sales of nearly three and a half million by 1955. The book concludes with anti-hero Frank slain by an erstwhile comrade, but the novel's success prompted Shulman to produce loose sequels, *Cry Tough!* (1949) and *The Big Brokers* (1951). *The Amboy Dukes* also caught Hollywood's attention. Universal Pictures quickly released a (bowdlerised) film adaptation, *City Across the River*

(1949), while Shulman himself branched into screenwriting, producing an early treatment for the iconic teen picture, *Rebel Without a Cause* (1955), before penning a 1961 novelization of *West Side Story*, the stage and screen musical smash.

But the success of *The Amboy Dukes* also heralded the rise of a tough, new genre in American popular fiction—the juvenile delinquency or 'JD' novel. From the early 1950s to the early 1960s US publishers cranked out literally hundreds of tales that paraded the sensational misdeeds of the nation's errant youth. With alluringly garish covers and eye-catching titles—*Juvenile Jungle* (1958), *The Little Caesars* (1961), *Teen-Age Mafia* (1959)—JD literature was a breathtaking world of switchblades, zip-guns and gang rumbles. Bold, brazen and brimming with brutality, the JD novels were spawned by a combination of the social, economic and political shifts that were transforming postwar America and revolutionising the world of US publishing.

Originally released as a hardback by the publishing giant Doubleday, *The Amboy Dukes* won moderate critical praise. But it was only two years later, in 1949, that Shulman's novel attracted significant attention, following Avon Books' launch of a paperback edition and a consequent leap in sales. The book's success was indicative of the way the paperback format was transforming American publishing. Of course, paperbound books were hardly new. The commercial possibilities of paperbacks had already been demonstrated in Germany during the 1930s, where John Holroyd-Reece, Max Wegner and Kurt Enoch had set up Albatross Books and successfully produced a range of mass-market paperbacks whose innovations in size, typography and layout became the industry standard. And in Britain the Albatross format was imitated by Allen Lane's launch of Penguin Books in 1935, which revolutionised British publishing through the introduction of high-quality, inexpensive paperbacks. But American talent was also quick to appreciate the paperback's potential.

Leading the way, entrepreneur Robert de Graff joined forces with publishers Richard Simon and Max Schuster in 1939 to found Pocket Books, which soon became a market leader with its paperback reprints of classics, light novels and popular non-fiction. The company's success was partly due to the low price of its books (25 cents) and their attractive presentation, but it was also a product of the firm's innovative distribution. Whereas hardback sales traditionally relied on bookshops, de Graff (a seasoned pressman) saw how a much broader market could be reached via the distribution systems used for newspapers and magazines. Hence, Pocket Books were racked up in newsstands and in drugstores and cigar shops; a strategic masterstroke that in the first year clocked up sales of more than 1.5 million.

Following Pocket Books' success, rivals vied for a share of the pie. For instance, Avon Books—publisher of *The Amboy Dukes*—started out as magazine publisher, J.S. Ogilvie Publications, but was bought up by the newspaper distributor American News Company (ANC) and relaunched in 1941 as Avon, a paperback imprint that directly challenged (and closely imitated) Pocket Books' releases. More competitors quickly appeared. Dell was launched in 1942, followed by Popular Library in 1943; while Ian Ballantine (formerly director of Penguin's American operations) set up Bantam Books in 1945, followed by Ballantine Books in 1952. And in 1948 Kurt Enoch (who had fled Nazi Germany and settled in the US) established New American Library, initially publishing paperback reprints of classics, then original mysteries, romances and adventure stories.

But it was Fawcett, a major magazine publisher and newsstand distributor, who most extensively blazed the trail of paperback originals. As the distributor of New American Library's Mentor and Signet imprints, Fawcett soon saw the potential of paperback sales and in 1950 launched its own Gold Medal Books— the industry's first major line of paperback originals. Specialising in westerns, mysteries and thrillers, Gold Medal had churned out over 9 million books by the end of 1951, with many novels quickly going to three or four editions. By 1953, then, the paperback trade was burgeoning and the business magazine *Fortune* could trumpet "The Boom in Paper Bound Books", estimating that the previous year had seen national paperback sales of 243 million in a market worth over $69 million.

The paperback bonanza was rooted in the economic upturn that followed World War Two. Disposable income and living standards rose, and publishers rode the tide of consumer affluence. One market was especially attractive. Wartime increases in youth's spending power were sustained throughout the 1940s and 50s, and by 1959 an awestruck *Life* magazine reckoned teen wallets to be worth around $10 billion per year. Industries scrambled to stake a claim in the teenage goldmine, and everything from rock-and-roll records to brothel-creeper shoes was pitched to young punters. Publishers, too, were keen to cash in. While paperbacks won a diverse readership, teenagers and young adults were squarely in the book trade's sights. In 1946, for example, Pocket Books launched the Teen-Age Book Show, a touring exhibition that pitched paperbacks to young readers; while throughout the 1950s New American Library had an educational sales department geared to penetrating the classroom market. Largely based on paperback reprints of classic titles, such initiatives were promoted as offering young readers easy access to literature deemed worthy and educational. But, alongside such earnest fare, there also existed a legion of titles whose sensibilities were less high-minded.

During the early 1950s critics regularly decried the flourishing paperback trade, arguing that the market was dominated by what was often dubbed "the three S's"—sex, sadism and the smoking gun. The point was not without foundation. Many paperbacks were gutsy tales of hardboiled tough-guys and racy dames; their scorching narratives matched by covers that bristled with sneering hoodlums and their improbably buxom molls. The formula had its roots in the traditions of pulp magazine publishers, many of whom had become major players in the new paperback business.

The 'pulps'—so called because of the low-cost, wood pulp paper they were originally printed on— were cheap fiction magazines renowned for their gripping themes and outré cover art. The genre's heyday was during the 1920s and 1930s when US newsstands were thronged with cheap, visually striking pulp titles such as *Argosy*, *Amazing Stories*, *Black Mask*, *Dime Detective* and *Startling Stories*, all proffering thrilling tales of mystery, crime and adventure. Paper shortages during World War Two brought a steady rise in costs and a decline in the pulps' circulation and, in peacetime, the pulps' sales were hit further by growing competition from television, comic books and paperbacks. But many pulp publishers survived by shifting into the paperback trade themselves. Pulp magazine specialists Leo Margulies and Ned Pines were quick off the mark, launching their paperback imprint, Popular Library, in 1942. Others soon followed. Pyramid Books, founded in 1949, was an offshoot of the pulp firm Almat Magazines, while Ace Books was set up in 1952 by A.A. Wyn, owner of the pulp publishing house Ace Magazines. Like Pocket Books and Fawcett, the pulp publishers exploited their established systems of magazine distribution and sales, and their new paperbacks did a brisk trade in newsstands and drugstores. And, as the companies' writers, artists and editors shifted from producing magazines to paperbacks, the pulps' generic themes, styles and subject matter were reincarnated.

Like the original pulp magazines, the new, pulp-*esque* paperbacks traded in the thrilling and the taboo. They were home to ruthless gangsters, hard-bitten detectives and brazen hussies. And, like the earlier pulps, the 50s paperbacks were adept at exploiting contemporary uproars and controversies, appropriating their concerns and motifs for narratives calculated to shock and sensationalise. It was a strategy to which delinquent teenagers were ideally suited. The theme of lawless street gangs offered a high octane mix of sex and violence, as well as a sharp bite of topicality at a time when America was seized by a wave of popular alarm about an apparent explosion of juvenile crime.

Unease about escalating levels of delinquency had bubbled since the late 1930s. In 1936, for example, the church-funded morality film *Reefer Madness* (originally titled *Tell Your Children*) had warned of the toll "evil" marijuana was taking on America's young. And in 1939, the upstanding publisher Little, Brown and Company released *Designs in Scarlet*. Written by Courtney Ryley Cooper (a close friend of J. Edgar Hoover, the FBI's redoubtable first director), the book lifted the lid on a world of CELLAR CLUBS AND JUKE JOINTS, where young thugs GET HOPPED UP ON LIQUOR AND DOPE, THEN ROB AND RAPE AND MURDER. Concern mounted during wartime, the FBI estimating that juvenile offending had leapt by as much as 40 per cent during the first six months of 1943. At the time the rise was widely seen as an insidious but temporary effect of social dislocation caused by the war. But when indices of youth crime continued to escalate during peacetime, alarm sharply intensified.

The early 1950s saw America gripped by the perception that delinquency was spiralling out of control. Gallup surveys show a brief peak of public concern in 1945, followed by a more sustained period of anxiety between 1953 and 1958. The fears were fanned by a tide of exposés in magazines, newspapers and newsreels, all purporting to depict a wave of juvenile crime frighteningly new in its scale and severity. The mood

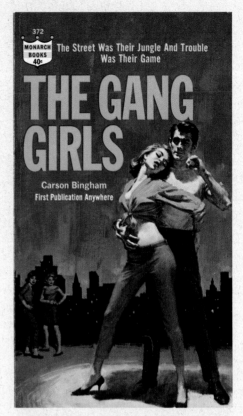

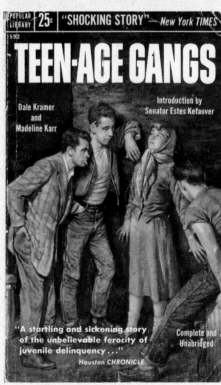

The Gang Girls (Monarch, 1963)
Teen-Age Gangs (Popular Library, 1954)

was captured by *1,000,000 Delinquents*, a non-fiction bestseller of 1955 written by Benjamin Fine, the education editor of the *New York Times*. Drawing on a welter of news reports, surveys and academic research, Fine presented youth crime as a national epidemic, a threat to the survival of the American way of life. In 1954, Fine estimated, the number of delinquents in America had already hit the million mark—a figure which was set to soar to 2,250,000 within the coming five years, he warned.

Concerns about youth crime were shared in the corridors of power; signalled in 1953 by the appointment of a Senate Subcommittee on Juvenile Delinquency to investigate the problem's nature and causes. The very existence of the Senate investigation helped to confirm the popular perception of delinquency as a major social issue, and the view was further confirmed in 1955 when Senator Estes Kefauver took over the Subcommittee's leadership. The Tennessee senator had earlier made his name heading a Senate investigation into organised crime and his appointment to head the Subcommittee on Delinquency lent the inquiry added energy and gravitas. Indeed, impressions of a quantum leap in the scale of delinquency seemed borne out by a relentless rise in the official indices of juvenile crime. But the figures were deceptive. In reality the 'juvenile crime wave' was largely a statistical phenomenon generated through new strategies of policing and changes in the collation of crime data. Rather than being a response to a genuine eruption of adolescent vice, the postwar panic surrounding juvenile delinquency is better seen as a controversy that became a symbolic focus for much broader anxieties in a period of rapid and disorienting change.

Popular perceptions of 1950s America as a land of confidence and cohesion obscure the way US society was actually shot through with conflict and contradiction. The global tensions of the Cold War and the explosion of consumer culture, together with the emergence of civil rights activism and profound shifts in gender roles and relationships, bred apprehension and suspicion. This atmosphere brought stern pressures to conform. In the political arena Senator Joseph McCarthy's witch-hunts ruthlessly gunned for "reds under the bed", but America's cultural agenda was also broadly infused with a shrill conservatism set on shutting down dissent and securing conformity.

At the heart of this cultural backlash stood archetypal images of straitlaced domesticity. Representations of traditional family life were ubiquitous in American culture throughout the 1950s, while academics, politicians and the mass media championed the nuclear family as the cornerstone of American liberty. As a consequence, any deviation from these norms risked charges of abnormality and deviance. In this context the burgeoning teenage culture was viewed with concern. Growing levels of disposable income, it seemed, had afforded American youngsters unprecedented independence from the traditional constraints of family life, and the rise of an autonomous peer culture at the edge of adult society seemed to threaten the fundamental anchors of social stability. For many critics, therefore, teenage culture and delinquency were virtually synonymous, and the perception of a new, dangerous divide between adults and adolescents galvanised the panic about juvenile crime.

Politicians and moral crusaders were not the only ones to be gripped by the spectre of delinquency. The world of entertainment quickly seized upon the topicality of juvenile crime. In Hollywood, for example, *City Across the River* (1949) was followed by a spate of JD pictures—*The Wild One* (1953), *Teenage Crime Wave* (1955), *Untamed Youth* (1957) and a host of others. And, in the world of publishing, *The Amboy Dukes* laid the way for a profusion of pulp delinquents.

Alongside Irving Shulman, other authors stand out as *meisters* of pulp delinquency. Hal Ellson was one of the foremost. Working as a recreational therapist at New York's Bellevue Hospital, Ellson was familiar with some of the city's most troubled youngsters. His experiences informed a succession of hard-hitting gang novels that kicked off with *Duke* in 1949. A portrait of the lawless lifestyle of a black 15-year-old in Harlem, *Duke* has little in the way of plot but proceeds through a series of stark episodes—reckless gang fights, seedy sex and dope sessions—that characterise the protagonist's grim reality and intersperse his descent into schizophrenia. In contrast to Shulman's measured, third-person narration, *Duke* (like many of Ellson's books) is written in the first person, its raw edge accentuated by clipped, hardboiled prose and street slang:

When we got back to the neighborhood everybody is high as hell. There's big news. Soon as we drew up to the curb boys who didn't come with us crowded around. The Skibos came through, they said. They raided and stomped hell out of a couple of our boys and ran.

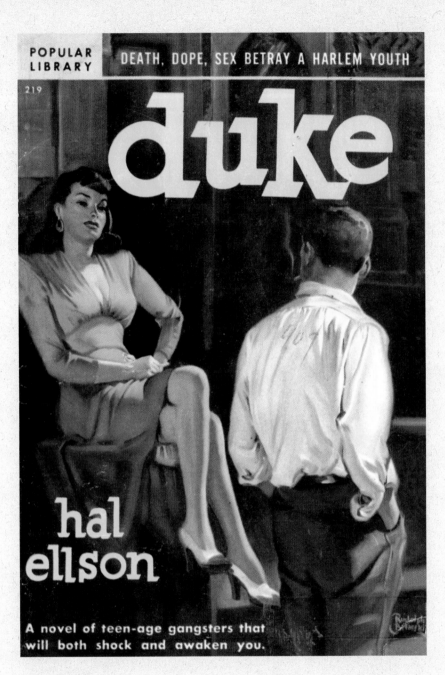

POPULAR LIBRARY

219

DEATH, DOPE, SEX BETRAY A HARLEM YOUTH

duke

hal ellson

A novel of teen-age gangsters that will both shock and awaken you.

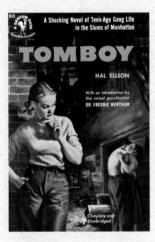

Duke (Popular Library, 1949)
Tomboy (Bantam, 1951)
Tomboy (Corgi, 1970)

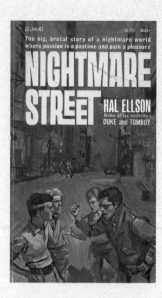

Nightmare Street (Belmont, 1964)
The Golden Spike (Ballantine, 1952)
The Knife (Lancer, 1961)

That got me wild. I told my cats to get their artillery . . . I went for my pistol . . . when I got back to the corner my boys are waiting for me. There was a real mob.

"The mighty Counts is ready," Chink said. "Do we rumble tonight or don't we?"

"Yeah, man!" I said. "Tonight we rumble!"

First released in hardback by the veteran publisher Scribner's, *Duke* became a bestseller in 1950 when Popular Library issued it in paperback. By 1955 the novel had clocked up sales of over 1.5 million, and Ellson quickly built on the success with a follow-up—*Tomboy* (1950). This time the attention switched to a 15-year-old girl's life in an Irish street gang—The Harps—among Manhattan's pitiless back streets. Again, Ellson takes the reader on a journey through a world of ruthless turf wars, audacious heists and torrid sleaze. But, as in *Duke*, he also explores the inner conflicts of the central character and throughout *Tomboy* the protagonist struggles with her sexual identity and disconsolate home life, finding haven in the sense of loyalty and belonging offered by the gang.

Tomboy was another Ellson hit. Quickly released as a paperback by Bantam, the novel had soon run to several editions. *The Golden Spike* (1952) came next. A graphic tale of New York's teenage drug addicts, the novel was a further success for Ellson but was also a landmark for its publisher, Ballantine Books. Established by publishing pioneer Ian Ballantine, the company startled industry traditionalists with its strategy of launching novels in hardbound and paperback editions simultaneously—a policy initiated with the release of *The Golden Spike*. The book also began a sustained relationship between Ellson and Ballantine, the company publishing many of the author's subsequent JD novels, including *Summer Street* (1953), *Rock* (1953) and *Tell Them Nothing* (1956). A prolific author, Ellson ultimately penned over a dozen JD novels, a roster that included genre classics such as *Jailbait Street* (1959), *A Nest of Fear* (1961) and *The Knife* (1961). By the mid-1960s, however, ill health was curtailing Ellson's output, though he signed off with one final JD outing, *Nightmare Street* (1965)—a book eloquently described by its front cover strapline as THE BIG BRUTAL STORY OF A NIGHTMARE WORLD WHERE PASSION IS A PASTIME AND PAIN IS A PLEASURE.

Ellson's JD novels were always a wild ride, their full-blooded drive underscored by breathless promotional blurbs—A RELENTLESS, SURREALISTIC NOVEL OF BITTER, BRUTAL TEEN-AGERS; CHICKS! COPS! THEY WERE ALL HIS MEAT AFTER HE GOT . . . THE KNIFE! But Ellson's narratives were also characterised by a critique of social injustice derived from his experiences working at Bellevue. Rather than being a gratuitous stream of sex and violence, Ellson's books skillfully explored the nature of teenage gang culture and its roots in the inequality and poverty endemic to America's urban sinkholes.

Ellson's approach was indicative of the diverse responses to delinquency. While authoritarian voices decried juvenile crime as the baleful outcome of moral decline, more liberal accounts highlighted the role of social and economic factors. In particular, leading sociologists and criminologists of the 1950s—for example, Albert Cohen, Richard Cloward and Lloyd Ohlin—argued that it was deprivation that pushed kids into the world of criminal street gangs. From this perspective the poverty and privations of ghetto neighbourhoods excluded youngsters from mainstream routes to success and so, looking for an alternative source of status and security, they gravitated to the gang subculture. By the beginning of the 1960s such theories had gained political traction and in 1961 informed the President's Commission on Juvenile Delinquency and Youth Crime. Set up by JFK, the Commission aimed to combat delinquency through an array of assistance programmes that offered new opportunities to disadvantaged youngsters. But, ten years earlier, the idea that juvenile crime was rooted in social and economic inequality was already evident in Hal Ellson's JD potboilers. In *Duke*, for example, Ellson's protagonist explains how life as a gang leader provides prestige and rewards in a world where the odds are stacked steadfastly against him:

I got my boys and they do like I say. I rule. And when we want something we take it. That's all. Cause nobody's giving you nothing. And you ain't going to get nothing by working, nothing more than peanuts anyhow. You ain't never going to be a millionaire shining shoes or mopping floors and being a janitor. You got to have white skin to have stuff, have shiny cars, live in a nice house and make big money. You got to be white. White kids got everything. White people run everything. White people own the world.

The arguments are even more explicit in Ellson's preface, where the author explains how he believes delinquency is rooted not in intrinsic evil or deep-seated criminality, but in deprivation and social exclusion:

How and why does a boy become a gang kid? In areas where the gang is everything a boy has little choice in the matter. In some neighborhoods every boy belongs and to be left out is to be unprotected. Where the gang exists as the 'biggest' thing there is, it is only natural for a boy to join for he is merely reacting logically to his own environment. He also finds acceptance in a world that otherwise rejects him, and this is perhaps the most important reason.

Social critique also surfaced in the JD output of Evan Hunter, a pseudonym adopted by Salvatore Albert Lombino. Growing up in Harlem and the Bronx during the 1930s, Lombino served in the navy during the war and, on returning to New York, took a variety of jobs as he developed a writing career under the 'Evan Hunter' pen name. A stint as a teacher at Bronx Vocational High School provided the basis for Hunter's first successful novel—*The Blackboard Jungle* (1954). The book focuses on an idealistic teacher, Richard Dadier, determined to do his job at a tough high school despite the apathy of his colleagues and the fierce resistance of his students. Violent confrontations between the teacher and the teenage hoodlums ensue, though Dadier is ultimately victorious after a showdown with Artie West, a particularly nasty knife-toting thug. But the real villain of the piece is the poverty of ghetto life, which is presented as locking kids into a cycle of violence and crime from which they have little hope of escape. A commercial hit, Hunter's book was quickly turned into a movie by MGM. Glenn Ford stars as the embattled Dadier, but the 1955 film became best known for featuring Bill Haley & His Comets' song 'Rock Around the Clock'—a number that was originally an obscure B-side, but became a rock-and-roll anthem as Hollywood exposure powered it up the *Billboard* chart.

In 1956 Pocket Books' *The Jungle Kids* collected the JD short stories Hunter had earlier produced for pulp magazines such as *Manhunt*. But a more extended JD treatment appeared in 1959 with Hunter's novel, *A Matter of Conviction*. The legal drama follows Assistant District Attorney Henry Bell as he prosecutes three members of an Italian street gang for the cold-blooded murder of a Puerto Rican rival. As before, a poignant social critique filters into Hunter's narrative; Bell struggling with moral uncertainty as

it becomes clear how the case is rooted in the prejudices of a neighbourhood blighted by decay. Again, the book was a hit and in 1961 led to a United Artists movie, *The Young Savages*, starring Burt Lancaster as the assistant DA. By then, however, Lombino had tired of the JD genre. Instead, he found even greater success under a new moniker—Ed McBain—whose hugely popular 87th Precinct crime series kicked off with the release of *Cop Hater* in 1956.

Harlan Ellison also cut his literary teeth on JD fiction. Growing up in Cleveland, Ellison attended Ohio State University in the early 1950s until he was (purportedly) expelled for hitting a professor who belittled his writing abilities. Undeterred, Ellison moved to New York to develop his career, penning short stories and magazine articles. With the newsworthiness of youth crime, in 1954 Ellison infiltrated a Brooklyn street gang to research what became his JD opus—*Rumble*. The taut, edgy plot sees teenager Rusty Santoro torn between the possibilities of a life away from his beleaguered neighbourhood and loyalty to his tough gang buddies, the Cougars; and Ellison's prose pulsate with turf war action:

It was like nothing but hell with screams.
The first bunch of Cherokees came sliding and stomping across the hardwood alleys, their heavy army boots leaving big black marks on the polished wood. The glitter of knife blades and the dull black of revolvers was mixed with the red of faces and the white of staring eyes. They came in fast and the Cougars met them without hesitation. Fish was the first one forward and the glass-end stick came down and jabbed a Cherokee with such impact, the point of the glass entered the boy's right eye, sending him spilling backward.

Rumble was published by Pyramid in 1958 while Ellison was completing his army service, and the book went through two editions before being reprinted as *Web of the City* (the title Ellison had originally intended). Returning to civilian life, Ellison resumed his writing career and, once again, drew on his gang experiences for a flurry of novels that delved the seamier depths of teenage culture—*The Deadly Streets* (a short story collection, 1958), *The Juvies* (another anthology, 1961), *Gentleman Junkie* (1961) and *Rockabilly* (1961)—though in the early 1960s the author moved to greener pastures, finding fame as a TV scriptwriter and science fiction luminary.

GIRL GANGS, BIKER BOYS, AND REAL COOL CATS

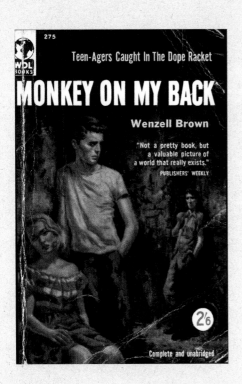

Monkey on My Back (WDL, 1954)

Gang Girl (Avon, 1954)

Jailbait Jungle (Belmont, 1962)

The Big Rumble (Popular Library, 1955)

THE ENFORCERS

Garvey Doyle followed Pat and Bugsy into the girl's flat. Her eyes were wide with terror. All she wore was a red negligee.

"You squealed on the mob," Pat began, slamming her onto the bed.

Bugsy unbuckled his leather belt. There was a whirr and then the belt lashed against her flesh.

Garvey wanted no part of what was coming. But he was one of Jango's mob now, and you did what the mob wanted, or else . . .

Wenzell Brown is the author of many recent best-sellers, including Monkey on my Back, Girls on the Rampage, and They Died in the Chair.

"His novels of teen-age crime in America are virtually required reading. For the purpose of pure entertainment, you can never beat Wenzell Brown."
— Leslie Charteris, Creator of "The Saint"

A BELMONT BOOK

Wenzell Brown was another top name in the JD genre. After studying in New York, London and Denmark, Brown had taught in China and Puerto Rico before traveling around the Caribbean. His travels provided material for his early books, including *Dark Drums* (1950) and *They Called Her Charity* (1951), historical melodramas set in Jamaica and the Virgin Islands. Brown found greater success with 'true crime' stories such as *Introduction to Murder* (1952) and his Edgar Allan Poe Award-winning profile of female killers, *They Died in the Chair* (1958). But he also carved out an impressive JD niche. Brown kicked off with *Run, Chico, Run* (1953), the tale of a good kid in a bad neighbourhood (Spanish Harlem) who slides into the mire of petty crime and drug-running. Brown revisited dope-sullied teens in *Monkey on My Back* (1953), while in *Gang Girl* (1954) he recounted the miscreant life of Rita, a 15-year-old hellion from New York's Lower East Side who **KNEW HOW TO FIGHT WITH HER KNEES, HER ELBOWS, HER TEETH, HOW TO HOLD A BLACKJACK, HOW TO SPOT A COP, HOW TO ROLL MARIJUANA, HOW TO LURE A MAN INTO A DARK HALLWAY.** Further JD sagas flowed, with Brown knocking out *The Big Rumble* (1955, republished as *Jailbait Jungle* in 1962), *Teenage Terror* (1958), *Cry Kill* (1959) and the magnificent *Teen-Age Mafia* (1959).

Edward DeRoo was also a JD pulp recidivist. (Note: his name appeared on paperback covers in slightly different versions, sometimes with a space, De Roo, sometimes without. —Eds.) An alumnus of the University of Denver and Yale (where he graduated as a Master of Fine Arts in 1950), DeRoo worked as a radio producer and dabbled in stage production before developing an academic career as a professor of communications. But during the late 1950s he also crafted a succession of JD gems—*Go, Man, Go* (1959), *The Young Wolves* (1959), *Rumble at the Housing Project* (1960) and *The Little Caesars* (1961).

A multitude of 'one hit wonders' also pepper the roll call of JD authors. Jay de Bekker, for example, proffered *Gutter Gang* (1954, **THEY CAME FROM FILTHY SLUMS—WHERE EVEN THEIR DREAMS WERE DIRTY!**), Bud Clifton gave us *D for Delinquent* (1958, **SHE WAS STRICTLY FOR THE BOYS!**), William Cox delivered *Hell to Pay* (1958, **THEY'RE HOPPED-UP PUNKS, AT WAR WITH THE SYNDICATE—AND THEY KILL JUST FOR KICKS**), Edward Ronns composed *Gang Rumble* (1958, **THE CITY STREETS BECAME A JUNGLE OF FEAR AND TERROR!**) and Morton Cooper dashed off *Delinquent!* (1958, **THE STARTLING STORY OF A**

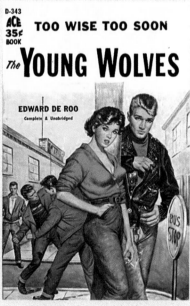

Teen-Age Terror (Gold Medal, 1958)
The Young Wolves (Ace, 1959)

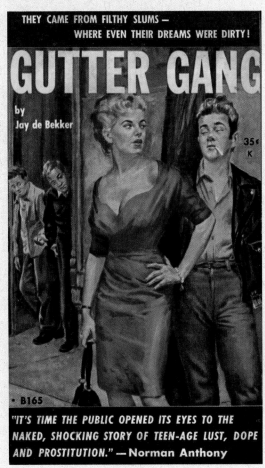

Young and Deadly (Crest, 1959)
Gutter Gang (Beacon, 1954)
The Young Punks (Pyramid, 1959)
Hell to Pay (Signet, 1958)
The Violent Ones (Ace, 1958)

A SHOCKING STORY OF YOUNG PEOPLE AND
THEIR MAD, RELENTLESS PURSUIT OF THRILLS

CARNIVAL BOOKS

SOCIAL CLUB

by ALBERT L. QUANDT

No. 930
35¢

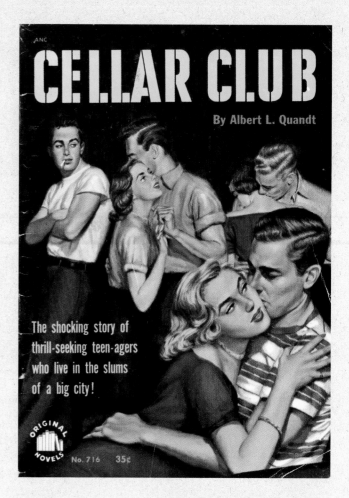

ANC

CELLAR CLUB

By Albert L. Quandt

The shocking story of
thrill-seeking teen-agers
who live in the slums
of a big city!

ORIGINAL NOVELS
No. 716   35¢

Social Club (Carnival, 1954)

Cellar Club (Original Novels, 1951)

The Cool Crowd, aka *Cellar Club*
(Paperback Library, 1963)

vinnie

At fourteen she was ripe with
knowledge of sex and every
kind of evil. Her companions
were cool, hard-eyed young
hoodlums. Her meeting places
were the cellar clubs of New
York's West Side. The price of
swinging with Vinnie was to
offer her a new kind of kick.

Shocking, explosive, savagely
realistic—a frightening novel of
today's thrill-hungry youth

50¢   32-224

The Cool Crowd

(formerly published as Cellar Club)

The story of Vinnie—
Lolita of the
New York streets

ALBERT T. QUANDT

OVER 1,000,000 COPIES IN PRINT

Angels in the Gutter (Gold Medal, 1955)

WALK DOWN ALL YOUR SIDE STREETS

through the raucous stone jungle of the city's backwash—and you'll meet her.

The delinquent. And hundreds like her, roaming the pavements in aggressive knots, schooled on reefers, zip guns, gutter rumbles.

At fifteen they are women, hard and cynical beyond their years, openly contemptuous of the law, eager for the glamour of the bigtime ways of violence.

The lucky ones get caught, maybe in time.

LITHO'D IN CANADA

They roamed in gangs, these lost girls, women at fifteen—too old at twenty

GOLD MEDAL BOOK

ANGELS IN THE **GUTTER**

JOSEPH HILTON

35¢

TEEN-AGE GANG!). Several collections of JD 'shorts' also appeared. Leo Margulies, for instance, compiled *The Young Punks* (1957, **A FRIGHTENING PORTRAIT OF OUR TEEN-AGE JUNGLE**) and followed it up with *Young and Deadly* (1959, **10 SEARING STORIES FROM TODAY'S KINGDOM OF HELL—AMERICA'S TEEN-AGE JUNGLE**), while Brant House anthologised *The Violent Ones* (1958, **POWERFUL STORIES OF THE TEEN-AGE JUNGLE**). Overall, the JD genre was dominated by a clutch of bigger publishers—Ace, Pyramid, Gold Medal, Popular Library and Ballantine—but many smaller paperback firms (Avon, Crest, Digit, Signet and numerous others) also chipped in, their endeavours ensuring that 1950s American newsstands were chock-full of fictional JD menace.

All JD novels shared a thirst for the wanton adventures of teenage hoodlums. But the line-up also included some distinctive subgenres. Dope peddling and narcotics were regular ingredients of JD fiction, but in some tales reefers and goofballs edged out switchblades and gang rumbles as the chief preoccupation of teen lowlife. Probably the best known 'druggie pulp' of the 1950s was beat icon William Burroughs's *Junkie: Confessions of an Unredeemed Drug Addict*, published (initially under the pseudonym 'William Lee') in 1953 by Ace. But Burroughs's semi-autobiographical portrait of heroin addiction was just one among a slew of paperbacks depicting ill-fated youngsters gripped by a desperate drug habit. Alongside novels such as *The Golden Spike*, *Monkey on My Back* and *Run Chico, Run* there also appeared first-person confessionals such as Leroy Street's *I Was a Drug Addict* (1953) and Valerie Jordan's *I Am a Teen-Age Dope Addict* (1962), as well as lurid exposés like Joachim Joesten's *Dope, Inc.* (1953) and Sloane Britain's *The Needle* (1959). Ostensibly, they sermonised against the perils of drug addiction; but their real appeal lay in their promise of a candid glimpse into a world of the risqué and the taboo.

Sex was a similar draw. JD fiction sizzled with accounts of sleazy, back-alley assignations which, for the time, were daringly racy. Albert Quandt had a particular gift for 'revelatory' accounts of lascivious teens; his lust-fixated oeuvre homed in *Girl of the Slums* (1951, **SIN STREET WAS HER BEAT**), *Cellar Club* (1951, **THE SHOCKING STORY OF THRILL-SEEKING TEEN-AGERS WHO LIVE IN THE SLUMS OF A BIG CITY!**), *Baby Sitter* (1952, **A SHOCKING STORY OF TEEN-AGERS IN SEARCH OF SECRET THRILLS!**), and *Social Club* (1954, **A SHOCKING STORY OF YOUNG PEOPLE AND THEIR MAD, RELENTLESS PURSUIT OF THRILLS**). Quandt's *Zip-Gun Angels* (1952, later reprinted as *Boy-Crazy*) was another spicy outing, but it also exemplified a further species of JD fiction—the 'girls gone bad' subgenre.

Alongside Hal Ellson's *Tomboy* and Wenzell Brown's *Gang Girl*, a stream of books charted the exploits of

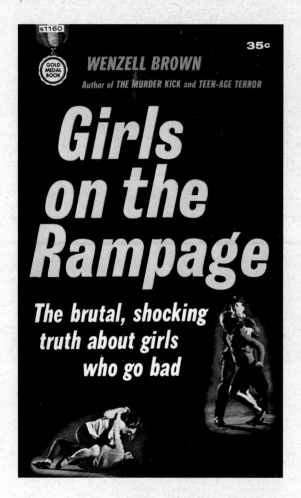

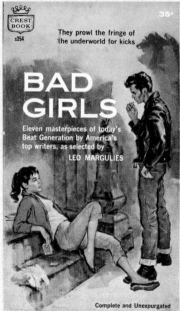

wild, young vixens—for example, Joseph Hilton's *Angels in the Gutter* (1955), Harry Whittington's *Halfway to Hell* (1959), Leo Margulies's short story collection *Bad Girls* (1958) and Wenzell Brown's 'gang girl' encore, *Girls on the Rampage* (1961). Like JD fiction more generally, the 'bad girl' subgenre capitalised on contemporary headlines. For the most part 1950s teen crime was characterised as a male problem—the stock delinquent portrayed as a swaggering, leather-jacketed hoodlum with a duck-tail haircut and a bad attitude. But the belief that girls were becoming "tougher", "harder" and "more vicious" was also widespread. Popularised in newspaper articles and magazine features, the image of the delinquent 'bad girl' also gained 'authoritative' weight from a number of professional pronouncements. Katherine Sullivan, for instance, drew on her experiences working on the Massachusetts Parole Board to deliver *Girls on Parole* (1956), a sobering account of **WHY GIRLS GO WRONG**; while *Rebels in the Streets* (1962) saw journalist Kitty Hanson scour the files of the New York City Youth Board to deliver a portrait of femininity run amok:

> Gang girls are becoming girl gangs, and the viciousness of girls in a gang often makes the boys' old style rumble a Sunday school picnic by comparison. Into lives starved of the necessities and barren of luxury, these girls have injected a substitute—excitement.

Such alarm was constituent in the wider tensions surrounding gender and sexuality throughout the 50s. Women's growing levels of social and economic independence were often configured as a threat to traditional ideals, and in this context the spectre of the tempestuous 'bad girl'—defiant, brazen and beyond control—seemed especially subversive. But the responses of officialdom worked to contain the threat. Psychoanalysis was widely used to explain the 'problem' of delinquent girls, so their criminality was diagnosed as less an act of wilful rebellion than a product of psychological 'confusion'. The same explanation filtered into much JD fiction. Not least Ellson's *Tomboy*, where the protagonist appears tough and dangerous on the streets but, at heart, is the lonely and vulnerable child of a dysfunctional home. Even Wenzell Brown's *Gang Girl* is more damaged than depraved. Rita might be a feisty, young hell-cat, but is she is still presented as a product of **FEAR, BEWILDERMENT AND A DESPERATE NEED FOR LOVE AND SECURITY**.

Girls on the Rampage (Gold Medal, 1961)
Bad Girls (Crest, 1958)

Many 'bad girl' books also pandered to prurience. On the covers, pouting lips and bulging cleavage were a titillating lure, and sex scenes that presented girls as boy-hungry hussies provided drooling readers with a rich seam of fantasy fodder. The output of firms on the fringes of the publishing industry—for example, Beacon, Midwood and Monarch—was especially salacious. With low production values (news stock print and poor bindings), their selling point was content more explicit than mainstream rivals, and they were sold under the counter or in cigar shops rather than on newsstands. Their titles ran the gamut of softcore sleaze, and predominant were 'bad girl' tales such as Orrie Hitt's *The Torrid Teens* (1960, **SHE CAME FROM A NICE HOME . . . YET AT SEVENTEEN SHE SUCCUMBED TO VILENESS AND TWISTED DESIRE. WHY?**), Julie Ellis's *Gang Girl* (credited to 'Joan Ellis',1960, **SHE HAD HER FIRST SORDID LESSONS IN LOVE ON THE DUSTY ROOFTOPS OF RUNDOWN TENEMENTS**) and Leo Rifkin and Tony Norman's *Gutter Girl* (1960, **THE WHOLE STORY OF THE WILD AND WANTON GIRLS WHO RUN WITH THE STREET PACKS AND THRONG THE CELLAR CLUBS**).

Undoubtedly, the 'girls gone bad' subgenre (like JD fiction more generally) was geared to a male readership. And its depictions of women were often shot-through with chauvinism and lechery. But, in the context of 1950s America, 'gang girl' tales also offered a beguiling walk on the wild side. The mainstream cultural tide relentlessly promoted images of docile femininity, with women configured as 'happy housewives' rooted in a life of subservient and achingly conventional domesticity. But 'gang girl' fiction was a thrilling alternative. Against the conservative grain, the JD paperbacks proffered a vision of outlaw girlhood that refused to toe the conformist line and flipped an insolent middle-finger to the puritanical moralists.

For the time, JD fiction's treatment of race and ethnicity could also be relatively liberal. Certainly, the genre included its fair share of hackneyed ethnic stereotypes. But many books were reasonably enlightened, with complex characters, convincing relationships and faithfully rendered settings. Philip Kaye's *Taffy* (1950), for instance, is a compelling depiction of Harlem street life and the central character's dog-eat-dog struggle to survive. Similarly, *Tiger in the Streets* (1957) sees Louis Malley (a native of New York's toughest neighbourhoods) produce a convincing account of Puerto Rican gang feuds among the rundown tenements of Spanish Harlem. And Shulman's *The Amboy Dukes*, of course, is a sharply observed

Tiger in the Streets (Ace, 1957)
Teen-Age Jungle (Avon, 1953)

account of Jewish gangs in wartime Brownsville. During the 1950s, however, some paperback editions of *Dukes* expunged its Jewish references—names, references to Passover, kosher meat and so on. But, rather than being rooted in antisemitism, the excision may have been designed to maintain the novel's sense of relevance. Since the mid-1940s (when *Dukes* is set) demographics had profoundly transformed blue-collar New York, and Shulman's depiction of thuggish Jewish teens may have seemed woefully passé to 1950s readers looking for a taste of contemporary grit. Instead, it was a new generation of black and Hispanic hoodlums who promised hard-hitting thrills of the moment.

Delinquent gangs were a perennial fixture in America's urban landscape, but during the 1950s they seized the popular consciousness. During wartime, concerns about adolescent street gangs had begun to intensify in response to the apparent escalation of juvenile crime and events such as the Los Angeles 'zoot suit riots' of 1943. In reality, the episode was a series of attacks on Mexican-American 'pachuco' youths by white servicemen infuriated by the kids' 'loud and proud' zoot suits (broad, tapered jackets with pleated, baggy trousers, tight at the ankle). The youngsters were victims of white brutality, but the 'riots' helped promulgate images of rebellious youth—'zoot suit gangs'—as a new criminal danger. And qualms grew as the style was steadily adopted as a symbol of cocksure cool by working-class whites (such as Shulman's Amboy Dukes). But it was during the 50s that fears of urban street gangs mushroomed. The anxieties were the sharp end of the panic that surrounded youth culture and delinquency more generally. Juvenile crime as a whole was perceived as a threatening social menace, but *gangs* seemed especially sinister. Organised, structured and unified by wicked purpose, the image of the teenage street gang condensed the murkiest fears of JD lawlessness. And public dread intensified as popular notions of the gang acquired increasingly 'racial' connotations.

Historically, America's urban gangs had been drawn from a spectrum of ethnic groups. But, in New York especially, the 1950s saw gang composition reconfigured. Demographic shifts saw older, white communities displaced by new (disproportionately young) African American and Puerto Rican migrants; while economic dislocation, urban renewal and slum clearance generated a sense of insecurity that pitted the new arrivals against one another. And, as ethnic hatreds rippled through New York's working-class neighbourhoods, evocatively named street gangs—Vampires, Heart Kings, Young Lords—proliferated to stake a claim on local turf and fight for personal respect and ethnic honour.

Popular fears of generational mayhem may have been overblown and histrionic, but (at least in New York) the intensification of violence between ethnically based street gangs was real. Reports of predatory, 'alien' gangs peppered the 50s media and stoked a public angst which, in turn, provided compelling inspiration for ranks of pulp writers. The work of some—Hal Ellson and Evan Hunter, for example—is almost sociological in its portrayal of tough gangs forged amid inner-city adversity. Others take a more sensationalised approach. Wenzell Brown's *Teen-Age Mafia*, for instance, is gloriously over-the-top in its account of 'punk kids' who give the mob a run for its money.

As a whole, the JD genre rode the tide of concern surrounding youth crime and street gangs during the 1950s, exploiting the hand-wringing anxieties of the moralists and offering armchair delinquents a taste of the illicit action. Even sober non-fiction was swept up in the sensationalism. As they shifted from hardback to paperback editions, solemn commentaries such as *1,000,000 Delinquents* and *Rebels in the Streets* were given a 'pulp makeover'; with new cover art and melodramatic straplines that aped the frenzied pitch of JD fiction. The strategy even gave a new lease of life to *Designs in Scarlet* (1939), Courtney Ryley Cooper's pre-war scoop on delinquent adolescence. Acquired by paperback kingpins Pyramid, the book was retitled *Teen-Age Vice* and republished several times throughout 1950s—with some especially slick artwork gracing the 1957 edition.

The JD pulps exploited America's obsession with juvenile crime. But the books themselves also fell foul of moral campaigners who saw paperbacks as a malign influence on the nation's youth. The early 1950s saw localised, uncoordinated censorship drives by parental groups and religious bodies such as the National Organization for Decent Literature (NODL, formed by Catholic priests), together with state-sponsored lawsuits against specific titles deemed 'obscene'. Censorship efforts occurred across the country, but were especially common in Midwestern and eastern states, where cops could seize armfuls of offending material from targeted newsstands. In 1952 the campaign was given focus by the appointment of a government inquiry—the House Select Committee on Current Pornographic Materials—tasked with investigating the paperback industry and the influence of lurid literature on impressionable young minds. Headed by Ezekiel C. Gathings (Democratic Representative for Arkansas), the committee gunned determinedly for the pulps, announcing at the outset:

> The so-called pocket-size books which originally started out as cheap reprints of standard works, have largely degenerated into media for the dissemination of artful appeals to sensuality, immorality, filth, perversion and degeneracy. The exaltation of passion above principle and the identification of lust with love are so prevalent that the casual reader of such 'literature' might easily conclude that all married persons are habitually adulterous and all teenagers completely devoid of any sex inhibitions.

The attitude epitomised the way popular culture served as a convenient whipping-boy during the 50s. In the face of rapid and disorienting social change, mainstream America's anxieties and anger were projected onto the media—films, TV and rock and roll were all routinely condemned as the malignant cause of the nation's ills. Estes Kefauver's Senate investigation into delinquency was typical. Televised from gavel-to-gavel, the Kefauver hearings considered a range of potential causes of juvenile crime, but they were preoccupied with the possible influence of the media. Comics, especially, attracted Kefauver's ire and, in response, a nervous Comics Magazine Association hurriedly introduced its infamous Comics Code in 1954, effectively outlawing the horror and crime comics beloved by thrill-hungry youngsters. Conducted a year earlier, Ezekiel Gathings's investigation had been determined to 'clean up' books in the same way.

From the start, the Gathings hearings were stacked against the paperbacks. Few witnesses were called from the publishing industry. Instead, a parade of religious leaders, police officials, teachers and judges testified to the pernicious influence of an array of paperback titles. Of the hundreds of books cited, a good number were JD pulps—including *The Amboy Dukes* and *Tomboy*—but the committee's final report, published in 1953, zeroed in on sex and drugs titles such as Treska Torres's *Women's Barracks* (1950) and N.R. De Mexico's *Marijuana Girl* (1951). Overall, the report was severe. Talking tough, the Gathings committee argued for a strengthened enforcement of federal obscenity laws, together with a new regime of

1,000,000 Delinquents (Signet, 1957); *Teen-Age Vice* (Pyramid, 1957)

self-regulation to be implemented by book publishers. The pressures for paperback censorship, however, ultimately fizzled out. In contrast to the comic trade, the book industry carried political and cultural weight and, citing First Amendment freedoms, publishers successfully lobbied against strengthened controls. Gathings, meanwhile, became a figure of press ridicule as his report was left to gather dust.

The paperbacks, then, prevailed over puritanical attempts to clip their wings. And, during the 1950s and early 1960s, court victories further rolled back the legal checks on literature. The JD pulps, then, were free to hit their high-watermark around 1958. As the panic around delinquency hit fever-pitch, the JD genre milked the furore for all it was worth, offering page-turning slices of youth-run-wild melodrama. But the glory days could not last. By the beginning of the 1960s leather-jacketed street gangs were old news and, as the delinquency panic steadily dissipated, readers' appetites for JD kicks also waned. Industry shifts during the early 60s were another nail in the JD pulps' coffin, as many smaller paperback firms fell by the economic wayside and others were absorbed by larger publishing houses whose aesthetic inclinations were lamentably tame.

Nevertheless, while 50s-style delinquents became a thing of wistful nostalgia, the attitude and approach of the pulps could still resurface. Indeed, throughout the 60s and 70s media-incited terror of new subcultural bogeymen brought successive waves of sensational paperbacks chronicling the malevolent menace of feral biker gangs, LSD-fuelled freak-outs and Charles Manson-esque hippie cults. The JD pulps may have gone, but the hunger for the frisson of the lawless lived on.

BILL OSGERBY

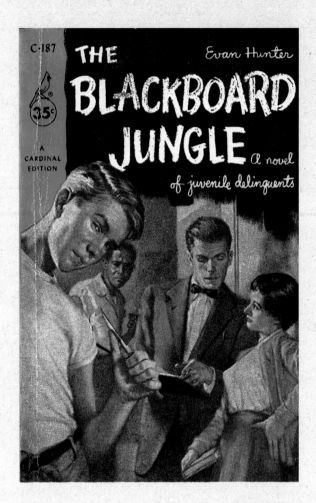

The Blackboard Jungle (Pocket Books, 1955)
The Blackboard Jungle (Panther, 1961)
The Blackboard Jungle (Panther, 1962)

EVAN HUNTER'S JUNGLE KIDS

Evan Hunter was one of America's most versatile, prolific and successful postwar novelists. Few other writers so shrewdly and industriously exploited the zeitgeist of the 1950s. In an era when popular and literary fiction were rigorously segregated by formats and channels of publication, Hunter uniquely conquered both the low and the middle-brow by distributing his voluminous writing through different pseudonyms and genres. He sold in huge quantities to men and women, in paperback and hardcover, in pulp digests and higher quality 'slick' magazines. He wrote topical fiction about crooks and cops, the city and the suburbs, marriage and adultery. And he hit the big time with *The Blackboard Jungle* (1954) on the hot theme of juvenile delinquency—it proved a reliable subject for the next decade.

'Evan Hunter' was itself a fiction, one of several personas created by Salvatore A. Lombino. The young Italian-American legally assumed this particularly WASP-ish handle in 1952 while working as an editor at the Scott Meredith Literary Agency, which would prove to be the incubator of a generation of crime writers that also included Donald E. Westlake and Lawrence Block. After Meredith became his agent, Hunter sold numerous science fiction, western and detective stories.

Beginning in January 1953 Hunter's stories appeared in the new monthly *Manhunt*, whose cover illustrations usually depicted large-breasted women, partially undressed and often threatened by violence. Hunter's stories (under his new name and other pseudonyms) appeared here for the rest of the 1950s alongside those of Mickey Spillane, Cornell Woolrich, Richard S. Prather, Ross MacDonald, David Goodis, Fredric Brown, Harlan Ellison, John D. MacDonald, Westlake and Block.

Public sentiment favoured repression. In 1954, psychologist Fredric Wertham published *Seduction of the Innocent*, a polemic that accused popular culture, particularly comic books, of encouraging violent behaviour in youth, and testified before the Senate Subcommittee on Juvenile Delinquency. *Manhunt* was published by an affiliate of the imperiled comic book publisher St. John. According to pulp historian Mike Ashley, the digest lived under threat of suppression on the basis of its lurid cover art and violent content. It skipped publication entirely in March and April 1954.

In 1957 *Manhunt* was charged with obscenity and the publisher fined.

A moral panic over teenage violence had created a market for juvenile delinquency stories. Hunter was one of the genre's earliest and most successful practitioners. The novel and film adaptation of *The Blackboard Jungle* appeared midway between *The Wild One* (1953) and *Rebel Without a Cause* (1955), films that enshrined the irresistible iconography of the delinquent in the popular imagination—Marlon Brando and James Dean, switchblades and bomber jackets.

Like almost everything else written or filmed within the JD genre, Hunter's work operated on the blurry border between moral condemnation of crime and lurid exploitation. The format in which Hunter's fiction was published—and sometimes republished under other names—largely determined its reception. It could be a serious 'sociological' look at a perceived social problem—or a contributor to the menace itself. The wily Hunter cashed in from both sides.

As befit a first hardcover novel from the prestigious firm of Simon & Schuster—and a *Ladies' Home Journal* serialization—Hunter's new legal name appeared on *The Blackboard Jungle* (1954). It built on his 1953 vocational school story, 'To Break the Wall', Hunter's only sale to a literary journal at that point. Hunter had saved $3,000 and decided, as he later told Don Swaim, "I'm going to try a serious novel." Hunter expanded his enterprise from the gutter to respectability with dazzling speed.

The story of a rookie teacher in a New York City trade high school, *Jungle* exposed the failings of this lowly section of the public education system—**one big, fat, overflowing garbage can**, according to one of its teacher characters—but more so the illiteracy, ill-discipline and mindless violence of the postwar teenage generation. The novel carried autobiographical cachet; Hunter had taught briefly and unhappily at Bronx Vocational High School in 1950 and this was mentioned in contemporary reviews. In its hardcover format, *Jungle* was essentially sold as novelised liberal sociology. Simon and Schuster advertised the novel by placing it in the tradition of *The Grapes of Wrath* and *Uncle Tom's Cabin*, novels that "opened fire on major social problems." In reality it is an overly earnest muckraking novel from a 27-year-old war veteran who was appalled and confused by a new generation of inner-city youth.

The Blackboard Jungle was adapted for the screen by Richard Brooks, working from prepublication galleys, and the film version was released in early 1955. Starring Glenn Ford and Sidney Poitier, *Blackboard Jungle* was the first Hollywood feature to include a rock-and-roll song (Bill Haley & His Comets' 'Rock Around the Clock'). Despite upfront disclaimers emphasising its moral purposefulness, the movie was controversial and widely attacked as an incitement to riot. When it was republished in paperback by Cardinal Books (the premium, 35-cent imprint of Pocket Books)—with a new subtitle, **A Novel of Juvenile Delinquents**, and featuring decidedly more exploitative artwork by Clark Hulings that emphasised switchblades and tight sweaters—Hunter's novel would sell two and a half million copies. Like most bestsellers, *The Blackboard Jungle* confirmed the status quo by flattering the prejudices of its readership. It tells us much more about 1950s misogyny and sexual repression than about the supposed contemporary menace of the teenager.

The novel begins with rookie teacher Rick Dadier applying for a teaching position at North Manual Trades High School in the East Bronx. Rick finds himself competing for the job with an old school chum. The chum is interviewed first; Rick averts his eyes lest he gain advantage learning from the other man's mistakes. But Rick doesn't need the angle; he lands the job because he knows *Henry V* from *Henry IV*. He's a winner in the Great American Meritocracy.

Rick returns to his low-income City Housing Project apartment where the Dadiers have friendly relations with their black neighbours. The building does not resemble a **craphouse** like other projects. We're introduced to Anne, Rick's pregnant housewife, a pre-Betty Friedan ideal. When she discovers Rick has the job, she does not have to **pretend vast joy because she was truly excited, the way she had only been excited on several occasions in her lifetime.** Anne's no snob, (**she saw the bottle of champagne, and she could read the delicately scripted Domestic, but that didn't matter to her at all**) and Rick, we're incessantly reminded, is without interest in other women (**and that included Hedy Lamarr and Rita Hayworth and anyone else you might care to name, sir**). They have celebratory sex despite her advanced pregnancy (**She was slender again for him tonight**).

But school proves tough. Rick acts the harsh sergeant with the kids and wonders about a black student, Gregory Miller, who is more intelligent than the others but just as disruptive and unwilling to learn. A fellow teacher and comic foil, Alan Manners, pines to be transferred to an all-girls school, perhaps an even worse prospect than an all-boys school (**"Yeah, but think of the pussy," Manners said honestly**). Soon Rick foils a student's attempted rape of a young teacher, Miss Hammond. The attack was foreseen in the interior monologue of another male teacher: the way Miss Hammond dresses, he thinks to himself, the rape would come **"either from the students or the teachers or maybe both."**

Miss Hammond's breasts are perhaps the novel's most skillfully drawn pair of characters. Rick encounters one during the battle to defend its bearer's virtue:

My God, he thought wildly, that's her breast. . . .

Miss Hammond screamed again, holding her hand up to cover the purple nipple and roseate of her breast behind the torn slip and brassiere. . . .

[Rick's] jacket was too large for her, but she clutched it to her exposed breast thankfully, her cheeks flushed with excitement . . . [Rick] hated [the boy] intensely, and he thought of the innocent exposure of Miss Hammond's breast as he had seen it, full and rounded, the torn silk of her underwear framing it, providing a cushion for it. A youthful breast it had been, firm, with the nipple large and erect.

Rick is generally uneasy with the role of **protector of the virgin**, as he is labeled at school. We learn he **had never stopped a rape before, except by changing his mind.** And his gallant defense of Miss Hammond is **regarded by the students . . . as nothing but the basest, most treacherous type of villainy.** Not for the last time are the students lumped into one unanimously mean bunch. But the **villainy** must also have been regarded as a bit of a joke, because Rick encounters **ribbing** and **good-natured sport** from his fellow male teachers, whose **humor closely paralleled that of the students . . . Rick had taken it all good-naturedly, smiling and parrying all their thrusts.**

Back home, Anne too is rather lacking in empathy.

[She] exhibited a womanlike contempt for Miss Hammond, blaming her for not wearing sackcloth and ashes to a teaching job in a school

like that. Even after Rick explained that Miss Hammond hadn't been dressed flashily at all, Anne still held to the theory that no woman gets raped or nearly raped unless she's looking for it.

Rick did not pause to analyze the psychology of the pregnant woman.

Fortunately for us, the author does make that analytical pit stop:

It had not occurred to [Rick] that pregnancy was a complete paradox. It was paradoxical in that only the female of the species could perform the amazing feat, while perhaps being less psychologically prepared for it than a male would have been. No woman enjoys the sight of sagging breasts and a bulging stomach, no matter how maternal her urge. A woman's good looks are a woman's good looks, and there is little good-looking about a pregnant woman . . .

As Anne is unhappy with her pregnant "unattractiveness", she can be excused for her contempt.

Miss Hammond's breasts were not tender to the touch, nor did they feel like heavy stones.

. . . No. Miss Hammond had been sufficiently attractive to provoke a rape. Anne had heard of pregnant women being raped, but she doubted very much if she could arouse any rampant male interest at this last stage of the motherhood game. So whereas she looked forward to the new addition with an almost childlike expectancy, she still possessed a woman's eye, and she could not trick that woman's eye into thinking all was well in the state of Denmark, or even in the state of her expanding middle.

Rick had been predictably gallant defending Miss Hammond's virginity. But for Anne:

That a slender, attractive, rape-provoking woman had been the cause of his gallantry—well, this did not sit too happily in her lactating breast.

One happy consequence is that Rick is now feared by the students. (Yes, that old rape might very well turn out to be the best thing that could have happened to him.) And Miss Hammond takes an immediate sexual interest in her defender. Rick is unsure whether she is an innocent or a lustful 'hussy':

She shrugged her shoulders, as if she honestly could not understand what had provoked lust. But in shrugging, her breasts moved, and Rick wondered for the second time if she were being artful, exhibiting her femininity while denying it. She seemed unaware of her breasts, though, like a little girl visiting a mature woman's body, living in it for a while, but not really getting used to all the furniture.

Rick pals with a fellow teacher named Josh Edwards, a trad jazz fan who rather foreshadowingly itemizes the collection of rare 78s he plans to spin for his ignorant students (**"Bet the kids today don't even know who Glenn Miller is,"** Rick said sadly.)

The men get staggeringly drunk on martinis and are set upon in the street by a gang of seven students in **an ideal trap, worthy of guerrillas, worthy of cutthroats anywhere.** The violence is explicit retribution for sending Miss Hammond's would-be rapist to reform school. The narrative voice lapses into the boys' collective point of view, a cynical hep-talking colloquial voice which, very clumsily, sometimes incorporates Rick's private memories (**Daddy-oh hadn't been in a street fight since that time in Panama when everyone on his ship had got drunk and turned on each other**). This collective voice recurs throughout the novel, usually in the classroom scenes. Anyway, Rick winds up **bleeding like a whore on her legitimate day off. The boys gave it to him until they felt they'd squashed his scrotum flat, and then they gave it to him equally around the head.**

Fortunately, Rick recovers upon Anne's lactating breast and goes back to school. Yet he feels that:

There was something shameful about the appearance of his face, and whereas he couldn't pinpoint the origin of the shamed feeling, he was guiltily aware of it. He felt like a pregnant woman wearing the badge of a bulging belly, the badge that proclaims to the world at large, "I've been layed." His face shouted, "I've been beaten," and he didn't want his face to advertise that slogan because it wasn't a true one.

Rumbled, perhaps, but not defeated. In the classroom, having given them a creative task, Rick realises the boys have no imagination at all. For some reason he experiments with recording their voices and is foiled by the class fool, Morales, who says "**fuck**" into the microphone.

Meanwhile, Miss Hammond tempts our hero when they find themselves side by side in a car.

He did not like this warm feeling within him, and he did not like the feeling of guilt that accompanied it. He knew that Lois Hammond was a woman, and it had been a long time since he'd looked at any woman as a woman, at least any woman other than Anne. He wondered if Anne's pregnancy had anything to do with this strange new awareness . . .

Miss Hammond moves closer, but a little rhapsody about Anne's hair, her eyes, etc., does the trick (**he forgot the pressure of Lois's thigh against his, forgot Lois completely**).

When Josh Edwards is back in *his* classroom, the collective voice narrates: "**There was another English drag with Mr. Edwards, little ol' Josh-wah fittin' the battle of Jericho. Man, these guys could think up more ways to bore a guy.**" Mr. Edwards has made the mistake of bringing his fragile 78s into a roomful of delinquents. He tells them: "**I've been a collector for a long time now, and there's some exciting stuff here.**" But the JDs don't dig Bunny Berigan. **So it's a guy singing. Does he stack up against [Perry] Como? Where does he shine to Tony Bennett?** The boys smash the seriously unhip shellac and leave Mr. Edwards crying on the floor, comforted by Rick, who **wanted to cry himself, but he didn't.**

Next Miss Hammond lures Rick into the office of the school newspaper.

And because the blouse was of the sheerest stuff, there was also no doubting that Lois Hammond was not wearing a slip, or if she was, it was a half-slip that began at her waist and did nothing to conceal the firm, abundant cones of her breasts caught tight in a white cotton bra. . . .

His palms were wet, and his eyes strayed back to the front of the blouse, and he again visualized the exposed white breast on that day of the attempted rape. The brassiere now

cupped her breasts firmly, and there was a deep shadow of warmth between the breasts, and he longed to touch that softly pocketed valley, longed for just an instant, and then turned his eyes away and felt the guilt spread into his face.

The cause of such lustful thoughts, Rick reasons, is his wife. In her untouchable pregnant state she is:

really the forbidden cookie jar, with no ifs, ands, or buts about it.
And so he walked the tightrope of the celibate, with desire on one side, and here, now, temptation on the other side. He would be lying to himself if he did not admit that Lois Hammond was temptation. One of the things Rick had never done was lie to himself.

Rick flees the newspaper office, feeling guilty (again) and flustered, and winds up pointlessly arguing with earnest young Miller and nearly coming to blows. The upset Miller threatens to not show up to class the next day. **The little bastard, [Rick] thought. The little black . . . He stopped abruptly.**

What was that? Of course, Rick *knows* he is not a racist, but he's racked by anxiety. After all, he doesn't want Miller to get the wrong idea that race-hate is the reason he treats the boy like shit. This might lead to trouble with the blacks, you see. Rick recalls the story of a white man who'd had his throat slit by blacks during a race riot. Alas, if only they'd known the man's true sympathies—he was married to a **"Negress"**!

In order to diffuse any suspicion of bigotry, Rick initiates a class discussion to condemn racial epithets. There'll be no **'wops'**, **'kikes'**, **'mockies'**, **'frogs'**, **'spics'**, **'krauts'**, **'micks'**, **'donkeys'**, or **'niggers'** in here. And naturally this leads to a student complaining to the school principal in a plot twist that anticipates Philip Roth's *The Human Stain* (2000) by nearly half a century. But that doesn't go very far.

Rick takes on responsibility for the school play. Miss Hammond becomes the wardrobe mistress, throwing out double entendres and pointed questions. Doesn't he like breaking rules? (**"No,"** [Rick] said, smiling, **"I don't particularly like breaking rules."**). By now Miss Hammond is seriously bored.

"Will you mind if I consider the first day of school the only true piece of excitement we've
had since I've been here? . . . I mean the time the stupid slob tried to rape me, Rick. That's exactly what I mean. My God, sometimes I wish he'd succeeded." She paused and said, **"Oh, not really, but damnit, I'm bored. I'm bored silly."**

Rick is uninterested in alleviating her boredom and does not take her up on her promise of a **'big present'** for Christmas. But he has a lingering feeling of unmanliness. After all, these days everybody seems to think it normal to succumb to extra-marital desire (**Thank you, Dr. Kinsey**). But Rick knows he has **blood**. He hears **his blood loud and strong** when he holds pregnant Anne at night, even if that is **"foolish"** and, yes, another thing to feel guilty about: **he felt somewhat ashamed of himself, as if he should not be feeling desire, not now when she was feeling nothing.**

Anne soon gives birth to a stillborn child and, when Rick finally reveals the fact to her (a day later), she begs her husband to forgive her. It's a guilty world, this 1954. The school drama culminates in a classroom switchblade fight between Rick and West, the class's worst-behaving kid. But rather than gang up on Rick, most of the other boys disarm West. A little hope. Rick and Miller become friends.

"It's an angry book in many ways," Hunter told American broadcaster and journalist Don Swaim in 1984. At the time it was widely denounced by teachers' groups as an inaccurate representation of the vocational school system.

In 1956 Hunter began publishing the very successful 87th Precinct police procedural series as Ed McBain, initially as paperback originals through Permabooks. That same year a dozen of Hunter's stories from *Manhunt* and other magazines were published as *The Jungle Kids*, a paperback-only collection from Pocket Books with a cover painting by Tom Dunn. In its design the book displays a clear continuity with the slightly more expensive paperback edition of *Blackboard Jungle*. The back-cover copy emphasised Hunter's youth (he was now 29) and claimed: HERE ARE A GROUP OF HIS SHORT STORIES CONCERNING YOUNGSTERS AND CRIME . . . HERE ARE THE STORIES BEHIND THE HEADLINES—TRAGIC, FRIGHTENING, ACCURATE EPISODES OF LIFE IN THE MODERN JUNGLE, THE STREETS AND CELLARS, THE HALLWAYS AND ROOF TOPS, THE PARKS AND SLUMS OF A BIG CITY.

The author's note asserts its basis in firsthand experience and says: I make no apologies for the

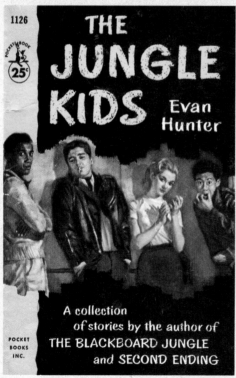

Second Ending (Corgi, 1957)
The Jungle Kids (Pocket Books, 1956)

violence I present. The violence was, and is, there on the streets. But I have tried, in these stories, to present much more than a bloody canvas.

Not every story directly concerned delinquency, but the JD angle provided the overriding theme: the threat of wild and unprovoked kid violence in the big bad city. You are given the impression America's inner city has been invaded by an alien force. The point of view varies from adult victims to the juveniles themselves. In 'The Follower' (*Manhunt*, July 1953), a seemingly invisible teenage stalker waits until everybody is convinced of a woman's paranoia before striking. 'The Jungle Kids' (*Adventure*, October 1955), revisits the classroom milieu of *The Blackboard Jungle*. An impromptu classroom court seeks to identify a schoolboy mugger, who intimidates the witnesses with **homemade brass knuckles, fashioned from the handle of a garbage can lid.** A crafty teacher puts a Hispanic patsy named Sanchez on the stand. When pushed, Sanchez fingers the mugger. It is left to a previously **mild** teacher to sock the mugger in the jaw before he can leap onto the stand. 'The Beatings' (*Manhunt,* October 1954) is one of Hunter's stories about Matt Cordell, a drunk ex-cop/amateur detective, investigating a particularly sadistic spate of attacks on alcoholic bums on the Bowery. After one drunk dies from the assault, Cordell decides to put himself on the street as a lure. Turns out the attackers are a quartet of youths out for **kicks from a deadly dull summer.** Who else has so much time on their hands? Cordell beats the shit out of them. One kid's fate: **I jack-knifed my leg, and then I shot out with my foot, and I felt the sole of my shoe collide with his crotch, and I was sure I'd squashed his scrotum flat.** Another: **He screamed when he tried to break his fall with his hands, spraining them, and then his head hit the concrete, and he wasn't doing any more screaming.** Another: **I had the little finger of his left hand between my own hands, and I shoved it back as far as it would go, and then some.** And he saves the worst violence (unspecified) for the last kid. Afterwards the local police detective closes the case and offers to buy Cordell a drink.

Paranoia about juveniles finds its extreme form in 'Kid Kill' (*Manhunt*, April 1953). A ten-year-old boy shoots his younger brother dead with a Luger. What appears to be a sad accident between innocent children is unmasked by a cop as cold, perfectly premeditated murder with Oedipal motivations (the killer's older brother died in the war and their father is already dead). **"Just him and Mum now,"** the cop says. **"But just take it to a judge . . . Just take the whole fantastic thing to a judge and see how fast he kicks you out of court."**

The stories are far more interesting when they take the point of view of the jungle kids themselves. 'See Him Die' (*Manhunt*, July 1955) would form the basis of the 87th Precinct novel *See Them Die* (1962), probably Hunter's most enduring JD narrative. The original story is written in first person JD argot:

> **[Officer Donlevy] had me in once because some jerk from the Blooded Royals took a slug from a zip gun, and he figured it was one of my boys, and he tried to hang it on me. I told Donlevy where he could hang his phony rap, and I also told him he better not walk alone on our block after dark or he'd be using his shield for a funeral emblem. He kicked me in the butt, and told me I was the one better watch out, so I spit at his feet and called him a name my old man always uses, and Donlevy wasn't hip to it so he didn't get too sore, even though he knew I was cursing . . .**

Danny, an Italian-American punk, takes the side of legendary local thug Django Manzetti, wanted by the cops. During a siege Danny directly assists Manzetti's murder of a policeman. Manzetti is killed. Danny is unrepentant. Others in Danny's gang have less admiration of Manzetti, so need to be fixed by Danny **just the way Django would have liked it.**

The theme of heroin addiction, which was subsequently the focus of Hunter's jazz novel *Second Ending* (aka *Quartet in H*, 1956), informs the cautionary'. . . Or Leave It Alone' (*Manhunt*, May 1954). A young addict in denial jumps out of a tenement window and finds himself stuck in a drain with a broken leg, just a few feet away from the fix that could take away the pain. Upstairs his junkie friend Annie, who is **built like a plastic latrine**, dozes on H. Our narrator nearly goes mad waiting for her help.

Two of the Hunter stories were adapted for 1957 episodes of *Alfred Hitchcock Presents*. In 'Vicious Circle' (*Real*, March 1953), a young hoodlum performs a hit for the mob and is ordered to kill his girlfriend when she threatens to go to the cops. By the end of the story the hoodlum is an emotional wreck.

'First Offense' (*Manhunt*, December 1955) is one of Hunter's most anthologized stories. Seven-teen-year-old Stevie has stabbed a candy store owner during a robbery. He is arrogant, unrepentant, stupidly ignorant, and does not heed the weary advice of an old 'bum' named Skinner. At the police lineup, one guy is interrogated about carrying an unregistered .45 Colt automatic. Next we meet a shifty unmarried couple caught with a carload of stolen goods. Then Skinner refuses to talk about his attempted robbery. We learn he's been in and out of prison for years. Finally Stevie takes the stage and learns the store owner has died of his wounds. A murder rap.

The two best and best-known JD short stories by Hunter are 'The Last Spin' and a story which just missed out on being included in *The Jungle Kids*, 'On the Sidewalk, Bleeding.' Both are simple but classic stories from the street.

'The Last Spin' (*Manhunt*, September 1956) relates a game of Russian roulette to settle a dispute between rival gangs: **This is how the club said we should settle it. Without a big street diddlebop, you dig?** Between increasingly higher-stake rounds of the game the two opposites find common ground. Before the last spin of the chamber they've agreed to go double dating with their respective chicks. But alas,

> **the explosion rocked the small basement room, ripping away half of Dave's head, shattering his face. A small cry escaped Tigo's throat, and a look of incredulous shock knifed his eyes. Then he put his head on the table and began weeping.**

In 'On the Sidewalk, Bleeding' (*Manhunt*, July 1957), a young gang member lies in the rain at night, the life leaking out of him from a stab wound received during a rumble. He thinks about his girl. Nobody helps him. A drunk mistakes him for one of his kind; a couple refuses to get involved in gang warfare; a homeless woman doesn't notice him at all. Dying, the boy renounces his affiliation with his gang, the Royals, and in excruciating pain removes his member's jacket (**the knife hated only the purple jacket**). He is eventually found by his girlfriend, who gets a cop. Alas, the boy is dead. The cop thinks of him only as a Royal.

One more story from the *Jungle Kids* period is particularly noteworthy. 'Sucker' (*Manhunt*, December 1953) is another rape-and-murder story, this time from the point of view of a lawyer duped by his defendant who, as it turns out, does lust after 16-year-old girls after all and *must* therefore be the killer. Unique among these stories, the violence is initiated by an adult against an innocent child—surely the real epidemic in 1953, as now.

In 1959 Hunter, by now very successful as Ed McBain, published *A Matter of Conviction*, another prestige hardcover about juvenile delinquency, presumably an attempt to recapture the success of *Jungle*. It became *The Young Savages*, a 1961 film directed by John Frankenheimer and starring Burt Lancaster.

Again a working-class liberal, risen by hard work, must deal with juvenile delinquents as the representative of a state institution. Hank Bell is a city prosecutor and, like Rick Dadier, a sexual square. He had met his German wife Karin during the war and is **disturbed** by **the puritanical fact that he had not been the first with Karin Brucker.** You know what happens during war. Fourteen years on, Hank still harbours thoughts of a lost love, Mary O'Brien, who **would not have.**

Out in Harlem, the July heat has not broken.

Now they came down the street, three tall boys walking rapidly and without fear . . . bursting into the mouth of the street like alien hand-grenade explosions. Their combat boots hit the pavement in regulated chaos, their fists were bunched, there was in each a high-riding excitement which threatened to blow the tops of their skulls and dissipate their generated anger. The tallest of the three pulled a knife, and the blade glittered in the paling light, and then there were three knives, the silent performers in a vaudeville pantomime, and a young girl shouted in Spanish "Mira! Cuidado!" and one of the boys yelled, "Shut up, you spic whore!" and a boy sitting on one of the stoops turned his head towards the sound of unaccented English then suddenly rose . . .

A blade flashed, penetrated, flesh ripped in silent protest as the knife gashed upwards from the gut. And now the other knives descended, tearing and slashing until the boy fell like an assassin-surrounded Caesar, crumpling to the pavement. The knives withdrew. Blood spattered like early rain to the sidewalk . . .

The rain drummed relentlessly on the figure balled against the stone of the stoop, diluting the rich red blood that ran from his open belly, washing the blood into the gutter that traversed the long street.

It is left to Hank to prosecute the three white teenage gang members for the murder of their Puerto Rican victim, a defenseless blind boy. But one of the defendants' mothers turns out to be Mary O'Brien—the same virginal ex-girlfriend Hank had just that morning been thinking about. This is complicated. Mary petitions for his mercy.

There is no legal impediment to the court sending children to the electric chair; this is a special case, and the city wants blood. As one of Hank's colleagues says, **"this whole damn juvenile-delinquency thing is giving the city a fat pain in the foot. Everybody's screaming about it, the cops, the schools, the judges, the press, the grand juries . . ."** What's more, **"tolerance groups have all piled on the bandwagon demanding equal justice"** for the blind Puerto Rican victim. The few 'liberal' anti-death-penalty-for-kids advocates we meet are shown to be actually motivated by anti-Puerto Rican racism.

Meanwhile, Hank seeks the true causes of ethnic violence in the city. He consults a psychologist to discuss the Glueck social prediction table on delinquency. He wanders into the competing gang districts. Like Dadier in *Blackboard Jungle*, he is savagely beaten by JDs, this time with tire chains.

A kick tore open his face. He could feel the skin ripping apart like the skin of a frankfurter on the outdoor barbeque grill of his home in Inwood, his face tearing, it was funny, the warm flow of blood, I must protect my teeth, the city swarming around him, all the sounds of the city rushing into the vortex of fifty-foot blackness on the path of the park, and the chains whipping, and the boots, the boots, and within him the outrage at the injustice, the impotent outrage suffocating him, rising inside him until a shocking star-shell explosion of pain rocked the back of his head and sent him soaring wildly into unconsciousness.

Fortunately Hank's scrotum escapes flattening.

As prosecutor, he finally discovers the truth on the witness stand: Danny, son of Mary, did not actually participate in the killing—he turned his knife-blade around. For Hank, representative of the state, it is a **matter of conviction** that the boy go free. It was society that killed the blind Puerto Rican. Or something.

With such astonishing early success under his own name and as Ed McBain, Hunter became a dashing figure to his younger admirers at Scott Meredith. Earl Kemp, the editor of softcore erotic novels supplied

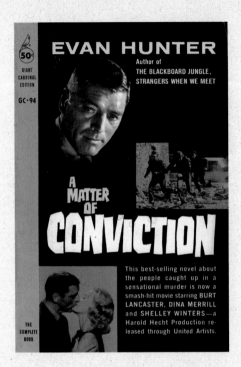

A Matter of Conviction (Pocket Books, 1960
The Young Savages movie poster (1961)

by the Meredith agency to Bill Hamling's various paperback imprints, wrote in 2006 of a "separation of awe" between the Meredith staff and their hugely successful predecessor at the agency. Both Kemp and Lawrence Block, in a 2011 article for *Mystery Scene*, claim Hunter ghost-wrote sex novels attributed to 'Dean Hudson' in exchange for envelopes of untaxable cash to finance extra-marital entanglements.

Despite superficial appearances, neither Rick Dadier or Hank Bell seem particularly autobiographical characters. The sexual conservatism of these early Hunter heroes seems calculated. Years later, discussing his Matthew Hope series, Hunter acknowledged the commercial mistake of putting forward an adulterer as a hero to a readership of mostly women. Maybe somebody had warned him early on.

When not publishing as Ed McBain, Hunter continued to publish hardcover novels that never recaptured the success of *Blackboard Jungle*. Delinquency narratives lost their commercial relevance in the 60s. If 'Ed McBain' was an easily quantifiable bestselling brand in the crime market, 'Evan Hunter' became uncategorisable. He worked diligently in many modes: the hefty potboiler romance (*Strangers When We Meet*, 1958), the generational saga (*Mothers and Daughters*, 1961; *Sons*, 1968), the courtroom drama (*The Paper Dragon*, 1966), the mafia farce (*A Horse's Head*, 1967; *Every Little Crook and Nanny*, 1972), the political thriller (*Nobody Knew They Were There*, 1971), the immi-

grant saga (*Streets of Gold*, 1974), the western (*The Chisholms*, 1976), the historical crime novel (*Lizzie*, 1984), the adulterous thriller (*Criminal Conversation*, 1994; *Privileged Conversation*, 1996), and family dramas such as *Far from the Sea* (1983), *Love, Dad* (1984), and *When She Was Gone* (2002). The Evan Hunter who had begun writing juvies was eclipsed. When Hunter made a final round-up of his early crime stories under the title *Learning to Kill* (2005), many of them from *The Jungle Kids*, it went out under the more familiar name Ed McBain, who had not even existed in those days.

A decade after Hunter's death in 2005, nearly all the Evan Hunter novels are out of print. Often topical and derivative of contemporary bestsellers, they are not without virtue. A strong case could also be made for the quality of Hunter's later work, particularly *Candyland* (2000), a 'collaboration' between Hunter and McBain. But for now Hunter's legacy is as the inventor of the 87th Precinct.

MATTHEW ASPREY GEAR

The Amboy Dukes—Irving Shulman (Doubleday, 1947)

Irving Shulman's novel about delinquent Jewish teenagers in the Brownsville section of Brooklyn was a publishing sensation upon its release in 1947, selling five million copies. It was also widely condemned as "pornographic" and reportedly banned in Canada. Almost seventy years later, the book still occasionally shocks with its brutality, but also with its pessimism: in the post-Depression urban ghetto, everyone is corrupted and no one will be redeemed.

Set early in the summer of 1944 (with a brief prologue in 1942), the book deals with the unexpected fallout of the wartime economic boom in poverty-ravaged Brownsville. After a decade of scraping by on Federal Relief, 16-year-old Frank Goldfarb's Depression-scarred parents eagerly take overtime shifts at the local munitions plant and the Brooklyn Navy Base, leaving Frank and his 11-year-old sister, Alice, more or less to fend for themselves. The Goldfarbs view the wartime economic boom as the opportunity to put aside money to move out of Brownsville and send their children to college; Frank takes the opportunity to start skipping school and running around with the Dukes, one of the many gangs that have sprung up in the absence of parental oversight.

The other authority figures in the neighborhood are ineffectual, to say the least: Mr. Bannon, the shop teacher at New Lots Vocational High School is both fed up with and overwhelmed by his charges. Stan Alberg, the former gym teacher who now runs the local JCC, naively believes that with enough basketballs he can cure Brownsville's societal ills.

Frank sets out each Monday morning by packing his voluminous suit with 'reefers', condoms, and a zip gun built in wood shop, for a day of cutting class. The first third of the book is a series of incidents predicated on shock value, as the boys grope a woman on the subway, pick a fight with a Puerto Rican gang from Ocean Hill, pick up some 'fast' high school girls at the local movie theater, get high, get drunk and round out the evening by beating up and robbing the middle-aged prostitute who has just serviced them.

When the plot finally gets started, it hinges on two incidents: the killing of shop teacher Mr. Bannon and subsequent rape of a gang member's 12-year-old 'girlfriend', Fanny Kane, at a dance thrown by the Dukes to raise bail for the members being held 'on suspicion' in Bannon's death.

By the next morning the entire neighborhood knows that Fanny was raped. Distressingly, most of the neighborhood is in agreement that Fanny was headed down a bad road and so this sort of thing was inevitable. Only Frank's parents seem to grasp the horror of the situation, and they hold their son responsible.

Turned away by his parents and younger sister, Frank flees to the roof of the apartment building, where a gang member known as Crazy suddenly appears and pushes him over the side. With remarkable economy of prose, Shulman depicts Frank's demise:

With flaying arms and legs Frank fell and hit the rail of the third-story fire escape, then caromed out in an arc toward the street, screaming his life away.

The book was adapted as a movie, *City Across the River* (1949); Shulman would later gain his most lasting fame by addressing affluent suburban delinquency in his screenplay for *Rebel Without a Cause* (1955).

MOLLY GRATTAN

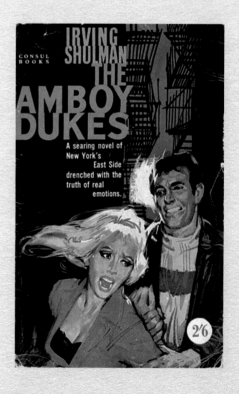

The Amboy Dukes (Avon, 1947)
The Amboy Dukes (Consul, 1962)
The Amboy Dukes (Pocket Books, 1971)

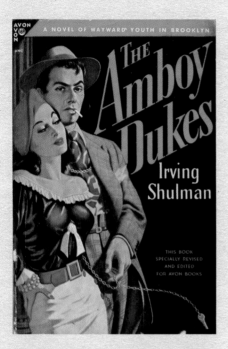

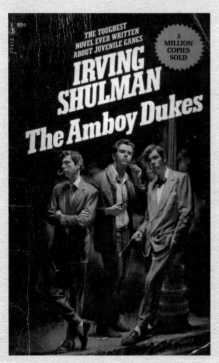

The neighborhoods of Brownsville, East New York and Ocean Hill were infested with gangs. The Pitkin Giants, the Amboy Dukes, the Sutter Kings, the Killers, the D-Rape Artists, the Zeros, the Enigmas, the Wildcats and the Patty Cakes were just a few of the gangs that fought, slugged and terrorized the neighborhood. They fought for the sheer joy of bloodying and mauling one another, and no insult was so slight that it could not be used as an excuse for a mass riot and free-for-all.

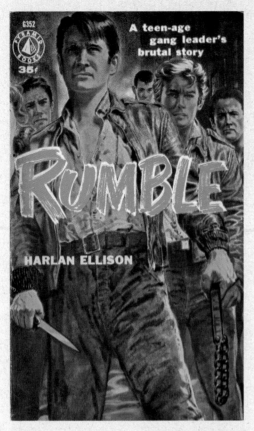

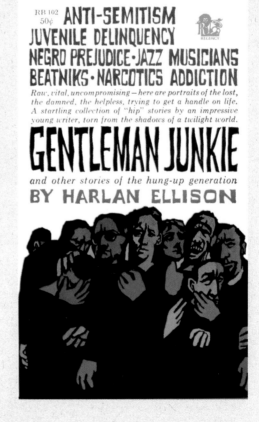

Rumble
(Pyramid, 1958)

Harlan Ellison in the 1990s (Photo by Chris Cuffaro)

Gentleman Junkie
(Regency, 1961)

The Deadly Streets
(Digit, 1958)

SOME SKETCHES OF THE DAMNED
The Early Pulp Fiction of Harlan Ellison

With over fifteen hundred works to his name, Harlan Ellison is an iconic figure in science fiction and fantasy circles. Best known for the stories '"Repent, Harlequin!" Said the Ticktockman' (1965), 'I Have No Mouth and I Must Scream' (1967), and 'A Boy and His Dog' (1969), as well as his trenchant criticism of literature, politics and television, he has won numerous prizes, including the Hugo Award eight times, the Nebula four times, and the Edgar Allan Poe twice. With a reputation as much for curmudgeonly sensitivity as for authorial and critical brilliance, he has regularly appeared on television and radio and at sci-fi conventions, often turning the tables on his interviewers in a manner as uncomfortable as it is entertaining.

Ellison's writing has touched on numerous topics in the realms of fiction and non-fiction with the distinction between the two, particularly regarding his own biography, often blurred. This article, which features extensive quotes from my 2013 interview with the author, provides an overview of his earliest work in the pulp field. A passion for life on the margins, along with his own experience of transiency and street life, led to him producing dozens of short stories in the 1950s and early 60s concerning youth gangs, musicians, beats and others, as well as the novels *Web of the City* (1958) and *Rockabilly* (1961), and the biographical *Memos from Purgatory* (1961).

Born in Cleveland, Ohio, on May 27, 1934, and raised in nearby Painesville, Ellison was an outsider from a young age. Small in stature and chafing at the restrictions that school placed on his intellect, he found himself the target of bullies fuelled by anti-semitism and contempt for his already defiant and unconventional nature. Constantly in trouble—and inspired by the writings of early 20th-century American bohemian writers Jim Tully and Jack London—he, like many young men of the period, sought escape by running away to join the carnival in 1947.

By the time I started kindergarten I could already read, and they put me in a room with children who were playing with blocks. On that first day I got into trouble and was called to the principal's office, the first of many hejiras to that place. Half an hour after she had dropped me off, my mother was called to take me home.

This is how I led my life until the age of 13 in Painesville, when I walked out the door and, with a hubris unparalleled since Adolf Hitler was born, looked at the world and said, 'This is all mine. I own all of this. All I have to do is go and get it.' The only glitch was that I was not allowed to cross the street.

Very soon thereafter I ran away from home. Not because I was beaten or mistreated, but because I was sick and tired of anti-semites busting my chops and ripping my clothes off in the snow. In my day there was no such thing as an electric guitar, so I couldn't form a rock band. In my day you ran away and joined the circus.

I couldn't find a circus, so I joined a carnival that did tri-state shows. I was with them for about four weeks, through Pennsylvania, Ohio, Michigan and parts of Kentucky, until the whole show got busted. It was what they called a 'burn the lot' operation with pickpockets, grifters and people who would cosh you over the noggin with a sock full of quarters to get your money. Everybody got sprung except me and a 'geek,' because they could find a kid to sweep up behind the elephant and a geek anywhere. A geek was a drunkard who is so far gone into alcoholism that his brain is literally turned into mush. He sweats sour mash out of his pores and bites the heads off chickens and sleeps with snakes so that they will give him his bottle of gin every day.

I was in a big freestanding cell for three days with this guy as he literally went insane, bashing his head against the bars until he went comatose. I was the most naive, tiny little person imaginable and was sitting in tears with my feet sticking out of the bars, because I wanted some part of me to be free, until I was located and sent home to my parents. It put me off drinking for life.

After the death of his father in 1949, Ellison's family returned to Cleveland. Already a voracious reader of everything from pulp novels to high philosophy, he became an avid member of the city's sci-fi scene, editing fanzines, corresponding with authors and publishers, and attending the kind of conventions he would one day headline. A self-described 'adolescent snot,' the young fanboy rapidly established a critical style that combined harsh reviews with insightful enthusiasm.

Unsuccessful in his initial attempts to break into professional story writing, Ellison began studying at Ohio State University in 1953. It was only 18 months before he was either expelled or left following numerous clashes with staff and fellow students, accounts of which vary greatly. By now he'd had articles printed in newspapers and a script used by EC Comics, so he moved to New York to pursue a full-time writing career.

Following the success of Irving Shulman's *The Amboy Dukes* (1947) and Hal Ellson's *Duke* (1949), stories about juvenile delinquency and gangs had developed into a whole genre. Inspired by the latter's work, and having observed members of a gang called the Blooded Royals in the street, Ellison decided to go undercover and join a gang himself. Settling in the Red Hook area of Brooklyn, he took on the persona of Phil 'Cheech' Baldone and, pretending he had previously been involved in gangs elsewhere, finagled his way into the ranks of an outfit he later dubbed 'the Barons.' Immersed in the subculture for ten weeks, Ellison was put through a three-part initiation, became the gang's war counsellor and survived a major rumble.

These experiences subsequently provided the fuel for Ellison's first professionally published story, 'I Ran with a Kid Gang' (1955), in the exposé magazine *Lowdown*. Over the next two years he would compose over 100 stories, many of them concerning youth gangs, for publications such as *Guilty*, *Manhunt* and *Dude*. A number of these were later gathered in the Ace collections *The Deadly Streets* (1958) and *The Juvies* (1961, later reissued as *The Children of the Streets*).

Although I wrote about them in a memoir and various stories, I've never revealed the true name of the gang I called the Barons because I didn't want to cause any harm to the people involved. I strongly believe you should never do anything to harm your friends.

At one point I needed to update my knowledge of the teen gangs. I've always felt it was very important to be *au courant* with slanguage as well as with the facial tics, eye tells and head movements. Anyone who knows my work knows that I pay great attention to facial expressions. I couldn't return to the Red Hook area because I had disappeared from the Barons suddenly, so I went to Queens, where I spent some time on the fringes of an assemblage called the Kicks.

They were what was known as a bopping gang. They existed to defend their territory, fight with other gangs and terrorize any citizens who had the *cojones* to stand up to them and tell them to get off the sidewalk.

Ellison's time with the Barons also provided the grist for his debut novel, 1958's *Rumble* (aka *Web of the City*), the plot of which sees former gang leader Rusty Santoro attempt to go 'straight' following a stint in reform school. Despite the mentorship of a trusted teacher he continually has to fend off the lure of the street and attacks from his former friends in the Cougars. After his sister—still involved with the gang—is murdered, Rusty hunts down her killer, delving into the world of drug dealing in the process.

The book was finished during 1957 while Ellison was completing basic training as a conscript in the army. In order to avoid disturbing his fellow draftees he worked in the toilet, using a typewriter placed on a board on his lap. A poorly constructed and self-admittedly flawed work, *Web of the City* was reissued by modern-day pulp specialist Hard Case Crime in 2013, with additional stories from the period.

Web of the City came out in 1958 while I was in the army. I was working in the Public Information Center at Fort Knox, Kentucky. I was constantly in trouble and had to figure my way out of the system—and managed to get a spot editing the newspaper at the base. I started a review column so I could read lots of books and wouldn't have to buy them.

One day I opened this box from Pyramid Books, who were one of the lower-echelon paperback houses . . . I pick up this book and it's got this horrible, garish juvenile delinquent coming at you with a switchblade knife and it says *Rumble*. I thought 'What is this piece of shit?' and then I looked at the author and it was me. I had sold *Web of the City* to Lion, but they had gone out of business and sold all the stuff in the drawers to Pyramid, who had renamed the book. It's been reissued a number of times since, and each time I've made sure it's been under the title *Web of the City*.

After getting out of the army in 1959, Ellison's next move was to Evanston, Illinois, where he edited the men's magazine *Rogue* for Greenleaf Publishing Company proprietor and longtime sci-fi fan and editor Bill

Hamling. During the same year Greenleaf imprint Nightstand Books produced, under the pseudonym Paul Merchant, an anthology of psychosexual stories Ellison had written for the magazine he was now editing and for other publications of a similar ilk. Originally titled *Sex Gang: Violent Stories of Naked Passions*, the collection was reissued in 2012 as two paperbacks, *Pulling a Train* and *Getting in the Wind*, by Norton Records' imprint Kicks.

Drawing on his experiences with the Barons, Ellison also continued to give lectures about juvenile delinquency for a variety of organisations.

After my time with the gangs I had begun lecturing in New York. Why did I do it? For the same reason anyone who's been around poverty or kids who are in peril, or who has a sense of needing to serve the Commonweal. Any decent human being should try and give back, and since my gifts are in writing and speaking I lectured frequently to chapters of the Police Athletic League, where they got kids off the streets or from gangs in a 1950s version of what they now call 'scared straight.' I'd talk to a room full of kids or go to the jail or Bellevue Hospital or wherever.

When I went to Chicago I lectured there about the same things, as well as against censorship. I had been lecturing since the early 1950s, either at science fiction conventions, charity drives or for the American Civil Liberties Union. When a 'morals campaigner' came to Evanston I attended his meeting. He was a very right-wing bible thumper who had a thing about pornography. He later appeared on the public scene a lot more but at this time was active in and around Chicago. I stood up at the public meeting and stripped him naked.

According to an introduction Ellison provided for a 1975 reissue of his 1961 anthology *Gentleman Junkie and Other Stories of the Hung-up Generation*, his time in Illinois editing *Rogue* was unhappy for the most part. Following a period of prolonged stress, an incident at a party pushed Ellison into a meltdown. Confronted by science-fiction author Frank Robinson over his dissolute ways, Ellison immediately sat down and began composing his next novel. Released in 1961 by Gold Medal under the title of *Rockabilly* (but retitled *Spider Kiss* in later editions), it follows the rise and fall of singer Luther Sellers, aka Stag Preston. After attaining stardom, the celebrity's music becomes

The Juvies (Ace, 1961)
Rumble (Pyramid, 1963)

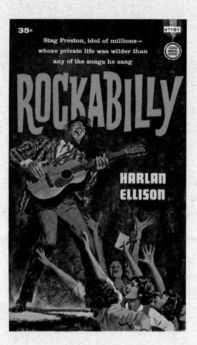

Rockabilly
(Gold Medal, 1961)

increasingly bland and his demeanor contemptuous. Despising his fans, he hides his calculating and malicious nature behind a bumpkin persona. Through a number of incidents, including paying off a singer he impregnates and buying back a stag film he appears in, the singer is revealed as a sociopathic liar, and his career takes a slide. Written after the 1959 congressional hearings into the payola scandal (illegal payments by record companies to DJs in return for airplay), it was the first mainstream novel to expose the manipulation, cynicism and exploitation at the heart of the music business.

Everybody thinks the book is about Elvis Presley, but it's closer to Jerry Lee Lewis. I had been into music since I was a child, beginning with swing and jazz. I was writing for magazines like *Downbeat*, *Metronome*, etc. and I also knew a lot of rock-and-roll people.

I wrote the novel with Jerry Lee as my image. It started out as a short story called 'Matinee Idyll' (1958) for *Trapped Detective Story Magazine,* who published it as 'Rock and Roll—and Murder.' I took as my keynote the fact Jerry Lee had married his 13-year-old cousin [then reputed to be 15] and created a character who attained success, but was amoral, self-consumed and filled with hubris. Characters like this do not understand their place in the universe and think they can do anything and get away with it. There had been a number of books dealing with jazz, but this was the first rock novel.

The year 1961 also saw Greenleaf's new imprint Regency publish Ellison's *Memos from Purgatory*, a non-fiction memoir divided into two halves: one a detailed retelling of his time with the Barons and the other concerning an arrest and stay in New York's infamous Tombs prison years later. Under pressure from his publisher, Ellison linked the two sections through an unlikely and invented meeting with the leader of the Barons during the evening behind bars, a revision he later revealed and rejected. The success of the memoir led to an 1964 episode of the *Alfred Hitchcock Hour*, slightly retitled as 'Memo from Purgatory,' in which a somewhat more straitlaced character, played by James Caan, infiltrates a JD gang.

When I was done with my first stint in Chicago I went back to New York. I was lecturing again about juvenile delinquency, but times were changing. Kid gangs were not what they had been. The rumbling gangs were now maturing into criminal enterprises.

Around this time (1960) I had a personal dustup with an idiot who called the police and told them I had a storehouse of armaments and narcotics, even though everybody knows I have

GIRL GANGS, BIKER BOYS, AND REAL COOL CATS

never used narcotics and never will. The weaponry I had was in a locked file case . . . items I used for demonstrations during my lectures. They were knives cut from steel girders, zip guns, and things of that nature. One of the items was a gun I had taken from a guy and never bothered to check. Its clip was gone but it was fireable.

One Sunday the police came to my door, took me in and I was arrested for the possession of a firearm. I spent a horrible night in jail, but when I went before the court they brought in a *nolo contendere*, that is a not guilty, no contest finding.

Following the memoir's publication, Ellison returned to Evanston to work for Bill Hamling again, despite his previous negative experiences. The author had married for the second time and needed a job, so he agreed to run Greenleaf's Regency imprint. In between dutifully editing titles on homosexuality, cults and scams, he also published original work by gifted writers such as Robert Bloch, Robert Sheckley and Clarence Cooper (for whom he wrote an introduction to the 1962 collection *Black*). He was also able to help out an early inspiration.

I had first become interested in juvenile delinquents after reading Hal Ellson's excellent novel *Tomboy* (1950). Hal was a youth adviser and worked at Bellevue Hospital in New York. When I became the editor for Regency Books I was able to publish one of his best books, *The Torment of the Kids* (1961). I was also able to champion a number of great writers' work and got to work with another of my favourite authors, Jim Thompson.

In the same crowded year, his anthology *Gentleman Junkie and Other Stories of the Hung-up Generation* was also published by Regency. The collection's release was delayed and fairly tortured, due to widening differences with Hamling, but it launched the next phase of Ellison's career. Featuring stories originally published in a variety of magazines, including *Rogue* and *Alfred Hitchcock's Mystery Magazine*, the anthology was Ellison's strongest outing yet, homing in on racial and other forms of discrimination in the US and providing plenty of wit and suspense in the process. Praised in *Esquire* by Dorothy Parker as "a good, honest, clean writer, putting down what he has seen and known, and with no sensationalism about it", Ellison had one of the stories optioned. Having returned to New York from Chicago, he sold a new collection of speculative fiction stories, *Ellison Wonderland* (1962), to Paperback Library and used the money to move to Hollywood.

Once in L.A. he became involved in scriptwriting telemovies as well as episodes for everything from *The Flying Nun* to *The Outer Limits* and *The Man from U.N.C.L.E.* At one point he was hired to work for Disney, a career move that did not last long.

I despise Walt Disney; he was a thief and a con man. And this is coming from someone who has great respect for most con men. I wrote about my time at Disney in an essay called 'The Three Most Important Things in Life,' which of course are sex, violence and labor relations. A lot of people think I lasted there a day, but it was actually only three hours from the moment I drove onto the lot and they said, 'Welcome, Mr. Ellison.' I didn't know what I was going to be writing or what the project was, but my name was on the parking spot and I went to the office and my name was on the door.

Whilst having lunch at the Disney commissary with four other writers, I described in detail my ideas for a pornographic Disney movie, doing all the voices out loud. Roy Disney, Walt's brother, who ran the studio, was sitting in the booth behind me and when I arrived back at my office there was a pink slip saying, 'You're fired. Get out of the studio.'

Based in Los Angeles, where he would remain for the rest of his life, Ellison wrote continuously in a variety of formats, winning his first Nebula and Hugo awards for '"Repent, Harlequin!" Said the Ticktockman' in 1965. A major supporter of the political and experimental 'New Wave' group of science fiction writers, he compiled the seminal *Dangerous Visions* (1967) and *Again, Dangerous Visions* (1972) collections, bringing together groundbreaking work by British authors such as J. G. Ballard and John Brunner with Americans such as Philip K. Dick and Ursula K. Le Guin.

Through the 1980s and beyond Ellison continued to write in various fields, as well as provide voiceovers, act, and work as a consultant for radio and TV shows including *The Twilight Zone* and *Babylon 5*. Ellen Weil and Gary K. Wolfe's *Harlan Ellison: The Edge of Forever* offers a critical study of his works, while 2008's must-see documentary *Dreams with Sharp Teeth* provides a career overview, highlighting Ellison's penetrating and combative nature.

IAIN McINTYRE

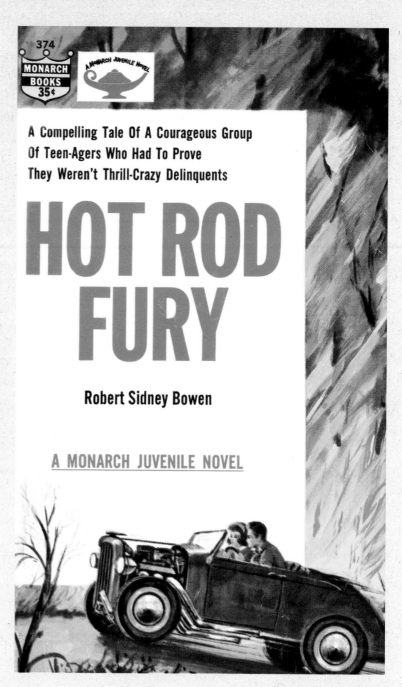

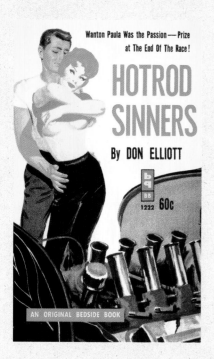

Crash Club (Bantam, 1960)
Hot Rod Fury (Monarch, 1963)
Hotrod Sinners (Bedside, 1962)

PLAYING CHICKEN
1950s Hot Rod Pulps

Along with drive-in movies, hamburger joints, rock and roll, and juvenile delinquency, hot rodding was one of the defining activities of the American youth movement of the 1950s. It had its origins in late-30s Southern California, but hot rodding ('hot rod' is believed to be a contraction of 'hot roadster') really came into its own after World War Two, in the late 1940s and early 50s. Kids who had grown up while dad was fighting overseas were now in their late teens and had acquired an independent streak—cars were a principal indicator of social status and freedom. An abundance of military air force bases, abruptly deserted across the United States after the war ended, provided perfect spots for local hot rod clubs to meet, race, and grow.

As rodding's popularity surged, magazines celebrating the culture appeared, starting with *Hot Rod* in 1948 and followed shortly by publications like *Car Craft* and *Rod and Custom*. The second half of the 1950s saw an explosion of low-budget B-movies cashing in on the craze: *Hot Rod Girl* (1956), *Hot Rod Rumble* (1957), *Dragstrip Riot* (1958) and many others. With so many teenagers making the drive-in their Saturday night destination of choice, hot rods and B-movies seemed a natural combination, especially if the theatre paired it with some American International creature feature like *The Beast with 1,000,000 Eyes* (1955) or *Invasion of the Saucer Men* (1957).

The emergence of the muscle car in the 1960s, combined with rising gas prices and an economic downturn in the 1970s, saw hot rodding's popularity decline. It was kept alive by a small but devoted band of die-hard enthusiasts and enjoyed a renaissance in the late 90s, spurred by a new generation's affinity for 1950s teen and rebel culture (which also included rockabilly music, burlesque, Bettie Page, and Sailor Jerry tattoos).

Intrinsically tied to the perceived increase in juvenile delinquency, hot rodding's original wave was perfect fodder for paperback publishers, who were always on the lookout for something new and controversial to exploit, especially if they could sensationalise it. Hot rod novels did not constitute a particularly large genre, but they certainly generated a few classic titles, which remain some of the most hotly sought-after books by paperback collectors.

Crash Club—Henry Gregor Felsen

During the 1950s, Iowan writer Henry Gregor Felsen (1916–1995) was the undisputed king of hot rod paperback fiction, with titles like *Hot Rod* (1950), *Street Rod* (1953) and *Fever Heat* (1954, as Angus Vicker) to his credit. Most of his books followed the same basic plot: a hot-headed, teenaged speed freak learns the dangers of fast and reckless driving the hard way, through the death of either himself or someone close to him (usually his best buddy or an innocent girlfriend).

Written at a time when concern over teenage driving habits was at an all-time high, Felsen's hot rod pulps could be found lining the shelves of many American high school libraries well into the 70s. Grim and preachy, they were a perfect companion piece to the gory driver education shorts being turned out by the likes of Highway Safety Films, Inc.—featuring titles like *Mechanized Death* (1961) and *Highways of Agony* (1969)—and shown to high school students at the time.

His books were often dedicated to his son, who seems to have inspired the characters for many of his hot rod adventures.

> To my teen-age son
> And his teen-age friends.
> Black leather boots,
> Blue denims,
> Turned-up jacket collars,
> And all . . .

Crash Club (Bantam, 1958) is perhaps Felsen's most curious and original work within the genre, centering on the deadly road game of 'chicken', where drivers would race towards a deadly destination (usually a high cliff top or brick wall), with the driver who waits the longest to slam their breaks on being declared the winner (and the loser being branded, naturally, as a 'chicken').

> "When you're top man," said Mike Revere, leader of the high school gang, "You've got to fight to keep it that way."
> The exhaust pipes of his bronze coupe blasted his victories in the drags. He set the

fads, made the decisions. And Donna Whittier, loveliest, coolest blonde in school, was his girl.

But then Dave 'Outlaw' Gale moved to town. Outlaw had utter contempt for authority. The gang was dazzled by his $4,000 Chevy FI.

Mike saw he had to fight for his title. His answer to Outlaw's bid for power was a new kind of hot rod club.

He called it Crash Club.

Hotrod Sinners—Don Elliott

WHAT DID ROMERO HAVE? A FOUR-CYLINDER SPORTS CAR AND TWO BEAUTIFUL WOMEN WHO LOVED HIM— AND ANYONE ELSE FOR THAT MATTER!

—cover blurb, *Les Floozies*
(1965 reprint of *Hotrod Sinners*)

Hotrod Sinners is one of the more collectible of the hot rod paperbacks, not just for its title and provocative cover art by Harold W. McCauley, but also because it is one of nearly 200 pulps written by science-fiction giant Robert Silverberg under a variety of pseudonyms (mostly Don Elliott, but his sleaze work was also published under the names John Dexter, David Challon and Dan Eliot).

Hotrod Sinners (Bedside Books, 1962) is more of a sleaze paperback than a youth-oriented hot rod adventure. Its main male character is a not-too-sharp 20-year-old named Romero, and while he does drive around in a rod, the bulk of the story deals with his attempts to be a pimp, working in a brothel to learn the tricks of the tricks trade, and dividing his affections between a backwoods hussy named Linda Lou and rebellious society girl Chastity, both of whom end up as part of his stable of working girls. The book was reprinted by Pad Library in 1965 with the more apt title of *Les Floozies*, under the pseudonym Loren Beauchamp.

Hot Rod Fury—Robert Sidney Bowen

A COMPELLING TALE OF A COURAGEOUS GROUP OF TEEN-AGERS WHO HAD TO PROVE THEY WEREN'T THRILL-CRAZY DELINQUENTS.

A prolific author of hot rod pulps, Robert Sidney Bowen was an ace pilot during World War One and reputedly turning to writing for adventure magazines as a way to keep his adrenaline pumping after the cessation of hostilities. He was 60 when he penned his first hot rod paperback, *Hot Rod Angels* (1960), but

it found an appreciative audience and he continued to turn out hot rod–themed paperbacks, mainly for Chilton and Criterion, throughout the 60s and even into the early 70s, including *Hot Rod Rodeo* (1964), *Hot Rod Patrol* (1966), *Hot Rod Showdown* (1967), *Hot Rod Outlaws* (1968) and *Hot Rod Doom* (1973).

Hot Rod Fury (Monarch, 1963) is fairly typical of Bowen's work in the genre: a fast-paced but simple tale of action and adventure, with the requisite hard-learned moral lesson at the end. Bowen, who wrote virtually up until his death in 1977, also authored *Top Secret*, a 1969 Whitman hardcover children's novel based on the popular television crime series *Hawaii Five-O*.

Go, Man, Go!—Edward DeRoo

THEIR JUNGLE WAS ON WHEELS.

THE SPEED DEMONS WERE A NON-ASSOCIATION GANG OF WILD, DAREDEVIL HOT-RODDERS. THEY HAD THE 100 M.P.H. CHARIOTS, THE CRAZY DRAG RACES, AND ALL THE THRILL-HUNGRY CHICKS IN THE NEIGHBORHOOD. THAT'S WHY PAUL SANDERS WAS READY TO DO ANYTHING TO GET IN WITH THEM AND DRIVE HIS OWN HYPED-UP BUCKET OF BOLTS. BUT WHAT THEY WANTED OF HIM WAS NOTHING SHORT OF A NIGHTMARE!

HERE'S THE LAWLESS SIDE OF THE HOT-ROD SET, AS SEEN BY THE AUTHOR OF THE FIRES OF YOUTH.

Not too much is known about Edward DeRoo. Born in Rochester, New York, in 1922, in the early 1950s he taught radio and television production at the University of Southern California. In conjunction with NBC, he also produced a television series at USC, *Halls of Science*, as well as producing, directing and narrating the radio series *America: Fifty Years of Growth*.

DeRoo's work in the pulp paperback field seems to be confined to the period 1955–1961, during which he authored several juvenile delinquency titles for the New York–based Ace Books, including *The Fires of Youth* (1955), *The Young Wolves* (1959), *Rumble at the Housing Project* (1960) and *The Little Caesars* (1961). *Go, Man, Go!* (Ace, 1959), DeRoo's contribution to the hot rod genre, has become highly sought-after among collectors thanks to its subject matter, its sensationalist title (which brings to mind the 1965 Russ Meyer movie *Faster, Pussycat! Kill! Kill!*), and the absolutely stunning, exciting and provocative cover art by John Willis. It was published in the UK in

1960 by Digit Books, who also published *Rumble at the Housing Project* under the title *The Big Rumble* (reusing the classic cover art from Bud Clifton's 1958 Ace paperback *D for Delinquent*).

DeRoo, who died in 1988, seems to have spent his later years writing plays and teaching communications at Nassau Community College. If the tough and gritty works such as *Go, Man, Go!* and *Rumble at the Housing Project* is anything to go by, his work for Ace Books deserves to be reprinted and rediscovered.

Drag Strip—William Campbell Gault

Born in 1910, William Campbell Gault was considered one of the best American writers of sports fiction, contributing many short stories to sports pulp magazines and writing novels like *Bruce Benedict, Halfback* (1957) and *Mr. Quarterback* (1963). Gault even incorporated sports into his later detective fiction work, more than a dozen novels written between 1955 and 1992 that featured his most famous creation, Brock Callahan, an L.A. football star who is forced to retire due to a bad knee and reinvents himself as a Beverly Hills private eye. The author also wrote a series of paperback originals during the 50s that featured Joe Puma, a private dick with a penchant for involving himself in luridly sleazy cases: *Shakedown* (1953), *End of a Call Girl* (1958), *Night Lady* (1958) and *Sweet Wild Wench* (1959).

Originally published in hardcover before being given the paperback treatment by Berkley Highland, *Drag Strip* (Dutton, 1959) was one of several hot rod/drag racing–themed books Gault penned between the late 50s and early 70s. It's a fairly predictable but exciting tale of a hot-rodding teen and his fight to establish a suitable, safe racing course for the people of his small California town. Responsible driving is one of the obvious underlying themes, as is the need to co-exist and embrace other cultures—demonstrated by the inclusion of a Mexican teen who, after being persecuted, is eventually accepted by the young neighborhood gringos and helps in their quest to secure a legal drag strip where they can indulge their hobby.

Gault wrote under his own name as well as under pseudonyms such as Will Duke and Rodney Scott. He died in 1995, three years after publishing his final Brock Callahan adventure, *Deaf Pigeon*. The original cover art for the first hardcover printing of *Drag Strip*, painted by Charles William Smith, was offered for sale in 2014 by a collector for more than $1,800.

JOHN HARRISON

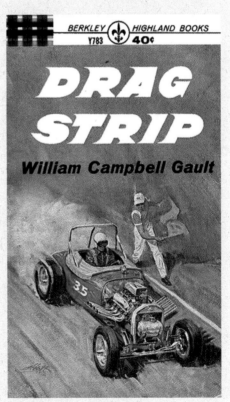

Go, Man, Go (Ace, 1959)
Drag Strip (Berkley Highland, 1964)

Rumble at the Housing Project—Edward DeRoo (Ace, 1960)

From the late 1940s through to the early 1970s a number of American inner-city areas underwent 'urban renewal'. The supposed vision of the city, state and federal authorities that funded and drove these programs was the eradication of dilapidated and hazardous housing and poverty traps through the creation of gleaming new housing projects free of slumlord exploitation.

In reality, such programs rarely had the best interests of those affected at heart. Paying little heed to residents' opinions or desires, 'slum clearance' served instead to further quarantine and ghettoize the poor, while adding to ethnic segregation as Anglo-Americans with enough money for a down payment joined their wealthier compatriots in 'white flight' to the suburbs. As existing communities were broken up and scattered, major profits were delivered to private developers constructing substandard high-rise apartments as well as new highways and developments on the sites they had cleared by demolition.

Given that the corrosive and supposedly inescapable effects of poverty and slum life were such a key theme of JD novels, the fact that barely any of them address the sweeping changes that took place at the time the genre was at its peak seems odd at first. But most of the books were produced by lazy hacks happy to stick with existing clichés, or by social workers with a belief or stake in the reforms, so perhaps it's not surprising that they failed to explore either the positive aspects of inner-city life or the negative consequences of its destruction.

The fourth of five novels that explored the teenage experience from the perspective of a middle-aged scribe, Edward DeRoo's *Rumble at the Housing Project* was one of the few to transplant the tried and tested JD formula into a modern setting. In the novel, slum clearance—combined with the jailing of teen gang the Scratchers' leader (the imaginatively named 'Big Tony')—allows a faction called the Spiders to break away from the gang and stake out a new housing project as their turf. At the centre of these changes is Larry, an unaffiliated 'coolie'. Larry falls in love with Cee-Cee, the daughter of his building superintendent, who also just happens to be Big Tony's former squeeze, at the same time he is trying to resist being press-ganged into the new gang. Unable to resist their pressure, Larry caves in and receives the gang's trademark tattoo of a splotched spider. Rapidly rising through the ranks, while maintaining a 'square' front to his parents, Larry is talked into organizing a youth dance by his naive mother and a social worker. Inevitably, his two worlds collide.

All the conventional features are present: a doomed, tragic romance, the brother with a promising future who is harbouring a secret that threatens to undo it all, an effete and clueless social worker, the candy store hangout, an obese mother, copious knife fights and rumbles, plenty of hep talk (especially from the female characters, for some reason), the inability of characters to rise above the conditions that surround them, and so on. Yet the author's description of life in the characters' new digs, his taut and engaging writing, and the use of urban renewal's disruption to provide fresh twists on the subject of gang warfare set the book apart from the pack. Written at a time when censorship was just beginning to ease, the book is also rather more risqué than many in the genre with slightly steamy sex scenes, a gay gang member, even the occasional swear word.

IAIN McINTYRE

Rumble at the Housing Project (Ace, 1960)
The Big Rumble (Digit, 1960)
The Little Caesars (Ace, 1961)

GIRL GANGS, BIKER BOYS, AND REAL COOL CATS

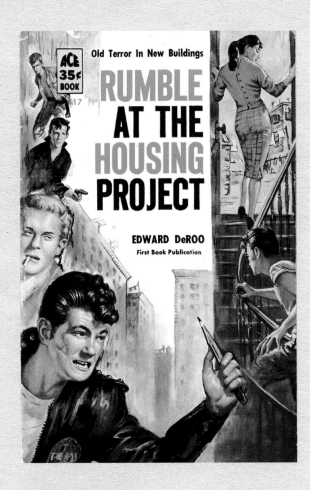

Fangs led him back across the street and down into the apartment house alley. Then he went around the corner of a building where they sat on the rubbish cans; Larry watched the rats scatter only to quietly come back and then boldly continue to forage for food while the two boys talked.

"Sure we're gonna live up to the goddamn pact," Fangs told him. "What you think I am runnin', a gang of cheesy punks?" He cocked a black devilish eyebrow. "What's your rumble plans?"

"Huh?" Larry knew what he meant but he wasn't ready to reveal Spider tactics.

Fangs shrugged. "Come on. We're nice and tight. Puke up. What you want us to do? You gonna general this thing?" He grinned. "Or I got somethin' to say, huh?"

Larry scratched his nose and rubbed his hand nervously over his face repeatedly. How should he put it to Fangs? He had to tell him what to do and yet not give away his plans for defense of the Spider turf. "Too many generals is like too many cooks, Fangs."

"What the hell's the matter with ya?" Fangs grinned weirdly. "Got the seven-year itch?" He pulled his knife. "Here, lemme operate. Make one less general."

Larry ignored the closeness of the blade. He sat still and looked at Fangs as if it wasn't there. It wasn't easy to stay cool. He concentrated on the plan and how to make good use of the Sharks.

It worked. Finally Fangs gave up his nonsense.

"You don't let 'em through the park, school yard, or your boundary to the project fence."

"That all?"

"Ain't that enough?"

Teddy Boy—Ernest Ryman (Ace, 1960)

Compared to the dark places British youthsploitation fiction would travel to by the early 70s, Ernest Ryman's *Teddy Boy*, first published in 1958, is a tame read. Although one of many local pulps published in the 50s that examined poverty and youth crime in the country's larger cities, it is one of the few to explicitly deal with a uniquely British youth subculture known as teddy boys.

The majority of the novel is told from the point of view of a teacher called Manry who, frustrated he's not doing enough to help some of his disadvantaged students, decides to apply for a position in an 'approved school'. Such schools were part of the British educational system, occupying a position between conventional schools and borstal, the juvenile prison service whose stated aim was to reform seriously delinquent youth.

This being the 1950s, a period of more of less full employment, Manry only has to pick up a copy of the newspaper and he sees an advertisement for a teaching position at Fulwood, an approved school on the outskirts of London. After a lengthy interview process, he gets the job and finds himself responsible for a class of young disadvantaged males, many of whom are teddy boys.

Parallel with this narrative are snippets from the life of Alban, a mentally unhinged teddy boy and recent Fulwood resident, who is being groomed by a criminal known as Gorab. Alban runs menial errands for Gorab's illegal gambling business, and seems to be on the criminal up until he is identified by the police, after which Gorab has no further use for him. Running out of money and desperate to make a name for himself, Alban buys a knife that he uses to murder the old lady who runs the local grocery store. He steals 30 pounds from the till, which allows him to live the high life for a few days until he is apprehended by the police.

Blink and you'll miss these sections of the book, which concentrates far more on drawn-out character analysis of Manry's various students and his somewhat bumbling attempts to help them. Alban's deviancy aside, the young folk in this novel are not a bad lot. They all come from poor backgrounds and broken families and the worst Manry has to deal with is truancy, petty theft and the occasional fight. The emphasis at Fulwood is on progressive Christian values and paternalistic moralising, mixed with a dash of psychiatry and electroshock therapy for those students whose behaviour doesn't improve.

Teddy boy style was a hybrid of various sartorial fashions, including that of Edwardian dandies and American zoot suit gangs. It originated in London in the late 1940s, in part as a reaction against the drab economic austerity of the period, and was looked upon favourably until the early 50s, when the style fused with aspects of working-class youth culture.

These included the influence of 'spivs', well-dressed petty criminals who traded illegal, usually black-market goods, and 'cosh boys', youth gangs with a reputation for robbery and gang violence (a cosh being a type of bludgeon). These gangs were popularised in a 1953 film, *Cosh Boy*, (released as *The Slasher* in the US), the tale of a 16-year-old delinquent and his gang in postwar London. The film was the first made in the UK after the war to receive a new X Certificate rating. A novel, *Cosh Boy*, was released by Ace in 1959 and purported to be **A GRAPHIC STORY OF LONDON'S JUVENILE JUNGLE.**

The term 'teddy boy' itself was coined in a 1953 newspaper headline that shortened 'Edwardian' to 'Teddy'. Teddy boys and girls (aka Judys) continued to be a major British youth subculture until the early 60s.

History has left us no clues about the identity of Ernest Ryman, although his evident familiarity with the approved school environment and the forensic detail with which he dissects the problems of his young characters would suggest that he had firsthand knowledge of what he was writing. *Teddy Boy* was his only novel.

ANDREW NETTE

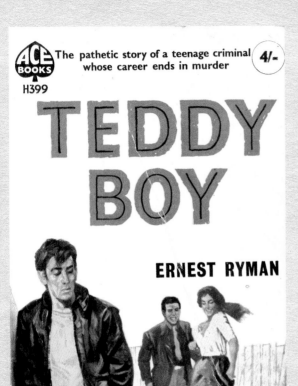

TEDDY BOY

ERNEST RYMAN

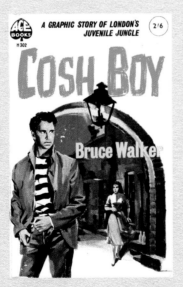

Teddy Boy (Ace, 1960)
Cosh Boy (Ace, 1959)

After lunch I entered into a very long afternoon session, much longer than normal school hours, and to help use the time purposefully, I decided to have some discussion and brought up the subject of Teddy-boy clothing. This special uniform of some sections of our youth consisted of black drainpipe trousers, a long, draped jacket, a waistcoat with a pocket to put the thumb in, and a very narrow tie, for which sometimes a bootlace was substituted. Only a minority of boys in my group had ever worn it but most of them were in favour of this type of clothing. I started by asking one of them why he liked it, and the following reply was very much to the point.

"Well, when you go out to work, yer want to buy somethin' ter make you look different; and when you've got a Teddy suit on people look at you in the street, 'specially the Judies. Some Judies won't look at you if you ain't wearin' 'em."

"I think they just look silly," joined in another. I looked at Charlie Bowker, who seemed to want to say something.

"What do you think, Charlie?" I asked.

"Well, I'm a Teddy boy. I think they're good. Look at the clothes you wear. They're just dull," he affirmed.

"You mean you don't like any of the clothes the instructors wear?" I queried.

"No, I don't," he replied firmly. "You're all peasants—that's what we call fellows that don't wear Teddy clothes," he explained.

"They cost around forty quid," informed another voice. "You have to have three or four fittings," he said with a touch of awe in his voice. "You need lolly all right!"

The Feather Pluckers—John Peter Jones (Eyre & Spottiswoode, 1964)

A key theme running through the better novels dealing with British youth from the 1950s to the early 1960s is the struggle waged by teens against the sheer boredom and ennui fostered by the austerity of the postwar years and by the psychological impact of war on their parents. Where most novelists focused on attempts by bohemians, jazzers and artists to rise above their surroundings and create something new, John Peter Jones's *The Feather Pluckers* describes the working-class treadmill of dull jobs, unemployment and prison from the standpoint of a trio of friends who try unsuccessfully to escape it.

Told in a series of first-person narratives, dominated by the perspective of white South Londoner George Perkins, the group are occasionally described as teddy boys by others but come across as work-shy scruffs of no particular subculture. Music features in their lives, but more important to them than adherence to a particular code or style is the desire to carve out autonomy amongst a world which offers them no public or private space. Constantly monitored and moved on from place to place by authority figures, the boys are forced to furtively take their pleasures in parks and bedrooms. Racism is also a recurring theme and while George's close friendship with Henry and Jimmy, of Jewish and West Indian heritage respectively, demonstrates he has risen above the era's bigotry, his adherence to contemporary masculine values fails to extend the same respect to women or gays.

Published in 1964, the book really belongs to an earlier era before the conspicuous consumption and creative upsurge exemplified by mod culture, the Beatles, and 'Swinging London' really kicked into gear. The novel begins with the boys spending aimless days killing time in parks and pools and on the street, while skirmishing with park keepers, the police and their parents. After Henry and Jimmy are attacked by a gang of racists for consorting with a pair of white women, George flees the scene to hide out in the West End. There he finds a sports car with the keys left in the ignition. Proceeding to take it for a joyride he picks up a pair of social climbers who convince him to drive them to a country club. Humiliated by those he finds there he trashes the car in a fit of class fury. Forced to hitchhike back to London, his lack of foresight and planning soon brings about his undoing.

Interviewed by US oral historian Studs Terkel for Chicago's WMFT radio station in 1965, Jones revealed that he hailed from a similar background to his characters. One consequence of this is how effectively he uses South London vernacular in the novel—*The Feather Pluckers* was subsequently used as a source by British slang dictionaries. Later turned into a stage play, with Bob Hoskins in an early starring role, the novel is fairly compelling up until the point at which George's narrative is interrupted by a series of vignettes from his parents, a journalist and others. These commentaries are forced and unnecessary and feel as if they've been inserted at the insistence of an editor keen for extra pages and explicit social commentary. But if you skip those 30 pages, you've got a great snapshot of dead-end 50s youth.

IAIN McINTYRE

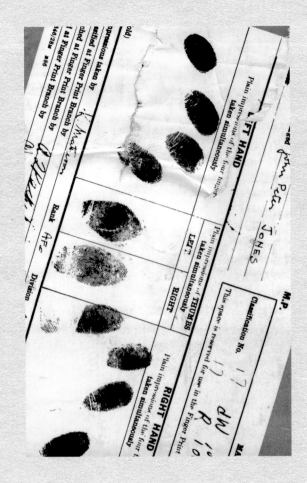

It ain't that I like work, or nothing like that, but I can do it if I have to. And it's what counts really, the work what gets done. It ain't the bloody nobs that makes the cars and houses and things what people need. It's blokes like my old man. So I don't reckon these gits got any right to go sneering at people like him.

But still I reckon only idiots work, that's why I don't go for the regular graft there; don't reckon it.

I mean, if it's the work what counts then it should be the people who does it that counts. But it ain't like that, is it? It's the other way round. All the gits who never works and never has to work is reckoned to be the cream.

And all the gits who does the work seems to reckon that's right. But it ain't, and I think they're idiots for thinking it.

I done jobs, plenty of 'em. But they're all the same when you gets right down to it. You got some horrible git over you all the time, who's always getting on to you. And when he isn't making your life a bleedin' misery, he's stickin' his nose up the guvnor's arse.

So I just does a job every now and again like. Get me fag money. I don't reckon on it regular. I wanna enjoy myself. Just like them rich bastards enjoy themselves. Nothing to worry about, just have a good time.

In Too Deep—Bruce Nicholson (Horwitz Publications, 1965)

In Too Deep is the tale of two young people with movie star looks and juvenile delinquent tendencies, who get sucked into the dangerous, twilight world of crime and drug addiction in Sydney's Kings Cross. As the quote on the inside front cover puts it:

> **Who cares? What the hell? Why bug me Daddio? If the Bomb doesn't finish us off, the Indonesians will. Only squares work for a lousy, tight fisted boss. So runs the philosophy of the young hoods on the motorbikes, who live to their own laws and lingo outside the pale of society. Beaten, rejected, different from the conformists of suburbanville. Like so many teenagers Carol and Smart Boy, spurned by their folks, drifted to the Cross. They took the easy road into the easy-beat life.**

It kicks off with a snarl, as 17-year-old 'Smart Boy' (so called because he did so well at school before dropping out) and his gang of 'Rev-men' engage in a vicious brawl with a rival crew in the street outside one of their regular haunts, a club called the Stomp House. Seeing off the interlopers, Smart Boy heads back inside to hang out with his girlfriend, Carol. (**She was sixteen and had more of a sort of animal attraction rather than conventional beauty.**) They groove to the sounds of house band 'The Tremendous Ones' before going their separate ways.

No sooner has Smart Boy got home, however, than he's accosted by his alcoholic father, who hates his **fighting, drinking, bike-riding bum of a son**. The father informs Smart Boy that he is, literally, a bastard. A fight ensues, and after knocking the old man to the ground Smart Boy storms out and rides his motorbike to another regular hang out, a milk bar *cum* hamburger joint *cum* SP bookie [off-track gambling] front, Devil's Den, run by a **short, dark haired new Australian** (i.e., migrant). It's not long before Smart Boy is in another fight, this time with a good-looking stranger called 'New Face'.

As the combatants are fairly evenly matched, the outcome results in a grudging respect between the two young men. New Face suggests Smart Boy and Carol move into his pad, a flat above the Comanche Espresso Bar in the heart of Kings Cross. New Face gets Smart Boy a night job bouncing at a rock-and-roll club called Sound Spot.

> **It was a typical Kings Cross dive. Smart Boy had been there before once or twice with the Rev-men. As it happened there had been a rumble too and the Rev-men had not exactly been the innocent party. Smart Boy was hoping they would not remember his face.**
>
> **There was a red sign about the doorway which read 'Sound Spot'. An early prostitute was standing, smoking by the door. There were large photographs on the exterior walls of bands that wailed therein and the paintwork was a bright, gaudy orange.**
>
> **They walked down several steps to the interior of the dive. It had little atmosphere. There was a kiosk near the door, a stage, and around the glittering walls were tables and, at this time of the morning there were chairs standing on the top of the tables. A fat, sloppy cleaning woman coughed as she mopped the floor.**

Smart Boy spends his nights keeping order at Sound Spot and his days hanging out in the Cross and talking with Hank, a commercial artist who lives in the flat next to theirs (**about thirty-five, balding, with an interesting, artistic looking face . . . He was quite tall and thin and wore a sharp, dark suit, thin, black tie and long pointed shoes**). This leads to one of the book's more bizarre scenes, an extended conversation between Hank and Smart Boy about the threat of nuclear war and the Sino-Soviet split.

Unbeknown to Smart Boy and Carol, New Face has a more sinister identity he has kept hidden from them, as a pimp and a smack dealer. This comes into the open one night when a gang of bodgies accost him, Carol and Smart Boy. Carol is wounded in the mêlée, and to relieve her pain while they wait for an ambulance New Face gives her a shot of heroin from a hypodermic needle he keeps strapped to his thigh.

She digs it and it's not long before Carol is hooked and Smart Boy is out rolling drunks to pay for her fix. One thing leads to another, and the two men decide to knock over a tobacconist in the Cross (another business owned by a 'New Australian'). They shoot the

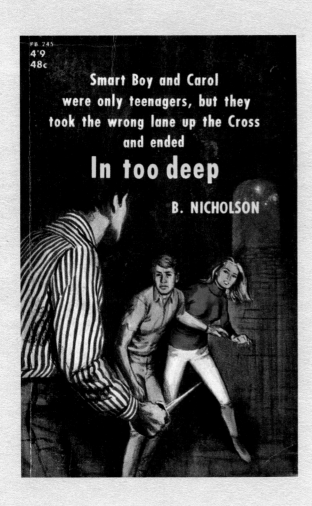

Smart Boy and Carol
were only teenagers, but they
took the wrong lane up the Cross
and ended

In too deep

B. NICHOLSON

owner and, thinking they have killed him, flee back to the apartment as machine gun–toting police surround the place.

In Too Deep would be lucky to crack 50,000 words. Despite its brevity, the book has a rough, mechanical energy and is packed with vivid descriptions of Sydney's underbelly and its young denizens: rockers, beatniks and surfies.

ANDREW NETTE

The Sound Spot was a glittering transformation from its mundane morning appearance. The neon signs over the entrance shone on the crowd of surfies, rockers and girls in skin tight slacks who loitered around the door.

The barefooted surfies with their bleached hair, cut down jeans and red checked shirts contrasted with the dark-haired rockers who wore long jeans, black cardigans and long triple point shoes.

Smart Boy wore his only suit, Carol wore contour hugging jeans and a white, loose fitting Surf City type shirt. New Face was in tight wheat coloured jeans, thongs and a shirt similar to Carol's.

An immature young surfie flirted with death as he whistled at Carol. Smart Boy went for him and would have pounded him into the ground had New Face not forcibly restrained him.

"Remember, dad," New Face said, "You're here to finish them, not start 'em."

Inside the transformation was even more apparent. The Interior strongly resembled the Stomp House. The glistening walls and violet light reflected the excitement soon to pervade. Most of the seats around the tables were occupied by the teenagers who frequented the establishment. On the stage a four piece band clad in bright red cardigans and black trousers were prepping their instruments. The name on the drum read "The Tremendous Ones."

Gunther Bahnemann, Coolum Beach, Queensland, early 1960s
(Image courtesy Heritage Library, Sunshine Coast Council)
Hoodlum (Horwitz, 1963)
Hoodlum (Horwitz, 1965)

BODGIES, WIDGIES AND BENT COPS

Gunther Bahnemann's *Hoodlum*

Many pulp novels feel like they have been researched from newspaper articles or a stool at the authors' local bar. Not Gunther Bahnemann's *Hoodlum* (1963). Set amongst the juvenile delinquent gangs of late-50s/early-60s Brisbane, Queensland, this book crackles with insider knowledge.

Hoodlum is noteworthy on many levels. To my knowledge, it is the only Australian pulp novel to deal in detail with bodgies and widgies, a uniquely Australian and New Zealand offshoot of UK rockers or US JDs as they were known in the 50s and early 60s.

The location of the story, Brisbane, with a side trip to the holiday town of Surfers Paradise to the south, is also unique. The majority of juvenile delinquent pulp fiction written in Australia in the 60s was set in Sydney, in particular the vice hot spot of Kings Cross.

Hoodlum was one of three books Bahnemann wrote and had published while serving a seven-year sentence in Brisbane's Boggo Road jail, back then one of Australia's most notorious prisons, for attempting to kill a Queensland police detective called Glen Patrick Hallahan. Hallahan and the other detective credited with disarming Bahnemann, Terry Lewis, were members of a powerful group of corrupt police known as the 'Rat Pack'. Lewis would go on to become Queensland police commissioner in 1976. His appointment is widely viewed as ushering in a period of major police corruption and abuse of power. He remained in the role until the findings of Tony Fitzgerald's Inquiry into Possible Illegal Activities and Associated Police Misconduct were tabled in Queensland's parliament in July 1989, which led to his trial and conviction on various charges, including accepting vast amounts in bribes to protect vice and illegal gambling.

From his own colourful accounts and what exists in the public record—especially journalist Matthew Condon's in-depth accounts of police and political corruption in Queensland, *Three Crooked Kings* (2013) and *Jacks and Jokers* (2014)—Bahnemann led a life that itself reads like a pulp novel.

A May 1993 article published in *Australasian Post*, a barbershop men's magazine that never let the truth get in the way of a good story, described Bahnemann as "happy to live the staid life of an Aussie pensioner. The 72-year-old retired adventurer, who won the German Iron Cross and then deserted from the Desert Fox, Erwin Rommel, has known enough danger, mayhem and fear for a dozen life-times. Gunther—or Gunner as he is commonly known—has roamed the world as a seafarer, crocodile shooter, pearl fisherman, gun runner and bestselling author."

Born in Germany, Bahnemann ran away from home at 13 and joined the merchant navy. He spent the next four years sailing around the world before jumping ship in Brazil. "Threatened with deportation soon after, Gunner travelled up the Amazon and married a 13-year-old native girl he plucked from a line-up of 'about one hundred available girls.'"

His "idyllic lifestyle" came to an end in 1939 with the news that his country of birth was at war. Volunteering to fight for Germany, he joined a parachute division and saw action in Norway, Holland, Belgium, France and Africa. *Australasian Post* reported he gained the Iron Cross First Class after knocking out four Renault tanks in France. Bahnemann had a change of heart after receiving a letter from his mother informing him of his father's execution at the hands of the Gestapo for political treason (the information turned out to be incorrect). He and another soldier hijacked two motorbikes and fled into the Libyan Desert.

His companion was killed when a British fighter plane strafed them, and Bahnemann went on alone. *Australasian Post* wrote, "Gunner was saved by a band of Arabs and he became one of them waging a relentless guerrilla war against Italian occupiers of their country." The story, also recounted in his 1961 book, *I Deserted Rommel*, goes that he went into league with an Arab called Ben Omar, who he had earlier rescued from a flogging and probably death by Italian Soldiers. Through this man he became involved in an Arab organisation selling British agents stolen arms and ammunition. Bahnemann was eventually taken prisoner by allied forces and in December 1941 landed in Australia as a prisoner of war. He spent the rest of the war in a camp for prisoners of war and Italian and German Australians, interned on suspicion of sympathising with the Axis powers, near Shepparton, central Victoria, before being released 'under supervision' into the community in late 1946.

In a report compiled by the director of the Commonwealth Investigation Service on Bahnemann in

1947, the former German war hero was described as having a "very unsavoury history", and as being totally unscrupulous and not to be trusted. According to Condon in *Three Crooked Kings*, Bahnemann settled in Mount Isa, a tough mining town, with his first wife, Vera "and became something of an eccentric local identity. Claiming he was a master mariner, he built a boat in the mining town and intended to use it for crocodile hunting in the waters of northern Australia and Papua New Guinea." He spent much of the 50s in Torres Strait, between the northern tip of Queensland and Papua New Guinea, "running illegal gun shipments to Indonesian rebels and poaching crocodiles."

He divorced Vera in June 1954 and quickly married Ada Louise Ruby in Brisbane. A Queensland police report compiled on Bahnemann claimed he had forced Ada into prostitution. "Ada entered a house of ill-fame in South Brisbane," wrote Condon, "funding him [Bahnemann] and his quixotic seafaring adventures. Police suspected Bahnemann was living off the immoral earnings of his wife, but they didn't have enough evidence to prosecute."

Ada plied her trade alongside another young woman Shirley Brifman, who would go on to become a successful brothel madam before dying of a mysterious drug overdose in 1972, soon after turning whistleblower on corrupt police she had previously been paying protection money to.

Prostitution in Queensland was at this time divided into two categories: highly organised establishments protected by police, and the rest of the trade. Condon asserts Ada was one of "a coterie of local prostitutes, along with Shirley Brifman, who were protected from prosecution by [then Queensland police commissioner Frank] Bischof and his trusted boys," including Lewis and Hallahan.

This may help explain the events that occurred in the early hours of Saturday, August 8, 1959.

According to a report on Bahnemann's sentencing in Brisbane's *Courier-Mail* newspaper on October 21, 1959, "The Crown alleged that he [Bahnemann] bailed-up two detectives [Lewis and Hallahan] and two other police officers in the bedroom of his house. He allegedly told them: 'I am going to kill my wife tonight and then die myself. I have killed people before and another one, especially her, would be easy.'"

"When Bahnemann pointed the rifle at detective Senior Constable T.M. Lewis Hallahan suddenly jumped at him", the court was told, "Bahnemann then swung the rifle towards Hallahan, fired, but missed. Lewis jumped over the end of the bed on to Bahnemann."

Bahnemann pleaded not guilty and, in his defence, "said he had taken 74 tablets, and had loaded the rifle to 'do himself in' because his wife had threatened to return to Kalgoorlie. He claimed that the rifle discharged when Hallahan grabbed it."

Lewis and Hallahan became celebrities in Brisbane after disarming Bahnemann. Mr. Justice Stanley, the presiding judge at the trial, commended them for "their courage and devotion to duty" and both were awarded the George Medal for Bravery, Queensland's highest honour for a policeman.

Three Crooked Kings goes into considerable detail about the circumstances of Bahnemann's alleged crime. While Condon dismisses Bahnemann's defence, he notes a number of significant inconsistencies in the four police statements concerning the incident. These included the almost certainly untrue assertion by Lewis and Hallahan that they'd had no prior interactions with Bahnemann and his wife, and conflicting accounts of how they had ended up at Bahnemann's house. Also telling is a statement made by Bahnemann, a decorated soldier, to a newspaper, "I made no threats. If I wanted to kill someone in that small room I couldn't have missed."

The most likely scenario, floated by Condon, is that the police were protecting Ada, one of Bischof's sanctioned prostitutes and hence and important asset, from threats made to her and her place of work by her husband.

Ada reportedly never visited Bahnemann in jail. She sold their Brisbane house and moved to New South Wales where, according to Condon, she continued in the brothel trade. She changed her name and married Joe 'the writer' Borg, the brothel king of east Sydney, reputed gunman and animal lover. She died in late 1967 of a drug overdose. Borg died several months later from injuries sustained when a massive gelignite bomb exploded under the driver seat of his car.

Bahnemann's time in jail was a productive one. He dubbed his cell, complete with a typewriter, desk and stationery, the 'publishing office'. *I Deserted Rommel*, was released to acclaim and serialised in several Australian newspapers, including the *Brisbane Telegraph*. *Hoodlum* was published by Horwitz Publications, Australia's premier pulp publisher in 1963, and republished in 1965.

New Guinea Crocodile Poacher appeared in 1964. The prologue states:

Some years or so ago, before the region was taken over by the Indonesian authorities, Gunther Bahnemann, the daring rebel who had once deserted the Afrika Korps, took a poaching expedition there, running the gauntlet of Dutch gunboats and the even more dangerous hazards of the jungle head hunters whose domain he invaded. Getting into that forbidding and forbidden territory was a nightmare. Getting out was infinitely worse.

The book was reportedly well received; the *Canberra Times* described it on August 1, 1964, as "a rattling racy adventure story . . . *Poacher* contains all the familiar elements of the paper backed 'popular novel', from a touch of sex to ritual violence and cannibal massacre." The author told *Australasia Post*, "I had scores of admirers coming into jail so I could autograph their books." This included Lewis, who got Bahnemann to sign his copy of *I Deserted Rommel*.

Bahnemann was released on parole in May 1963. He told the press he held no animosity to Lewis or Hallahan. "I hope to go up to police headquarters sometime and say hello to Glen [Hallahan]."

The prologue to the 1965 edition of *Hoodlum* states:

An outbreak of juvenile crime in Brisbane Australia, has provided the author of HOODLUM with the material for this remarkable novel, which exposes the "Bodgie" and "Widgie" cult. The facts on which the story is based are authenticated from police and press reports. The anti-social behaviour of the "juvenile delinquents", who use motor bikes as a means of transport for orgies of vandalism, violent assault, and sexual indulgence, was not limited to Brisbane, but was a world-wide occurrence in various forms, curiously alike in their main aspects.

The causes of this cult of adolescent frenzies have never been satisfactorily explained. Gunther Bahnemann, though not himself a "bodgie", had opportunities of observing the peculiarities of this cult.

No doubt in the hope it would encourage sales, the foreword attempts to position *Hoodlum* as a book about an important social issue, with Bahnemann as the messenger.

He was convicted and imprisoned in Brisbane in 1959, but for an offence not related to the events described in this novel, which he has written to draw public attention to one of the most disturbing problems in modern times.

Hoodlum opens with 18-year-old Larry leaving the Home for Juvenile Delinquency where he's just done a stint for theft. He visits his parents. His father, a foundry worker, is, in Larry's eyes, **just another stupid working horse**, and his mother is exhausted from trying to keep the family together. He lies that he has a job in a machine shop over the border in NSW. Next stop is his pregnant girlfriend, on whom he releases the lust built up during his time in reform school before dumping her. He then steals a motorbike and visits a Greek-owned milk bar and space for bodgies and widgies to hang out.

Even the various gangs who hated each other behaved peacefully at Nick's place, and that meant a lot . . . Nick's outsize jukebox made enough noise to drown out the rattle and roar of arriving trains in the station across the road. In fact his place was so famous that it even charmed the cops, with usually one or two hanging around outside the joint. Uniformed men mostly, but some wore mufti [slang for civilian clothing]. One developed a nose for that kind of cop.

Not that Larry has any love for Nick or any of the 'New Australians' (recent migrants). **What he [Larry] did not admit, even to himself, was that he was jealous of them. They always seemed to have more money and business than anybody else . . . the place was lousy with them.**

Larry returns to the milk bar late at night and successfully robs it. Larry's mate, Rob Lee, then takes him to a gathering to initiate a couple of young widgie women into a gang. The initiation is preceded by a beer-fuelled rampage through an outer suburban shopping strip, the owners of which have complained to the authorities about the disruptive presence of the gang on their business. The local cinema owner, who has banned the gang members from his establishment, is the target of particularly fierce violence.

Larry hatches a plan to get a mate, Jonno, out of the same Home for Juvenile Delinquency he's just gotten out of, using the money he got from the milk bar robbery. Jonno, who is a few years older than Larry and originally from Sydney, is there for a crime he does not talk about, which leads Larry to suspect it must be more serious compared to his own misdemeanours. He is particularly impressed with Jonno's dismissive attitude towards the bodgies and widgies, and believes his older friend offers him a chance at the big time. **"Kid stuff, Larry, just kid stuff!"** he recalls Jonno saying. **"Long-haired, tight-pants, leather jacketed show offs, that's what they amount to and no more. You stick with me, Larry, and you'll make some coin."**

Larry and Jonno's sophisticated girlfriend, Lorraine, travel to nearby Surfers Paradise, even then **a haunt of the rich**. Larry steals a car and buys an old M1 carbine from an ex-US serviceman. After a bit of pre-job sexual tension, in which Larry starts to fancy his chances with Lorraine (**This girl was class, real class at that, not one of those silly mouthed widgies**), they successfully bust Jonno out. Larry wounds a guard in the process.

But instead of escaping together, his best friend and Lorraine abscond with the stolen car and the proceeds of the milk bar robbery and leave Larry stranded at the scene of the crime. His dreams of getting out of Queensland and hitting the big time dashed, Larry has no choice but to go back to Brisbane and resume his criminal ways. He, Rob and Lorna, a young widgie woman, mug a tram conductor, a crime that gets major newspaper attention and drives anti-bodgie feeling to a fever pitch. They try and escape by stealing a yacht, but a fire kills Larry's accomplices and leaves him back in the hands of the police, this time facing adult criminal charges.

"I've been a fool," he groaned to himself as he stared desperately through his tears at the bare wall. At the moment of truth he meant it.

Hoodlum's descriptions of bodgie and widgie culture are vivid. Particularly interesting is the extended sequence in which Larry attends the gathering on the outskirts of Brisbane to initiate a couple of young widgie women. The get-together takes place in a derelict boathouse on a secluded beach and opens with Hank, the head of the gang (his seniority signalled by a death's head on the back of his leather jacket), taking up a collection to pay the fine of one their members, Kane, who has been nabbed by the cops. While this is going on, Larry observes the social hierarchy amongst the gang.

Some of the bodgies were well supplied with the female species of the wedgy class, having two or three of the tight skirted, or pedal-pusher-trousered molls hanging onto them. A bodgy's [sic] fame was dependent on his haircut, his clothes, his motor bike, his manner of speech and the outrages he committed in true bodgie tradition. Money was one of the lesser requirements that made one a proper bodgie. As long as he had the other accessories and qualifications, his widgies would subsidise his extravagances, and supply him with the necessary padding for his nearly always empty pockets.

The initiation ceremony is described in great detail.

Silence fell like a heavy cloak over the assembled bodgies and widgies as they watched Rob Lee leading the two new girls to the centre of the floor. For a brief moment many feet shuffled over the floor, bringing the onlookers closer towards the performers of the act to be staged.

The two candidates for initiation were dressed in tight jeans and blouses that buttoned up in front. As they stood there within the circle of the many staring eyes, neither of them showed the slightest hesitation of shame.

One of the two girls, a red head, was pretty to look at, slender and scarcely more than fifteen years of age. The other girl as Larry observed, was getting closer to being at least seventeen years of age. She possessed an extremely curvaceous body, emphasised by the tight clothes she was wearing.

At a wave from Hank, two widgies of the old clan walked up to the new comers, whilst Rob Lee, who so far had done the chaperoning stepped back.

"You wanted to be one of us?" the two widgies said loudly to the newcomers.

"Yes, we want to be one of you!" came their reply.

"You'll do at any time what we'll want you to do?"

"Yes, we'll do whatever is asked of us!"

"You'll never speak of our doings to an outsider?"

"No!"

"You'll not give us away even if you have to go to jail?"

"We will not give you away!"

"You'll do the boys' bidding any time, whatever?"

"We shall!" . . .

Suddenly a bodgie crashed through the door. "Cops are on the way!" he screamed. The party broke up quickly.

Bahnemann does not attempt to paint his main character as moral in any way. Larry is a violent racist and a pathological liar, devoid of even a shred of decency. This is clear early on when he first visits his parents after his release from the Home for Juvenile Delinquency. His reaction to his mother is described thus:

Larry looked down on the uplifted face, wrinkled, not so much with age, but worries. It was convulsed now with happiness, streaked with tears. For a moment, a brief one only, Larry thought he felt his heart collapsing into sentimental pulp. But eight months of lessons in incarceration froze him back into the semblance he had adopted, studied and pictured himself to be. The tough, icy and unapproachable, the cynical I'll knock you down chap, who felt far too superior to accept as genuine, a mother's love and sentiments. To him it was just so much mush.

The other interesting aspect of *Hoodlum* is the way Bahnemann describes the fashions and the almost dandyish way in which the bodgie men are concerned with their appearance. This scene, for example, when Larry prepares to go out for the first time since getting out of reform school:

He smiled at himself as he pushed his legs down inside the tight tubes of his jeans— the hallmark of the bodgy! Then he zipped the fly shut and adjusted the narrow white leather belt. Frowningly he glanced at the well-worn, ripple soled, suede shoes, the moccasin type, renowned amongst the *Element* as *Brothel-Creepers* because of their inch-thick crepe soles . . .

The combing of his black hair, now short and stiff from the Reformatory regulation-cut, had him somewhat bothered. He realised it would be some time before the missing inches of hair left behind in the barber's cubicle in Block C, would grow to the length which the element considered fashionable and necessary.

Slipping into his leather jacket, he turned his back to the mirror. Looking over his shoulders, observed the Golden Eagle spreading its wings across his shoulders. It made him feel big, and exhilarated him with a strange power— akin to invincibility. Just like old times again, he mused, looking again at the reflection in the mirror, before he turned and left the room.

Or this scene, when Larry is holing up in a Surfers Paradise hotel until the heat from busting Jonno out of the Home for Juvenile delinquents passes:

At that moment Larry was resting on his bed in his flat. He was fully dressed, his clothes reflecting the latest fashion acceptable within the circle of the element. He wore tight black jeans, fitted with chromium-plated zips on slanted pockets. **Ex RAAF** [Royal Australian Air Force] flying boots protruded from the narrow turned over cuffs of his jeans, with the lot topped by a black shirt lined with red piping. All of this was enhanced by the true hallmark of the bodgie, a leather jacket.

Bahnemann's bodgies and widgies are, literally, at war with 'square' society. 'The jacks' or 'blue shirts' as the police are variously described, are depicted as an invading power, out to crush them. Brisbane is rife with rumours that returned servicemen are forming vigilante groups to conduct their own campaign against the youth gangs and the cops are telling milk bar owners to remove jukeboxes from their premises.

According to Dr. Keith Moore's 2004 paper 'Bodgies, Widgies and Moral Panic in Australia 1955–1959', the term 'bodgie' was originally slang for something fake or poor quality. The female equivalent, 'widgie', possibly originated as an abbreviation of the word 'wigeon' used for girl or female teenager after World War Two.

Bodgies first appeared in inner Sydney just after World War Two and were initially Australian seamen who impersonated American black marketers. Moore states that "By 1948, about 200 bodgies were regularly frequenting Kings Cross milk bars. Soon, bodgie gangs formed at other inner Sydney locations . . . For bodgies, almost all of whom were working class, emulating the high status Americans who had so recently occupied Australia as military personnel was easier than achieving upward social mobility."

By the 1950s, bodgies and widgies had become a manifestation of larger social trends sweeping much of the West, including the growing financial independence of young people, shifting social mores and rapid urbanisation. Increasing rates of juvenile delinquency and sexual promiscuity became a great concern to many Western governments and, parallel with the growing threat of communism internationally, rebellious youth were identified as a major domestic threat. Governments unleashed a barrage of official inquires to identify the key causes of teenage unrest. So-called illicit culture, comics, pulp novels, rock music, film, particularly popular movies such as *The Wild One* (1953) and *Rebel Without a Cause* (1955), and lack of parental supervision, were usually identified as the major culprits.

Heavily sensationalised reports of teen delinquency began appearing in the Australian press in the early 1950s. The media was particularly obsessed with razor attacks, sexual promiscuity and violent clashes between young people and police. "Concerned psychologists discussed the causes of the bodgie phenomenon at length," according to Moore. In August 1955, NSW Director General of Education Wyndham suggested, "Bodgie and widgie cults were symptoms of a malaise in the whole community and not just the teenage group." According to his analysis, youth lacked a "common objective." He added: "Hitler and Mussolini gave youth a goal as had communist Russia."

The Bodgie: A Study in Abnormal Psychology (1958) by Auckland psychologist A.E. Manning was another prominent example of official attitudes towards the phenomenon of bodgies and widgies. Based on a six-month study of 15 young men and women in Australia and New Zealand, it concluded that young people who identified as bodgies and widgies were juvenile delinquents who needed psychiatric treatment. "Bodgies and widgies can be regarded as social 'boils' on the body of a tense and emotional society," wrote Manning. He also noted young people thought life had no real purpose "except to have a good time, and the majority were of the hopeless opinion that all the future held for them was the possibility of death and mutilation in war . . . Life lacked a real purpose for them and a real security."

Brisbane in the late 50s was a deeply conservative, semi-rural backwater, but even it was not immune to the problem. The same edition of the *Courier-Mail* that reported Bahnemann's trial and conviction carried an article on the findings of a parliamentary committee into youth unrest. "Comparatively small but dangerously unruly groups of delinquent teenagers were active in Brisbane and must be curbed," it intoned. This includes delinquents, larrikins, bodgies and widgies. "Inadequate parental direction and guidance were major causes of youth problems."

In November 1956, Brisbane experienced its first rock-and-roll riot, when hundreds of teenagers began jiving in the street after a concert, then started abusing the police who arrived on the scene to disperse them. "One fan threw a stone that hit a policeman's head and another smashed a bottle over a police car while yet another jumped onto the back of a detective while he was trying to arrest a demonstrator," as Moore summarised newspaper reports of the incident. "The police charged six young men and two women."

Police Commissioner Bischof was particularly aggrieved that rock and roll was gaining a foothold in Brisbane and, according to *Three Crooked Kings*, assigned police, including Hallahan and Lewis, to stamp out the craze. What was colloquially known as Bischof's 'Bodgie Squad' prevented rock concerts from taking place and detained young men wearing dark shirts and with longish hair.

Given that Bahnemann spent most of the 1950s at sea, it is unlikely he had much personal interaction with Brisbane's bodgie and widgie culture. He probably came into contact with bodgies, and absorbed their stories, while doing his time in Boggo Road.

Bahnemann was a natural storyteller but, by all accounts, not a particularly competent writer. The prose in *Hoodlum* is clear and competent. He was helped in this regard through his association with Queensland writer, editor and publisher Percy Reginald Stephensen, nicknamed 'Inky'. Stephensen was a member of the Australian Communist Party in the 1920s and continued his left-wing activities when he went to the UK to read philosophy, politics and economics at Queens College Oxford, where he was in the same university branch of the Communist Party as historian A.J.P. Taylor and Graham Greene. He returned to Australia in the early 1930s, set himself up in the publishing business and released books by prominent local authors Banjo Paterson, Miles Franklin and Eleanor Dark, among others.

For reasons that are unclear, Stephensen's political sympathies shifted right in the late 30s. In 1941 he formed the Australia First Movement, which opposed Australia's alliance with Britain in World War Two. Under security surveillance for several years, he was arrested in early 1942 on suspicion of subversion and interned without trial for over three years in the same camp near Shepparton as prisoner of war Bahnemann.

In the years after World War Two, Stephensen made a living mainly from ghostwriting. He returned to Sydney in 1956, continued to write, was a foundation member of the Australian Society of Authors and worked as a literary agent. He died in 1965.

A May 2013 post ('Books from Behind Barbed Wire') on the Book Collectors' Society of Australia website states:

> In 1959 Bahnemann approached Stephensen to edit and to arrange publication of his remarkable adventure tale of escape and survival, *Tonight I Desert*. Stephensen rewrote the book from his rookie author's 'rough German sort of Australian English'. He then sent copies of the manuscript to his agents in London and New York. Shortly afterwards, the American actor Marlon Brando expressed interest in the film rights to the unpublished book. Bahnemann corresponded with Brando, his preferred Hollywood star to play him on the screen after seeing the actor's performance as a German soldier in the movie *The Young Lions* (1958) . . . Although Bahnemann's *macho* story was tailor made for Brando, the actor declined to take the role.

Tonight I Desert was retitled *I Deserted Rommel* and became the first of Bahnemann's books to be published. "Stephensen puffed the book in a letter to an American agent, Armitage Watkins, on 5 September 1961: 'Some booksellers are saying this could be the *All Quiet on the Western Front* of the 1939–1945 War: a revelation of the German soldier's mentality. I believe this is the only book ever written by an Army deserter, and it is absolutely authentic.'"

In all likelihood, Stephensen played a major role in rewriting and placing Bahnemann's other books, *New Guinea Crocodile Poacher* and *Hoodlum*.

According to *An Island Surrounded by Land: The History of an Earlier Coolum*, an unpublished local history by Frances and John Windolf, "On his release from prison, and as an established author, [Bahnemann] came to Coolum, where he spent a large amount of his time attempting to build a yacht behind his house. The yacht was still unfinished when he moved on to other areas and other adventures, but local residents, enthralled by his colourful past, still remember his time in this area."

Bahnemann married for a fourth time, to a much younger woman, with whom he had three children. Moving to north Queensland, he started a boat building business, but the advent of fibreglass wiped him out. He would publish one other title, *The Calling Reef* (1970), based on a legend from the Torres Straight Islands, and reportedly completed a number of other manuscripts, including a fiction trilogy set in West Papua. All were destroyed when the shed they were stored in was hit by one of northern Queensland's periodic cyclones. Bahnemann died in poverty in 1994.

Bizarrely, Bahnemann had continued to correspond with the man who had helped put him in prison, Terry Lewis, sending him regular Christmas cards. Condon wrote in *Jacks and Jokers*: "Lewis says he took pity on Bahnemann following his imprisonment all those years ago. Bahnemann may have been keeping his options open. By fate, the man who had helped imprison him was now the most powerful police officer in the state. To his family, Bahnemann . . . expressed his innocence regarding the shooting incident in 1959, although he offered little in the way of detail regarding his former wife, the prostitute Ada, and the night of his arrest. Perhaps it was a case of both men—Lewis and Bahnemann—keeping their enemies close."

By the early 1980s Bahnemann was living in Bellenden Ker, a mountainous area 50 kilometres south of Cairns, in far north Queensland. His correspondence with Lewis included a letter in late 1980 with the news he had been in contact with police in northern Queensland to share his opinions about likely locations for drug plantations and trafficking routes.

It is interesting to speculate whether Bahnemann knew that one of the men involved in drug importation into northern Queensland at the time, according to Condon, was none other than the (now ex-) detective Bahnemann had been accused of trying to kill over two decades earlier, Glen Patrick Hallahan.

ANDREW NETTE

The Delinquents—Criena Rohan (Gollancz, 1962)

Published in 1962, *The Delinquents* was one of only two books by Criena Rohan, the pseudonym adopted by Melbourne writer Deirdre Cash. A second, *Down by Dockside*, appeared in 1963. She supposedly wrote a third book, but the manuscript has never been found.

A former singer and nightclub dancer, Cash turned to writing to pay medical bills for what she thought was tuberculosis; in fact it was the cancer that would claim her life at the age of 38. She succeeded in having *The Delinquents* published in London under a pseudonym after several Australian publishers rejected it, no doubt because its content jarred with the more bucolic version of Australian culture favoured by local publishers at the time.

The book was widely praised on first publication. *The Daily Mail* described it as "a backstreet Tristan and Isolde". Yet despite being made into a movie in 1989, starring former *Neighbours* regular and then-up-and-coming pop diva Kylie Minogue, the book was out of print for much of the last half century. Recently republished by Melbourne publisher Text, it is now regarded as a classic of Australian literature.

But like many works of so-called literature, *The Delinquents* had a furtive semi-pulp existence. It appeared in paperback at least twice in the 60s, in 1964 and 1968, with sexed-up covers designed to make the story out to be another seedy tale of debauched, out-of-control youth. As the cover blurb on both editions stated: TEENAGE LOW LIFE—ITS LOVES, ITS DESIRES, ITS SINS. One can imagine the publisher, Panther, hoping to cash in on English readers getting a vicarious kick out of the sexual goings-on of young people in one of the far flung former colonies.

Not that marketing *The Delinquents* as juvenile delinquency pulp was much of a stretch, given the plot. Brownie, a young bodgie, and Lola, an even younger widgie, meet one night in their hometown of Bundaberg in northern Queensland. Soon after they have consummated their romance, Lola falls pregnant and the couple are separated. Lola's mother carts her off to have a backyard abortion, while Brownie goes off to become a merchant seaman. What follows is a series of encounters up and down the eastern sea-board of Australia, as the two young lovers reunite, only to be separated again by police, sanctimonious welfare workers and various other representatives of repressive adult society.

What separates *The Delinquents* from the mass of JD pulp in the early 60s, and gives it claim to literary merit, is the prose, which is excellent, if at times overly flowery, and the sense of character and social place it evokes. The poverty of the postwar years, the run-down bedsits, cheap clothes and bad food, is starkly rendered. At one point towards the end of the book, Brownie and Lola go to live with Mavis and Lyle, a couple of 'Ten Pound Poms', the colloquial term given to British subjects who migrated to Australia after World War Two under an assisted passage scheme.

So Brisbane was not like the tropical islands Mavis had seen on the movies; nor was it the roaring pioneer town for which Lyle had hoped. There was no pioneering to do, there were no wonders to see—just the housing shortage; the neighbours who ignored them, the poor pregnant Mavis. No stimulation except the stimulation of disapproval—the locals looking with intolerant amusement at his pegged trousers and duck-tail haircut.

There's no sign of either Brownie's or Lola's fathers and both mothers have been left to raise their children as best they can. Lola is half Asian, something her mother is desperate to keep hidden in deeply racist northern Queensland. Brownie's status-obsessed mum is still paying the price for having seen to have being **carrying on with the Yanks** during the war.

The Delinquents is liberally sprinkled with allegorical sex and in another of the book's incarnations, excerpts appeared in an anthology of Australian women's erotic writing in the 80s. There are also some remarkably hard-hitting passages, particularly around the difficulty and danger of getting an abortion, illegal in 1960s Australia.

ANDREW NETTE

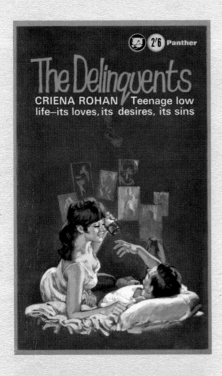

The Delinquents (Panther, 1964)
The Delinquents (Panther, 1968)

He became moody and had his backside kicked for it several times, for moodiness is not encouraged in deck boys. He bought the leather jacket in Sydney and the jack-knife in Melbourne, and always wore them when he went ashore. Big Emile the Norske said he had the makings of a good seaman. He kept so quiet when they spoke of women that his shipmates decided that he must be a virgin, loath to reveal his ignorance. Virginity is fraught with dangers aboard ship, so the first night back in Brisbane they decided to buy him a woman. He remembered drinking in a round of hotels, and in some lounge or another they collected the woman—a real old sailor's sweetheart dating back to the time of Lord Nelson. They put her into a taxi with Brownie and packed them off.

"Don't let him get away," they said.

He was too drunk to care very much, and once alone with the woman it was a case of noblesse oblige—after all his mates had paid for her. When he woke sober and saw her in the daylight he rose and dressed and went back to the ship without waking her. She slept on in the tumbled bed, her face blotchy and obscene against the pillows.

Coming along the dock in the cleanness of the dawn, Brownie prayed: "Oh God, if You are there and if You are listening, please let me find her soon, and let her be happy. Wherever she is, let her be happy."

The Rebels—Carl Ruhen (Scripts, 1967)

Sydney's Kings Cross was ground zero for Australia's pulp paperback publishing industry in the 60s and early 70s. Its heady mixture of bohemian culture, flourishing nightlife and organised crime meant the area was constantly in the headlines. And constantly on the minds of pulp writers under pressure to churn out another manuscript.

Publishing houses such as Calvert and Horwitz issued a large number of books set in Kings Cross. Many centered on the fate of innocent young women and men, lured from the country to the bright neon lights of the Cross, where they inevitably became ensnared in drug use and prostitution. Another popular trope was the activities of uncontrollable youth gangs.

The Rebels is told in the first person by Bernie, a working-class 17-year-old. A Brylcreemed bodgie (even though the young people on the front cover have longer hair), Bernie spends his weekdays living a boring suburban existence with his parents and working as a storeman in a department store, and his weekends in a blur of sex, alcohol, car theft, and fighting. He and his gang pick up two girls at Luna Park and gang-rape them, then they beat up a North Shore mod.

With the guilt of the rape hanging over him, Bernie meets Sandra. She challenges Bernie's masculinity and his conceptions of women. Sandra is upper-middle-class, from Sydney's North Shore, is learning French, and wants to travel. But she also likes the wild life, likes to slum it with working-class boys like Bernie and drive her mother's car at dangerous speeds.

"It would be so much better if this were a convertible," Sandra yells above the roar of the engine. **"We could let the hood down and wind would stream through our hair. The marvellous sense of *freedom* it gives."**

That's one thing I don't fancy, having the wind stream through my hair. I take too much care and worry over it as it is without having the wind streaming through it, ruining all the good work. No, thank you.

Bernie starts to think about giving up the gang life, saving his money and travelling to Europe, perhaps with Sandra.

She takes Bernie to a North Shore mod party, where a group of men beat him up for messing with their women. Swearing revenge, Bernie and his gang return the following Saturday, and a major brawl ensures. **"This is developing into a proper orgy of destruction,"** thinks Bernie in the midst of the violence. **"All the girls have disappeared, maybe out of the flat to get some help, we can't stay here much longer."** Before Bernie knows it, one of the opposing gang is dead and he is now implicated in a murder.

Ruhen's prose is clean and crisp and the story has a rough cultural authenticity. Also notable is the way Ruhen avoids the heavy-handed moralising of similar juvenile delinquent stories—in which the characters realise the error of their ways and embrace mainstream society—in favour of a much more sombre ending.

Like many aspiring local writers in the early 60s, Ruhen, who died in late 2013, got his start submitting short fiction and articles to *Man* magazine, a local version of the 'barber shop magazines' that were popular in the United States at the time. Import restrictions on foreign print material, which had been in place in Australia since 1938, began to be lifted in the late 50s. Increased competition saw many local pulp publishers close. Others, such as Horwitz, readjusted their business model, stopped relying on reprinted overseas material and published more Australian books. Ruhen was part of a stable of authors put together by Horwitz to write these. The group also included James Holledge, J.E. Macdonnell, W.R. Bennett, James Workman, Leonard Mears and Rena Cross.

Ruhen is credited with 78 books. In addition to writing under his own name, he worked under numerous pseudonyms, across all subgenres. He was an editor at Horwitz from 1968 to 1969. From 1969 to 1971, he edited *Man* magazine.

The Rebels is one of several juvenile delinquent themed pulps he wrote. *The Violent Ones* dealt with the story of two gangs of female motorcycle riders in New York, "in total rebellion against their slum like environment" and each other. *Wild Beat*, the tale of a young gang girl called Elaine (THEY WERE ONLY KIDS, BUT THEY WERE CAPABLE OF MURDER—AND WORSE. THE STORY OF TODAY'S VIOLENT GENERATION), was published in 1967.

The introduction of the 'R' classification in Australia in 1971 meant that mainstream films, books and television increasingly dealt with subject matter that had previously been the preserve of pulp. In order to compete, pulp became more salacious and sexually

They took the law into their own hands in a running orgy of lust and destruction

Carl Ruhen

THE REBELS

50c
PB295

explicit. Ruhen spent the 1970s writing smut for Scripts Publications and another Horwitz offshoot, Stag Publications: titles included *Orgy Farm*, *Bar Stud*, *Sex Parlour*, *Saturday Sex Club*, *Wife Swap Orgy*, *Porno Girls* and *Society Stud*. He also wrote a number of biker books under the name 'Peter Brand', horror under the pseudonym Caroline Farr, and romance as Alison Hart.

In addition, Ruhen wrote film paperback tie-ins—popular before the advent of VHS—for *Alvin Purple*, *Mad Max 2*, and *Melvin, Son of Alvin*, as well as paperback versions of Australian TV soap operas such as *The Young Doctors*, *Neighbours*, and *Sons and Daughters*, for the UK market. He also wrote children's books and local histories. He even wrote a book on baby names. The last book credited to Ruhen on the AustLit website was the ninth book in the *Neighbours* series, published in 1989.

ANDREW NETTE

Hell, what a drag. What a bore. I mean, here they all are knocking themselves out, falling all over the place, all sweaty and shiny—for what? A few lousy miserable kicks, that's what. Not even that if you ask me. It's a drag. Hey Mister, where can I buy some LSD? I keep reading about LSD in the newspapers. Like the time I got mixed up in that marijuana party. I don't know how I got mixed up in it, but there I was. It was only about a year ago, when I was sixteen. All these kids there, some of them real fancy talking, a bit older than me, university students and beatniks, some of them, thinking it was real smart smoking reefers and drifting off into bedrooms. Sometimes, they didn't bother going off into the bedrooms, but did it right there on the floor. Real smart. I had a puff, too. Gas. I don't know what was so marvellous about it, but on top of all the sweet sherry I had been drinking I felt like I was going to be sick.

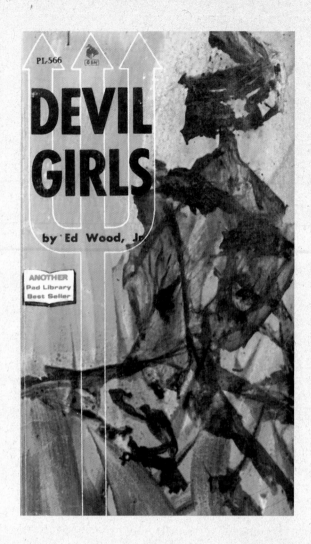

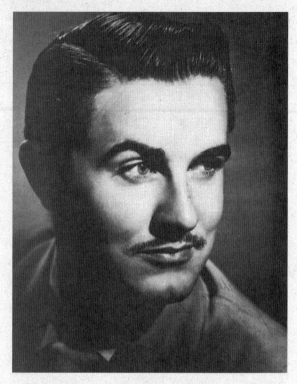

Devil Girls (Pad Library, 1967)
Publicity shot of Ed Wood which circulated in the 1950s
Sex Shrouds and Caskets (Viceroy, 1968)
Drag Trade (Triumph, 1967)
Orgy of the Dead (Greenleaf, 1966)

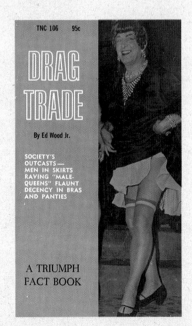

THE TYPEWRITER WAS HIS CAMERA

Devil Girls and the Shadowy Literary Career of Edward D. Wood, Jr.

Director Samuel Fuller once declared, "I write with the camera. It is my typewriter." For Edward D. Wood, Jr. (1924–1978), who once did a single day's work as an uncredited stunt double for Fuller on *The Baron of Arizona* (1950), the very opposite might have been true. Chiefly known as a filmmaker, Ed was also a writer who spent more hours hunched over his trusty Underhill or (later) his IBM Electric than he ever did behind a movie camera.

From an early age, Eddie showed a remarkable talent for using these clicking, clacking, dinging devices. At 17, the ambitious lad from Poughkeepsie, NY, joined the Marines in order to do his part in World War Two and soon distinguished himself as, in the words of his second wife Kathy, "the fastest typist in the Marines". To be clear, Ed did some killing in addition to clerical work while in the military, and once he was back stateside, he used these experiences as the basis of his first novel, *The Casual Company*. While this work was never published (excerpts were serialized in *Cult Movies* magazine in the 1990s), Ed knew even then to get every bit of mileage he could out of his work and thus adapted *The Casual Company* into a play in 1948, a year after he'd migrated to Hollywood to make it in the entertainment industry. The play was produced at a small Los Angeles theater, thus providing Ed's first experience as a professional writer.

Within a few years of moving to California and working in the theater, mostly as an actor, Ed Wood made a few crucial showbiz contacts—including producer George Weiss, cinematographer Bill Thompson, and fading Hungarian screen legend Bela Lugosi—which would allow him to launch a career as a low-budget, independent movie director. By some latter-day accounts, he was the worst ever to pursue that particular line of work. Still, it was this profession which would give Eddie his strange but durable fame. Though Ed Wood still continued to produce, if not publish, occasional short stories during the 1950s, it was his work in motion pictures that defined and dominated that decade of his life.

What fans would one day refer to as Ed's "classic period" stretched from about 1953 to 1960. That's the period during which he was writing, producing, and directing feature-length, theatre-released films under his own name. It's an era which started with *Glen or Glenda?* (1953), a surprisingly enlightened faux-documentary shocker about transvestism and transgenderism, and ended with *The Sinister Urge* (1960), a grim crime thriller about the seedy underground world of pornography. Both were semi-autobiographical. Wood's own cross-dressing, which some have declared merely recreational and others deemed obsessional, is legendary; and like the doomed director in *The Sinister Urge*, Ed also descended into the notorious 'smut racket' to make his living.

Due to changing tastes and fading fortunes, Ed Wood's filmography thinned out considerably in the 1960s, after *The Sinister Urge*. For the last 18 years of his life, he contributed to the cinematic world mainly as a writer whose scripts were directed by others, such as prolific B-movie journeymen Stephen C. Apostolof, Don Davis, Boris Petroff, and Ed De Priest. Wood's efforts as a screenwriter nearly all fall under the heading of pornography, mostly softcore, but occasionally hardcore. When he could find the backing, Wood also wrote and directed X-rated features and loops (i.e. short films) well into the 1970s, though these assignments were not as common.

Some of Ed's screenwriting jobs were done under his own name, especially those done for Apostolof, but several more were written under pen names such as 'Don Miller' and 'Adkov Telmig' (the latter is a near-reversal of 'vodka gimlet'). For legal reasons, given the prudish tenor of the times, Ed's stag films were made anonymously or pseudonymously. And these lowly, disreputable jobs were sporadic and unreliable, since even the cheapest movie can be a logistical nightmare. You need actors, technicians, and either sets or locations in which to film. Then there's developing and distribution to consider. You have to make the prints and send them out to theatres, all without attracting unwanted attention from John Law.

Meanwhile, Ed Wood had very pressing expenses. By the 1960s, his raging alcoholism, long a concern, had grown to epic proportions. The neighbourhood bars and corner liquor stores he frequented weren't exactly giving the stuff away, and pesky landlords kept demanding rent for the increasingly sketchy hovels he occupied with the loyal, long-suffering Kathy.

In short, Ed Wood needed a quick and certain source of income. He found one at the lower end of the publishing business. Starting in 1963 with a grotesque thriller called *Killer in Drag*, Eddie began moonlighting as the author of pulp paperbacks brimming with sex and violence. It was a field in which he would toil, productively if not profitably, for the next 15 years until the year he died at the age of 54 in December 1978. In that time, in addition to various articles and short stories, Ed Wood may have written as many as 75 books, ranging from pseudo-educational volumes about salacious subjects like *Bloodiest Sex Crimes of History* (1967), to full-length novels drenched in debauchery and sadism (*Side-Show Siren*, 1966).

Ed Wood was a natural for the paperback market, since it relied on his two greatest strengths: his incredible talent for typing and his seemingly inexhaustible ability to generate massive amounts of verbiage in a brief amount of time. Seemingly no Ed Wood documentary is complete without a testimonial from a friend or co-worker expressing astonishment at the way the man could continue typing at lightning speed while smoking, drinking, and carrying on an unrelated conversation.

In such anecdotes, Ed almost comes across as superhuman. If Ed's research methods were dubious or his plots less than airtight, neither his readers nor his editors seemed to raise any objections. What mattered was that they could depend upon Eddie to churn out those precious pages of sin and vice. They flowed from him like water from a spigot. All the publishing company needed to do with an Ed Wood manuscript was set it into type, slap on an eye-catching cover with a suggestive title and some lurid artwork, and sell it to the dirty old men of America at 95 cents a pop.

Unfortunately, even though they represent such a large part of his creative output, Ed Wood's books are not nearly so accessible or well curated as his movies. Many of Ed's fans were not even aware of their hero's prolific second career until 1992, when Rudolph Grey published *Nightmare of Ecstasy: The Life and Art of Edward D. Wood, Jr.*, an oral history which functions as the closest thing we have to a biography of the man. Along with its filmography, Grey's book contains a lengthy and detailed bibliography and representative excerpts from some of Ed's books. Since then, there have been at least two published guidebooks devoted to Eddie's literary life: David C. Hayes's utilitarian but handy *Muddled Mind: The Complete Works of Edward D. Wood, Jr.* (2001; revised 2006), plus Michael Daley and Johan Kugelberg's *Ed Wood's Sleaze Paperbacks* (2013). The latter is a belated promotional tie-in to a 2011 New York art exhibit in which Ed's books were displayed in glass cases like rare gems.

The books themselves, however, remain frustratingly inaccessible to most readers. Vintage Wood-penned paperbacks routinely fetch hundreds of dollars on eBay and Amazon when they're available at all. Circa 2001, a company called Ramble House embarked upon a reissue campaign called Woodpile Reproductions, which would have put several of Wood's books, both fiction and non-fiction, back in print. But this project seems to have ended almost as soon as it began, with only a few copies ever reaching readers. These reproductions have yet to appear on the secondary market. As of this writing, only about four of Eddie's paperbacks are easily and affordably procured by fans.

One of these available titles is a quirky and quaint crime novel entitled *Devil Girls* (1967), which was reprinted in England by a company called Gorse in 1995 in order to capitalize on the release of the Tim Burton–directed biopic *Ed Wood* (1994). This particular work was a product of Eddie's most fecund time as a writer. Between 1967 and 1968, he published at least 21 books—many under his own name—for a whole host of small-time publishers, including Private Edition, Viceroy and Pendulum. *Devil Girls* happened to be a release from Pad Library, which also published Wood's *Security Risk, Watts . . . The Difference* (1967) and *It Takes One to Know One* (1967), among others, that same busy year.

Since Ed's other books are not currently available, the aspiring Wood-ologist must take the ones that are still accessible and draw from them larger conclusions about Ed's writing style and career, in much the same way that a palaeontologist might construct an extinct creature's entire skeleton from a few stray fragments of bone.

What, then, can we learn about the mysterious and elusive Ed Wood from a musty old fossil like *Devil Girls*? Well, we can safely say that as an author of crime fiction, Ed presented no particular threat to the legacies of Hammett, Chandler and Cain. In their most devious moments, however, *Killer in Drag* (1963) and its sequel, *Death of a Transvestite* (1967), bear some resemblance to the truly eccentric and depraved novels of another hard drinker with a fevered imagination,

Jim Thompson (1906–1977). But even at his wildest, Ed is a lot squarer and less nihilistic than Thompson. Fans of Ed's movies may be surprised to learn that, as Wood creations go, *Devil Girls* is remarkably focused and coherent, almost sensible. *Killer in Drag* and *Death of a Transvestite* may offer these folks the kind of hallucinatory, stream-of-consciousness experiences they would expect from the director of *Glen or Glenda?* and *Plan 9 from Outer Space* (completed 1957; released 1959).

Devil Girls is much closer in tone and structure to Ed's more straightforward, less-heralded crime films, such as *Jail Bait* (1954), the aforementioned *Sinister Urge* and most especially *The Violent Years* (1956), which was written by Ed, but directed by a British director named William L. Morgan. Like that surprisingly successful juvenile delinquent drive-in flick, *Devil Girls* deals with an all-girl teenage gang whose members act and talk in a coarse, violent way we might deem stereotypically 'male'. Gender fluidity is one of the overriding motifs of Ed Wood's career, but we must not think that Ed was limited in this respect to the depiction of feminized men. One is just as likely to encounter masculinized women in the Ed Wood oeuvre. In both his scripts and his novels, Ed often wrote about ballsy, take-charge broads eager to prove they're as tough as any man. For a splendid, late-career example of this, please see the Ed Wood–scripted, Steve Apostolof–directed exploitation film *Fugitive Girls* (1974), in which Ed also plays multiple roles.

What elapsed during the decade-plus between *The Violent Years* and *Devil Girls* was a period of unprecedented social change in America. The former is an artefact from the neat-and-tidy Eisenhower years, when the sudden rise to economic and social prominence of the American teenager represented a distinct threat to the repressed, 'perfect' world that adults were so desperately trying to build in the years following World War Two. Appropriately, the protagonist of *The Violent Years* is a spoiled, privileged brat (her catchphrase is "So what?") who takes to a life of crime not out of economic necessity but simply for kicks. It's a way for her to escape the anesthetizing boredom of her suburban life.

By the late 1960s, the schism between America's young people and their parents had acquired a name, 'the generation gap', and had both deepened and taken on added political significance, catalyzed by such hot-button issues as the Vietnam War and the

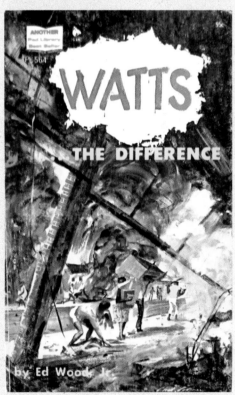

It Takes One to Know One (Pad Library, 1967)
Watts . . . The Difference (Pad Library, 1967)

civil rights movement. History popularly remembers 1967, the year of *Devil Girls'* ignominious debut, as a high point of the so-called counterculture—a time of joyous sexual, philosophical, artistic, and pharmaceutical experimentation, the days of *Sgt. Pepper* and the Summer of Love.

But for Edward D. Wood, Jr., there was no Summer of Love, and the counterculture was just a continuation of the juvenile delinquency scare of the 1950s—a bunch of no-good, irresponsible, ungrateful kids causing trouble. This attitude is a product of Ed Wood's unwavering, law-and-order conservatism. A proud war veteran with a Purple Heart and other honors to his name, he had no sympathy whatsoever with the draft dodgers of the LBJ years and nothing but contempt for mind-altering drugs and those who used them.

If this seems at odds with Ed's own nonconformist lifestyle, which included plenty of alcohol, cross-dressing and pornography, then consider that Wood was an enigma to all who knew him, even to his wife of 22 years. It is Rob Craig, author of the fascinating book *Ed Wood, Mad Genius: A Critical Study of the Films* (2006), who gives us the most apt description of the man: "a unique cross between libertine and prude".

Devil Girls is the very type of book a prudish libertine would write. On its face, it is a *Dragnet*-inspired cautionary tale about a gang of wayward teenage girls, the Chicks, under the sway of a sleazy, Svengali-like crook named Lark, a mid-level mobster. Under the destructive influence of illicit drugs and loose sex, Lark and the Chicks lay waste to the small Texas border town in which they live and terrorize its adult population. Like *Dragnet* creator Jack Webb, Ed Wood gives us a fallen, corrupt world in which an overtaxed and underappreciated law enforcement community is all that separates us from the complete breakdown of civilized society. Unlike Webb, however, Ed also takes a certain amount of fetishistic or voyeuristic glee in depicting the 'bad' behavior he professes to despise. Every single scene of *Dragnet* is shown from the perspective of its hard-nosed cop hero, Joe Friday. Viewers never leave his side or see the events from anyone else's vantage point. In *Devil Girls*, even though the book has a Friday-type hero in the 'ruggedly handsome' Sheriff Buck Rhodes and follows him through his investigations, readers get to spend some quality time alone with the Chicks as well.

In the pages of *Devil Girls* the audience is treated to numerous murders, many of them quite twisted and sadistic in nature, alongside rampant drug use and widespread sexual impropriety, including forced lesbianism. Naturally, of course, these actions carry with them heavy consequences. There is no such thing as crime without punishment in Ed Wood's universe. The guilty are vanquished with extreme prejudice here, but the innocent are frequently made to suffer and die as well. Not only is the local schoolmarm murdered in *Devil Girls*, for instance, but her sister is harassed and her replacement winds up in intensive care, horribly mangled!

We are meant to be disgusted by these acts, but there is an undeniable titillation factor in them as well. With the arguable exception of the sleazy sex farces he wrote for Steve Apostolof in the 1970s, true optimism is rare in Ed's writing, and upbeat endings are noticeably scarce. The best the reader or viewer can expect is that the incorruptible forces of virtue—represented by the police, military, medical community and clergy—will quell a particular threat and restore some kind of neutral or default moral state to their surroundings. *Plan 9 from Outer Space, Jail Bait, Bride of the Monster* (1955) and its sequel *Night of the Ghouls* (1959) all explored this theme. Even the sensitive, positive-minded *Glen or Glenda?* ends on a melancholy note, as narrator/godhead Bela Lugosi laments the uncertain fate of transvestites "the world over," even though the film's nominal hero, Glen (portrayed by Ed Wood himself), finds redemption in his own narrative.

So it is with *Devil Girls*. Though Wood's stiff writing style and imperfect grasp of slang (e.g., using 'jazz' as a silly euphemism for 'fuck') may lend the novel an aura of laughable camp, this is not a light-hearted book. The setting is the blighted fictional community of Almanac. That's the type of name a stumped writer might devise if he were working under a looming deadline and glanced around the room in search of inspiration. Had Eddie's eyes landed elsewhere, *Devil Girls* might have been set in a town called Dictionary or Atlas.

Whatever its name, Almanac is supposedly close to the Mexican border and is therefore a popular entry point for the illegal importation of heroin and marijuana—drugs treated with equal revulsion by boozehound Ed. The town, as bleak and comfortless a locale as any I've encountered in pulp literature outside the works of Jim Thompson, has been shaken to its very core by a juvenile crime wave. Teens rule the streets, while adults cower indoors.

The erstwhile leader of the Chicks, the brash and ruthless Lila, is in prison for murdering her own father, so her role in the gang has been usurped by the dippy, drug-crazed Babs, who has recurring visions of **pink clouds** while high and is really not capable of managing this small-scale organization. A pivotal character in *Devil Girls* is Rhoda, Lila's younger sister and a recent inductee to the Chicks. Though she talks tough, Rhoda is not quite completely beyond salvation yet. As a seeming indication of the character's inner goodness, Ed Wood makes sure to point out that Rhoda is the prettiest member of the gang.

After a striking escape scene, in which she brutally and cunningly murders a nurse, Lila returns to Almanac and the Chicks just in time for a major drug-smuggling operation spearheaded by mastermind Lark, in which the girls will board a small boat and hide the deadly contraband, including large bricks of marijuana, in their bras, panties and girdles. Given Ed Wood's lifelong fixation on women's undergarments, this plan comes as no great surprise. As this plot unfolds, the members of the Chicks commit any number of additional crimes and murder anyone who interferes with their plans. Victims are not limited to the grown-up population; members of a counterpart male gang are also eliminated in creative ways.

One particular escapade by the Chicks, the vandalizing of a classroom, is imported directly from the screenplay for *The Violent Years*. The duty of restoring order in Almanac falls to a number of male authority figures: the tireless lawman Buck Rhodes, but also a man of the cloth, the pious and incorruptible Reverend Steele, and an ex-athlete named Jockey, who runs the local (drug-free) teen hangout and has a criminal past of his own. One important subplot running through *Devil Girls* involves Mrs. Purdue, Lila and Rhoda's beleaguered immigrant mother, a widow who runs the family delicatessen and is horrified to see her daughters fall into criminality. This character epitomizes the theme of the innocent being made to suffer in Ed Wood's universe.

In addition to women's underwear, gender reversal and juvenile crime, *Devil Girls* contains Ed Wood's other trademark themes: funerals and the symbolic resurrection of the dead.

As Rob Craig astutely points out in *Ed Wood, Mad Genius*, Wood was endlessly fascinated with the rituals surrounding death. This can be seen in his screenplays for such erotic films as *Orgy of the Dead* (1965), which takes place in a cemetery, and *Necromania* (1971), which ends with a couple making love in a closed casket. As one might expect, considering the story's high body count, there are numerous funeral services scattered throughout *Devil Girls*, just as there are in *Plan 9 from Outer Space* and even Ed Wood's earliest filmmaking endeavour, the crude proto-western *Crossroads of Laredo* (1948).

As for the issue of the resurrection of the dead, there are two kinds to be found in Ed's work: literal and symbolic. Of course, *Plan 9* and *Night of the Ghouls* feature characters that rise from the grave through supernatural means. But there are other types of resurrection in Eddie's scripts, too, such as the climax of *Jail Bait*, in which a plastic surgeon uses his skills to transform a gangster into a living, breathing doppelganger of the doctor's own late son.

Devil Girls has at least two major examples of symbolic resurrection. Relatively early in the book, Lila murders a nurse in a prison hospital and escapes from the institution by donning the dead woman's uniform and impersonating her. And during the story's bloody climax, a character assumed to be dead also makes an unexpected reappearance.

But there are less-grim reminders of Ed Wood's other movies to be found in *Devil Girls* as well. One memorable supporting character, for instance, is Jockey's brawny, towering Native American sidekick 'Chief,' who is highly reminiscent of the hulking, inarticulate Lobo character portrayed by Swedish wrestler Tor Johnson in *Bride of the Monster* and *Night of the Ghouls*. In fact, when director Andre Perkowski adapted *Devil Girls* into a semi-parodic movie in 1999, he simply substituted Lobo for Chief and gave the role to *Muddled Mind* author David C. Hayes.

If this is not enough to appease his fans, *Devil Girls* contains the one crucial element needed to qualify a work as a quintessential Ed Wood creation: the protracted and loving description of a pink angora sweater worn by one of the female characters. That's the kind of detail which will make any Wood fan feel instantly at home in the musty, yellowing pages of this cheap and sordid novel.

JOE BLEVINS

The Warriors—Sol Yurick (Holt, Rinehart & Winston, 1965)

The Warriors is probably best known as a 1979 cult film by one of the masters of the intelligent B-movie, Walter Hill. The book on which the film is very loosely based, is one of the stranger and more original takes on the trope of out-of-control youth gangs that dominated pulp fiction in the 50s and early 60s.

First published in 1965, *The Warriors* was New Yorker Sol Yurick's debut novel. It was obviously deeply influenced by his radical politics (he was born into a politically aware working-class Jewish immigrant family and was active in Students for a Democratic Society and the opposition to the war in Vietnam) and by his time working for the New York welfare department in the early 60s.

Ismael Rivera, leader of a New York gang called the Delancy Thrones, has called a meeting of all the youth gangs in New York. Gang representatives have gathered in a pre-arranged meeting in a park in the Bronx (signalled by the playing of a particular Beatles song on the radio). Among those in attendance are representatives of the Coney Island Dominators, an African American/Hispanic gang.

Ismael believes that if all the gangs could see past their differences and unite they would have enough strength to really challenge **the man**. In an impassioned speech he tells the assembled delegates they would number **forty thousand counting regular affiliates, sixty thousand counting the unorganized but ready-to-fight**, more than enough to take over the city.

Midway through his audacious pitch, the police arrive in force and start arresting those present. Believing he has betrayed them, the gangs turn on Ismael and kill him. In the ensuring chaos, the Dominators' leader disappears and it is up to their second-in-command, Hector, to lead the gang safely back to their home turf. This journey, which takes up most of the book, involves the gang having to evade not just the city's police force, but hostile gangs with whom they must parley for safe passage through their territory.

Unlike the film, the book has no heroes and there is no sense of relief or victory when the surviving Dominators make it home. There's just a brief reprieve before they sink back into the squalid poverty that is their everyday reality. While the book makes it clear that terrible living conditions and complete lack of hope or opportunity are the reasons why young men and women join gangs, Yurick doesn't glamorise their motives or actions. Indeed, he pulls no punches in his depiction of their activities, which includes nearly killing a passing man who looks at them the wrong way and the brutal rape of a woman from a rival gang.

The gangs are like small armies, highly militarised, right down to ranks and insignia (the Dominators have Mercedes symbols stolen from cars as their symbol). The book's great strength is its ability to conjure a parallel New York, a secret underground geography, invisible to **the others** (as straight society is referred to), but understood down to the last detail by the myriad of gangs that inhabit it: the Borinquen Blazers, Castro Stompers, Jackson Street Masai and Intervale Avenue Lesbos, to name a few.

ANDREW NETTE

The Warriors (W.H. Allen, 1966)
The Warriors (Panther, 1967)
The Warriors (Star, 1979)

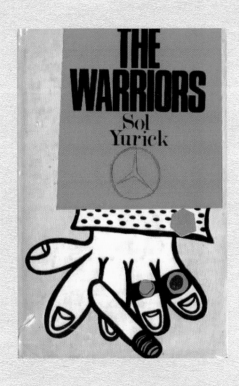

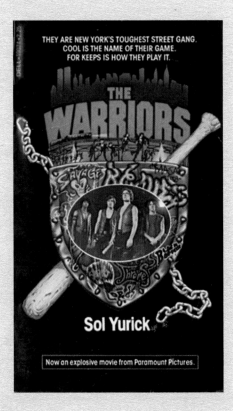

They reached the end of their turf and stopped. No one had lined it, like on school maps, and there were no visible border guards. The only sign of permanent divisiveness was the usual scum of oily motor leakings, dirty paper, white crossing lines, but the frontier was there, good as any little newsreel guardhouse with a striped swinging gate. The eyes of the Colonial Lord were hard and hostile, even though they were allowed free passage today. They couldn't help feeling that old pre-battle nervousness. Their backs prickled; their shoulders went into that old hard-man, can't-put-me-down-man hunch; their stomachs fluttered; they perspired, plucking the tight paints away from their crotches. Bricks might come raining down from the roofs, chains could lash out from doorways as they passed, baseball bats would crack their heads, and knives were whickering.

The delegates put on their jackets; they were the new short ones, buttoning up to the neck and monkey-jacket tight. They fussed, twitching their shoulders, pulling down on the jacket skirts to make them lie better, flicking spots of dust, pulling up on their shirt collars, checking to see if every button was buttoned and every buckle was tight and gleaming while their women fidgeted, helping. Bimbo made sure that the bottles were strapped in well. Their uncomfortable ankle-high, elastic sided boots were glossed. Their hats sat cocky, high on their heads.

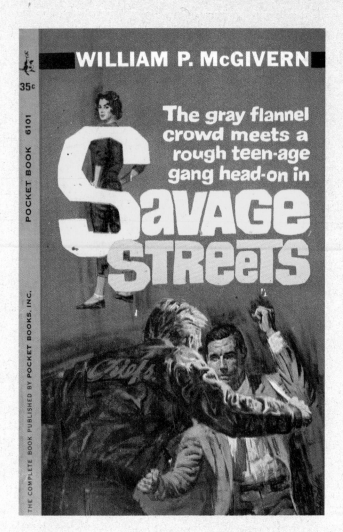

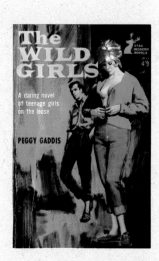

Savage Streets
(Pocket Books, 1961)

The Desire Years
(Gold Medal, 1962)

Walk Back with Me
(Horwitz, 1967)

The Wild Girls
(Stage, 1963)

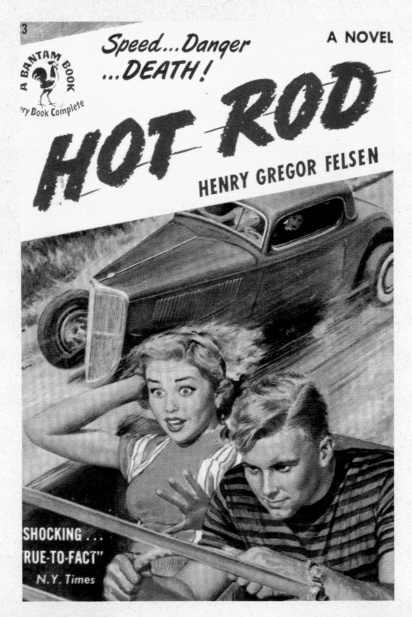

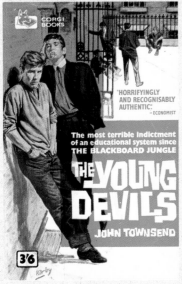

I'll Fix You (Pedigree, 1958)

Hot Rod (Bantam, 1950)

End of a J.D. (Gold Medal, 1960)

The Cool World (Ace, 1959)

Road Rocket
(Bantam Pathfinder, 1963)

The Young Devils (Corgi, 1961)

TEENAGE JUNGLE

1960s Beats and Bohemians

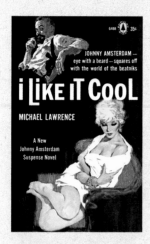
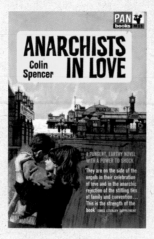

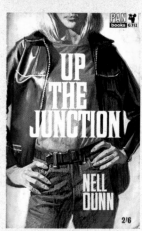

I Like It Cool (Popular Library, 1960), *Anarchists in Love* (Pan, 1965), *Like Crazy, Man* (Newsstand Library, 1960), *Beatnik Wanton* (Greenleaf Classics, 1964), *Not by the Hair of My Chinny, Chin Chin* (W.H. Allen, 1968), *Expresso Bongo* (Ace, 1960), *Through Beatnik Eyeballs* (Pedigree Books, 1961), *Bongo Bum* (Brandon House, 1966), *A Twilight Affair* (Midwood, 1960), *The Dharma Bums* (Mayflower/Dell, 1965), *The Real Gone Goose* (Perma Books, 1960), *Up the Junction* (Pan, 1966)

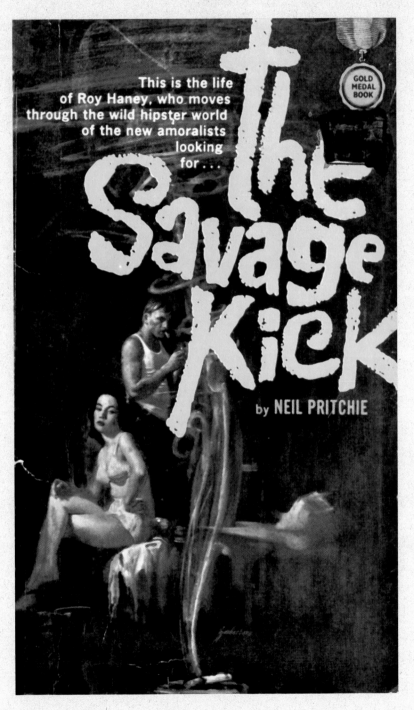

The Savage Kick
(Gold Medal, 1962)

THE BEAT GENERATION is the searing story of the restless, jaded men and women, with no aim in life except a new sensation—drugs, "way-out" jazz, perverted sex, actual crime.

THE BEAT GENERATION is especially the story of rich, young Stan Belmont, who had known every thrill. Now his only kick was—rape.

THE BEAT GENERATION is an MGM release, a spectacular Albert Zugsmith production starring Steve Cochran, Mamie Van Doren, Ray Danton, Fay Spain, Maggie Hayes, Jackie Coogan, and Louis Armstrong and his All-Stars.

The Beat Generation (Bantam, 1959)

Poster from the 1959 MGM film *The Beat Generation*, produced by Albert Zugsmith, co-written by *I Am Legend* author Richard Matheson

GIRL GANGS, BIKER BOYS, AND REAL COOL CATS

TOMORROW IS A DRAG
Beats and Bohemians in 1960s Pulp Fiction

While juvenile delinquency would continue to provide fertile ground for pulp writers until well into the 1960s, by the late 1950s publishers were already searching for the next big thing that would sell paperbacks. They found it in the emergence of a new youth cultural movement: the 'beat generation'.

The beat generation initially referred to a group of poets and writers who met in New York in the forties, including Jack Kerouac, William Burroughs, Lucien Carr, Neal Cassady, Allen Ginsberg and John Clellon Holmes (the author of Go, published in 1952 and generally considered the first 'beat novel'). The term 'beat generation' appeared several times in Go, but gained wider public currency after a November 1952 article by Holmes in the New York Times Magazine, 'This is the Beat Generation'. The article attributed the term 'beat' to Kerouac, although he had reportedly appropriated it from a street hustler called Herbert Huncke, who, in turn, drew on the African American slang term for 'tired' or 'worn down'.

The beats incubated throughout the 1950s. As the original group travelled to the West Coast, particularly San Francisco, they met and formed friendships with other poets, writers and artists. The year 1957 was an important one in the development of the beat generation as Kerouac's On The Road was published and became a success. His next two novels, The Dharma Bums and The Subterraneans, both appeared the following year. The year 1957 also saw Ginsberg's controversial poem "Howl" become the focus of a highly publicised obscenity trial.

As the beat generation seeped into America's cultural consciousness, it became associated with a collection of behaviours bound up in an emerging sense of rebellion against the conformity and paranoia of American mainstream life as it had come to be defined in the 50s. This included drug use, sexual experimentation and an interest in alternative spiritualities.

Interestingly, the original beats, particularly Kerouac and Burroughs, opposed the merging of their sensibilities with the nascent counterculture. But regardless of what particular individuals thought, the beats became intertwined with a broader cultural movement and would soon influence literature, film, art and sexuality. As Simon Warner put it in his book Text and Drugs and Rock'n'Roll: The Beats and Rock Culture

(2013): "The spirit of Kerouac, as traveller and seeker after truth, and Burroughs, as a living embodiment of narcotic adventure, would still be adopted as guides and heroes by musicians and their fans alike, even if they, as writers, could find little of value in these alliances and transformations."

Herb Caen, a columnist for the San Francisco Chronicle, reportedly coined the term 'beatnik' in April of 1958 by fusing 'beat' from the beat generation with the 'nik' suffix of the Soviet Satellite Sputnik that had been launched into space by Moscow the previous year. Whether he meant to imply the beats were subversive in the same way that communism was viewed or was aiming for a modernist twist is unclear.

The media latched on to the term and soon 'beatnik' became synonymous with a lifestyle involving shallow, goateed, black beret-wearing, bongo-playing hipsters, who had their own rituals and hep-cat patois, and spent most of their time in dimly lit jazz clubs and coffee-houses. Like all mainstream takes on youth culture, it was a mixture of myth and reality, with a heavy emphasis on the seedier sides of the 'beat lifestyle' that both fascinated and appalled mainstream society: drug use, communal living, blurring of gender roles and sexual experimentation (the sex, especially).

And where mainstream society's voyeuristic attentions drifted, pulp publishers followed. The earliest example of pulp fiction capitalising on emerging interest in the beats is arguably The Beat Generation, by Albert Zugsmith, published by Bantam Books in 1959. Based on an MGM film of the same name released earlier in the year, produced by Zugsmith and co-written by I Am Legend author Richard Matheson, it promised to be the **SHOCKING AND REVEALING NOVEL OF A GENERATION GONE WILD**. The film poster claimed to take viewers, "Behind the weird 'way out' world of the Beatniks" and, to emphasis the point, cinema audiences were given free 'beatnik dictionaries' which explained 'beat' terms and phrases used in the story.

The Beat Generation concerns a thrill-seeking serial rapist (Stan Belmont in the book) at large in Los Angeles, whose MO is to gain entrance to the homes of married women while their husbands are out and attack them. Leaving the scene of his latest crime, Belmont is nearly hit by a car being driven by hardened cop Dave Culloran. As a way of making amends for the near accident, Culloran offers Belmont a lift. The two men get talking, during which Culloran reveals he is married. Belmont, who gives the cop a false name, gets Culloran's address from a disused envelope in the car. He later visits Culloran's wife, Francee, and rapes her. Bizarrely, the case is assigned to Culloran and his partner.

Culloran's previous relationship, to **a tramp** called Lila, has left him with deep emotional wounds and a thinly veiled hostility to women. As part of this, Culloran prides himself on the ability to **distinguish between the wanton and the decent.** Coincidentally, the crime scene Culloran was leaving when he nearly hit Belmont was the house of the rapist's last victim, an innocent woman to whom Culloran gave the third degree about the rape and accused of playing around while her salesman husband was out bowling.

She's the victim, not the criminal, cautions Culloran's partner.

Maybe, Culloran replies.

His attitude comes back to haunt him after his own wife, Francee, is raped. The resulting existential torment is made worse when she informs him she is pregnant and isn't sure whether her husband or the rapist is the father. At first she wants an abortion but struggles with guilt and the logistics of organising the procedure. Their marriage disintegrates under the pressure of her decision to have the child and his obsession with tracking down the rapist. Culloran eventually arrests Belmont and Francee has a baby girl, whom Culloran accepts as the couple reunite.

A former reporter and lawyer, Zugsmith's movie production credits included *The Incredible Shrinking Man* (1957) and *Touch of Evil* (1958), after which he went on to do a string of exploitation titles, such as *College Confidential* and *Sex Kittens Go to College* (both of which appeared in 1960) and the 1962 cult film *Confessions of an Opium Eater,* starring Vincent Price. The novelisation of *The Beat Generation* was his only book.

The Beat Generation may be a fascinating study of masculinity in post–Kinsey Report America but has little to do with beat culture in any form other than incorporating aspects of its aesthetics and parodying its supposed worldview.

Belmont, the spoiled child of a rich family, dropped out of college because he believes **it's a drag.** He has a beach pad, paid for by his father, that he has turned into a haven for his retinue of hangers-on, including young women in black crewneck jumpers who sit around and recite bad poetry. **Laws were passed for them to flout,** thinks Belmont. **Social taboos existed for them to reject. The past was hoary with laughs and lies. The future promised H-bombs or hideous mediocrity. There was only now. To learn the beat you had to suck the last drop of juice from the present.**

Belmont's pad is decorated with giant oil paintings and wallpaper simulating exposed brickwork. Belmont's cronies are blissfully ignorant of his double life as a rapist. The ease with which he can fool his friends shows the susceptibility of young people to decadent cultural influences.

A wave of pulp novels appropriating aspects of the so-called beat culture followed *The Beat Generation. A Twilight Affair* (1960) was set in New York's Greenwich Village, the hub of so-called beat culture; according to its back cover blurb it depicted **THAT TWILIGHT WORLD WHERE WOMEN ARE IN LOVE . . . WITH OTHER WOMEN.** *The Far Out Ones* (1963) claimed that **9 TO 5 AT THE OFFICE WASN'T FOR HER . . . NOT WHEN BELLY DANCING COULD SHIMMY HER INTO THE BIG TIME.** *Beatnik Wanton* (1964) was advertised on the basis that its heroine **LUSTED IN SIN ORGIES AND REEFER BRAWLS,** and *All Kinds of Loving* (1965) was marketed as **A SHOCKING PEEK AT THE WAY THE BEAT GENERATION LIVES AND LOVES IN GREENWICH VILLAGE.** *I Like It Cool* (1960) featured private investigator and Korean War veteran Johnny Amsterdam, the 'eye with a beard', who agrees to help the vaguely beat sister of a dead army buddy track down her missing friend.

Beat culture met the spy novel in Jay Flynn's *A Body for McHugh* (1960). McHugh tends bar in a dive on the San Francisco waterfront as a cover for his real job as the agent of a nameless Washington-based intelligence organisation. The second of five books featuring McHugh, *A Body for McHugh* sees the character come under suspicion of murder when a foreign man (McHugh can tell this from the deceased's fancy clothes) turns up dead in his bar. The clue to discovering the murdered man's identity, and clearing McHugh's name, rests with finding a woman called Cece, last seen in the bar moments before the man's death. She's a beatnik artist who specialises in driftwood sculptures. McHugh tracks her down to a large house by the sea. As he arrives a party is in full swing.

McHugh stood just inside the door. His eyes sorted over the dozen or so people in this front room. They were young. They looked strong. Happy young animals. Sweatshirts and jeans

were their uniforms . . . He felt out of place in his Brooks Brothers suit, and the button down collar of his short seemed to choke him.

He spies the girl.

She was wearing a dark turtle-neck sweater and narrow chino slacks that emphasised the slenderness of her waist, the length of her legs. She was barefoot and without make-up.

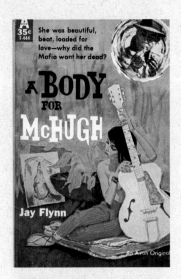

Pulp publishers were particularly keen to play up the sexuality of beat women, the way they combined what, for the early 60s, was a somewhat masculine dress sense and manners with the sexual promiscuity that came with their immersion in an alternative cultural milieu. For the straight, white, suburban working stiffs who populated the world of pulp (and made up the majority of its readership), these women were both feared and secretly lusted after.

A good example of this is Jerry Weil's *A Real Cool Cat*, originally published by Signet in 1960 and re-issued by Scripts, the adult-oriented imprint of Australian pulp publisher Horwitz, in 1967. The cover of the Scripts edition features a suggestive photograph and the blurb: THE EROTIC DESIRE AND PASSION OF A BEATNIK WANTON SHATTER A FAITHFUL HUSBAND.

An advertising copywriter for a New York pharmaceutical company leaves his Manhattan office one night, stops to buy a newspaper and decides he doesn't want to go home. Clutching his paper, he is overcome by what has obviously been a long simmering midlife crisis and wants a break from his suburban existence, his kids and his pregnant wife.

He just couldn't go home and that was all there was to it . . . He wanted, he needed, he was desperate for a deviation, however slight, from the main highway of his life, just a small winding road that he could travel for now more than a speck of time, only to see some fresh scenery.

He wanders the streets that evening, does the same the next night, and it becomes a habit with him. In the process, he discovers another world that exists parallel to his weekend activities, playing golf and hosting backyard barbecues with the neighbours. He becomes obsessed with a stripper at a friend's stag party, obtains her number and, after several false starts, works up the courage to call her. 'Cat'

A Body for McHugh
(Avon, 1960)

A Real Cool Cat
(Scripts, 1967)

Pads Are for Passion
(Beacon, 1961)

is straight out of beatnik central casting. Part sexual ingénue, part hedonist, she smokes, drinks, swears, and, most perplexing to the man, refuses to take his money, despite having sex with him. She even wears the uniform, jeans and a turtleneck sweater. Cat's philosophy is simple: **"The only thing to do is joy and joy and joy," she said softly and rhythmically to the motion of her body. "Joy and joy and joy until you're so tired and then you can sleep".**

She nicknames the man 'Mister Joy'. They hang out in Mexican restaurants and jazz clubs, smoke reefer, drink cheap wine, sit on the floor of her apartment and talk beat philosophy. And, of course, they have a lot of sex. She introduces him to her friend, a beatnik poet and artist called Mole who dresses like a hobo and recites poetry. The man's suburban life starts to seem dull and meaningless—that is, until a sexually abusive cop busts Cat on a drugs charge and threatens to expose him. Cat ends up going to jail, and he goes home to his wife, who was beginning to suspect something.

Amid the inevitable focus on sex, drugs and violence, some pulp managed to capture slightly more authentic aspects of beat culture. *Pads Are for Passion* by Sheldon Lord aka Lawrence Block—published in 1961 and reissued in 2011 by Hard Case as *A Diet of Treacle*—is one example. Joe Milani is a dissolute Korean War veteran and college dropout who can't handle returning to 'squaresville'. He spends his days hanging out in coffee bars, smoking reefer, bumming meals, 'balling chicks' and reading in Washington Square. His current book is a copy of Henry Miller's *Sexus* **that someone had carefully smuggled in on a return trip from Europe.** Milani's cellmate in beatnik hell is 'Shank', a psychotic small-time drug pusher, so called because of the switchblade he carries.

Milani is sitting in his favourite 'coffee pot', the Palermo, at three in the morning, stoned and drinking espresso, when he spots Anita Carbone, an attractive dark-haired woman from East Harlem. They strike up a conversation, start seeing each other, and soon the two of them are living together in a tiny apartment with Shank. Anita wants to escape the boredom and consumerism of the suburbs—a husband, two kids, and everything she thinks goes with it. Joe is not entirely sure what he wants. He has a bad case of the beat condition . . . immobility. He found himself wondering why

nobody had bothered to describe it in a novel. The beat writers were uniformly lousy, but one of them nevertheless should have managed to get hipped on the notion of transferring that marvellous state of nothingness to paper.

Anita starts taking drugs and loses her inhibitions, something she is doing to please Joe and fit in with his friends, but it only seems to alienate him. Meanwhile, Shank, unbeknown to his flatmates, has graduated from selling weed to heroin. This only comes into the open when a cop visits their apartment and Shank kills him in front of Joe and Anita. They have no choice but to go on the run, but what will they do for money?

Block was in New York as a young university student in the 50s. "I lived in the Village, I knew a lot of people who hung out in and around Washington Square, and never having seen the milieu treated in fiction, wanted to write something about it," Block told me in May 2013. "There were a lot of people who were hip to one degree or another. I don't know that they'd come under the heading of 'beats'."

Ostensibly a crime novel, *Pads Are for Passion*, has the seeds of Block's later talent and is well written. There are also some interesting observations about the dynamics of the drug trade and the emerging counterculture of Greenwich Village:

There weren't that many—of the others. You could walk all over the Village and never notice them, not unless you were one yourself and consequently knew what to look for. They varied in age, appearance and dress, but a boy like Shank knew how to spot them.

They were lost people, bored people, tired people, angry young people, Zen people, beat people. They were tagged with more labels than you could shake a stick of pot at, but the people themselves scorned the labels and spent little time worrying about them. Shank himself shrugged at labels. He knew there were two classes of people in the world—the ones he liked and the ones he didn't.

The ones he didn't could go in a body to hell, as far as he was concerned. The ones he liked were going to hell, too, but he happened to be going on the same boat they were—and that made the difference.

The people he gravitated to smoked marijuana or gobbled Benzedrine or drank cough syrup

or chewed peyote. They talked with each other, walked with each other, sat with each other and slept with each other. They listened to jazz, deep and grinding hard bop, and they spoke their own language, the inner language of Hip.

Another interesting take on New York's early-60s alternative scene is J. Nicholas Iannuzzi's *What's Happening?*, published in 1964 and republished in 1966. While the cover of the latter version, a vulnerable-looking semi-naked blonde nymph, would appear to hold the promise of lashings of steamy sex, *What's Happening?* is an almost anthropological tract about contemporary life in Greenwich Village ('the Village', as the locals call it). The main characters are a group of female flatmates, most prominent of whom is Rita, who has fled the suburbs of Brooklyn to realise her dream of being an actress.

What's Happening? (the title comes from the way Village locals in the book commonly greet each other) appears to be Iannuzzi's only book. The beats hardly rate a mention, but the book is packed with significant details of the changing times: young women who drink in public (straight from the beer bottle, no less), open interracial relationships, casual sex, even a gay bar. There are also some vivid descriptive passages of the Greenwich Village scene, such as this portrayal of a late-night bar:

Men and women, racially interlaced like pawns on a chessboard, were crammed about tables covered with red-checked cloths. The entire room rumbled with conversation which spasmodically burst into laughter. Some people sat on isolated chairs in the aisles. Others stood in the back against the wooden bar which was illuminated from behind by a dim red bulb.

These were the Villagers. They were veiled in a face-absorbing dimness . . . many people wore sunglasses. Light-colored clothing and jewelry appeared through the cloaked atmosphere. White pants and shirts could be distinguished; so too could tennis sneakers on feet resting on chairs. Many women wore long, silver earrings and twists of silver around their fingers. The men wore tight pants; some had beards.

And this passage about the fluid nature of the Village's population:

Just as the waiters and bartenders and cooks were replaced constantly, so were the people living in the Village. The values and ideals remained, the principles, the rules, the code of the revolutionaries, but the people believing in them varied. The people living there last week had gone away, perhaps to surrender and live home again, or to go to California to get away from the grind of the Village, or to be closer to nature, or to tour with Summer Stock, or to live with someone who lives in another part of town, or to do any number of things in further search of peace. Their places were eagerly filled by others. Male and female flee to the Village attracted by the lure of excitement, of freedom, of tolerance, of peace and security, to escape from the harsh, unthinking world—but many leave very soon, most leave after a while, with more tolerance for the world, but some never go away and never find it.

Iannuzzi also displays awareness of the illicit attraction of the Village and its lifestyle for 'Uptowners', as locals describe other New Yorkers.

Many girls from Uptown come to the village to get picked up and taken to a wild party, to meet the 'weirdo' guys, to have some different, very exciting kicks. Men from Uptown come to the Village to meet some wild, way-out women.

One of the most realistic and gripping portrayals of the underbelly of the emerging counterculture in the early 60s is *Shake Him Till He Rattles* (1963) by Malcolm Braly. Set in the San Francisco suburb of North Beach, the main character is a dissolute horn player, Lee Cabiness, who attempts make sense of relationships and his music while being stalked by a narcotics cop called Carver. Carver wants to make Cabiness his snitch in the war against the North Beach drug trade, and the story opens with the cop casing out an after-hours jazz club in the hope of catching sight of the musician.

Through the large windows of the coffee-houses he studied his quarry. Most of them wore old clothes, deliberately shabby, khakis, denims and army-surplus jackets. The girls dressed the same as the men; they would be indistinguishable from the back, except for the loose

What's Happening? (Paperback Library, 1966)
Easy Living (Corgi, 1962)

hair around their shoulders. There were exceptions to the uniform—a number of young men in very tight slacks and sweaters—and he passed a light-skinned Negro standing in a doorway who wore an immaculate riding habit . . . Another group brought Carver's gorge up, hot and fast. Three grotesque celebrants from some private masquerade wandered arm in arm, but they were still masked and glittering with theatrical jewelry, impossible to identify as to the gender, except that they were so aggressively female they must have been male.

Shake Him Till He Rattles is well written, and the way the characters think and speak, their interactions with the police and the drug scene feel authentic—not surprisingly, given how much time Braly spent in prison.

"There is no big [drug] **connection," Sullivan replied dully. "That's funny paper stuff. Maybe at one time there was, but you've got everyone on a panic kick. Every once in a while someone drives South, over the border at TJ or Mexicali. They sell about half of what they bring back to pay for the next trip. You know all this."**

Some young Americans went further afield to escape the boredom of 1950s America. Maitland Zane's *Easy Living* (1959) is the story of a couple of young men in Paris, Harry Steiner, a New York–born trumpet player whose career has been deep-sixed by his earlier addiction to heroin, and his friend, Irving Wyeth. They spend their days sitting in cafes, drinking cheap espresso and doing the *Herald Tribune* crossword. It's such a meaningless, dissolute lifestyle that even the characters don't seem to know why they do it: **Today, though, I'm not in the least interested in Gina, I feel lazy, enervated, drugged,** thinks Steiner at one point. **My eyes feel puffy and I've been yawning since I got up from lumpy mouldering little bed. I slept too long, just as I always sleep too long; sleeping late shortens the day, makes it possible to get by on two meals. But mostly it just shortens the day.**

For kicks, Steiner and Wyeth smoke reefer (they talk about heroin or 'horse' but don't indulge in it—Steiner is once bitten, twice shy on that score) and hang out in jazz clubs:

We rode the Metro back to Montparnasse, got off at Vavin and walked to the Etats-Unis, a

ground floor, oddly laid-out bar in the hotel of the same name. We took a table near the grand-piano, ordered wine and listened for a few minutes to the trio, two Americans and a Frenchman. The pianist blew an eclectic style, half Monk, half Garner, a little of this and a little of that.

The people in there that night were mostly Left Bankers, salted liberally with Algerian hash-pushers, Negro GI's stationed in and around Paris, and the sort of French who live with and off Americans. It was not the kind of bar American Express nightclub buses stopped at, which was a reason why I went there. Nonetheless, the place was too noisy, the people febrile, "Everybody I see in here," I said morosely, "is sick. Sick, sick, sick."

Steiner strikes up a semi-serious relationship with Delores, a British girl who has moved to Paris to escape an abusive alcoholic husband. She's a Communist Party member, an intellectual and is traumatised by the death of her eight-month old baby, who choked on a safety pin while her drunken husband was looking after the child. Steiner briefly travels back to the UK with Delores. He moves into an apartment in Earl's Court and encounters a bohemian scene that is more downwardly mobile, grottier and poorer than the one he left in Paris:

With Delores working again, it meant that I couldn't see her until the evenings, unless we met for lunch, and I had again to start finding ways to kill the days. Killing time in London isn't as easy—or wasn't for me—as it was in Paris. The liquor laws are different, for one thing, and they don't have sidewalk cafés and the coffee shops don't open up until later. You can walk and you can read in your room or go to the movies or sit in Hyde Park and look at the grandmas sunning themselves or you can sleep. I did all these things, alone and with Wyeth, who seldom went outside the apartment except to eat and buy more books.

Being back in the UK brings Delores into close proximity to her ex-husband, which cools her sex life with Steiner. He eventually ends their relationship and decides to move back to New York.

Although it took different forms, the changes sweeping youth culture in the US in the early 60s extended further afield. The late 50s saw many British youths also gripped by a desire for change. Many left their suburban surroundings and headed to London, where they immersed themselves in the emerging bohemian scene. Some of these young people put pen to paper in attempt to describe their experiences. In 1961 three of these accounts were published: Terry Taylor's *Baron's Court, All Change*, Laura Del-Rivo's *The Furnished Room* and Colin Wilson's *Adrift in Soho*.

In an article marking the reissue of all three books by New London Editions in 2011, British author Cathi Unsworth wrote: "The spark that crackles through all three books is the yearning for change and difference, of finding a way of living in the centre of all happening without resorting to the drudge of work—by far the biggest fault line in this generation was the one that opened up between the baby-boomers and their parents. The protagonists of each, while hanging in similar locations and social milieus, find differing solutions to this crucial problem, to varying degrees of success and disaster."

Taylor worked as a passport photographer in Soho, a cosmopolitan suburb of London that was to British bohemians what Greenwich Village was to America's beats. *Baron's Court, All Change*, his only published work, was, according to English writer Stewart Home, "a novel so groovy and ahead of its time that it joined the Legion of the Reforgotten faster than the publisher was able to dispatch it to the shops." Set on the cusp of the 60s, the story is narrated by an unnamed 16-year-old who leaves the suburbs and a dead-end sales assistant job to come to London. He becomes ensconced in Soho, where he listens to a lot of jazz, investigates alternative spirituality, and deals marijuana. He makes £38 from one sale, a fortune to him, most of which he spends on new clothes.

In Del-Rivo's *The Furnished Room*, a young Irishman, who has lost his faith in life, lives a meaningless existence in a dingy London bedsit. He meets a con man, with whom he devises a violent scheme to make money. It was filmed in 1963 by Michael Winner as *West 11*, from a screenplay co-written by Keith Waterhouse, author of the 1959 novel *Billy Liar*.

The best known of the three books, Colin Wilson's *Adrift in Soho* is a semi-autobiographical coming of age story set in the late-50s London. The book opens with the main character, Harry Preston, leaving the

Royal Air Force to work on a building site in Nottingham. Soon fed up with this, he travels to London with £30 in his pocket and a suitcase full of philosophy books. Renting an attic room in Earl's Court, he is intent on writing a book about outsiders in cult literature, but ends up spending as much time in the cafés and bars of Soho as he does in the Reading Room of the British Museum.

In one of these establishments he meets James, a flamboyant 'blagger' (a British version of a hustler) who has given his life over to the pursuit of freedom. James crashes at various friends' houses and spends most of his time bumming meals and drinks, and seducing impressionable young women who wander into London from the suburbs.

James teaches Harry how to fend for himself and tries to imbue him with his anti-bourgeois views. **They're all hypocrites and frauds**, James says about the middle classes. **They spend their lives fighting to make money so that they can buy television sets and washing machines, but the one thing they can't buy is human dignity, because a slave can't have dignity. That's why they can't stand our sort. They know we refuse to sell out to the great illusion. We won't support the sham. We're a perpetual reproach to them.**

The title, *Adrift in Soho*, is an accurate description of the novel, made up as it is of a series of meandering conversations in pubs and cafés between Harry and James and various characters they come into contact with, including con men, writers and downwardly mobile aristocrats. The most memorable supporting character is 'Ironfoot Jack', the self-styled 'King of the Bohemians', supposedly based on a real individual who frequented Soho at the time Wilson was writing his novel:

> He was a strange looking man, a cross between a tramp and a character out of *The Prisoner of Zenda*. A dirty cravat was held by an enormous brass ring. He was a big man, with the shoulders of a wrestler; and his bulk contrasted oddly with his voice, which was that of an old Cockney woman, slow, tremulous, as if he were on the point of bursting into tears.

Harry also strikes up a rather tepid romance with a New Zealand woman, Doreen, his first encounter **with the directness of colonials**, and moves into a house in Notting Hill full of unsuccessful artists, writers and journalists.

Adrift in Soho followed in the wake of the success of Wilson's first book, *The Outsider* (1956), which had made the author an overnight sensation. Before that, however, he had been sleeping rough on Hampstead Heath, working in a café, and spending as much time as possible in the British Museum.

Compared to America, Soho's bohemian scene is generally portrayed as less hedonistic, more intellectual and, like the rest of the country, still gripped by a sense of drab austerity. A good meal consists of greasy fish and chips and a cup of tea, with only beer, the occasional glass of red or a joint to liven things up.

In much the same way as in the US, Australian pulp writers in the 60s used 'beat' as a loose signifier for any young person who spent time in coffee-houses, took drugs, stayed up late listening to jazz or rock and roll, and wanted to rebel against the prevailing cultural mores. As in the UK, most importantly, this meant not defining your identity according to your day job.

Charles Barrett's *Address: Kings Cross* (1964) is a case in point. The main character, Claudine, is a nice middle-class girl. The product of an Adelaide convent school education, she is lured to Sydney by the prospect of a **groovy, way out lifestyle**, and the chance to avoid the 'nine to five' slog endured by her parents. Upon her arrival she meets Greg, a boy from the posh eastern suburb of Vaucluse. It's inferred that he's a bit of a beatnik because he has dropped out of university. He serves the useful role of introducing Claudine to the various cultural tribes of Sydney's notorious vice strip, Kings Cross, but the relationship doesn't last.

Claudine's attraction to Kings Cross is spelled out soon after she arrives:

> This was a big, exciting city. Maybe New York, Paris and Rome were bigger or more exciting but Sydney had everything you could get in an international city. Little more than a mile away from Sam's apartment was the Cross—Kings Cross, the vibrant, kaleidoscopic hub of Sydney's night-life where people lived in a way I'd only dreamed about back in old fogy Adelaide. At the Cross, things Happened. That's what I liked and needed, things happening all the time so that there were no empty hours to fill, no time to remember what a lousy deal life really was, anyway. That's why the kids roamed the streets there for hours, I thought, hanging the

Adrift in Soho
(Houghton Mifflin, 1961)
Adrift in Soho
(Pan, 1964)

brightly lit corners. They collected in espresso bars and twisting, stomping and shouting in dimly lit dance halls, so they could forget how little life had to offer all vital young animals who wanted to be up and doing something.

She goes on to say: **It struck me that the Cross wasn't nice, in a way that I'd been taught about niceness at schools. It was a blaring, bawdy, vulgar, honky tonk strip, but it was exciting and it filled a need in me . . .** [especially in comparison to the outer suburbs] **where people lived in neat fibro boxes of houses with tiny gardens and a dull routine that has nothing to offer lively kids.** By the book's end, Claudine is popping purple hearts (an amphetamine popular in the 60s and available on prescription) and working as a high-priced call girl.

Charles Barrett was one of the many pseudonyms of local pulp writer Marcia McEwan, who for several years in the 60s penned novels for Horwitz Publications. Her specialty was stories about the perils faced by young people like Claudine, lured by the bright lights and fast life of Sydney's Kings Cross.

Prior to the early 21st century, when substantial gentrification began to transform the area, Kings Cross had a well-earned reputation as Australia's foremost centre of prostitution, sly grog (alcohol sales outside permitted hours) and illegal gambling. From the 1930s to the 60s, it was also one of the few places in Australia where alternative sexualities and lifestyles were openly tolerated. It had a thriving communist scene and was a haven for Italian, Greek and Jewish migrants, as well as for German refugees from Nazism. In addition, Kings Cross was the first place in Australia where apartment living predominated, which not only made the Cross the most heavily populated part of the country, but also allowed young men and women to live unsupervised in close proximity. This was anathema to the prevailing mainstream view of family life, and generated a moral panic focused on the sexual implications of such a lifestyle, especially for young women.

The combination of low rents and closeness to the heart of the city made the Cross a sought-after location for artists and bohemians. This in turn fuelled a vibrant culture of jazz, folk, art, poetry and literature. It was also favoured by the closest thing Australia had to beats, the Push. A loose grouping of bohemian intellectuals, academics, journalists and writers, the Push formed in the 1940s and flourished during the conservative 50s and early 60s.

The Push had a more explicitly libertarian outlook than its American and British counterparts and was less focused on music, literature and the arts than those Australians tagged as beatniks. Its members despised middle-class values, considered themselves intellectuals and were anti-careerist, as well as opposed to monogamy, censorship and political activism. Historian Jim Franklin notes in *Corrupting the Youth: A History of Philosophy in Australia* (University of NSW, 2003) that the group provided a rare case in Australian society of people who took debate and ideas seriously, offering "an island of excitement in a sea of dullness." He cites a 1959 assessment by the Australian Security Intelligence Organisation [Australia's equivalent of the FBI or MI5], which claims:

At first meeting with these people one is inclined to regard them as an offshoot of the 'beatniks', but after knowing them a short while it becomes obvious that they are well above the average 'beatnik' intellectually. Their knowledge of Marxism is surprising and their ability to discuss this subject on levels not encountered in the Communist Party of Australia is both stimulating and educational . . . [They] have absolutely no standard of ethics. Their behaviour and conversation in mixed company would be regarded as 'shocking' even in 'modern' society.

Others found them less shocking or intellectually challenging. Anne Coombs's study, *Sex and Anarchy: the Life and Death of the Sydney Push* (1996), includes the observation by one former participant that the Push were "a dreary lot who wore dreary clothes, drank in dreary pubs and lived in dreary dwellings with nothing on the walls."

The Push faded as the 60s wore on and Australians slowly became more cosmopolitan. Anti-authoritarian and anarchist in its outlook, many of its significant members abandoned their initial cynicism and anti-activist stance to become involved in broader struggles, such as feminism, squatting, and the movement against the war in Vietnam.

In Julian Spencer's *The Spungers* (1967), remnants of the Push are described as living in dark apartments . . . **old ladies and queens and buyers of dirty books and party givers and money spenders.** At another point in *The Spungers* a young surfie who is spending his holidays slumming it in the Cross goes to a party, where he confuses the Push with mods and the bohemian scene more generally:

Phil didn't know where he was, only that he was very drunk. It was a party of some description, music ("Would you believe: the Rolling Stones, baby," someone shouts from somewhere and Phil has another mouthful of whatever), people, this pressing push of people, this sudden revelation in Phil's brain, hey, is this the Push? Is this the mythical Push then?

The most significant mention of the Push and beatnik-style bohemians in Australian pulp fiction is *Beat Girl* (1965), by the aforementioned Marcia McEwan (this time using the pseudonym Marcia Wayne). An American sailor, Eric Eriksson, is on shore leave in Kings Cross. He gets separated from the other sailors from his ship and picks up a girl named Jan. They go skinny-dipping in the ocean and dancing at an illegal casino. Next thing he knows, he wakes up in a **Darlo alley** with a splitting headache, his fleet has sailed, and he's in danger of being considered a deserter. To make matters worse, someone has stolen his watch, a keepsake from a friend who was killed in Korea.

There is no sign of Jan, but as he wakes up he notices a young woman, **a zombie faced beatnik blonde,** watching him from the alley entrance. The woman, Lois, takes pity on the stranger and lets him crash at her 'pad'. With her as his guide, Eric embarks on a one-man crusade to get the watch back.

Eric is a farm boy, out of place in the big smoke. He views inner Sydney as a sort of modern Sodom and Gomorrah. Eric's perceptions of the people that Lois hangs out with are that they're:

Off-beat types . . . supercilious-looking intellectual characters with beards, wearing elastic sided boots and clothes that had a vague Mark Twainish or Southern gentlemen flavour about them. Jan seemed to know them and positively panted to join the group, dragging Eric in with her. Excitedly she explained that they were in The Push, really Way Out Intellectuals . . . Eric didn't go for them. They were beatniks, whether they called themselves Beats or Degenerates or The Push or The Drift. In his book they were lousy no hopers.

He goes to a party full of guys in shorts and thongs and girls in tight blue jeans and black-rimmed glare glasses. A folk band is playing.

They swayed and wailed over their guitars while one odd bod sat on the floor with bongo

BEAT GIRL

PB201
4'6

Marcia Wayne

She lived with a wild push in a pad near the Cross—living by their law

Dimly he remembered the events of the previous night

. . . or was it nights? Out of the haze that came and went with the painful throbbing of his head, vivid pictures formed in his mind.

Jan, tall and golden and tempting, her body brown as an island girl's against the white of the sand.

Tracy, small and voluptuous, green eyes glittering unnaturally, her dark hair a swirling cloud of night around her pale oval face.

Vague memories of having too much to drink and of cigarettes which tasted like no ordinary cigarette. Of lank-headed, bare-footed beatniks and of a dirty room . . . and then the blackness won. He moved his head gingerly and groaned.

"As if it's not enough to have lost all your money," he thought bitterly, "now you're a deserter as well!"

Beat Girl
(Horwitz, 1965)

drums clasped between his knees, his fingers drumming the hypnotic beat without faltering, his vacant eyes fixed unseeingly on a point in mid-air as if concentration on the primitive, jungle drumming had drained him of all intelligence and humanity.

In keeping with the sexism of the era, Eric is particularly critical of the Push women. **Betty [their host] was a grubby, fortyish, divorcee in tight purple stretch slacks, black skivvy which clung to pointed rubber and nylon cups masquerading hopelessly as a bosom, dangling gold earrings, dangling chain pendant and a mass of thin gold and silver bracelets jingling on her bony wrists.**

Eric's suspicions about who stole his watch eventually fall on a man called Karl Essen and his girl, Tracy. Karl is a habitué of the local Push pub, the Grenadier. As Lois puts it, the pub is full of young men who:

Drift around in gangs, hang around places like the Grenadier and talk, talk, talk, trying to find

out what life's all about. I used to think it was exciting, that they were all potential geniuses and there was real significance in the Push, like you don't find in the suburbs . . . Lately, I'm beginning to wonder. I'm getting tired of the way they say and do the same things, over and over and it still doesn't make sense.

It turns out Karl used Tracy to slip Eric a knockout drug so her boyfriend could rob him. In revenge for Karl abusing her one night, Tracy helps Eric retrieve his watch. In the resulting confrontation, Karl and Eric fight on the balcony of Karl's inner Sydney terrace. Karl falls to his death. Eric gets his watch back and is taken into custody by US military police who promise not to be too hard on him. Lois commits to waiting for him. She has now renounced the Push altogether and thinks Eric looks good in his uniform.

The only thing that could jeopardise their plans to be together is a war in a faraway Asian country called Vietnam.

ANDREW NETTE

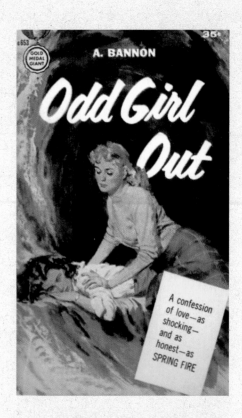

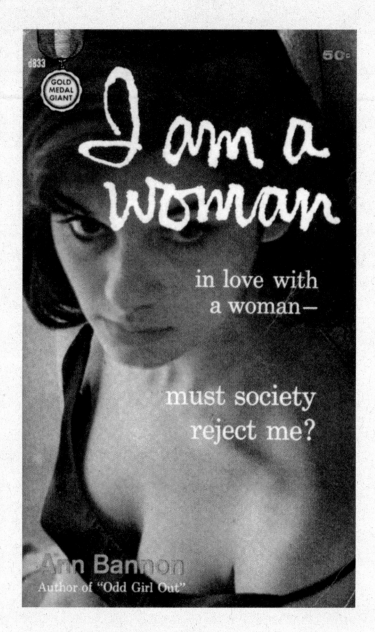

I Am a Woman (Gold Medal, 1959)
Odd Girl Out (Gold Medal, 1957)
Beebo Brinker (Gold Medal, 1962)

GIRL GANGS, BIKER BOYS, AND REAL COOL CATS

ANN BANNON AND THE BEEBO BRINKER CHRONICLES

Having emerged as a creative enclave in the late 19th century, Greenwich Village came into its own in the immediate postwar era. Allen Ginsberg, Jack Kerouac, William Burroughs and other writers belonging to what became known as the beat generation gathered there from the late 1940s, joining avant-garde artists and political radicals. The area's long association with theatre spawned a distinctly experimental 'Off-Off-Broadway' scene while its music and cabaret venues nurtured key folk, jazz and rock performers.

Amongst these thriving alternative subcultures were those concerning sexuality. As with so many other scenes, the Village came to represent a magnet for people seeking to escape the sexual repression of rural and suburban American. Although many heterosexual artists and folkies frequented different venues and scenes to those associated with gays and lesbians, there was some crossover, and sexual diversity added to the area's overall bohemian reputation.

With so much going on there it is hardly surprising that Greenwich Village came to be heavily chronicled in the literature of the time. Some of this emerged from the area itself, but much of it dealt in crude stereotypes, cashing in on the media and public interest which had burgeoned from the late 1950s onwards.

One writer who provided a rare and sympathetic insight into gay and lesbian life of the period was Ann Weldy, better known as Ann Bannon, whose Beebo Brinker Chronicles are now regarded as pulp classics. After *Odd Girl Out* (1957), Bannon went on to pen four more in the series for paperback publishers Gold Medal—*I Am a Woman* (*In Love with a Woman—Must Society Reject Me?*), (1959), *Women in the Shadows* (1959), *Journey to a Woman* (1960), and *Beebo Brinker* (1962)—as well as a stand-alone novel, *The Marriage* (1960).

In the following interview, Bannon discusses the repressiveness of society at large during this period and the lifeline that the reality and the mythology of Greenwich Village, as well as the novels about it, provided to gays and lesbians across the world.

When did you first come across novels being published in the lesbian pulp genre, and what inspired you to start writing in the field yourself?
Like a lot of people back then, I first found one of these novels when I was poking around in a pharma-

cy in the mid-1950s. There were a lot of paperback books on the shelves then that had started to be published as original stories instead of just reprints of the classics.

One of the genres that proved most successful was the lesbian pulp novel. This was a remarkable phenomenon because it was such a taboo subject. It was okay to write about policemen, romance, cowboys, science fiction and all the other things that were starting to come out as original paperbacks. Lesbian novels however were extremely unusual and there were only two out there, one of which was a reprint. That was a book called *Women's Barracks* (1950) by Tereska Torres. And then there was Marijane Meaker's book *Spring Fire* (1952), which she wrote as Vin Packer. This was the first time books on the topic were easily found and distributed the way that magazines were.

So I picked up Marijane's book and it was about girls in a boarding school. I had just graduated from college straight into the arms of my husband, but while I was in college I was in an all-girl sorority so a lot of what Marijane wrote about seemed familiar to me. I thought: I can do this too. I wanted to use my writing in a creative way, instead of just academically, so I sat down at the table with my husband's portable typewriter and just jumped in.

Once you'd written the novel, how did you get to know Marijane Meaker? How did your friendship lead to Odd Girl Out *being published in 1957?*
I was impressed by her work—she is a very good writer and still earning a living that way. I wrote to her care of her publisher. It was kind of a fan letter. I did not realise she was getting them by the bushel from young women all around the world, but she responded. She was living in New York and I was in nearby Philadelphia. She said, if you have a manuscript and you can visit me, then I'd like to see it and maybe you can get to meet my editor. This was of course music to the ears of an aspiring young writer, since one of my perplexities had been how to get into print.

My husband took some persuading because he was unenthused about sending me off to New York, but finally—when I convinced him I would stay at a women's hotel—he took heart, perhaps mistakenly, and said all right. I went to New York and spent most of the visit with Marijane. It was the beginning of a terrific friendship and she did in fact introduce me to the editor-in-chief at her publisher, Gold Medal Books.

What was Gold Medal's response to your manuscript?
In the view of Dick Carroll, the twinkly old Irishman who was running that show, the manuscript was twice as long as they wanted. He also felt that I hadn't recognised my story. I had told a kind of straightforward coming-of-age type novel, and rather cautiously and timidly put a small romance between two young women in the corners of the background. He said cut the length by half and tell the story of the two young women, Beth and Laura, and then maybe we'll have something. I was a bit abashed because I was very cautious about writing about any kind of lesbian romance, but it was clearly what I wanted to do and where the energy of the book was. I went home and followed his advice, brought it back to Dick and they published it immediately. They didn't edit it, they didn't cut it, and I was amazed. I look back when I read it now and think it really did need a little editing (laughter). The book was tremendously successful and got a very warm reception, much to my amazement.

This was of course a period in which gay and lesbian relationships and identities were extremely taboo.
That's very true. In the US we were living through a time of congressional investigations—gay people were being fired from jobs in the State Department under the ruse that they could be blackmailed. Of course they could only be blackmailed because they were held in contempt and put under investigation.

It was a very repressed and frightening time. After World War Two ended, the country had made a frightening turn and embraced the most conservative and traditional roles. All the girls were supposed to be home having babies and making soup and casseroles. Everyone was supposed to be as conventional as is possible to imagine. People whose nature led them to a same-sex attraction were forced to put up a conventional façade. The danger was very severe, and gay attraction was frankly illegal in a lot of places. You could be jailed, you could certainly be publicly humiliated and everything could be thrown into jeopardy in terms of your job your family. You were treated almost as if you had a disease, and if you were known to be gay then your friends had to abandon you because they might catch it too. If you happened to be a parent then you certainly stood to lose your children.

Odd Girl Out established some of the characters that would recur throughout the series. Where did the inspiration for the characters come from?
Having been a member of a sorority, I inevitably saw a little bit of the attraction between the small number of girls who felt romantic about others in the house. There were some very attractive and confident young women, and it was easy to blend one or two of them into someone along the lines of Laura, who was terribly pretty but lacking in self-confidence. On the other end of the spectrum was a character like Beth, who was kind of the campus sweetheart. A beautiful outgoing and highly talented girl who was in authority in many of the campus organisations. All the boys were in love with her, and about half the girls. I do think to some degree, like with all authors, I myself am in those characters. If you write at all well, and your characters catch fire with the readers, then that has to be part of what makes it all viable.

Laura and Beth are the main two characters in Odd Girl Out. They have a relationship, but in the end go off in different directions.
They do, but that was a step forward because in those days to write about gay characters at all you had to make sure that even though they might have a beautiful love affair at the end of the book they could not be together. It had previously been required that they suffer for having loved each other. That usually meant that one of them went crazy or committed suicide and that all kinds of things went amiss. If writers didn't do this, the United States Post Office, which was delivering the books, would refuse to carry them. It wasn't like the aristocratic old hardcover houses. They delivered their own books straight to the bookstores. The Post Office was under the governance of the federal government and that government heartily disapproved of anything to do with homosexuality. When Marijane Meeker was writing *Spring Fire*, she was constrained very heavily in having to end her book on a very negative note.

Writing five years later, I found things had loosened up. I was able to, in a sense, have a happy ending. Laura understands even though she is shy and life is going to be difficult for her, she is not going to change her nature. So she decides to go for it. Having heard of the mecca of Greenwich Village, which was one of the gay strongholds, and known around the world even then for being artistic and bohemian, and where young people—straight and gay—gathered to exercise their freedom and creativity, that's where she decides to head.

How did you choose your pen name?
My husband at the time was in sales and had a list of potential customers sitting on his desk. We had moved to California when I was finishing the manuscript for *Odd Girl Out*. I went through this list and saw a familiar old Irish name, Bannon. There is some Irish in my family and it had the advantage of encapsulating my first name.

Once the book became successful, Gold Medal commissioned more work from you. Given that you had received some suggestions from them concerning the first novel, how much did they direct you from this point on, and were there any conventions you were expected to stick to?
There was generally very little direction. I actually launched into the second book at the suggestion of Dick Carroll. I had tried a book which I thought would be a straight romance, but it didn't seem to gel very well. Dick said, "You sent Laura to Greenwich Village so why don't you follow her there and let us know what happened?" That was as far as he intervened. I think in all of the six books I wrote, there was only one time they censored anything. That was because I had tried to use the phrase 'shit list'. They took that out and substituted 'blacklist'. That's as far as they ever went. The books sold very well and they were delighted, so I think it was mainly a case of just trying to get them into print expeditiously.

You mentioned before that the books were sold in pharmacies. Where else could they be found?
They were sold on the shelves of news stands, available in train stations and airports. Anywhere that you could buy magazines, pulp fiction was available as well. It was kind of an ephemeral literature. People would pick up a paperback novel to read on the train, on their way to work, keep it for a day or two until they finished it and then throw it away.

The remarkable thing was that people in the most remote little villages across the country were for the first time able to read both the good and the bad in original paperbacks. There were a lot of fine writers working in the field because the pay was so good—people like Gore Vidal, Patricia Highsmith and Marion Zimmer Bradley.

Ann Bannon (above) at college in 1953 and (below)in Pennsylvania during the mid-1950s.

During the war, young people were scattered all over the world with long periods of waiting, so what they did was read reprints of the classics and whatever the Modern Library and other publishers put out in paperback. This fed a hunger for good characters and good stories which continued after the war and was met by the new original paperbacks.

Readers who weren't likely to go into bookstores or didn't have one in their home town could walk into their drug store and pick up a lesbian novel. Of course it was likely that the clerk knew your mother so people would hide that novel between a couple of boxes of Kleenex, some toothpaste, and hope the clerk skipped over it quickly. Anybody could find them, so you didn't have to go into the library and request access to the rare and naughty books they held in the back.

Previously a great many people were denied any information at all about gay life. If you were a young woman living out in the country and didn't know if you had any lesbian friends, and felt as if you were alone in the world, then these books gave you a sense of where the gay communities were and what people wore, how they talked, how to find the gay bars. By happenstance, these gay communities were where my books were primarily set, and as such they not only spoke to young people who needed advice and information, but also gave them some hope.

Just as you had originally written to Marijane, you now received a lot of letters, didn't you?
Yes I did, much to the dismay of my long-suffering husband. He just didn't know what to make of it. He never read the books, although he gathered what they were about by looking at the covers. The postman would arrive with bags full of mail that came from all over. The books were all published in other countries and languages. So I would hear from people from all corners of the world.

The letters were very touching and what everyone wanted to know was: How does one declare oneself? How does one know for sure if one is a gay person? Of course, I needed the same kind of book. To tell you the truth I needed *Lesbianism for Dummies* [*laughter*] . . . I was winging it too. Here I was, a young mother, married. Of course, I recognised had taken a misstep, but once there were children in the mix I felt I had to tough it out until they were young adults, and I did. In the meantime I was hearing from an awful lot of women who had done the same thing. There were

a great many men as well who thought by getting married they would automatically make themselves straight . . . They were very surprised that their feelings were unchanged towards members of the same sex. I was expected to be Dear Abby, when my own opportunities of enjoying gay life were so limited.

Nevertheless, I did try to comfort people and answer their questions as well as I could. It might not have been the best advice, but it was kind and supportive and certainly well meant.

One of the things that set your novels aside from other pulp novels covering same-sex relationships was that many in the genre were written by men for men and so tended to be titillating and negative. Who do you think made up your audience?
I sat down, in a sense, to write a story that I would have liked to have read. There were so few of them. I wasn't so much consciously writing for other women, although I knew that they would pick up the books, so much as writing a love letter to the women I thought I would never meet.

In many regards, the books were sweet and tender romances. I didn't really think about the vast number of men who would pick these books up [*laughter*]. It seems to be a proverbial truth that many men find the idea of two women in bed together fascinating. I was astounded to find how many men bought these books and wrote to me, but what I was seeing was just the tip of the iceberg. It was something that publishers caught on to immediately. One of the reasons many of these books had sleazy covers was that the publishers marketed the books to a male audience knowing full well that the women would buy them anyway. Had it not been for this crossover audience the books may not have been financially successful. The business model was entirely different to a hardcover publishing company, they needed to sell hundreds of thousands of books.

There were men writing lesbian pulps as well, and most of theirs were the worst of the worst. Extremely sensational and cheaply thought through, with very little character development. Essentially they were going chapter to chapter from climax to climax. They really had nothing else to say. One exception was Lawrence Block. His books were very well done.

Other than Marijane, were you aware of other women writing in the field?
There were a few, and some of the more quite good writers like Valerie Taylor, Paula Christian and Claire

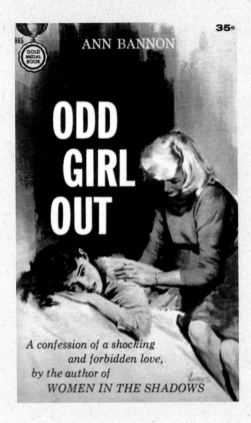

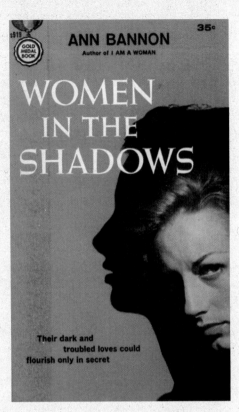

Odd Girl Out
(Gold Medal, 1960)

Women in the Shadows
(Gold Medal, 1959)

Morgan, which was Patricia Highsmith's pen name. Very little of this work has been picked up and republished over the decades.

Your second book had an unwieldy title, I Am a Woman in Love with a Woman—Must Society Reject Me? *Better known simply as* I Am a Woman, *it came out in 1959. Set in Greenwich Village, it was the first to feature the characters Beebo Brinker and Jack Mann.*

I was not allowed to choose the title [*laughter*]. Dick Carroll chose all my titles except the last book, *Beebo Brinker*. He allowed me to choose that one.

Jack Mann is a world-weary, wry and goodhearted gay man who takes young, frightened and confused gay people under his wing and helps them get oriented. Jack was based on a friend who used to come to my family's home on weekends. My stepdad was a wonderful jazz pianist and we had all kinds of bright and lively young people there on weekends, including a friend named Jack Hutchinson. He was a very funny person with a great sense of humour, but kind of a loner in a sense. Jack went to work for the CIA and they sent him to Southeast Asia where he disap-

peared. I have no idea of what happened to him, but my suspicion is that he was a gay man. He was a great man and I loved him.

As for Beebo, I kind of wished her into existence. I hadn't yet met her coming around a corner in Greenwich Village, but I had seen young women that could have filled the bill. When I was trying to get a handle on my second novel, I was in Manhattan. I'd been invited to stay with friends of friends who had an apartment near Columbia University. You could go up on the roof of that building and look out over the whole island of Manhattan. I would do that and I would stand out there thinking, "Who is she, what does she look like?" I couldn't quite get a fix on her until I thought of the name, which came from a childhood friend whose family named her Beverley. She couldn't say Beverley so she named herself Beebo. Once I thought of that name she popped from my brow like Athena from the brow of Zeus. After that, I could see her and understand her.

In the forewords you've written for some of the reprints of your novels you've talked a bit about the butch/femme dichotomies of the times. How were they reflected in your novels, and how have attitudes towards these roles differed over time?

When I was writing, there really were two models. Women were expected to sort themselves into either a 'femme' or 'butch' role. Femmes were feminine girls who could easily pass in society at large as straight. They would wear lipstick, high heels and skirts and would take the traditional woman's role in any partnership. To be butch was to emulate young working-class men. To wear jeans, cut your hair short, have a cigarette dangling from your lip. Whether you smoked or not you carried them around and presented yourself in as masculine a way as you could. Young gay men went through the same kind of constraints, you either had to be a 'top' or a 'bottom'.

These dichotomies were fun, and in a way romantic, but they were also a very restrictive view of the options of living one's life. So when the women's movement intervened, and was tremendously influential in both straight and gay life from the late 60s, being butch or femme was deeply frowned upon. It was thought that the butch women had all the power and authority and the femmes were subservient. This was seen as dreadful, because the movement did not want any disparity of power in relationships. So there were perhaps two decades in which nobody who enjoyed being butch or femme were allowed to admit it [laughter].

Somewhere around the 1990s women began rethinking this. There are many different ways to be in a relationship, as Dr. Kinsey pointed out many years ago, and people began to think that maybe butch and femme were among those ways. If the roles were freely chosen, knowing that there are other options, then it was okay. In the 21st century women know that there are many ways to be, and they can even be both butch and femme if they like.

Given that Greenwich Village assumed great significance in American gay and lesbian life, as well as in your novels, did you get to spend much time there?

Not as much as I would have liked [laughter]. I would go up for a weekend or two weeks and spend a limited amount of time. I cannot tell you how wide open my eyes were, how receptive I was to everything, how stamped upon my memory all of the little streets, the little bars, craft shops, all of it is. It was so vivid and lively to see two young men walking down the street holding hands or two girls kissing in a doorway. That was just spine-tingling. It was of course also a time when the folk music wave was rolling, when the beat

generation was happening. They were just as young and dumb and excited and eager as we were.

To a significant degree there was crossover with the folk and beat scenes. There were people with fluid gender and sexual identity amongst all the scenes. You had everyone from the poet W.H. Auden to Peter, Paul and Mary spending time in the same place. There is no question that a lot of beats were in and out of the gay bars.

Years later I met Allen Ginsberg and told him that we were hanging out in the same area at the same time. I told him about a friend who would teach 'Howl' (1956) and how he almost got fired from his job for doing so. He remembered my books as well. So we were all probably rubbing shoulders, but I could not be there long enough at any time to sustain acquaintances that could be shepherded into long-lasting friendships.

What were some of the more memorable venues and coffee shops?

Marijane introduced me to most of them. She was no longer living down in the Village, but she knew where everything was. There was one called the Bagatelle and one called the Seven Steps Down, another called the Sea Colony. There was a wonderful old restaurant and men's bar called Fedora which is still there. Another was Julius's, and there was a restaurant called Portofino where Edie Windsor—the woman who won the case in the Supreme Court against the Defense of Marriage Act over the right not to pay taxes on inheritance from her partner, because their marriage had not been recognised at the time of her wife's death—had met her wife originally. Of course, there was also the famous Stonewall Inn, right in the centre of the Village, which was more for the drag queens.

The bars really were the social clubs, they played the role the gay and lesbian bookstores and other venues would play later. It was sad to realise that most of them were owned by the Mafia and were kept open because they had a deal with the police.

The police would come and do their raids on a sort of schedule. They would publish the names of the people arrested in the newspapers the next day and crow about cleaning up Greenwich Village and then everyone would reopen and go back to normal. The first thing you wanted to know when you went into a bar would be how long had it been since they were last raided [laughter].

In 1959 Women in the Shadows *was published, so you had two books out that year. This novel approached some of the grittier aspects of lesbian life as well as issues regarding interracial relationships, alcoholism and lavender marriages, those in which a gay man and a lesbian masqueraded as a straight couple.*

By this time I had become well enough acquainted with the scene to get the stars out of my eyes and realise that many gay relationships had problems analogous to those in straight ones. Alcoholism was certainly a problem amongst the scene, and went back to the bars being the social hub of life. For some people the alcohol got a grip. There were also butches outside bars having fistfights over femmes. On the weekends, high school kids from the suburbs would come into Greenwich Village and terrorise gay people. I wanted to capture those kinds of stresses.

I also recognised that sometimes lesbians wanted children and that society denied them any real way to do that, as they could easily lose custody of their children. For the characters of Laura and Jack, marrying in order to have children was important. Laura simply loved children, and Jack, who had lived his life in a dissolute way but always worked, loved the idea of being settled outside of Village life. From his point of view it was something for the young. Because of their deep friendship they thought, "Well let's make a life."

I think I was very gauche and inexperienced in trying to develop a love affair between Laura and Tris, the dancer from an African American background who had troubles of her own in attempting to pass as Indian. These were issues that I think show the age of the novel, but at the same time they demonstrate the lengths that people would go to try and find some stability.

Your next book, Journey to a Woman, *came out in 1960 and saw the return of the character of Beth, who left her marriage to seek out her first love Laura.*

I had presented Beth in the first novel in such a way that she was deeply moved by her emotions towards Laura, but at the same time was being wooed by a very attractive man. Where Laura, the shy, uncertain girl, found her courage and embraced a lesbian life, Beth turned away from it thinking, as so many of us did back then, that by an act of will and her fondness for a man she could become straight.

However, as the years went by, Beth was tortured by the memories of her early feelings. Like me, she had two young children and felt she couldn't leave, but finally does seize the moment and turns away from a marriage to follow her heart. Although in many ways I was in her shoes, she did what I never did, which was leave her children. In her search for the young and innocent love she knew, she finds the years have moved on and, even though only in their late 20s, her and Laura's lives have been shaped in very different ways.

I thought it would be interesting to explore what fireworks would fly when the two of them got back together. Then, of course, it was irresistible to put Beebo in the mix.

The year 1960 also saw you produce The Marriage, *the only one of your novels not to have been reprinted. Can you tell us why you decided to write something outside of the genre for which you had become known?*

This was my attempt to go straight [*laughter*]. I had been a little abashed by my mother's reaction to my string of gay novels. She had been very sweet, accepting and patient. When I was writing *Odd Girl Out* she had told all her friends that I was writing a book. I tried to soft pedal it and cautiously let her know what it was about, but it was hard for her to then tell her friends that maybe the book wasn't for them, and they might not want to read it after all. So I thought maybe I could write a straight story that would kind of redeem me.

The idea I came up with, which I still think has promise, but which I did not handle very well, was to again go back to my college roots and look at the lives of a young couple. She's very bright, thoughtful, and desirable, and he is the college hotshot. I'm making them sound a little artificial, but they weren't. They meet, fall in love and get married, and their families are delighted.

I had to sustain that very vanilla introduction for about 50 pages before introducing the nub of the problem. The novel revolves around the fact that this young couple are full brother and sister, but don't find out until they are married and she is pregnant and they don't know what to do. Having spent so long establishing a very conventional romance, I think I lost most of my readers before the novel became more interesting.

By this time my original editor, Dick Carroll, had died. Knox Burger was now in charge of Gold Medal. He liked the book and published it, but it never found a wider audience. The gay audience and the straight

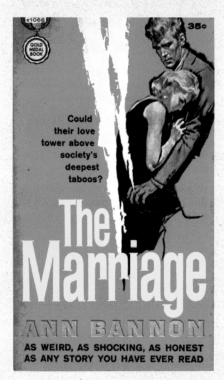

Journey to a Woman (Gold Medal, 1960)
The Marriage (Gold Medal, 1960)

men who had enjoyed my earlier books didn't know what to make of it, and it didn't have enough of a strong introduction to hold new readers. It's not really part of the series, so I don't mind that it hasn't been republished.

There was a two-year gap between The Marriage *and your final novel,* Beebo Brinker, *which came out in 1962. During this time you had some material published in lesbian and gay activist publications.*
They were fairly limited, but a number of small magazines existed. There were great difficulties involved in sending these through the mail. They had to be placed in small brown envelopes without even an identifying return address. You could put the street address, but you couldn't put the name of your organisation. This was so that anyone receiving the publication wouldn't have to explain to their parents or families why they were receiving gay material. Despite being very modest and sensible, and trying to establish connections with the broader community, the mere fact they were addressing the question of homosexuality meant that the magazines were considered completely outrageous.

One was called *The Ladder* and was published by a lesbian group called the Daughters of Bilitis. That was an organisation founded by Del Martin and Phyllis Lyon, two wonderful women who many years later were the first to be married in the state of California. It began in San Francisco and developed chapters across the country. Ultimately the organisation was very influential, although at the time this would have seemed very unlikely.

The Ladder was mainly taken up with short articles about lesbian life and a great many book reviews. I didn't actually write for the magazine, but my books were reviewed in it. Among the reviewers was a woman who called herself Gene Damon, but whose real name was Barbara Grier. She went on to form the first women's press called Naiad Press, which in the 1980s republished my books. In the 1950s and 1960s she reviewed my books and later helped put together a very influential bibliography called *The Lesbian in Literature* (1967).

Another magazine was called *One.* This was put out by the men's organisation the Mattachine society. Their organisation included some of the well-known founders of the gay movement, such as Harry Hay, Frank Kameny and Don Slater. They used to have regular monthly meetings in Los Angeles. As I was living in Southern California, I was able to attend some of them. Subsequently I wrote some short stories for *One*.

Beebo Brinker was a prequel, in which you explored the title character's arrival in Greenwich Village and her subsequent friendship with Jack. Given that this became one of your best-known novels, why did you stop writing?
I had fun with that novel. Beebo has a wonderful romance with a movie star. As fantastic as that sounds, women like Greta Garbo and Marlene Dietrich would come through New York, and believe me when I say that a handsome young butch like Beebo would be in demand [*laughter*].

It was my last book because my children were just getting of an age to wonder why I was spending so much time at the typewriter and I didn't want to have to explain to five—and seven-year-olds what I was writing about. Part of it was also that I had run out of creative energy. Greenwich Village had been my source and, although I did make the occasional trip to New York, living in California meant I felt quite cut off from my inspiration. Following a move to Northern California, and then Oregon, I began to think more about working in academia, which subsequently happened. Finally, my husband had never welcomed my interest in these topics, although he welcomed the royalty cheques [*laughter*].

Your books have gone through a series of reprints beginning with Arno Press in the 1970s, Naiad Press in the 1980s, the Quality Paperback Book Club in the 1990s, and most recently Cleis Books in the 2000s. Have you been surprised by the enduring popularity of the series, despite the fact that society has changed so much?
Yes, I have. Like my readers, I really thought what I was writing was ephemeral literature, although I wrote it as best I could. I understood the rules, and the rules were that these were throwaway books. They were made of shoddy paper and had outrageous covers—which, I should mention, I had no input into—and many of them were associated with sleazy topics that were deemed unworthy. Critics ignored us and we flew beneath the radar, which is probably one of the reasons we were allowed to exist. So I had no real belief that they would have a life beyond their initial 6 to 12 month period of publication. We were surprised if a book was given a second or third run by our publishers.

As a result, when the Arno Press reprints happened in the 1970s I was astounded. They brought the books out in hardcover editions as part of a series on homosexuality, literature, and society in America. The books then ended up in libraries. In the 1980s Barbara Grier founded Naiad Press, which became very successful. She mainly published romances for women, but she also did reprints of lesbian pulps. At that point I realised that the books already had a life somewhat longer than that which I'd imagined for them.

By the 1990s, when the Book Club brought the books out again, I decided that though aspects of them were a little bit embarrassing, they were mine and I had to own up. My own university had copies of them in the library, and I was starting to receive Masters theses and term papers from young readers who were using them for academic credit. By the beginning of the new century, I had yet another publisher in Cleis Press and was now getting doctoral dissertations.

The novels obviously speak differently to this new generation of readers than they did to those who were originally desperately seeking anything about the lesbian experience. I think their current attraction is two-fold. They firstly serve as a social history of a particular time and place that came to be very significant in gay and lesbian history. Above and beyond that, I think the characters have an ability to speak to people who are young and—believe it or not, with all the changes and all the information available—still frightened, still uncertain, and still unable to approach their parents. One woman who approached me after a lecture told me that when she was young she had come across *Odd Girl Out* in a bookshop, and that after finding it went home to have dinner instead of jumping off a bridge. Something like that really turns your heart over.

In turn what effect has the interest in these books had on your own life?
It's been quite a remarkable ride. Just in the last ten or twelve years, three of the books have been turned into a play called *The Beebo Brinker Chronicles*, written by Kate Moira Ryan and Linda S. Chapman. The play has been presented around the country with 14 or 15 different productions. I'm regularly invited to give lectures and be on panels, and it has been wonderful to meet young writers as well as some of the old-timers. It's all come rather late in life, but better late than not at all.

IAIN McINTYRE

BY JOHN TRINIAN

a game of flesh

THEY PAID FOR HIS LOVE—
WITH MONEY AND SHAME.

LANCER DOMINO BOOKS 72-678 50¢

A SEARING NOVEL OF MAN-HUNGRY
WOMEN AND A HEARTLESS GIGOLO

north beach girl

35¢

GOLD MEDAL BOOK

Where did she belong, this
kid called Erin? What did
she want? Was it what
Bruno had to offer? The
casual kicks of San
Francisco's Beatnik
underworld . . .
(continued on back cover)

john trinian

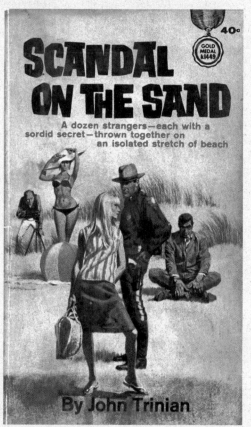

SCANDAL ON THE SAND

A dozen strangers—each with a
sordid secret—thrown together on
an isolated stretch of beach

GOLD MEDAL k1449 40¢

By John Trinian

North Beach Girl (Gold Medal, 1960)
A Game of Flesh (Lancer, 1963)
Scandal on the Sand (Gold Medal, 1964)
John Trinian in the early 1970s

'BEAT' IN FICTION AND FACT
The Books of John Trinian

It would be a stretch to call John Trinian (1933–2008) a beat writer. But the San Francisco–based author, who wrote seven pulp novels from 1959 to 1964, definitely lived a bohemian life. He palled around with Jack Kerouac, and one of his books, *North Beach Girl* (1960), explored the environs of what was in the early 60s the epicenter of the city's beat culture.

All Trinian's books are worthy, however you care to classify them, and several featured offbeat characters with whom rebellious youth of the day could have identified. The full body of literary work produced by Trinian—a neighbor of John Steinbeck's in Salinas, California, in his boyhood years—makes him a noteworthy San Francisco pulp author.

North Beach Girl was Trinian's third novel but the first one in which he fully explored the neighborhood name-checked in the title and its beat scene. Readers approaching this book in hopes of finding Kerouac-ian exuberance or *Dobie Gillis*–like zaniness will be disappointed. In keeping with the author's overall literary output, *North Beach Girl* is a pointedly downbeat, even sinister, tale.

Erin, a 21-year-old North Beach denizen, is an attractive, disillusioned young woman. Guys are always hitting on her but she's been wary of male company since her stepfather (now dead, along with her mother) entered her bedroom one too many times when she was a teenager. She shares a North Beach garage apartment with a woman named Bruno: a butch man-hater who is overprotective of Erin and who runs an art gallery. As the novel begins, Erin quits her job as an art school model, because she'd rather 'just be'. She has a rich, dying grandmother who lives nearby. Bruno wants them to hit the granny up for some cash so they can move to Sausalito and open a second gallery there, but Erin's not too hip on that idea.

Meanwhile Erin gets to know a talented, irresistible beat painter whose company she can't help but enjoy, even though he's a man and even though Bruno doesn't want him around. Early in the book we get a feel for Erin's defiant worldview, when the third-person narrator follows her thoughts just after she's walked out on her present job:

> She began to walk down the steep hill towards North Beach. It was at times like this, when she sensed the righteous resentment of others directed at her, that her otherwise slipping convictions strengthened. It was at times like this that she felt justifiably rebellious, and the more resentment people felt towards her, the more convinced she became that she was right. She certainly didn't want the phony alternative that others were trying to shove on her.
>
> Erin smiled secretly to herself.

Part of what makes *North Beach Girl* such a fine read is that its characters are believable people who happen to be part of the beat scene, rather than 'beatnik' caricatures. Also, Trinian's writing is spot-on. There's plenty of story, but also vivid interior scenes, such as when his narrator goes inside Erin's head while she's drunk and high and lets us follow her stoned thought patterns and sensations. We don't get an inane 'wow, man, this is wild' sentiment from these passages, but rather a realistic look at the disorientation of a conflicted young woman's drugged mind:

> The tip of her nose tingled and she felt sluggish and delicate at the same time. She was light on her feet . . . and yet she wasn't standing. She felt safe and secure. Everything was all right. Bruno and the crazy blue light, all alone in the grotto with the shells outside the door. Hell, why was she always plodding around like a zombie? She should take a greater interest in things. Maybe she should play tennis . . . That was a rip. She could see herself out on the courts with a tennis racket and a bronze face, batting the ball around and smiling like the women in *McCall's* advertisements. She wondered whom she could play with. She was sure that Bruno didn't play tennis. Billiards maybe, but not tennis.
>
> The blue light rested her.

Likewise, the rest of the novel strikes a compelling and realistic chord. *North Beach Girl* should be viewed as a parallel to Malcolm Braly's *Shake Him Till He Rattles* (1963). Both are gritty novels that lay bare the underbelly of the North Beach beatnik scene.

Trinian's first two published novels, *A Game of Flesh* (1959) and *The Big Grab* (1960), had incidental beat characters and dialogue, but they were hard-nosed crime stories. *A Game of Flesh* concerns a former reform school kid who becomes a San Francisco male escort and gets pulled into the middle of a drug war between a kingpin and one of the crime boss's former associates. *The Big Grab* is a heist novel about two cons fresh out of prison planning the big swindle that could put them on easy street. Both are at the same time edgy and meditative, a duality characteristic of Trinian's work. Writing in this vein, Trinian started to work the beats into his fiction. *The Big Grab* features a character who speaks in bop lingo, often using words like 'dad' and 'dig'. It was made into the excellent 1963 film *Any Number Can Win*, starring Jean Gabin and Alain Delon.

Some of the scenes in Trinian's next book, *The Savage Breast* (1961), also take place in North Beach. The fact that it's a Fawcett Gold Medal title suggests a work of pulp fiction, but the writing here makes it into a literary social novel closer to John O'Hara than Trinian's fellow pulp writer Orrie Hitt. The story focuses on a challenged love affair between a young woman trying to break free from her wealthy father's controlling ways and a classical music composer who struggles to make it with his music and keep tabs on his dangerous, mentally ill brother. Money and influence come up against personal and artistic integrity, familial obligations against freedom to pursue happiness. Eccentric San Francisco art world characters abound, and just about everyone in the book is constantly drunk. The lead female character, D.B. Sadder, is something of a champion for the countercultural, willing to give up the creature comforts and social status offered by her father in favor of striking out on her own and leading a genuine and non-materialistic life.

Trinian returned to the crime fiction milieu for his next novel, *Scratch a Thief* (1961). Similar to *The Big Grab*, the tale involves a former criminal and jailbird, Eddie Slezak, who's trying to make a straight life in San Francisco, working regular jobs and being a good family man to his wife and their daughter. But a cop with a longstanding grudge, as well as his former underworld colleagues (including his brother) won't let him be. Slezak is about as beaten down as a character could be. *Scratch a Thief* is a grim story of a person fighting the uphill battle to escape his troubled past. It's Trinian's strongest work of crime fiction, again showcasing his ability to write with a duality of edginess and reverie; in 1965 it was made into the film *Once a Thief*, Trinian (using the name Zekial Marko)

wrote the screenplay and had a bit part; other actors included Alain Delon, Ann-Margret and Jack Palance.

House of Evil (1962) is Trinian at his wildest. A pair of longtime hucksters set up a religious commune outside Los Angeles, with one of them as the resident guru and the other his right-hand man. The crowd they attract to their retreat includes some seedy Hollywood types with a jones for occult play and sex games. The whole story builds in the direction of a climactic battle between a B-movie actor, who is on to the shysters, and the cult leader. The plot and characters are all outrageous, yet believable enough to keep it from becoming a mere campy read. Roger Corman should have made a film from it; in fact, some of the characters are straight out of Corman's troupe of low-budget thespians.

Trinian's finest novel was also the last he published. *Scandal on the Sand* (1964) is a brooding, atmospheric story that centers on a whale that washes ashore on a Los Angeles beach. Brief enough to be considered a novella, the story looks into the souls of the characters who turn up on the scene, through how they respond to the whale. A couple on a tense date, a gangster on the lam, a hungover lifeguard, a Russ Meyer–type nudie photographer and two of his models, a struggling actor and his young wife, a surly cop with a cowboy complex, are among those who happen upon the whale and get involved in one way or another. Most people reading the book at the time would likely have been moved by Trinian's clear sympathy with the whale versus most of the humans in the story; by his showing how much of humankind is uninterested in dealing with the natural world and other life forms in a sympathetic way. It's a beautifully written book, one that makes you wonder why it was its author's last published novel, when he lived for more than four decades after its release.

Trinian was born Marvin Leroy Schmoker. John Trinian was a pen name used by the man known in his adult years as Zekial Marko. He seems to have led a bohemian kind of existence his entire adult life, long after it was fashionable (or, some would say, appropriate) to carry on in such a way. Trinian's daughter, visual artist Belle Marko, who was interviewed for this article, gives the impression that Trinian was a classic example of the artist who couldn't cut it in the real world. He was a charmer and a con man, as well as both a talented guy and a ne'er-do-well. He also appears to have been a haunted man who wrestled with bouts of depression and could never get the better of his addictions (alcohol, mostly). "My mom tried to help him get grounded, but he just wouldn't. He was like a wild animal. He never could settle down, could never be faithful, could never be a good parent or husband. But he was a great writer."

Trinian wrote for TV shows in the 70s, including *Toma, Kolchak: The Night Stalker,* and *The Rockford Files.* "When he tried to get into Hollywood and TV work he was always screwing up," recounts Marko. "He always managed to mess up at the most inopportune moments, whether it was because he turned up to a meeting drunk, or flirted with the producer's wife, or peed in a potted plant in the studio, or crashed his car into somebody's trailer. He just couldn't keep it together. He would have been such an incredible guy if he had cleaned up his act, but he just couldn't."

In her youth, Marko, her mother and her siblings generally lived a hand-to-mouth existence without any material support from Trinian. Belle relates a revealing anecdote that shows part of her dad's character:

I was about eight years old and we were really poor. He was living apart from us by then. He was living in an abandoned school bus in Sausalito. He gathered a bunch of poets and writers and musicians and me, and said, 'Let's go have a nice breakfast.' So we all went to this place in Sausalito and he told everybody to just order whatever they want. I figured he must have made some money from his writing and he was treating everybody. I ordered all this food and I was sitting there in this pink coat, and feeling really cool. We were all eating all this food and people were wearing berets and smoking. Then, when everybody was finishing up, my dad suddenly said, 'Alright everybody, split!' Dine and dash. I was so embarrassed. Here's somebody I'm supposed to look up to, and I knew this was totally wrong. But that's the way he rolled. He thought it was funny.

Trinian stopped writing novels after 1964. "He just couldn't do it," says Marko. "He deteriorated. His demons were taking over, and I don't know if it was more drugs or alcohol, but he got more and more bitter and more and more sensitive. His skin got more and more thin and he couldn't take it anymore. He was against commercialization, was against a lot of writers. His standards were very high. I think he was afraid of success, or of failure. He moved to New York

Once a Thief (Manor, 1973)

and was living with his second wife there, and there was a big writing project he was working on that was going to be the granddaddy of them all, his big one. But it never happened."

According to Marko, Trinian never really settled down. "He got estranged. He ran away. He ended up in a town near Santa Cruz. He was staying in a room he got through this woman. She had this property and had a kind of a roadside attraction where she sold carved bowls and things. She had a lot of plants and things on the property and my dad loved plants and flowers. So he tended to the plants and helped her make the bowls she sold, and in exchange he got to live in the little workhouse. He just had a cot, under a bench. He never had a real home unless he was with a woman. He was pretty much homeless most of his life. He was always making friends with people who could give him a place to stay without him having to pay."

John Trinian was not vaguely close to what one would call a good parent. But he was a colorful character. However you want to view him as a person, he was an excellent writer.

BRIAN GREENE

Shake Him Till He Rattles—Malcolm Braly (Fawcett Publications, 1963)

Shake Him Till He Rattles is a bleak story of sexual jealously, drug use, lost opportunities and jazz, set in the San Francisco suburb of North Beach, ground zero of the West Coast beat scene in the early 60s.

In the opening scene a vice cop called Carver is staking out an after-hours jazz club, the Hoof, **where the hard-core hip hang out**. He corners a failed playwright, Sullivan, who is on his way to the club. In the space of a couple of pages, Carver has turned Sullivan into his snitch, loading him up with drugs, which he orders Sullivan to take into the Hoof and spread around as incriminating evidence for a raid Carver plans to undertake of the establishment later than night.

Carver's main target is a saxophone player called Lee Cabiness. Carver has a major thing against jazz musicians who he regards as **the original carriers of the Beat infection**. If this wasn't enough, he also has Cabiness pegged as **"big connection"** in the North Beach drug scene.

Cabiness eventually turns up at the Hoof with another musician, 'Furg'. Soon after Cabiness enters the club the police raid takes place. Carver hauls Cabiness down to the station and threatens to plant drugs on him unless he turns snitch for Carver's campaign to clean up North Beach.

Cabiness is not a major criminal. He's not a major anything, really. His only aim in life is to **"smoke a little pot and blow my horn"**, much to the chagrin of his girlfriend, Jean, who is getting tired of the scene. She hassles him about wasting his talent. To which he replies: **"Music is just music until you start trying to sell it; then it changes in a lot of ways. A lot of things change. You end up with a product . . . I'd have to be some other person, Change myself in some ways. You dig?"**

Their relationship breaks up and at another after-hours club, the Bird's Nest, Cabiness hooks up with Clair, a rich girl and wannabe painter, slumming it amid the North Beach beat scene. Carver busts Cabiness again and this time the musician is holding a number of marijuana joints. While in the 'hype tank', the worst cell in the police station, he compare notes with his cellmate, a black horn player nicknamed 'Bear', and the two identify the central role played by Sullivan in both their busts. Clair bails Cabiness out, sets him up with a lawyer to fight the drug charges

and starts a relationship with him. It soon becomes apparent his potential ability to score drugs is what attracts her as much as his aura of hip coolness.

Cabiness gets a band together and starts gigging at the Bird's Nest. He even thinks about trying to get a record deal. But with the drug charge hanging over him, Cabiness also considers taking off for Mexico: **Guadalajara, a swinging town he'd heard . . . But there were two feds for every civilian American. It was nowhere.**

Cabiness is finally shaken from his torpor when Furg overdoses on strychnine-laced heroin, bought from Sullivan. After anonymously dumping Furg's body in a park so the overdose won't be traced back to him, Cabiness braces Sullivan, who tells him the drugs came from Carver, himself a junkie. Cabiness sets up Carver to OD on his own bad drugs. With his main accuser dead, Cabiness ends up only doing six months in county jail. After his release he gets back with Jean.

Shake Him Till He Rattles is a well-written, shrewdly observed tale. The characters, the way they speak, the descriptions of the drug milieu and jail, are vivid and real, as is the writing about jazz, something most pulp books dealing with beat culture pay only cursory attention to in order to signify a cultural time and place.

The title comes from a scene in which Carver orders a police officer to search Cabiness for drugs, to **"shake this guy till he rattles"**. It's something the author, Malcolm Braly, once called "the patron saint of losers", had first hand experience of. Abandoned by his parents, he spent his youth in foster homes and institutions for delinquent children and by the time he was 40, had spent 17 years in various jails for burglary related offences.

Shake Him Till He Rattles was one of three novels Braly wrote behind bars. The others include *Felony Tank* (1961) and *It's Cold Out There* (1966). Upon his release in 1965 he began his best-known book, *On the Yard*, about his time in prison. Prison authorities threatened to revoke his parole when they found out what he was doing and he completed it in secret. It was published after the end of his parole in 1967. He died in 1980 at the age of 54 following a traffic accident.

ANDREW NETTE

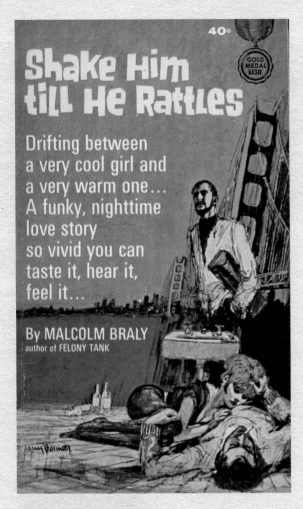

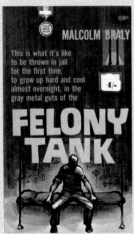
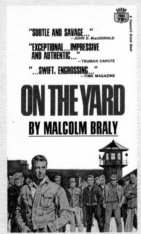

Shake Him Till He Rattles (Gold Medal, 1963)

On the Yard (Fawcett Crest, 1967)

Felony Tank (Gold Medal, 1961)

W hoever was paying the rent on the basement—if anyone was—hadn't done much more than rig up a light, a naked hundred-and-fifty watt bulb strung over a pipe, and set up some makeshift furniture. The cement walls were dirty and water-stained, and up near the ceiling someone had scrawled the motto: BIRD LIVES!

It was in black letters, dashed on with a big brush, and celebrated the resurrection of Charlie Parker, the first Beat saint.

Someone else with a red crayon had contributed: SCOWL! YOWL! HOWL! BOWEL!

Probably derived from Ginsberg's "Howl." His place in the hagiology hadn't been computed since he had the misfortune to be alive.

At the end of the room, a dismantled furnace lay on its side, with the vent pipes stacked up around it like the skeleton of a tepee.

There were over thirty people pressed together in the room. C saw the same people he was always seeing, those that made a point of being on the inside hub: fellow musicians too cool to join the honking contest; painters; a near famous poet; and half the cast of one of the current little-theatre hits, out of costume, but still made up; as well as a good smattering of just talkers and hangers on, and probably an occasional office girl or young accountant from the Shell Oil Company, nervously waiting for the orgy to start and meanwhile straining to maintain a supercilious smile.

Marijuana Girl—N.R. De Mexico (Universal Publishing, 1951)

Suburban Long Island high school senior Joyce Taylor would seem to have the world on a string: she's smart, privileged, and very sexy. And her brainy boyfriend Tony has a rich dad and snazzy convertible. But she's also defiant, and this gets her tossed out of school when she decides to perform a bump-and-grind routine in front of an unsupervised study hour in the school auditorium. A teacher had happened by, seen Joyce, and reported her to the dean, who promptly took her name off the graduation roster. Since Joyce's parents are abroad as usual, and her guardian aunt is ineffectual, she takes a job as copy girl at the local newspaper, where the attractive, hip, 31-year-old city editor, Frank Burdette, takes a shockingly inevitable "mentorly" interest in her.

A true aficionado of the new jazz (bebop) and a devotee of the sweet weed, marijuana, Burdette soon introduces Joyce to Greenwich Village, where the jazz combos **were writing history in marijuana smoke and music.** Joyce is much taken by the music and **the scene** in general; recognizing this, the musicians—all serious and black—make her one of them and, before long, become the family she had always longed for. And they, like Burdette, are scrupulous to teach her the differences between pot and 'hook' drugs like heroin ('horse'). It doesn't take long for Joyce to get into the groove: talking jive in style, even *thinking in jive*; hitting the Harlem jam joints after hours; and, always, smoking weed. Meanwhile she has taken a menial job in the City and rented an apartment in the Village.

Alas, Joyce's surrogate family of black musicians depart New York for distant gigs, leaving the teenage girl a social isolate in the big city. In despair she turns to the drug she had been repeatedly warned against, heroin, and this predictably deepens her desperation by turning her into a circumstantial prostitute.

Remarkably, her johns (like her pushers and other traditional bad guys) are solicitous of Joyce, until the day one of her favorite preppy patrons rejects her for the damage she's doing to herself, making her believe she's not worthy to be wanted even at this desultory level. Enter the avenging duo, Burdette and Tony, who in the interim have become friends. They have quite coincidentally learned of Joyce's plight and devised a plan of rescue designed to lead her back in the direction of a socially respectable future. Many readers today, especially feminists, will regard Joyce's transformation and likely return to a complacent existence as capitulation to suburban cliché. After all, the road Joyce is traveling down at the end of the book runs in the opposite direction to the one Jack Kerouac and his beatnik buddies are on at the same time, in their quest for the ineffable freedom of the open road, far from society's restraints.

Marijuana Girl qualifies for pulp status largely by virtue of its title, cover art, scarcity and subject matter. Unlike many other pop fictions of the time, it avoids sensationalizing or glamorizing the events in the protagonist's life. Author Robert Campbell Bragg, writing under the pseudonym N. R. De Mexico, assiduously avoids profanity and stereotypes (even the bad guys seem decent at heart), and even depicts the drug-jazz culture authentically without caricaturing the hipster argot. It also promotes racial harmony. It's still a pretty good, albeit nostalgic, read. Witness the passage quoted here in which Joyce turns on for the first time; it *feels* as if the writer had 'been there' and wanted to render the experience as truthfully as, say, Hemingway might have if he'd turned his attention from bulls and booze to recreational drugs.

DAVID RIFE

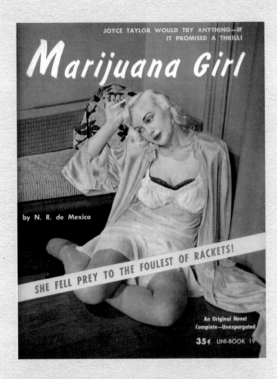

JOYCE TAYLOR WOULD TRY ANYTHING—IF IT PROMISED A THRILL!

Marijuana Girl

by N. R. de Mexico

SHE FELL PREY TO THE FOULEST OF RACKETS!

An Original Novel
Complete—Unexpurgated

35¢ UNI-BOOK 19

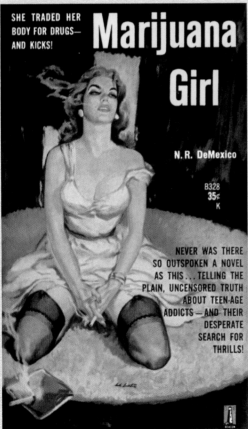

SHE TRADED HER BODY FOR DRUGS— AND KICKS!

Marijuana Girl

N. R. DeMexico

B328
35¢
K

NEVER WAS THERE SO OUTSPOKEN A NOVEL AS THIS... TELLING THE PLAIN, UNCENSORED TRUTH ABOUT TEEN-AGE ADDICTS—AND THEIR DESPERATE SEARCH FOR THRILLS!

Marijuana Girl (Universal Publishing, 1951)
Marijuana Girl (Beacon, 1960)

Joyce took two more drags on the stick, watching the little amber fire creep upward on the thin roll. The strange odor and unpleasant taste were gone now. It felt almost as though she were drawing very cold air into her chest. But nothing was happening. She said it. "Nothing's happening."

"Maybe it won't," Frank said, discouragingly.

"Will I do anything funny—I mean silly?"

"Of course not," Frank said. "It's not like liquor. You don't lose control or anything."

She drew again, still aware that it had no effect, then let her hand hang down holding the tiny cigarette. Suddenly she became aware of the night beauty of Washington Square Park. The cross atop the Judson church, glowing against the deep blue of the sky caught her eye, and the street lamps against the façade of the arch. Each was a detail worth infinite attention. There was a faint, warm haze lying low against the ground, lending the whole park an atmosphere of unreality. Beyond the Square the lighted windows of a row of tall apartment buildings had a crystalline clarity—so clear were they that even from where she sat, nearly a sixth of a mile away, she could see well into the rooms, see people moving about, see what they were doing.

It was as though every window of those huge apartment buildings were a stage on which a special performance was taking place for her benefit. Even the sky was richer and more velvety ease. How strangely wonderful and lovelier than any she had seen before, with deep-glowing blue stars—all warm and close and friendly—peering down at her. "God!" she said. "It's beautiful here." Then she remembered the stick and drew on it again. She turned to Frank. "But nothing's happening."

"Are you kidding?" he said. "No."

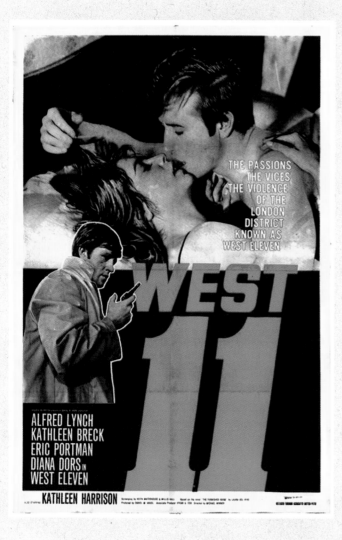

The Furnished Room

LAURA DEL-RIVO

NOW FILMED AS

WEST 11

Set amongst the beats and angries of London's bedsitter-land — a devastating novel of a young man who stops at nothing in his feverish search for meaning to life

The film is for Warner-Pathe release and stars Alfred Lynch, Eric Portman, Kathleen Breck, Diana Dors

3'6

The Furnished Room (Pan, 1963)

Poster for *West 11*, 1963 film adaption of *The Furnished Room*, directed by Michael Winner

LAURA DEL-RIVO'S *THE FURNISHED ROOM*

The London of Laura Del-Rivo's first novel, *The Furnished Room* (1961), is that of the late 1950s, when racial tensions became highly visible in Notting Hill and the signs of swinging—and swingeing—London, in sexual behaviour, in popular music, in fashion, and in respectable outrage, began to appear. But life in the capital for young people with jobs as clerks and typists and shop assistants was still repressed, with a repetitive working week shadowed by the recurrent inertia of Sundays and a sporadic pursuit of pleasure in cafés and at parties.

Laura Del-Rivo knew this London. Born on 13 February 1934, she grew up in Cheam, in a respectable family that had rather come down in the world. Her grandfather was an Italian who had married Mary O'Connell, a granddaughter of Daniel O'Connell, the Irish political leader known as 'The Liberator', but her father, as Del-Rivo herself puts it, "was a complex man who wore without complaint the homburg hat and the overcoat appropriate to a bank employee of the middle rank. He played bowls, and pursued his interest in Greek and Roman classical history." Del-Rivo was educated at Holy Cross Convent in New Malden, but left at 16, at the start of the 1950s, to work in a range of London jobs—assistant in Foyles bookshop, counter hand in a J. Lyons tearoom, art-school model, office clerk, messenger and char (housecleaner)—and to spend her evenings in Soho cafés, where would-be writers exchanged manuscripts.

Here she met two unknowns, Colin Wilson and Bill Hopkins, who, with Stuart Holroyd, were to emerge briefly, after the success of Wilson's *The Outsider* (1956), as the trio of young men whom Kenneth Allsop, in *The Angry Decade* (1958), dubbed 'the law-givers', because they seemed to issue edicts to what they saw as a slack society in need of new heroes—an approach that smacked of fascism. This was a very macho cultural formation, but studies of the period, and of this group, make it even more so by largely ignoring Del-Rivo, a woman writer of distinction, with a gentle disposition, who was close to the heart of 'the law-givers' and who, in *The Furnished Room*, provided both an exemplum and a critique of their attitudes.

The title of Del-Rivo's novel suggests an interior focus, but the name of Michael Winner's 1963 film adaptation firmly locates this furnished room in a particular London district: West 11. In fact, *The Furnished Room* features six main London settings: Notting Hill, Holborn, Earl's Court, Camden Town, Fitzrovia, and SW1, a postcode-designated area of southwest London that includes the centres of British prestige and power: Buckingham Palace, Westminster and Whitehall. Each is the territory of different characters and represents a different set of existential and social possibilities.

The first setting, Notting Hill, is where the novel's twenty-something anti-hero, Joseph Ignatius (known as Joe) Beckett, rents the furnished room of the novel's title. Beckett has escaped from a provincial Catholic family which he finds oppressive, to London and a succession of furnished rooms, all **much the same**. He suffers from a strong sense of unreality relieved by occasional epiphanies. A once ardent Catholic, he had decided, at the age of 15, to be a priest. The collapse of his faith has left a void that nothing can fill. Though he seems to lack literary aspirations, he keeps a green notebook in which he enters **his disbelief in God and in everything, his sensations of unreality and lack of meaning, and his inability to love or feel.**

His neighbour in a nearby boarding house, an elderly eccentric called Gash, left a good career, wife, and family to pursue mystical insights in squalid poverty. Beckett finds Gash, and his room, with its odour of **thug cat and Dettol and the stale smell of insanity**, physically repellent but talks at length with him because Gash grasps Beckett's plight, even though Beckett cannot accept Gash's mysticism.

Beckett is strongly aware of his violent urges. **Once, seeing a bald baby, the impulse to smash its skull had been so strong that he had clenched his fists in fear of giving way to it.** When three West Indians walk with an easy swagger through a hostile white crowd in Notting Hill, Beckett, though he denies being a racist, tenses **like a dog ready to spring. Like the others, he had shared in the mob hatred at the cool effrontery of the West Indians.** He feels **a burst of sadistic joy** when reading about a Nazi concentration camp in which a guard shot a whole detachment of panicking women prisoners. Sooner or later, he believes, he will **commit a violent crime** but, for most of the novel, he stays on the plane of fantasy.

In the earlier chapters, Beckett is boxed into a clerical job at Union Cartons & Packaging (Great Britain) Ltd in Holborn—the parenthesis suggesting a national rather than merely personal inertia, an ironic inflation of the Little Britain that Pip enters when he goes to London in Dickens's *Great Expectations* (1861).

A third key London setting in *The Furnished Room* is what the novel calls **the grey wastes of SW5**—Earl's Court, where Beckett's 19-year-old on-off girlfriend, Ilsa Barnes, shares a flat with another young woman. Ilsa has come to London to escape her family, whose Sussex farm figures as a place of constraint rather than naturalness. Originally she chose the art-school route out of conformity, studying at Saint Martin's with the idea of becoming a teacher; but she left, averse to the poverty of student life and lacking artistic talent or commitment, and now works in an office.

Ilsa likes taking men from other women, making them fall in love with her, and then dumping them, though she acknowledges she has met her match in Beckett, who finds her desirable but, as she recognizes, **only gave an imitation** of loving her. There is a strained quality about Ilsa's **gaiety and her pale taut face** that evokes the London of the Blitz. **She was like a woman in wartime, living it up in order to forget that she might die tomorrow.**

The décor of her Earl's Court flat, however, is kitsch-contemporary rather than 1940-ish. It has red **curtains patterned with drink labels: Martini, Cinzano, Dubonnet**; its ornaments include **glass tumblers with a playing-card design, bowls of peanuts, a wooden dachshund with a corkscrew for a tail, and a doll dressed in bra and pants.** Beckett has a patronizing vision of Ilsa's future: **This hard-drinking, hard-living, desperately young product of the modern age would become a middle-class housewife.**

A fourth London setting is Camden Town, the location of the larger flat of another, older girlfriend of Beckett's, Georgia, and of the communal house where Reg Wainwright, a left-wing novelist, lives with his wife and children and others. Georgia, **experienced in double beds and saloon bars and in being combined mistress and mother to many men** is about 35 and has escaped the fate Beckett predicts for Ilsa. Separated from her husband, Georgia lives with her six-year-old daughter, Teresa. She admires Beckett's self-important discourses without really understanding them. After he holds forth on the collapse of the sense of an absolute value, which religion alone can provide, as a cause of crime, she says only, in a deflating compliment: **"You are clever, Joe."** Her furnished room is more welcoming than Beckett's, less kitsch-contemporary than Ilsa's, aspiring towards a bourgeois interior: it **looks more like a drawing-room than a bedsitter.**

Beckett, however, is on the run from bourgeois interiors and finds solace in Mick's Café in Charlotte Street, which is in Fitzrovia but also representative of some Soho cafés on the south side of Oxford Street. Its oddly assorted clientele had one thing in common:

> **They were all misfits of one sort or another. Because of this, Baroness Tania, who drank methylated spirit, could share a table with Tom, who was a porter and wore a British Railways uniform, with Dutchie, whose face bore the scar of a razor slash, and with an ageing young man named Flora who wore make-up and had tinted hair.**

But while Beckett is glad to move among misfits because they ask no questions, he cannot commit himself to the misfit life.

An alternative commitment is represented by 45-year-old ex-army captain Dick Dyce, who is a chancer (as his surname, a homophone for 'dice', suggests) and who has an expensive service flat in Grosvenor Court Gardens, SW1. On one level, Dyce is a stock post-1945 English type, **the fake major in the Tudor roadhouse who slaps you on the back and asks you to cash his cheque.** But his idolization of lucre makes him a harbinger of post-1980 London, the Dionysian capital of capital. He tells Beckett:

> **"I look at life through money-coloured spectacles. I see the money like the ether, permeating everything. Collecting in pockets here, banks there, financing industry, changing into power like matter changing into energy. And obtained by wits, work, or violence."**

When Beckett visits Dyce's flat, Dyce stresses the link between affluence and crime: **"The front flats are the classiest, but the back are the most popular because they have fire escapes . . . I never met so many crooks as I have since I moved in here"** and the fire escapes enable them to make a quick getaway. Dyce will come to be the chance element, the roll of the dice, which determines Beckett's future.

After Beckett insults his boss at United Cartons and gets the sack, he becomes a sick, penniless flâneur:

> **Often he walked in Kensington Gardens, liking the feathery sunlight on the grass. In his mouth and nostrils was a flavour like soda-water that**

Laura Del-Rivo, 1961. Image by Ida Kar © National Portrait Gallery, London, reproduced with permission.

belonged to sickness. Sometimes he went to Speakers' Corner where he engaged in arguments with strangers. Sometimes he went to Brompton Oratory because he liked the Victorian cherubs that ornamented the candelabra. . . . Sometimes he spent the night in Covent Garden, which smelled like an orchard. There was an all-night café for the market workers, with yellow-topped tables with bottles of O.K. sauce on them, and thick crockery. He sat in a corner, grim and unspeaking like a secret agent . . . Beckett the tramp wandered down dustbin night streets, stole milk and a loaf from a crate outside a café, and saw the dawn break over London.

Then Beckett's father writes to tell him that his mother, with whom he still feels strong bonds despite his rejection of her attempt to make him respectable, is dying of leukemia. Beckett thinks that taking her to Lourdes might cure her by auto-suggestion. But a Lourdes trip would cost money, and Beckett cannot even pay his rent. When his landlady threatens to call in the police, he does a moonlight flit.

A homeless wanderer in London streets, he runs into Dick Dyce again. In Dyce's flat, they discuss a scheme that Dyce had floated earlier: that Beckett should murder Dyce's wealthy aunt, Kathleen Dyce Grantley, so that Dyce can inherit her money and give Beckett a cut. Beckett, hoping to obtain both cash and a clear sense of purpose, agrees to the scheme.

Beckett breaks into the home of Dyce's aunt in a nearby town and confronts her with a revolver. But he never pulls the trigger; she drops dead from a heart attack. He recognizes the irony of the situation:

The crime, intended to dynamite the way to freedom, had instead been the ultimate unreality, the concentration of all the previous unreality into a sickening unreal nightmare. He had tried to commit an act of will, but instead events had been taken out of his control.

Moreover, Beckett realizes that, at the crime scene, he has dropped, from the portable chess set that he is known to carry, a broken white bishop; an ironic ecclesiastical self-incrimination by the young man who had once wanted to be a priest. He returns to Notting Hill to give himself up at the local police station, without implicating Dyce; he wants **to complete his circuit; to return to the district where he had fought the looming walls of his bedsitter.**

Beckett meets Gash's landlady, who tells him Gash is dead. In Tewkesbury Road, Becket notices someone, whom he suspects is a plainclothes policeman, watching his former boarding house. Then Ilsa, who has been looking for him, hails him by name, and runs into his arms, an inadvertent Judas revealing his identity to the watcher and thwarting Beckett's desire to give himself up of his own volition. The watcher walks towards him, presumably to arrest him, but the end of the novel does not confirm this, shifting from Beckett's existential melodrama to a last paragraph evoking the circumambient daily life of the capital:

The children were wheeling and shouting as always; their screams ricocheted from the buildings. Two women walked along the pavement, pushing their shopping in wheeled baskets. A front door banged, a radio played. The sky was London grey over Tewkesbury Road on a Saturday morning.

The tension between the quotidian and the extraordinary in London life runs through *The Furnished Room* and throughout Del-Rivo's career. Now in her eighties, she still lives in West 11, runs a clothing stall in the Portobello Road, and continues to write. Her story collection *Where Is My Mask of an Honest Man?* was published in September 2013 and is set in and around—where else?—West 11.

NICOLAS TREDELL

Baron's Court, All Change—Terry Taylor (MacGibbon & McKee, 1961)

In the early 1960s, swathes of British nonconformists had not yet appeared, but the seeds of the counterculture were being sown by the small knots of proto-mods and dropouts making up London's jazz and art underground. Colin MacInnes's *Absolute Beginners* (1959) has long been lauded for its portrayal of those chafing against postwar austerity and repression by creating alternatives to the emerging galaxy of cheap materialistic pop kicks otherwise on offer to the young. It is less well known that the inspiration for that novel's narrator was provided by the life and deeds of a young free spirit named Terry Taylor. Even more obscure—until Stewart Home began championing it in the 1990s—was the fact Taylor had documented his city's emerging alternative scenes in his own novel, *Baron's Court, All Change*.

According to Home's foreword to the New London Editions 2011 reissue of the book, Taylor was born in 1933 and entered the jazz scene as a teenager. He met MacInnes in 1956 and their friendship saw the 23-year-old join the bohemian set based around Victor Musgrave's Gallery One. Taylor subsequently served as an assistant to Musgrave's wife, noted photographer Ida Kar, and became her lover, despite their quarter-century age difference. After a period of living at Gallery One, Taylor moved to Notting Hill, where he formed a relationship with another member of London's avant-garde, Detta Whybrow, and—presumably inspired by the success of *Absolute Beginners*—wrote *Baron's Court, All Change*.

After the novel was published, Taylor began to spend extended periods in Tangiers, where he associated with William Burroughs and was involved in devising a series of magic rituals involving marijuana. Via Detta's contacts, he and others associated with Gallery One began to use LSD as part of further occult experimentation in London in the mid-60s. Many in their circle were targeted when the drug was banned in 1966, but his long stints overseas saw Taylor avoid the raids that led Detta and others to face court and in some cases serve prison time. Although he wrote at least two further novels, they were rejected by his publisher due to their increasingly experimental nature. Taylor continued to travel before eventually settling in Wales in the 1980s; he died in 2014.

First published in hardcover in 1961, *Baron's Court, All Change* did not appear in paperback until Four Square issued it in 1965. A cracking read, the novel is narrated by an unnamed teen who initially seeks relief from the suburban drudgery of his parents' house and the tedium of retail wage slavery by taking part in spiritualist meetings and attending jazz gigs. Sussed and sarcastic, he begins an affair with an older woman he meets at a séance, but an even more attractive path to liberation appears to open up when he is turned on to the joys of dope-smoking by new found friends after a gig at the Katz Kradle.

After a low-level dealer is arrested our protagonist and his best friend Dusty Miller seize the opportunity to enter the business themselves. Although this initially allows him to ditch his job and furnishes him with his own digs, a high-end hi-fi system and all the 'charge' he can smoke, the risks involved in bucking the nation's drug laws eventually exact a toll on the narrator and his young girlfriend, Miss Roach.

Baron's Court, All Change is an insider's take on the nascent new breed of hipsters whose love of black music, rejection of the sloppy look and intellectualism of the beats and trad jazzers, and predilection for drugs would prove a forerunner of the mass cult of mod and the psychedelic experimentalism that followed in its wake. The novel features copious drug taking, including references to junkies, who in the 1950s and 60s were still able to obtain a basic fix from the National Health Service, and possibly the first mention of LSD in British fiction.

IAIN McINTYRE

Baron's Court, All Change (Four Square, 1965)
Baron's Court, All Change (MacGibbon & Kee, 1961)

"I hate the youth club," I told him. "What don't you hate?" he asked, with an 'I-hate-you' sound in his voice.

"I don't hate freedom," I answered. "I don't hate truth or people that live their own lives, and I don't hate people like my sister Liz, who are so weak they can do bugger all about it. I don't hate you because you're one of those—I just feel sorry for you."

The poor fellow just didn't know what to say—you could see that from the expression on his face. He walked along, with his going-greasy mac, with all the buttons done up on, showing his highly starched white collar, that pulled so tight around his neck that I thought it was going to choke him any minute; his face was red from embarrassment, too. "I don't need any of your sympathy, thank you very much," he managed to get out. "It's right what Young George said. You're the original crazy mixed-up kid!"

"Not for long, don't you worry. I'll escape from this stagnated cesspool they call the suburbs! I'll ride out one day—and when I do, nothing will give me greater pleasure than to leave you and Young George behind, to your unreal life of television and peeping behind the curtains and your suburban respectability!"

"I think you're trying to be rude," he answered back in a small voice.

I couldn't stand any more of this idiot. "You bet I am! Why don't you wake up? You're dead before you've ever lived! You've had it, matey. And like the stupid fucker you are, you don't care. The suburb's bug will bite you if you don't watch out—and you're bit, boy! You've caught an incurable dose! But not me—oh no! Me? Never! I've had my inoculation against it! And I'll get away from this disease-infested land before long—so help me, I will!"

Vice trap, Kings Cross

The Purple Garter Club provided more than sexy striptease and topless go go. Young Chuck Waters gets mixed up in murder and mayhem at The Cross

Jean-Paul Severn

PB 285 60¢

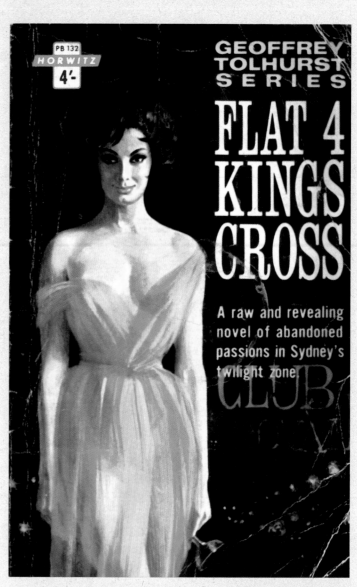

PB 132

HORWITZ 4'-

GEOFFREY TOLHURST SERIES

FLAT 4 KINGS CROSS

A raw and revealing novel of abandoned passions in Sydney's twilight zone.

CLUB

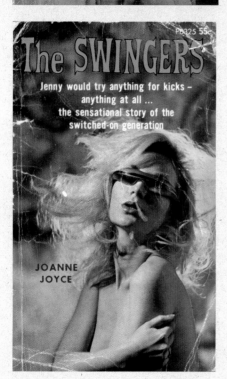

PB325 55¢

The SWINGERS

Jenny would try anything for kicks – anything at all ... the sensational story of the switched-on generation

JOANNE JOYCE

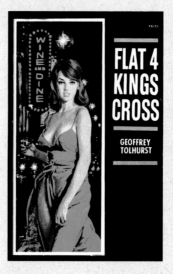

Vice Trap, Kings Cross (Scripts, 1966)

Flat 4 Kings Cross (Horwitz 1963)

Flat 4 Kings Cross (Horwitz, 1963)

Flat 4 Kings Cross (Horwitz, 1966)

The Swingers (Scripts, 1967)

GIRL GANGS, BIKER BOYS, AND REAL COOL CATS

PARTY GIRLS AND PASSION PITS
The Pulp Fiction of Sydney's Kings Cross

The trouble is, once you start caring too much about people it screws you up. You don't feel free anymore because all the time you're kind of responsible to them, and this stops you from doing a lot of things which otherwise you wouldn't think twice about. People and the relationships between them are the cause of all the problems in the world. I'm convinced.

Philosophy a-go-go from Joanne Joyce's
The Swingers (Scripts, 1967)

During the rise of the so-called switched-on generation (circa 1963), before they became the wacked-out generation (circa 1970), a strangely compelling genre of literature emerged, based largely on the area of Sydney known as Kings Cross.

The name of the suburb usually featured in the cover blurb, if not in the book's title, as if the mere mention of the glittering mile would make it sell more. It probably did too. I, for one, would pick up any book that had at least three of the following words in the title: Kings Cross, sex, vice, delinquency, strip club, drugs, topless and (although this word never appeared, to my knowledge) speedway.

If you can believe what you read in cheap, exploitation novels—and I certainly did—the glittering mile was a mass of sex, drugs and self-destruction. Sorry, make that **orgy of self-destruction**, the phrase of choice in Joanne Joyce's 1967 novel, *The Swingers*, perhaps the best of this small but cool collection of Kings Cross literature. It's one of the few you can read cover to cover, instead of flicking through looking for the good bits.

The front cover is dominated by a topless ice-cool blonde in mod wrap-around shades. On the back cover is the hard sell: SYDNEY THE SAVAGE CITY . . . SEX PARTIES, DRUG PARTIES, SUICIDE PARTIES . . . THE STUNNING STORY OF THE PSYCHEDELIC SWINGERS AND THEIR WILD, WILD WAYS.

Yeah, let's grab an RSL cab and go there right now. Kings Cross has traditionally been Australia's epicenter of vice but the 60s gave it a hard edge and a killer soundtrack. Check out the Missing Links at Surf City, or Python Lee Jackson around the corner at Whiskey Au Go Go.

This fertile period saw the emergence of an open gay scene at the Rex Hotel (meet you at the Bottoms Up Bar) and those "all-singing, all-dancing trannies" at Les Girls in Roslyn Street. Strip Clubs like the Pink Pussycat and the Paradise Club sprang up at the start of the decade, allegedly started by promoter Lee Gordon with the backing of organized crime figures Sammy Lee and Abe Saffron. Prostitutes paraded in designer clothes on the footpaths. A network of illegal gambling clubs—baccarat was the game of choice—operated more or less openly, supported by bent cops and corrupt New South Wales premier Bob Askin. Crime was a spectator sport, with gangland slayings on a regular basis, occasionally in the middle of a nightclub packed with celebrities.

This was the world I followed, at age 13, from the security of my bedroom in Adelaide. The scene was celebrated in a series of cheap paperbacks, available at your nearest railway station bookstall or second-hand bookshop. Without quite knowing what I was doing, I started collecting these books, plus the trashy magazines that documented the Kings Cross scene. I created my own virtual world with the aid of my 1966 copy of *Gregory's Sydney Street Directory*.

Neighbouring suburbs like Double Bay were included in my imaginary map because, as I read in *Man* magazine, this was where exotic dancers did their Saturday morning shopping in bikinis before hopping into powder-blue MGB sports cars and speeding down the New South Head Road to Watsons Bay for lunch. It's true. There were photos to prove it. I studied the list of motels in the front pages of my street directory and decided that when I moved to Kings Cross I'd stay at the Florida Car-O-Tel in Victoria Street. This was where I was pretty sure that all the visiting TV personalities, wrestlers and Roller Game stars would stay. Not so, as I later discovered.

One of the first novels I picked up was *Model School* by Christine James. It was published in 1963 by Horwitz and obviously inspired by the Profumo scandal that had rocked England that year and made celebrities of Christine Keeler and Mandy Rice-Davies. This was a typical trash-novel gimmick, basing a fictional story on a factual event. It was rare for a woman to write pulp fiction, so whoever Christine James is, she was a literary pioneer. Unless she was a bloke writing under a woman's name to boost sales. That was another gimmick.

According to the blurb, this story is about **the world of Party Girls and Prostitutes** or **the other side of modeling in the dim twilight world of Sydney's vice world**. It's a traditional tale . . . young girl called June Palmer, 18, comes from the country to the Cross to make it big in the world of showbiz . . . **a real country kid, pretty naive and innocent to boot**, as she describes herself.

She gets a job in a Kings Cross Casting Agency then discovers that some of the girls on the books are making lots of money by attending private parties. That's one of them on the cover, Nina, with her hair dyed so blonde it was almost white.

> **"Do they have to?" asks Little Miss Innocent. "I mean, are they . . .?**
>
> **"We don't set standards of morality on our clients," is the reply. "If they want to make a little extra on the side, that's their business."**

In other words, yes to both the above questions.

It's a tame read but does suggest that, even in 1963, some girls were more than happy to take money for sex and there was a local porno-movie industry. June is asked to appear in one but, typically, chickens out at the last minute. Peroxide party girl Nina is more than happy to take her place and the hundred pounds in cash.

This theme was repeated, with a few minor changes, in *Flat 4 Kings Cross* (1963) by Geoffrey Tolhurst. According to the back-cover blurb: DRUGS, PROSTITUTION, GAMBLING . . . THIS WAS THE LIFE CARLA FOUND AT KINGS CROSS IN THE NEON JUNGLE OF AUSTRALIA'S NOTORIOUS NETWORK OF VICE.

Carla grew up in a small country town in northern New South Wales.

> **And I was as naive as only a 15-year-old country girl can be. I reckoned that all I had to do was step to the junction of Darlinghurst Road and Macleay Street and my fortune was made.**

She did make her fortune, as a high-class call girl, operating from Flat 4, Kings Cross. The flat was dominated by a huge white satin bed in the shape of a shell (Carla was the pearl).

> **My telephone rang almost constantly, although I took it off the hook when I had a guest. If I**

> **liked the voice at the other end of the phone, and the voices were always male, I would arrange to meet him at the Rex or the Chevron, and I would take my time getting dressed and going to meet him.**
>
> **I could have worked every night of the week, if I had chosen. But I was still fussy over the men I met. I turned down more than I took home. I got the reputation for being very exclusive and I heard that men even laid bets as to whether they could 'make me' or not.**

This is 1963, so there has to be a moral message. Carla is eventually arrested and faces three years in prison although the tone of the book is optimistic enough to inspire real-life 15-year-old girls from the bush to make the trip to the Cross. Thousands did. In *Model School*, June Palmer managed to survive her Kings Cross experience with her innocence—and her virginity—intact, but only four years later it was okay for women in paperbacks to have casual sex and enjoy it, as Jenny Adamson does in *The Swingers*.

Jenny is the switched-on chick who relates this story. The swinging starts when she goes to a party and meets Mick, who plays guitar in an undiscovered garage band.

> **All the blokes—there were five of them—were wearing t-shirts and jeans.**
>
> **"These are the Uglies," Anna said with a gesture which included all of them. "They're playing at Poppy's now."**
>
> **I was rather at sea at first, and then I remembered where I'd heard the name before— Poppy's. It was the new discoteque which had just opened in Paddington. From all accounts pretty swinging, and The Uglies were a really wild group. They'd just cut their first record and were thinking of going to London.**

Later, after the inevitable one-night-stand, Jenny goes to see them play. This then is an accurate description of what a 1967 discotheque was like:

> **Poppy's, Saturday night. Music crashing, bouncing off the walls, filling the packed room. So loud that talking was impossible, you only wanted to dance. The whole place rocking, bursting with noise, lights—red, orange, purple—flashing from throbbing drums**

over twisting faces, into eyes, onto skin, over bodies, walls, clothes, feet moving in rhythm, Phil the singer swaying drunkenly with the mike, words running together, lashing out of twisted lips, urging drums beating in a rising frenzy, rising crescendo of shrieking sound, lights flashing faster, faster. Silence.

Then she focuses on the band, all wearing the mandatory black wrap-around sunglasses and the first symbols of psychedelia.

Tonight four of them were wearing huge paisley ties that one of the kids from Tech had made. Swirls of colour—pink, orange and purple—with the swirly parts outlined in scarlet sequins and crystal beads. Ralph, the new drummer, was the only one who was without a tie—he had on a white t-shirt with the picture of a caveman-like person on the front, and underneath in big black letters—HERE COMES THE INCREDIBLE HULK.

The top records of the time are mentioned throughout as a kind of unheard soundtrack . . . The Who's 'I'm a Boy', the Rolling Stones 'Mother's Little Helper', the Beatles' *Revolver*.

While the switched-on generation was doing their thing at Poppy's, my 13-year-old batteries were still charging. Through these books, handed around at school as if they were contraband, we could get a taste of the thrills that, hopefully, lay ahead. Others worthy of a mention include Gordon Flanagan's *The Kings Cross Caper (1962)*, Jean-Paul Severn's *Vice Trap*, *Kings Cross* (1966), Carl Ruhen's *The Rebels* (1967), and Julian Spencer's *The Spungers* (1967).

Some historical background is included in Donald Hann's *The Deserters*, published in 1964 by Horwitz, although it deals with Sydney in the World War Two period. Nothing much has changed. **Kings Cross during the Yank invasion was a tawdry hotbed of sex, sin, silk stockings and Scotch,** says the blurb.

Julian Spencer wrote a series of wonderful trash novels, including *Cross Section*, *Clik* (1966) and *Shooting Sequence* (1967). All were set in actual locations in and around the Cross, which gave them a televisual quality, like grainy old episodes of the Australian crime show, *Homicide*. *The Spungers* is typical subject matter. **CONFLICT EXPLODES**

Model School (Horwitz, 1963)
Model School (Horwitz, 1965)

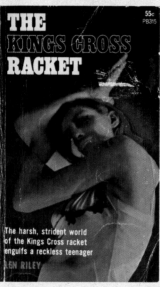

The Kings Cross Caper (Calvert, 1962)
The Deserters (Horwitz, 1965)
Kings Cross Affair (Horwitz, 1965)
The Kings Cross Racket (Scripts, 1965)
An Ornament of Grace (Sun, 1966)

BETWEEN A BEATNIK CON-MAN AND A YOUNG REBEL AT KINGS CROSS, says the cover. Spencer, like Joanne Joyce, wrote in a hipster style somewhere between Mickey Spillane and Jack Kerouac.

It really was macabre, Spotty thought. Here he was in Phil's pad with Phil's bird, and Phil had gone off on some fool errand. It was his own fault if he couldn't look after his girlfriends, and the least he, Spotty, could do was do the right thing by the poor girl. She wanted it. Poor bloody Phil. After all the world was full of people like that. In a way Spotty was glad. He needed them. Where would he be without them? And old ladies and queens and buyers of dirty books and party-givers and money-spenders. Spotty needed them all.

Spotty is so studiously immoral he's lovable. It almost seems a pity when he dies at the end of the book, crashing his stolen MGB into a stone wall on Darling Point Road. He was my favourite anti-hero in 1967.

Vice Trap, Kings Cross is set in the Purple Garter Club in the heart of Kings Cross (the Pink Pussycat by another name) which, **seemed to be just another strip club, yet hidden behind its dim façade was a million dollar vice empire**. This was another common theme, the anonymous criminals who controlled the Cross, versus those from out of town, like Chuck Walters, who get mixed up in their world. Chuck meets Toni, topless waitress at the Purple Garter, who tells him how things operate around here:

> "When you work around the Cross you mix with all types, artists, entertainment people, beatniks, underworld fringe characters. Only a dill could fail to know what goes on . . . vice rackets, drug-peddling, smuggling."

Chuck is a 'dill', and you feel disappointed when he emerges as the victor in the battle of the moral codes. This would never happen in real life.

The strip club was such a common setting that it now appears as cliché, except they really were where the action happened. A more accurate account appears in *The Strippers*, another quickie release by Horwitz, bashed out by hack writer James Holledge in 1965 . . . promoted as **the Naked Truth on the girls who strip for a living**. **Naked Truth** in big, bold letters to attract the perverts. The book mainly rehashes the history of strip around the world but the publisher Horwitz adds a chapter on the emerging Australian scene at the end. This was a relatively recent phenomenon. The first clubs had appeared there in 1960.

> Up at Sydney's Kings Cross new strip clubs sprout with bewildering rapidity and the entrepreneurs who run them will tell you that they are almost embarrassed by the number of young ladies who approach them for the chance to show their undressing ability.

You could also explore this underworld through the pages of James Workman's *Shark Bait*, a 1968 Horwitz paperback based on the Australian Broadcasting Corporation television series *Contrabandits*. **A fast action suspense drama**, as they describe it on the back cover. I can't remember seeing this show on the box, although I recall it was based on the newly formed narcotics squad, so regular visits to the meaner streets of the Cross were essential. Bob Piper, played in the series by John Bonney, is the most interesting character, a young plain-clothes cop with a liking for the dark side.

> Piper was whistling softly to himself as, with hands thrust deep into his pockets, he slouched along Darlinghurst Road towards the Cross. His shoulders were slumped deliberately forward and he was un-shaven. His fair curly hair was tousled. His top shirt button was unfastened and his tie was crooked. As he walked he swayed slightly as if drunk. He wasn't drunk. Far from it. He had had a few beers down the road at the Rex, but not enough to make him fuzzy.

He's a man on a mission. Five minutes later he wandered in to Manfred's disco in William Street.

> Inside the place was, as usual, dimly lit. Suffused lighting dribbled out from brackets at various points around the walls and fell limply down to the outer edges of the tables which surrounded the dance floor. Most of the tables were occupied, mainly by kids, and the loud, near deafening music seemed to be vibrating up through the floor.

Manfred's was where the cool kids scored their pep pills, so Piper, pretending to be drunk, wasn't entirely out of place. This series was one of the first to reveal that organised crime had moved into the drug scene.

By 1970 heroin was the drug of choice. This was when Kevin Mackey's novel, *The Cure: Recollections of an Addict* (1970), was published. This non-fiction work is a much heavier text, but it speaks the same language, although for Kevin it's the dull agony of waiting to score smack in the drizzle, rather than grooving with the happening crowd at Poppy's or Manfred's.

> Misty, humid rain. Kings Cross. I'm waiting and I'm experienced at waiting, spent a great deal of my life waiting. I sit by the fountain in the village. Nine thirty. She'll be on time. Not many people about. Weekday morning, off peak. TAB shit, bookshop shut, cafés all shut except the ice-cream and refreshment kiosk. I'm shut tight and tensely clutching so I buy a choc-mint ice-cream.

By now the hard reality of drug addiction had set in, both in the pages of cheap paperbacks and in the deserted back streets of the glittering sewer. Kings Cross literature somehow wasn't selling anymore. Teenage fantasists like me didn't want to go there anymore.

JAMES COCKINGTON

The Spungers—Julian Spencer (Scripts, 1967)

CONFLICT EXPLODES BETWEEN A BEATNIK CON-MAN AND A YOUNG REBEL AT KINGS CROSS, screams the front cover blurb of *The Spungers*. This being pulp, both labels, 'beatnik' and 'rebel', only apply loosely. That said, *The Spungers* is one of the better local pulps set in inner-city Sydney in the late 60s.

The beatnik of the story is 19-year-old Spotty, a failed art student and 'spunger' (Australian slang, usually spelled 'sponger', for a parasite or freeloader), existing on the fringes of Sydney's inner city. As the story opens, he's sleeping on a mattress on the floor of a mate's flat and cadging money, drinks and meals from the other low-life denizens of Kings Cross.

Phil is the young rebel. He has a day job as an accountant, hails from Sydney's affluent North Shore, but feels his life lacks something. He is disgusted with his parent's snobbish attitude to life and craves new experiences, social and sexual. His yearnings are an early sign of the youth-driven discontent and protest politics that would hit Australia a couple of years later. When Phil's annual vacation comes up, he lies to his parents about going surfing and instead hangs out at Kings Cross, where he meets up with Spotty.

Spotty agrees to let Phil stay in his friend's flat in return for Phil paying for drinks and food. Phil realises his new friend's true nature when Spotty accompanies Phil and his girlfriend to a university student party at Darling Point. Phil becomes separated from Spotty, giving the latter the opportunity to slip away and bed his girlfriend.

The two eventually fall out, and Spotty goes to live with an older rich woman who thinks he is cool, while Phil goes back to his other life. It looks like Spotty has landed on his feet, nice pad, nice clothes, even an MG to drive. Spotty bumps into Phil and his new girlfriend one night, drives away from the encounter furious, crashes the car and is killed.

The Spungers has a great sense of Sydney's geography and the class gap, far more pronounced in the 60s than today, between different parts of the city, and some cameo appearances by the various subcultures that inhabit the city, rockers, upper-class university students and the last remnants of Sydney's small beatnik scene.

ANDREW NETTE

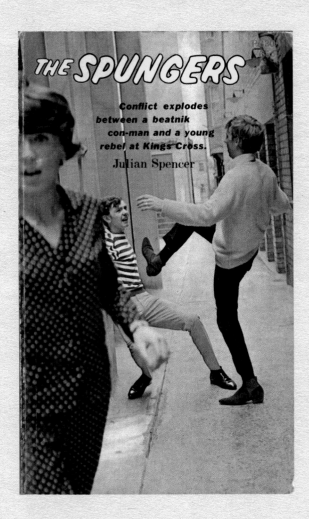

The Spungers (Scripts, 1967)
Shooting Sequence (Horwitz, 1967)
Cross Section (Horwitz, 1966)
Clik (Horwitz, 1966)

H e passed the Rex Hotel on the other side. Someone he knew might be in there having a first Saturday evening drink. Spotty knew lots of people, because he was so friendly. It paid to have a wide circle of friends. He turned into Tusculum Street, trying to remember which way the numbers went. It was a short street with lots of trees, it looked good in the early morning, and there was a view out over the excavation which was going to be part of the Chevron Hotel eventually. The monstrosity reared up into the sky, and every time Spotty passed it he thought of what it represented, all the things he was opposed to or was at the moment because he didn't have them. Expense accounts, swisho food, cocktails, suave old fatties in dinner suits, rough looking bouncers disguised in uniforms of commissionaires, all that old crap. All designed for interstate fatties, the turbo-jet set, conferences in swinging Melbourne, company meetings in swinging Sydney, and then a night out on the town at the Cross, and all from a comfortable base at the Chevron, where the furniture was designed for overweight executives. He told himself to stop being so bitter and twisted, his father was like that, he might even finish up like that himself.

Hippies and the Pulp Fiction of the Late-60s and Early-70s Counterculture

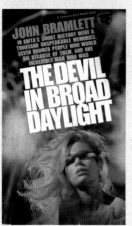

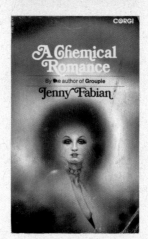

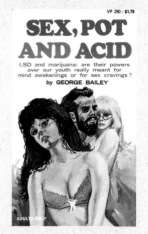

The Wildest Street (Brandon House, 1967), *The Secret Swinger* (Signet Books, 1967), *Hippie Doctor* (Calvert, 1972), *Teenocracy* (Ace, 1969), *Tripper* (Exposition Press, 1973), *The Devil in Broad Daylight* (Gold Medal, 1969), *The Acid Nightmare* (Paperback Library, 1972), *Jacklove* (Panther, 1970), *A Chemical Romance* (Corgi, 1971), *The Groovy Genius* (Pyramid Books, 1971), *Sex, Pot and Acid* (Viceroy, 1968), *Pulling Taffy* (Midwood, 1970)

The Love Tribe
(Signet, 1968)

Flower Power — Ernest Tidyman

They destroyed her innocence, then rechristened her 'Flower'

PYRAMID BOOKS   T-1614   75¢

HAPPENING AT SAN REMO

A daring novel of today's Young Underground—its sexual and mental excesses—its search for sensation and conflict ▇ BRUCE CASSIDAY

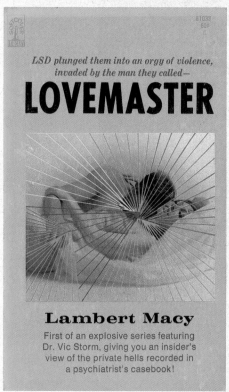

LSD plunged them into an orgy of violence, invaded by the man they called—

LOVEMASTER

Lambert Macy

First of an explosive series featuring Dr. Vic Storm, giving you an insider's view of the private hells recorded in a psychiatrist's casebook!

Flower Power (Mayflower, 1969)
Happening at San Remo (Pyramid, 1967)
Lovemaster (Softcover Library, 1967)

TURN ON, FREAK OUT
Late-60s Hippie Pulp

At some point in the 1960s, 'beat' became 'hip' and a new subculture was born: the anti-establishment, countercultural, hippie movement. As with beats, hippies had their 'bibles', books that everyone read, or claimed to have read. Many a bookshelf in a hippie pad housed mystical and consciousness-expanding titles such as *Siddhartha* by Herman Hesse, Aldous Huxley's *The Doors of Perception* (which inspired the name of the band, the Doors) and *The Teachings of Don Juan: A Yaqui Way of Knowledge* by Carlos Castaneda. For a generation born following World War Two, and living under the spectre of MAD (Mutually Assured Destruction) in a nuclear war, there had to be a better way. A groundswell of youth were inspired by the technicolour message of countercultural revolutionary and one-time university professor Timothy Leary to "tune in, turn on, and drop out".

Hippies sought to generate a cultural revolution and encouraged people to "make love not war". In surprising numbers, and with surprising cultural impact, hippies explored other ways of being, including new (at least to the West) philosophies, new music, new drugs, new fashions, and new social mores—peace, communal living and 'free love'. Hippies wanted the things frowned upon by squares and those on the wrong side of the generation gap.

As with other youth subcultures, the hippie movement spawned its own literature: hippie pulp. Like other pulp genres, its products were often exploitative and salacious rather than progressive and insightful. The focus on (promiscuous) sex, (mind-expanding) drugs and (psychedelic) rock and roll in novel settings and situations means that hippie pulps continue to have considerable appeal. Eight very different books that illustrate these themes in various ways are: Bruce Cassidy's *Happening at San Remo* (1967); *The Love Tribe* by Joseph Mathewson (1968); Lambert Macy's *Lovemaster* (1967); *Acid Temple Ball*, by the imaginatively named 'Mary Sativa' (1969); Ernest Tidyman's *Flower Power* (1969); Doug Lang's *Freaks* (1973); Douglas Orgill's *Jasius Pursuit* (1973); and Hugh Pentecost's *The Girl with Six Fingers* (1969).

Happening at San Remo is described as **a daring novel of today's young underground—its sexual and mental excesses—its search for sensation and conflict**. It focuses on events leading up to a planned concert by the band the Surfers Three as part of the 50th anniversary celebrations at Peel University. Peel is located on the American West Coast in San Remo, California (apparently somewhere between Santa Barbara and Monterey), which situates it perfectly within the West Coast hippie movement. The Surfers Three are a free-wheeling band featuring the surf-loving Brendan Tom, El Greco and Stingaree: an emerging folk rock trio with a small, but growing cult following who tread the line between artistic freedom and commercial success. Their growing reputation is bolstered by the way they belt out (ad-libbed) lyrics such as:

> Now listen to my song of gloom
> I wrote it in the muck and gloom
> And here's the burden of my tune: we're dying, comrades, dying soon!
> Doom, gloom, tune, soon!
> Whoo-ee! Whoo-ee!
> Gonna catch that rattler to the moon.
> Whoo-ee! Whoo-ee!

Lead singer Brendon Tom's encounters with Evita Navarra, a passionate and rebellious señorita of Mexican descent, and the well-heeled Lora Lee, who happens to be a student journalist, provide momentum for the story, with Tom's dilemma described as follows:

> I looked at Lora Lee. She was my pick of the crop, my top draw. But Evita's tricks were provocative too, and had more in keeping with my speciality. I would have to make a hard decision.

However, much more than romance is at stake: Peel University is a divided place, and not everyone is looking forward to the arrival of the Surfers Three. Indeed, conservative interests are exerting considerable pressure in numerous ways to ensure that the 'happening' does not go ahead. Further fuelling the fire is the fact that arch-conservative Cornelius Oakes also carries a torch for both Evita and Lora.

The rising tensions are accompanied by various combinations of sex, drugs and rock and roll, as the following encounters illustrate:

Mist swirled about me and I looked up to see the heavens receding. Yes, the pot was taking effect. Then my limbs lengthened, my torso grew wide and strong. I had the height of ten men, the strength of giants, and my body burst against my clothes. I turned to her but she floated away, almost vanished and then came in close, laughing, eyeing me with pupils wide and bottomless . . . Sweat beaded out on her upper lip, an obscenity of instant duration. "I'm hot" she said.

I smelt the faint odour of nasturtiums, their pungent earthy odour omnipotent and all-pervasive. The acid was taking effect. A far off buzzing grew in volume. Wheels revolved in the blackness, coloured wheels with arrows as spokes.

Other noteworthy features of *Happening at San Remo* include the presence of a malevolent Timothy Leary–type character, the characterisations of student subcultures, and some sense of class politics. In addition it was written by well-known pulp writer Bruce Cassidy (1920–2005), whose obituary in *The Independent* stated: "He was one of the last generation of writers who not only read and enjoyed the enormous variety of pulp magazines as they were being produced, but saw them as a useful as well as entertaining entry into the writing business."

In contrast to the West Coast setting of *Happening at San Remo*, *The Love Tribe* is set in New York's East Village (517 East 6th St., apparently) and is concerned with a small communal family/tribe living in a crash pad. Joseph Mathewson's book, which invites readers to **Freak out, love in, do your thing the way it is in the East Village** charts the emergence (and disintegration?) of a loose-knit but loving family of **runaways, drifters,** and **dropouts from the adult world.** Part of the charm is the setting, which is described room by room, with one space described as **a darkish chamber with half a dozen mattresses, some army blankets and pillows—all the things, in short, that make life worth living.**

Notably, the distinction between hippies and beatniks is made; this difference is presented as a matter of philosophy and outlook, rather than merely the passing of time. George, the central character, was inspired to establish the 'family' as a consequence of his disillusionment with the San Francisco beats: **He wants to love, but could not, felt himself be-coming like the San Francisco beats, hopeless and forlorn.**

In place of this nihilism, George (**the son of a sometime communist, an unwashed, shaggy-haired, bisexual pothead with a firm belief in the power of love**), aims to live a life based on love, as this exchange with housemate Flicker indicates:

First of all I'd say we look around for some more people to live here.

Which won't be hard. In a month or so you'll have to fight them off.

But the sort who'll—you know—be able to live together, be a real family.

Down here—yes—easy. That's what most of us want in a way. A family. But the kids I've met turn green if you say the word. Bad vibrations.

A tribe then George tapped a little pot from the bottle into the trough he'd formed at the bottom of the paper. Then he rolled the paper tight, licked the joint all over, and twisted one end to a point.

A tribe. OK, that's better. But what do we do together as a tribe?

Live. For now at least. Just try to stick together and live the good life.

That's all?

I think it's a lot. I mean, in the middle of New York City in the middle of the twentieth century—a tribal family based on love. Christ man, that's unheard of.

The story proceeds via a series of biographical vignettes about each member of the family, and how they came to join this family, with its foundations based on love, trust, and 'not trying to own each other'. As expected, these vignettes are littered with tales of sex, drugs and rock and roll, such as **George undressed her slowly, licking every inch of her body, making sure he knew what he was possessing before he possessed it;** and **we all trooped off to the music room, where Dial put on a Jefferson Airplane record and Bucky started rolling joints.**

The most (inadvertently) humorous scene, in what is otherwise a seemingly earnest book, takes place at a gig where the band, The Manhattan Project (composed of three brothers, with long hair dyed platinum blonde and dressed in coats of scarlet, purple, and pink), somehow manage to exercise **absolute control over the crowd** with deep and meaningful lyrics such as: Time is now, baby, yeah, baby, now! Move on in, baby, now, baby, now, now, now! and: Time, ohhh, time, time, time!

Lovemaster by Lambert Macy offers a different perspective on the hippie lifestyle. It seeks to assess the benefits, or otherwise, of 'turning on' to psychedelic drugs, with the story revolving around psychiatrist Doctor Vic Storm, who is **A daring explorer in that most dangerous of all areas, the sexual jungle.** The sex, drugs, and rock and roll associated with LSD are mainly explored as a consequence of the 'fieldwork' activities undertaken by the good Doctor and his sexy sidekick, nurse Madge Broun, as well as from recorded therapy sessions with patients. Ron and Petty Castle, a young couple flirting with the LSD lifestyle courtesy of trips provided by Svengali Tod Billum, come to Vic Storm's attention due to the fallout associated with a very nasty earlier encounter with the thug-like Joe Lacey. As a consequence, Dr. Storm declares to Madge, **"I want to find out what happened to Ron Castle that night. I want to find out what drives this man Joe. I want to find out how much damage Tod Billum is doing. I want to help Petty."**

In response, Madge queries whether his views about hallucinogens are fixed, to which he replies, **"Whatever we may think about the hallucinogens, we have to face facts. The acid age is here and when you can't see, smell, or taste the stuff in a cube of sugar, a drink of vodka—how are they going to control it?"**

Madge's commitment to her work, and her interest in making out with Dr. Storm means that she goes well beyond the call of duty in her efforts to understand LSD and its effects. First she dances flirtatiously with the Sleazy Joe Lacey at a happening nightclub in order to get insights into how he thinks: **In the cages the go-go girls worked hard, bare breasts bobbing, hips frantically emulating copulation. One the floor Madge and Joe Lacey began to emulate the girls in the cages.**

Later, she attends an Acid Test, where she takes what Tod deceives her into believing is a small trip, saying, **"Here—drink up. I hope there's enough for you to feel it. I mean a very short trip. Just a sample."**

When the acid hits, the effects are startling:

With unexpected joy she discovered that the lights changed with the music. The lights were the music and the music became the lights.

The notes were brilliant red, yellow, deep purple . . . The room began to change shape. It became a huge diamond containing her. Next it oozed into a great ovate form . . . She wanted to put her arms out and hold the light. She wanted to speak but could not. The room became a great flower and she was a butterfly in the heart of the flower, watching multi-coloured petals sway with the music.

Despite the effects of the acid trip, Madge, ever the professional, thinks to herself, **"She must try to remember to tell Vic".** If the adventures of Dr. Storm and Nurse Broun are to your taste, the cover indicates that *Lovemaster* was the "first of an explosive series featuring Doctor Vic Storm", although the series may not have extended beyond a second book, *The Love Pack* (1967).

Acid Temple Ball, attributed to 'Mary Sativa', is a drug-fuelled sex romp through the late 60s told from the perspective of a liberated young art student. The story takes the reader from the East Village to San Francisco via a road trip, and documents various and numerous encounters with friends and lovers, with plenty of drugs and multiple references to the music of the day. Musicians referred to include: Jefferson Airplane, Vanilla Fudge, Janis Joplin, Jimi Hendrix, Bob Dylan and Country Joe. The sex, drugs and music are seamlessly interwoven in *Acid Temple Ball*:

Davey puts on Jimi Hendrix. I roll my skirt down, slip out of my underpants, pull off my soft sweater and remove the cowboy boots. I stand naked moving to the music, touching my hard nipples with my fingertips.

I put the Vanilla Fudge record on my favourite cut, and begin slowly stripping off my clothes and dancing to the music in the orange light. The Fudge does a psychedelic extension of the Detroit spade blues, it's like hearing the original Supremes version with superimposed acid hallucinations: a huge echoing room, flashing lights, the music stretching with the movement of hands and torso. Arch my back, flutter my hands like a temple dancer, through my hair back and forth with the jerks of my hips and belly. My soft wool dress, unzipped, slips down over my hips to the floor. Stockings rolled down inch by inch. I wear no bra, touch my breasts with my hands as I slide off my black bikini underpants . . . Lightly he

takes my shoulders and I climb on to his lap, crossing my legs behind his back. The record changer is playing the last half of the record over and over, in response to our needs.

With its explicit and plentiful sex, copious drug taking ('Mary' apparently has sex while under the influence of seven separate drugs), and frequent music references, *Acid Temple Ball* has the elements of a classic. This status is confirmed by the fact it is well written and the relations between the characters are believable and generally respectful. This should actually come as no surprise, since it turns out that Sharon Rudahl, one of the creators of *Wimmen's Comix*, has been identified as the author behind the pseudonym 'Mary Sativa'.

Like *Acid Temple Ball*, Ernest Tidyman's *Flower Power* also tells a young woman's story, in this case Phyllis Greenfield's metamorphosis from dutiful daughter in an uptight upper-middle-class family into Rainbow Flower, a beautiful young peacenik. The story begins with 16-year-old Phyllis arriving in San Francisco, after escaping school on a bus from Dayton, Ohio. Here she chances upon Furman, a young African American hippie, who befriends her. Following a quick visit to 'The Snatch' (the nickname given to a coffee shop because it is dark and wet) Furman takes Phyllis back to his share house somewhere in the Haight-Ashbury for the night. There she meets the other members of the household: Moby, the aptly named Tripper, Me (a beautiful young woman in search of truth and love) and Signal (a cat with an interest in electronics). What follows is a light-hearted account of the events over the course of a drug-fuelled summer of love, which culminates in a riotous party in which hippies, bikers, Italian mamas, FBI agents, an eastern guru, mobsters, and an undercover patrolman, somehow come together. As part of her journey to becoming 'Rainbow Flower', Phyllis crosses a number of Rubicons. She takes drugs for the first time: **Pot? Oh, God, she was only in San Francisco an hour and here she was smoking marijuana!**

She watches Moby and Me having sex: **But they couldn't be doing that, Phyllis thought, watching them do exactly that. Not with all of us sitting right here. Not that. Not here.** She goes bare-breasted in front of people for the first time, and soon after, also for the first time, she 'makes love' with Furman in front of Moby, Tripper, Me, and Signal.

Like other hippie pulps, *Flower Power* describes the effects of drugs:

Every cell of her brain moved, melted, reached out of her skull and felt the freedom. God she thought, my mind is bending! Then the focus of her eyes returned and Tripper was somehow four and five or six dimensional.

Tidyman also provides frequent description of Me's 'charms': **The girl's breasts were elegantly round, as if they had been poured into small Jello molds to firm, then dotted with pink raisins.**

The punk-prescient lyrics of a band called Wild Asparagus and the correspondence between Phyllis/Rainbow Flower and her parents are also noteworthy for their humorous insights into the 'generation gap'. At the house party, Signal plays Wild Asparagus's smash hit which includes the following lyrics:

You tell me I'm too fat,
You laugh at all my pimples,
You never use to do that
When baby still had dimples.
Up yours, Up yours! Up yours!

In Phyllis's letters to her parents, wonderfully 'rose-coloured' explanations of the household's domestic circumstances and activities are provided in an attempt to reassure her parents that everything is okay. The house is described as a place that is **kind of like a youth hostel, except it isn't really** and Me is described as a young girl **who is very interested in religion** and who has a **green thumb**.

In addition to being a fun read, what makes *Flower Power* collectible is that Ernest Tidyman was also the author of the Blaxploitation classic *Shaft* and associated sequels, as well as writing the screenplay for the movie *The French Connection*, for which he won an Academy Award. He also wrote books on the Jim Jones cult, the Guyana tragedy, and Alcatraz.

Across the Atlantic, a hippie pulp that continues to attract interest is the New English Library offering *Freaks*, by Doug Lang. The back cover says it all:

THE TIME: two months of chaos and crisis in the summer of 1972
THE PLACE: a communal house in London
THE PEOPLE: five men and two women
THE PROBLEMS: drug abuse, sexual antics and political activism

Freaks
(New English Library, 1973)
The Girl with Six Fingers
(Zebra, 1974)
The Jasius Pursuit
(Sphere, 1975)

Part of this book's charm is that the author, and central character, is/was a Welsh poet, who now lives in the United States. As suggested by the back-cover blurb, the plot centres on events following the return to London of a young poet, Calvin Longbow, from a lucrative poetry reading tour of the US, during which he dabbled with a cocktail of assorted drugs: "The mescaline chills have got me in their clammy grinding grip" to such an extent that **I was so fucked up it didn't matter**. Stylistically, the narrative is free-flowing and sparse, but *Freaks* is also relatively experimental for pulp fiction, with some very short chapters (sometimes a single paragraph) and a poetic tone to some of the text, as these two extracts illustrate:

> **Sitting in my study, stoned, I would listen to the sounds inside my head. I read a lot of books. I smoked a lot of dope.**
>
> **I had a little private party with Tristy that evening. A fancy dress party. I came as a seal and Tristy came—rapturously.**

Hippies also provided a useful vehicle for crime and mystery novels, such as *The Jasius Pursuit* by Oxford educated Douglas Orgill (1973) and crime writer Hugh Pentecost's 1969 book, *The Girl with Six Fingers*. The French Riviera provides the setting for *The Jasius Pursuit*, with the action focused on the holding hostage of **a lone Englishman and two beautiful women** by a gang of crazed hippies, led by the Mansonesque cult leader, Starbuck. A nice feature of this surprisingly readable book is that the cover hints at the climax, with it showing Starbuck, the leader of the hippie cult grimacing amongst encircling flames (you can tell he's a hippie by the long hair and beard and assorted beads and chains around his neck).

The Girl with Six Fingers (Pinnacle Books, 1969) is number five in the John Jericho Mystery Series. It involves Jericho investigating the violent kidnapping of a model at a Happening, which is described on the back cover as follows:

> **Drums were throbbing and psychedelic lights excited the youthful audience at the Happening of the year. The artist's model, Linda, hired for the occasion, had just been sloshed with scarlet, green and purple paint—the audience was roaring its approval. The screams of pleasure turned to cries of hysteria, as over fifty raiders, armed with clubs, broke into the building and dragged the screaming Linda into the woods. It was the last time anyone would see her live.**

The cover features a drawing of a curvaceous, but surprisingly androgynous young woman dancing, her body reflecting the swirling colours of a psychedelic light show (although, incongruously, her long flowing blonde hair doesn't reflect the coloured lights).

BRIAN COFFEY

Moonbabies (Midwood, 1970)

Two Travel Through; or, The Skinny Shall Inherit the Earth —Glen Gainsburgh & Peter Whitehead (Signet, 1968)

The intriguing *Two Travel Through* follows rebellious daydreamers Warren and David from their suburban Boston high school through to a New York crash-pad, before one of the pair descends into the hell of heroin abuse. The book clearly aims at a little *Catcher in the Rye* adolescent profundity—indeed that work is referenced on one occasion as the central pair struggle to define themselves in an unforgiving world. Of course this is nowhere near that classic, but there are some very evocative and well-written passages, particularly around David's drug addiction, which is convincingly portrayed in a non-sensationalist manner.

The plot of the book is very episodic and almost directionless, leading me to wonder if it was a semi-autobiographical tome (real life is rarely as well plotted as fiction). It captures the fear that one might experience prior to a first drug experience in realistic detail, rather than the hackneyed descriptions one generally reads in hippie-exploitation novels. The lack of sex in the book is also telling. Every 17-year-old knows that much more time is spent thinking about sex than actually having it.

The back of the novel claims the two authors have **tried it all and lived to tell the tale**, while the blurb inside the cover ominously states: **Peter Whitehead and Glen Gainsburgh were juniors at a well known prep school in New England when they wrote this novel of the teenybop drug scene. Peter Whitehead is currently a student at Brown University. Glen Gainsburgh, at last report, had disappeared into the underground.** This atypical book has an insider's feel and stays away from all the genre's usual sex and drug clichés.

AUSTIN MATTHEWS

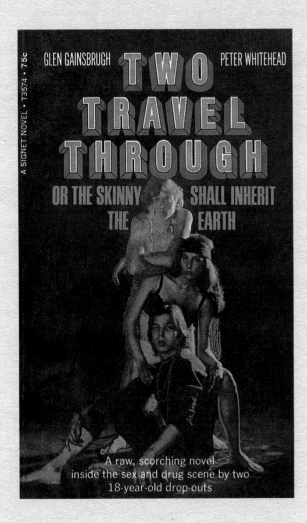

The silence was broken by Allan asking if we wanted to "turn on." David and I looked at each other and then at Allan and the three of us started to laugh.

David managed to ask, "What the hell is turning on?"

Allan, still laughing, held out a thin home-rolled cigarette.

"Marijuana," he said.

Dope! Holy shit! I couldn't believe that this little white stick in Allan's hand was the real thing, the thing everybody talked about, but nobody ever saw. I pictured smoke-filled opium dens in China and scenes from the high-school movies on drugs that showed all the stiffs laid out on the slabs with their arms ripped open and the girls fainting all over the place. I looked at Allan and his outstretched arms and placed a mental caption under him in stark black and white letters: 'This is an addict. He may be dangerous and is known to carry weapons.'

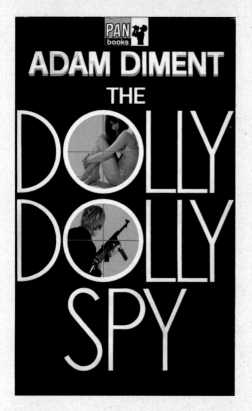

The Dolly, Dolly Spy (Dutton, 1967)
The Dolly, Dolly Spy (Bantam, 1968)
The Dolly, Dolly Spy (Pan, 1967)

THE DISAPPEARANCE OF ADAM DIMENT

The October 1967 issue of Michael Heseltine's *Town* magazine featured an interview with fashionable 23-year-old author Adam Diment. The introduction said that he was "Hoping to move from his Fulham Road flat to trendy King's Road, where his tight pink trousers and matching floral shirt will be more appreciated."

In the late 60s, moving a few hundred yards from one part of west London to another was like travelling to a different country. Diment knew he could afford the expensive move, because after the publication of his first novel, *The Dolly, Dolly Spy* (1967), he suddenly became the most talked-about author in town. That year *Publishers Weekly* wrote about the novel: "A kinky, cool mod flare that is outrageously entertaining . . . If you appreciate clever plotting, plenty of excitement, sex at its most uninhibited, a dollop or two of explicit sadism, Adam Diment is a name to remember."

Except he wasn't, and Diment is almost totally forgotten about these days. He wrote three more books, *The Great Spy Race* and *The Bang Bang Birds*, both published in 1968, and *Think Inc.*, which appeared in 1971. After which he completely disappeared from public view.

Diment's novels, while entertaining romps through the swinging sixties, appear hugely dated now; they're peppered with enough of the era's casual sexism and racism to make the James Bond novels seem as if they were written by Andrea Dworkin. This passage from the *Bang Bang Birds* is a case in point:

> Despite her lovely body it was her face which had me hooked. I do not belong to that philistine philosophy which propounds the 'put a sack over their heads and they're all the same' nonsense. I like to watch something pretty and interesting when collecting my oats, and her face is certainly that. At present she was doing a languorous chameleon change from perplexed to pout.

Or this from *The Dolly, Dolly Spy*:

> She was wearing her latest acquisition, bought in a boutique in King's Road which is a cross between an Eastern bazaar and a rugger scrum. It was very short and covered with overlapping

Adam Diment and friends, London, late 60s

blue and yellow flowers. Over her heart, which was almost visible because it was as low at the breast as it was short at the thighs, was a bright pink heart . . . as she was so brown, she had given up wearing stockings. Veronica was about as naked as you can get these days without being nicked for indecency.

The books were all thrillers featuring a reluctant spy called Philip McAlpine. The sex-hungry hero was suspiciously similar in appearance to the writer, and Diment was evidently quite happy for this blurred confusion to continue, especially given the character's marijuana smoking and the preponderance of girls.

Fleet Street seemed genuinely intrigued by the similarity between hero and author; the 'Atticus' column in the *Sunday Times* noted: "Adam Diment is 23; his hero, Philip McAlpine, is based on himself. That is to say he's tall, good-looking, with a taste for fast cars, planes, girls and pot." While the *Daily Mirror* wrote, "McAlpine is the most modern hero in years. He's hip, he's hard, he likes birds and, sometimes, marijuana."

On the inside cover of the 1969 edition of *The Bang Bang Birds* it says: At present *The Dolly, Dolly Spy* is being filmed with David Hemmings as

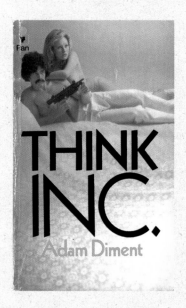

The Bang Bang Birds
(Pan, 1969)

The Great Spy Race
(Bantam, 1968)

Think Inc.
(Pan, 1971)

Philip McAlpine. A Stanley Canter/Desmond Elliott production for release by United Artists. David Hemmings was at the peak of his career at this point. *Blow Up* had premiered in October 1967 and both *The Charge of the Light Brigade* and *Barbarella* were released in 1968. The Diment film evidently came to nothing—whether filming ever took place, or was halted halfway through, nobody seems to remember, although pictures exist of Diment with David Hemmings and one of the producers, Desmond Elliott.

After publishing his final novel, *Think Inc.*, Adam Diment vanished without trace. Well, almost. In 2008 a few documents relating to Adam Diment (F.A. Diment) were released by the US National Archives, including two anonymous letters written in March 1969 to the Bank of England's Department of Exchange Control. The letters accuse Adam Diment of some kind of currency swindle involving the export of $2,400 which had been paid by the film producer Stanley Canter; one letter insinuates that it was related to some kind of drug deal.

There seems to be no clue about whether the purported currency swindle had anything to do with the non-completion of the film of *The Dolly, Dolly Spy*, or was the cause of Diment's disappearance. One of the letters does however impart the important detail that Adam Diment, despite what he told *Town*, never made the move to the King's Road: according to the anonymous informant, he was still living at 28 Tregunter Road—in tight-pink-trousers-fearing Fulham.

Since this piece on Diment first appeared in 2011 on the website *Another Nickel in the Machine*, there have been many comments from various readers. Initially people presumed that 'Adam Diment' was just a publisher's construct, but slowly people who knew Adam started to come out of the woodwork. One remembered Adam's glamorous girlfriend Susie Mandrake. Another remembered him driving at breakneck speed through the Knightsbridge underpass and that he drank, along with the rest of the 'Chelsea Set', at the Markham Arms on the King's Road, next to the Mary Quant shop. And some of these comments, from people who have seen him relatively recently, suggest that Adam Diment is alive, maybe living in Kent with his wife. He's just happy to stay out of the limelight.

ROBERT BAKER

THE CARNABY STREET SPY

The 60s spy boom, inspired by the James Bond movies, reached its peak in 1965. After that, people were looking for the next big thing, and one way to achieve that was to distance your product from Bond as much as you could. After all, Bond worked for the government. He took orders from *the Man*.

One of the most successful anti-Bonds of the late 60s was a sandy-haired character called Philip McAlpine, the creation of author, Adam Diment. McAlpine worked for an outfit called 6 (NC/NAC), which was an offshoot of MI6. But unlike Bond, McAlpine was not a willing spy. He was a hash user, and when he bought his last block, he chiselled off a small portion and sold it to his younger sister. Even though it was only a small quantity, this made him a drug peddler, and as such he could be sent to prison for three years. The head of 6 (NC/NAC), a man named Rupert Quine (often referred to as **Quine the Swine**), assures him that through his contacts, he can arrange for the prison sentence to be extended to five years. So McAlpine is blackmailed into working for the organization.

> **Now I knew what the threat was and I knew I was going to have to work for this man. I sat there staring at the little block of hash and nibbling the inside of my cheek with frustration.**
>
> **Hash smoking was a small vice I picked up at University, way back, when it was the ultimate debauched experience and Acid was something jilted lovers still threw in each other's faces. I smoke it because it makes a change from alcohol, I like mild hallucinations and not waking up with a hang-over. It is non-narcotic, but whether or not it leads you on to the hang up drugs I don't know. I've never itched for the hypo yet. I suppose the probability of this happening is about the same as the first, innocent glass of Cypriot sherry ending one up under Waterloo Bridge taking meths straight from the bottle.**
>
> **Either way, Hash, like booze, is best hit not too often, too hard or too young. Unless you like life anaesthetized . . .**

Put simply, in McAlpine, we have a drug-taking Carnaby Street hipster who is forced to work for the authorities, a very different creature to the stiff militaristic duty-bound character of James Bond.

Diment is somewhat of an enigma, disappearing into the ether. There has even some speculation that he was not even a real person, but rather a house name for several authors. When he burst onto the scene in the mid to late 60s he was heralded as the hippest thing since the Beatles. The author biography at the start of his last book, *Think Inc.* (1971), states that he "went to live for a period in India, where he studied at Ashram Aurobindo. He now lives in Zurich and is at work on another novel." That fifth novel never saw the light of day, at least not credited to Adam Diment.

The first book in the McAlpine quartet, *The Dolly, Dolly Spy* (1967), is fast-paced and well-written, with tongue firmly in cheek. While not written as out-and-out comedy, it can read that way now because it uses a lot of 60s jargon, like 'luv', 'lovey', 'baby', etc.

The story starts with McAlpine trying to land a plane in Rhodesia. McAlpine is working as a pilot for a shady airline called International Charter. His passenger is some kind of politician or revolutionary who intends to shake things up a bit. Therefore they are not greeted with open arms when they try to land. In fact, they are fired on. McAlpine pulls up and they divert to a secondary airfield. On the return leg of the journey, McAlpine recalls how he got into this caper.

The plot culminates with McAlpine collecting a renegade Nazi named Dettman. Rather than fly him to the pre-arranged destination, McAlpine is to deliver the Nazi to his superior. Of course, complications ensue.

The story is told in a very relaxed and casual first-person style. It is almost as if you had bumped into the character at a bar and he was now telling you his tale, at several points stepping out of the narrative to address the reader directly. And this works. It makes the story seem real. The author also manages to juggle a multitude of flashbacks as the story progresses. However, at no point does the time or place in the narrative become confusing. Toward the end, the story has a few twists, one rather predictable, telegraphed from the beginning, but the next quite unique.

In the second book, *The Great Spy Race* (1968), Philip McAlpine is once again coerced into doing something he doesn't want to do by Quine. This time it is to compete in the Great Spy Race, an event organised by a retired super-spy named Peters. Peters's prize for the winning competitor is a list of names and locations of all the Red Chinese agents in the Far East. Of course, every spy agency in the world wants the list, so the competition is fierce. Peters explains the rules:

"While I have tried to individualize targets as far as possible, you may find other competitors after the same objective. This should enliven the early stages of the race. One other rule; should you wish to extract information from any person you will kindly do so without the use of truth-serum, mind-benders or any other combination of drugs. You will stick to the tried if not proven methods developed during earlier and less chemically inclined eras."

This little gem really sent me cold. I couldn't torture a bed bug—I just haven't got it in me. While extracting information through LSD and scopolamine is right up my street. Painless betrayal with pleasant dreams thrown in. By this time, any pleasure I might have received from either the food or the luscious Lallia had evaporated like spilt ether. I was frankly horrified at the prospect of going up against the best the rest of the world had entered. I am a coward and yet again I made an oath to get square with Rupert Quine who had dropped me in all this.

The third book, possibly the weakest in the series, was *The Bang Bang Birds* (1969) which found McAlpine investigating a chain of aviary themed clubs which believe in sex as an art form, and are staffed by titular 'Bang Bang Birds'. The final book in the series, *Think Inc.* finds the reluctant spy in central Italy and out of a job, hiding under an assumed name after he botched his last mission and was promptly dropped by 6 (NC/NAC). But an ex-spy is a nuisance, so his ex-boss Rupert Quine, tries to have him killed.

McAlpine explains the pitfalls of being a free agent:

Despite the money I had conned out of 6 (NC/NAC)—may their loathsome name live long in the anus of infamy—I would soon be broke. One of the less amusing aspects of my dismissal from the department had been the freezing of most of my assets which were not as well hidden as I had thought. Ever since devaluation and the gold rush those Swiss banks have become too bloody cooperative for my liking. It made me gnash my rodent fangs with rage to imagine Rupert's slimy vassals collaring my hard-earned gelt.

The question of defection was answered when I realized how little I had to sell. I was, when employed, basically a humble operator in the field, and a simple bit man, and none of the highly saleable esoterica of future plans and policy, which they argued about at such prissy length in London, ever came my way. And even if the Russkies took me on, after spieling the few goodies I knew it would be a file clerk's job on pay an English typist would turn down, and living with a family in Moscow. They'd never give me a place of my own; and with that climate and those ghastly Moscow birds it was out of the question.

McAlpine ends up being discovered and working for a criminal named Faustas. As with all the McAlpine books, the story is fast paced, filled with dry humour, and has a high old time thumbing its nose at authority and authority figures. But as Diment only wrote a book a year, rather than cranking out two, three or even four a year like some of his colleagues, by this, the fourth year, his countercultural zing had been diluted by competitors all vying for the same shelf space—James Eastwood's Anna Zordan series, James Yardley's Kiss Darling series, and even the Callan series, written by James Mitchell. Each of these series have one thing in common, and that is their heroes or heroines have been bullied, conned or blackmailed into being a spy.

The Bang Bang Birds would be the end for the wild, swinging, pot-smoking, reluctant spy Philip McAlpine.

DAVID JAMES FOSTER

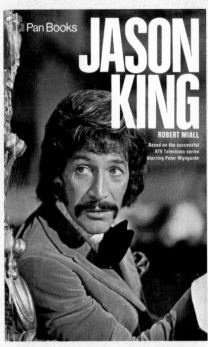

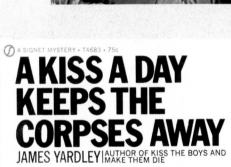

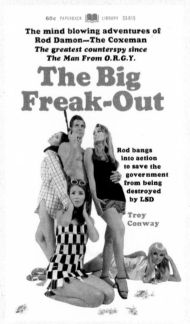

Jason King (Pan, 1972)

The Psychedelic Spy (Lancer, 1967)

The Big Freak-Out (Paperback Library, 1968)

A Kiss a Day Keeps the Corpses Away (Signet, 1971)

"WHOEVER WAS IN CONTROL WAS THE ONE TO WATCH"

An Interview with Floyd Salas

Floyd Salas grew up in a working-class, literarily in-clined family in the San Francisco Bay Area. He was in trouble with the law as a youth, but developed the ambition to be a writer while working as a library page in Oakland. He has written eight novels and several hundred poems, taught English in several major colleges and prisons, and coached boxing. Salas was also briefly involved as a screenwriter for a short-lived 2003 TV crime miniseries, *Kingpin*, the story of a Mex-ican drug trafficker and his family life.

Two of his books, *Tattoo the Wicked Cross* (1967) and *What Now My Love* (1968), occupy the blurred area between high—and lowbrow literary culture that was particularly pronounced in the late 60s and early 70s. New York's Grove Press, best known for putting out high-end alternative or edgy material, published both of them. Grove had introduced many French existentialist writers to the US market and published Malcolm X and Frantz Fanon. They were also involved in high-profile censorship fights over books such as *Lady Chatterley's Lover* and *Naked Lunch*.

Tattoo the Wicked Cross is the story of a 15-year-old prizefighter named Aaron D'Aragon, an inmate of a California prison farm. *What Now My Love* opens with the narrator, Miles, and his girlfriend, Carole, caught in a police raid on an acid factory in a house in San Francisco's Haight-Ashbury. The two of them, along with one of the dealers, flee to Mexico where they must contend with various pimps and hustlers, as well as US and Mexican undercover police. It was described by the *San Francisco Chronicle* as "a grandchild of the hardboiled school of American fic-tion whose most celebrated practitioner was James M. Cain", and the *Berkeley Barb* as "A chronicle of the dark side of the hippie phenomenon . . . direct, sometimes rough, hinged directly to the facts."

Salas was deeply involved in radical politics, includ-ing the student and anti-war politics of the 60s. *Lay My Body on the Line* (1978), told through the eyes of an idealistic teacher and ex-boxer, is set amid the San Francisco State College uprising of 1968. This lasted from November 1968 to March 1969, and was triggered by the suspension of English instruc-tor George Mason Murray, the Black Panther Party's Minister of Education, for allegedly saying at a rally that black students should bring guns to campus to protect themselves from white conservative college administrators. A student strike was followed by an official strike by members of the American Federation of Teachers. The strike, which saw a number of con-frontations with the police, is one of the longest in American higher education history and resulted in the creation of a Black Studies Department at the college.

The following interview with Salas was conducted by e-mail in early 2014.

Your first two novels were published by Grove Press, the American publisher of Henry Miller, Samuel Beck-ett, William S. Burroughs, Jean Genet, and so many of the most daring writers of the international avant-gar-de. How did you come to be published by Grove and later in their paperback imprint Evergreen Black Cat? Was it a satisfactory relationship?

My agent, Robert Lesher in New York City (NYC), said to me on the phone—long distance, of course—that he was going to send *Tattoo the Wicked Cross* to Harper. The editor at Harper communicated by mail and said that Aaron [the main character] should get in a knife fight with the Buzzer [a character in the book] at the end, and I wrote back and told him that that was a clichéd ending and that you would expect something like that to fit a Hollywood script.

I said no, man, that it wasn't like that and that the Buzzer was going to die as I wrote it. I wasn't nasty but I was steadfast. I said no, and so he then said no to the book. I think he commented on the attitude of the writer as somebody he didn't want to work with. So adios, motherfucker. He was going to guide me into writing a conventional book. Now, I didn't say it to him, I don't think, but Aaron was a little guy. The Buzzer was a big guy, a big black motherfucker and he could kick ass, he was tough, a bully. I understood when the underclass goes to jail they get revenge. They don't take shit from someone they have to cater to on the outside. Aaron, when he had a fight with the Buzzer, had to roll underneath the bunk so he wouldn't get killed, beat to death. That's how little he was. And it was autobiographical in that when I was 15, I was 4 foot 11 and weighed 90 pounds. That's small. In the next couple of years, I really grew. I grew about 6 inches.

My agent had said at one time that he didn't want to send it to an obvious press like Grove. But because of

Floyd Salas in the late 1960s

Tattoo the Wicked Cross (Grove Press, Evergreen Black Cat edition, 1968)

Floyd Salas in 2014 (photos courtesy of Floyd Salas)

my attitude toward the Harper editor, he sent it to Grove because he was sick of me. I just threw away a big-money prize by being too authoritarian, I guess he could have said, in a typical first-novelist response. So he went to the obvious place, and lo and behold, the Grove Press editor on the West Coast was Don Allen, who was very instrumental in the publishing world and the primary North Beach figure in terms of publishing. And he liked it right away. And they promised they wouldn't change one word of it. They were going to stand by me, instead of being mad at me, like the Harper editor.

Was it a satisfactory relationship? Don Allen and I had a good relationship at first. He was just right for me because he was dealing with those beat generation poets who wrote about drugs and crime, too. And [Allen] Ginsberg was a well-known drug user. I could have said fiend, because that's how mainstream society looked at drug use in the 60s. So Don tried to be my editor. "I'll be your editor from now on and we won't change a word of what you've written". It was a great relationship. We were at his place near North Beach, and we hugged, because as far as I was concerned, I had the perfect editor for my work. It was a chance to move in publishing circles.

I had a big breakthrough in my poetry writing during this time. [Before,] there had been metaphorical, complex statements, images, etc—in a sense, traditional literary writing. I felt that my poetry was too traditional in its speech, so I decided to just write poems without giving any thought at all to whether it was poetic or normal speech. So at the time I am speaking about I was living in Bolinas, at a house by the sea, and it cost me $75 a month. It was bare, with no furniture, and cold, though I had a lovely young 19-year-old to share it with me, Juliet Calabi, who had writing talent. And I think that's probably why I was

attracted to her. I discovered I'm one of those people who gets attracted to people with talent, as far as girls are concerned. I love those who make lovely art out of their feelings. When I first read her initial work in my class, I thought she was really good in terms of the beauty of her language and the ease with which she used it. She was vibrant. She had energy.

At this time, I sent Don Allen a poem based upon this breakthrough in the writing of my poetry. And the main difference was that the art form of traditional poetry came first previously, and now only the statement itself was primary and first in all regards. So I sent him a poem based upon this. At that time, I think we were communicating by mail because I was out in Bolinas and he was in San Francisco. So I sent him a poem called 'Steve Nash'. And there was no answer. Now I was living in different places in California. I said, "Did you get the poem?" And I think he said "Yes" and then he didn't say another word, as if he was putting it down. To me, that was my breakthrough poem, brand new in form and language:

Out of a tent of wind
came a tuxedoed scarecrow
dancing for me
with hinged limbs of broom

to:

STEVE NASH
HOMOSEXUAL TRANSIENT

Executed San Quentin gas chamber
August 21st 1959
for killing eleven men
and a little boy

This is about the killer who gets away
This is it from the viewpoint of the murderer

Dedicated to Tony Curtis and the Boston
Strangler
and to Johnny Weissmuller
and Jane
with thanks to Jack Micheline

"There are much worse things to be
than a swinger of birches." Robert Frost

I am a big cat
six-four
long stringy body
with sloping shoulders and big hands
hands that hang down like small paddles
like balls of weight with big knuckles
big hands
I can spread around a basketball
knobby hands
from having to work all my life
in canneries
and on constructions jobs
out on the farm picking grapes
or prunes
bussing dishes

So I never sent him another poem as long as I lived because I thought he was a phony motherfucker and a Federal Bureau of Investigation [FBI] stool pigeon. Grove Press was a perfect publisher for this material and he played that game on me. So I then went to Europe for a year, and never wrote him once from Europe, and wrote about 20 or 30 poems and never sent him one, not one. Now I recall he did say he didn't get it and I didn't believe it. I thought he was lying.

So all the time I was in Europe and writing those poems, I didn't send him one poem, not one letter, nothing. I was in Paris, London, etc. I could have met all those French poets and English poets, but he was a phony motherfucker, an FBI fink stool pigeon, that's what he was. The FBI decided what happened to me and they chilled the relationship with Don Allen. And when I came back from Europe one year later, to Berkeley, I get a phone call and it was from him, Don Allen, and he invited me to his house for some literary get-together. We found the poem on the Internet years later. He'd had it all along.

What inspired your 1968 novel What Now My Love? *How much of the book is autobiographical?*
I think the book was inspired by the same impulse that led me to change the style of my poetry writing: to catch the tempo of the times, which was a healthy revolt, however civilized, of the downtrodden masses.

How much of it was autobiographical? All of it, in a way, meaning it springs from autobiographical experiences. But like all true fiction, it is dramatized and shaped to make an artistic whole. Different parts of the book are autobiographical. I really did have a girlfriend named Carole and she really was tall. I said six feet, she said five ten. So it's based upon that relationship, but more than that. I had been in Mexico, in Tijuana with a couple of my buddies on a weekend jaunt from Los Angeles, having some fun in a famous Mexican border town, TJ [Tijuana], which it was commonly referred to among hip Americans.

So me and my buddies went down there and went to score some pot. No problem, but one younger blond-headed dude who was about 18 or 19 wanted to score some smack. Me and the guy who was actually going to be my brother-in-law, John Gamborini, a poet himself, weren't into the heavy drug thing but it ended up with us trying to get the smack for this punk, us being robbed by some Mexican hustlers, a chance to rip off some rich Americans. So we ended up getting ripped off by these two dudes and fighting them back and getting our goodies back and having to fight them off and some cab drivers who came to help them, at the end of a mile-long line of American tourists trying to get back across the border in the United States. And when they came after us, I ran out them to fight them. The other two dudes froze. I had to fight them off but got held up by the same Mexican cop who had ripped us off on a main street in TJ a couple of hours earlier. So that was a true experience that I dramatized into art by making that little blond spoiled bastard into a tall, spoiled young woman, Carole.

That's art. Now Carole and I had had an affair of a sort, though we were never really committed to each other so I decided to write about this exciting experience in Mexico in which I'd been held up by a Mexican cop. So it sprang from true experience that I shaped into a dramatic whole called *What Now My Love*. It should have been a bestseller. The acid factory bust was taken from a newspaper article.

How long did What Now My Love *take to write? Where were you and what were you doing when you* wrote it? What was your involvement in the hippie scene?

Ah, this is fun. *Love* was my second novel following the four and a half years I'd spent writing *Tattoo* and I didn't want that enslavement anymore at that time. So I decided to write something that wouldn't enslave me for years. I wrote it in six weeks, and I did it by just enjoying telling a story with pleasure, not the monkish commitment that I had made to my first novel.

At that time, I was living in San Francisco with some buddies. There were two houses right next to each other and everybody was smoking pot now. I think it was about 1966–67, and all my friends would be there. I wrote every day. I got up early every day. I would get up at seven and take a shower and begin to write. I did that every day. Now a couple of people that I lived with and around, one was a writer, one was an artist—a pretty fine artist, too—and they smoked pot every day. I lived up on the top floor, a third floor area. They would come up, and we would all smoke and talk, and I would walk over to my typewriter (I wrote standing up with my typewriter on a crate about four and half feet high) and write some words, then go back and hang out and talk and smoke some more pot, and go back and type some more words. I was enjoying writing this one rather than writing as if I was sentenced to hard labor. So I wrote it high in six weeks. It was sure fun to write a draft in six weeks instead of six months. Then I sent it to Don Allen in San Francisco, and he really liked it. I went to see him and said, "I hope Grove Press takes it", and he said, "They'll take it". I succeeded in what I set out to do in writing the second novel, which was to switch from the formal style of the first novel to the freewheeling beat-generation hippie style type of living and writing.

Tell me about your involvement in the radical politics of San Francisco and Berkeley in the late 60s. What were your observations of the time?

Me and a student by the name of Don AuClaire started the Student Peace Union at San Francisco State, I think early 60s, maybe 1961 or 1962, to oppose the hydrogen bomb. And that brought me in contact with other peace-loving, young, mainly students and other ongoing peace groups that included old-time commies and young idealists, mainly from the universities, and some old-time professional reds.

I recall, later, when the Panthers and the Brown Berets [the radical Chicano/Mexican-American community organization active during the 1960s] were doing their thing, as well as the old-time radical groupies, I did not trust them. I felt that all of them, every one of them, bar none, would cooperate with whatever suited their intentions, in whatever situation might come up. So when I would appear at some of these radical things that were happening in the late 60s, I would oppose not just the administration in these strikes but whatever group or students or whoever were seeking control. So I would go to these meetings, spontaneous meetings, not formal, and not take either side, and one young student leader said, "He's a Trotskyite", and that's really what I basically was. Whoever was in control was the one to watch, no matter what side they said they were on.

By the time of the 60s, one of the reasons why I was so critical was that I didn't trust any of them. But I was willing to work with them if they fought for freedom. So I was called a Trotskyite by one guy and by golly, I really was with Trotsky on most issues, if I thought about them. In going to Europe to pursue my own roots, all my great-grandparents came from Europe in the first half of the 19th century, from Spain, France, Belgium and the anarchist movement was strong in Spain, I think Barcelona, and I realized one of the reasons I was like I was, a dissenter. I basically was an anarchist. I was against all authority that was heavy-handed of any size. All this was the basis for my third novel, *Lay My Body on the Line* (1978), about the San Francisco State student strike.

Now my inclusion in politics drew the attention of the FBI so I came under surveillance. I was a dangerous dude. I not only smoked pot but I objected to authoritarianism of any kind.

How hard was it to stand aside from the drug culture of the late 60s and write about what was going on? Did you want to stand aside?

There were two aspects of the drug culture. One was the drug dealers and crime, and the other where those who used drugs simply for pleasure and harmony. (When I was in the nuthouse [California's Napa Hospital after an altercation involving the police], the doctors asked me why I smoked pot, and I said, "Because it makes me love everybody.") I am an artist, a writer, who wants to make a better society. In the meantime, although I could have fun and great friendship with smokers, I always had to fear getting busted by the cops of any kind. I myself had found the cultural milieu of being able to smoke pot without having to be involved in crime and going to prison for it. So I was able from that essentially safe position of being both in and out of the drug culture, even though I had to remain on guard, forever and still do. The same attitude as that time.

What was the response of critics to Tattoo the Wicked Cross *and* What Now My Love*? Was there any reaction from within the countercultural scene?*
Tattoo created a great positive reaction. It was first-rate literature. *What Now My Love* was called "a stunner." So in that sense I was riding high. The *Kansas City Star* said *Tattoo* was an autobiographical rendition of my time in a juvenile prison facility, essentially. And I wrote back and told him that it wasn't about my life in reform school, because I had never been in reform school and I'd never seen a reform school. Critics wrote that *What Now My Love* was about the dark side of the hippie phenomenon and compared me to James M. Cain.

One of the most interesting aspects of What Now My Love *is the class tension between the characters. Carole is obviously middle-class, and so is the dealer, Sam. In contrast, the narrator Miles is part-Hispanic, has working-class origins, and got into academia via a boxing scholarship. Unlike middle-class Carole, he's also brushed up against the law before. Is this something you were very conscious of wanting to inject into the book? Is the class and racial tension in the novel something that you felt yourself in countercultural circles in the 60s? If so, how did this manifest?*
I did not feel any class or racial tension in counterculture circles in the 60s. None. Racism was not big. And race or racism was not at all a factor in *What Now My Love*. Not between the characters. What there is, is a contrasting of the poverty of Mexico, TJ, as opposed to the comfort of the hero and his girl who were there in an MG, [who] don't work, don't sweat out paychecks.

One of the reviews in the *Berkeley Barb* was a put-down—because the characters were obviously middle class, could afford to drive MGs and not work and were therefore bourgeois . . . [but] it's an economic class distinction; the racial tension is with the Mexicans themselves, who are poorer than the Americans, particularly these young hippie types who lived well off the well-being of their parents.

ANDREW NETTE & MATTHEW ASPREY GEAR

What Now My Love—Floyd Salas
(Grove Press, 1969)

The counterculture and protest politics of the late 60s and early 70s resulted in some fascinating pulp fiction. *What Now My Love* by Floyd Salas, published in 1969, is a good example.

The book opens with the narrator, Miles, and his girlfriend, Carole, visiting an acid factory in a house off San Francisco's Haight-Ashbury. Carole is immediately seduced by the excitement of being in proximity to such a large amount of drugs. Miles just wants to score and get out. Although he lectures in creative writing at one of the local universities, Miles is part Hispanic, has working-class origins, and got into academia via a boxing scholarship. Unlike middle-class Carole, he's also brushed up against the law before. As he tells Carole:

> **"You've never been through this before, baby. I have. I tried to score some grass down in West Oakland one time when most of the college kids didn't smoke it, and you had to go down to the underworld to get it."**

He nearly gets busted, setting in train

> **a five year run from them up and down California and even down to Mexico City, where they didn't let up, and tried to set me up every way they could, and finally got to my family through my brother-in-law, and finally even my wife, until there wasn't a person in the whole world who didn't try to help them bust me.**

The drug factory has psychedelic posters on the walls, the dealers are wearing Nehru shirts, and Herb Albert is on the record player. As evidenced by the surly biker bodyguard in a cut-off Levi denim jacket, there's also a palpable feeling of paranoia. One of the dealers, Sam, is particularly cautious of the new arrivals.

Everyone is right to be paranoid, because the police raid the place, shots are fired, and Miles and Carole end up fleeing with Sam to Mexico. They cross the border without incident, but any hopes Miles has of getting to Mazatlan as quickly as possible are derailed by Sam and Carole's desire to score drugs for the journey. The second half of *What Now My Love* chronicles these efforts. Miles is already fearful of arrest and his paranoia only gets worse as they try to navigate the

B-305-N

What Now My Love
a novel by Floyd Salas
"Brilliant..." –Los Angeles Times

hellish world of pimps, hustlers, and US and Mexican undercover police, all of whom appear to be on the take. Class tensions and unresolved sexual frustrations increase with every misstep.

It is a well-written book, with some great passages. A description of Miles and Carole having sex in the front of their car, as Sam lies drunk and passed out in the back, is particularly evocative.

ANDREW NETTE

I didn't blame him for being uptight. The word went down Haight Street like the wind when somebody had a new stash of acid. There'd be pushers on every block, whispering the name of the new brand in your ear when you walked by, some big dealers giving away free samples, and the heat would be by in a few days at the latest. So he better be empty or clean by then or know everybody he sold to personally or he'd be busted within a week. I didn't want to be around when it happened either, but couldn't leave because instead of making her buy so we could split, Carole got hung up on the capping and was having so much fun making the illegal dope scene that she teased Sam by pretending to lick the powder off her fingers.

Dress Her in Indigo—John D. MacDonald (Gold Medal, 1969)

Such was its pervasiveness that by the late 60s even popular mainstream writers working at the time touched on the counterculture in their books or used it as a setting for their stories. This is certainly the case with John D. MacDonald's 1969 novel *Dress Her in Indigo*.

MacDonald got his start writing for pulp magazines in the late 1940s, and rode the paperback boom of the 50s and early 60s. He authored over 60 books, a number of which were adapted for television and the big screen, including *The Executioners* (1957), which was filmed as *Cape Fear* in 1962 (and again by Martin Scorsese in 1991). MacDonald is best known for creating the fictional private investigator Travis McGee, who featured in 21 of his books, including *Dress Her in Indigo*.

McGee is hired by Harlan Bowie, a rich, self-absorbed Florida businessman to investigate the last months in the life of his daughter, Beatrice or 'Bix' as she was known. Harlan last saw Bix before she headed to Mexico, very much against his wishes, with a bunch of friends and $20,000 of her late mother's money. She subsequently died in a car accident near Oaxaca, southern Mexico.

McGee, accompanied by an old friend, Meyer, heads down to the scene of the accident. The paperwork relating to her death seems in order and there doesn't seem much to do except eat, drink, and observe Oaxaca's bizarre expatriate US culture, a collection of hippie runaways and bored, rich people.

But his suspicions are aroused when he discovers all the people Bix originally travelled to Mexico with are dead except Rockland (or Rocko), the leader of the group. Rocko is a mean drunk and sexual predator who has previous form smuggling narcotics into the United States from Mexico. The Summer of Love is well and truly over, as McGee uncovers the real nature of the last months of Bix's life, a sordid tale of sexual abuse and drug addiction.

Dress Her in Indigo is a well-written hardboiled crime novel and an evocative portrayal of one aspect of the decaying counterculture. Affluent Americans of all ages fled to Mexico to escape the meaninglessness of their lives. Once there, some needed money and had little choice but to smuggle narcotics to get by. McGee's age makes him a 'square' and he doesn't pretend to understand or particularly sympathize with the young runaways. In keeping with Woody Haut's description in *Pulp Culture and the Cold War* (1995) of McGee's character as "pulp culture's most humane, if not realistic, private detective", the story largely avoids judgment and stereotyping. Interestingly, as part of this, the Mexican police are not portrayed as corrupt. They are helpful and genuinely concerned, both about the welfare of the young runaways and the impact of their freewheeling on the local culture.

ANDREW NETTE

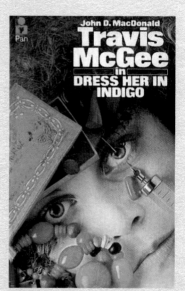

Dress Her in Indigo (Pan, 1969)
Dress Her in Indigo (Pan, 1972)
Dress Her in Indigo (Gold Medal, 1969)

It was a group of four young men and three girls. The college-age men were wearing faded Mexican work shirts, bleached khakis. The girls wore shorts with bright cotton Indian blouses, and the boys were extravagantly bearded, long-haired. This, as Meyer pointed out, was a clear indication they had been in Mexico for a long time. The Government had long since closed the border to what were called 'heepees', so the shorn locks and whiskers had to be regrown south of the border.

clockwise from top left:
Acid Temple Ball (Olympia Press, 1969)
Acid Temple Ball (Olympia Press, 1972)
Acid Temple Ball (Freeway Press, 1973)

GIRL GANGS, BIKER BOYS, AND REAL COOL CATS

FROM *ACID TEMPLE BALL* TO *WIMMEN'S COMIX*
Sharon Rudahl's Adventures in the Underground

Originating in Paris in 1953, Olympia Press and its founder, Maurice Girodias, rapidly built a reputation for controversy by being the first to publish such works as Vladimir Nabokov's *Lolita* (1955), Terry Southern and Mason Hoffenberg's *Candy* (1958), and William Burroughs's *Naked Lunch* (1959).

Obelisk Books, the company owned by Girodias's British-born father, Jack Kahane, had in previous decades similarly dealt with English versions of books banned or censored elsewhere, including works by Henry Miller and Anaïs Nin. Following in his footsteps, Girodias translated and reprinted classics by the likes of the Marquis de Sade, as well as publishing new works covering a wide range of sexual practices. Olympia also released avant-garde and literary works, often with sexual and contentious themes, by the likes of Alexander Trocchi, Samuel Beckett, Georges Bataille and J.P. Donleavy.

Hounded by the censors, Girodias moved to the US in 1964. Maintaining his interest in experimental and innovative writing, while seeking a level of prurience that would satisfy his customer base, he continued to publish works by writers with connections to artistic and countercultural milieux. Amongst these were titles from women such as Diane di Prima, whose *Memoirs of a Beatnik* came out in 1969, and Valerie Solanas, whose *SCUM Manifesto* was issued in 1968.

Artist Sharon Rudahl, writing under the name of Mary Sativa, produced two works for Olympia Press, *Acid Temple Ball* (1969) and *The Lovers' Crusade* (1971). The latter was a medieval piece, but her debut, narrated by a young woman with a voracious appetite for sex, drugs and good times, was a solidly countercultural affair. Unusual in the erotic and pulp fields for its consensual approach to sex, as well as the author's goofy take on the 60s underground, *Acid Temple Ball* was initially issued as part of the publisher's Traveller's Companion series.

In the following interview, Rudahl discusses working with Girodias, as well as her later experiences in the San Francisco underground comix scene that gave rise to a new wave of artists and publishers during the late 1960s and early 1970s.

When did you first become involved in alternative and political scenes?
I grew up in Virginia and Maryland, quite close to Washington, DC. As a child in the 1950s I remember seeing water fountains at the train stations designated for 'Whites Only' or 'Coloreds Only,' with the latter being really corroded and horrible. I had this visceral feeling that something was very wrong.

The first demonstration I took part in was when Kennedy was president. It was the first major demonstration in Washington since the Rosenbergs had been executed [for espionage in 1953]. The protest was against atmospheric nuclear weapons tests. There had been lots of articles in the newspapers accessible to people like me about the dangers of radiation and yet people were afraid to speak out. Most of the demonstrators came from New York. I was 13 or 14 and heard about it on the radio. I felt a passionate desire to join in, and took the two-hour bus trip to do so. It was a wonderful experience.

What brought you to New York's East Village in the 60s? Can you tell us about the flavour of the area at the time?
I went to New York in 1965 to attend the art school at Cooper Union. It was a 100 per cent free scholarship college which had an engineering department and an art department. I had read an article about it and with my political sensibilities I thought, "A free college in New York, that'll be great, I'll be with the working class"—but of course the real working class didn't let its children go to art school.

It had no dorm so I had to find myself a place to live. It was in the part of the Lower East Side that was just becoming the East Village when I moved there. It was almost like a science-fiction story. The first time I saw a head shop [a store selling smoking implements, posters and other countercultural paraphernalia] on the street I thought it was like something from a Philip K. Dick novel. They were selling marijuana pipes and had lots of pink and green and psychedelic-coloured things in the windows. I felt like a spaceship had landed from another planet. I liked that planet.

This would have been just around the time the counterculture was emerging?
Well, with me it was like I was already that way and then everyone caught up. It had been clear to me that there shouldn't be separate water fountains, that bras were uncomfortable, that repressing sex was fascist, and that marijuana was wonderful. Suddenly, instead

of being a loner there were people all around me thinking the same things. Unfortunately it didn't last, and it hasn't happened since. I'm just as alienated now as when I was a young teeny [laughter].

When did you first come across books by Olympia Press? How did you come to decide that you could write for them yourself?
I first encountered Olympia Press through them publishing writers like Nabokov and Henry Miller. I was aware of them as a revolutionary force concerning the sexual instinct. I never thought about writing for them until I had to cover my living expenses. I had worked doing childcare and then as a file clerk.

At the same time, as part of general experimentation, I read some porn. I liked the idea of porn, but I would just start to be getting turned on when there would be something really violent or nasty, or someone would say something really awful about women, which would break the mood. So I decided it would be good if someone wrote a porn book that would be fun for people like me to read.

I also wanted to make some money, so I quite cold-bloodedly counted out the pages in one of Olympia's books and counted out the chapters and wrote an outline. I'd come home from my clerk job, do my homework, and write my pages. One innovation was to write it all in first-person present tense, which was my attempt to show what the hippie experience was like. When I had six chapters and an outline, I dropped them off at Olympia Press.

Shortly after I got a call from Girodias, which was very exciting. I went to see him in his office in midtown and he was very charming and debonair. Instead of taking this attitude that, "You're going to turn out trash for money", he said, "You're my latest discovery and you're going to be like Nabokov and Miller." I felt quite glamorised by it all and gained a very small amount of notoriety around the scene. I also made enough money to quit being a file clerk, that was the best thing.

Olympia always ripped off their writer's royalties and I never received any additional royalties beyond the initial advance. The book sold something like 100,000 copies and was sold all over Europe. In the US it was sold in regular bookstores and was available in a lot of places where ordinary porn wasn't.

Acid Temple Ball details the sexual adventures of a young woman whose various encounters take place under the influence of drugs such as marijuana, am-

phetamines and mescaline. *The book is initially set in New York, but then the characters take a road trip to California's Bay Area, where they soak up the more relaxed atmosphere and attend a Be-In.*
The book was marketed as a memoir, but wasn't really. Whatever experiences I'd had informed it. I'd had no experience of hard drugs, but some of the others I had had many times. Many of the characters were based on people I knew. Friends and acquaintances, or somebody I saw on the subway who was handsome, were recruited as characters.

I was happy with the book, but I wasn't trying to convince anyone it was a literary work or anything. I basically sat down every night after doing the dishes and thought, "What position or drug haven't I written about yet? Who amongst my acquaintances can I recruit to be in this?" I've always been quite disciplined about my work. It's sort of a cliché that everybody has a novel in them, but I think it's true that everyone has at least one erotic novel in them. By drawing on your own experiences, and those that you would like to have, I think that almost anyone could patch one together.

Did Olympia edit or shape the book at all? Diane di Prima has talked about how she was pushed to increase the sexual content in Memoirs of a Beatnik.
That wasn't an issue for me because I wanted to write in the erotic genre, but to do it in a form that would address my complaints about the genre as it existed at that time. I will say to my credit that I had feminist friends who were generally totally opposed to pornography but told me they loved my book [laughter]. So I think I accomplished what I set out to do.

Looking back on those times, one thing I think we had wrong was that we believed because fascists repressed sex, releasing repressions would help lead to an anarchist or socialist paradise. It turned out sex could be co-opted as much as anything else. Not knowing that at the time, I thought that changes in attitudes to sex could make people less competitive, less interested in material things, less interested in going to war.

The book was published exactly as I wrote it. I think the only limits Olympia would have imposed would have been if I had become boring by going on too much about politics. I had to work in the politics and philosophy around the sex and drugs. With genre writing, whether it's detective novels or porn or the Martians landing, you have to follow the conventions and do the best you can.

Did you have any input into the cover or the title or your pseudonym?

No, none at all. In France it was sold as *Une saison en paradis*. This was a play on Rimbaud: in English it translates to *A Season in Paradise*, after his *A Season in Hell*. I much preferred that title. I liked the German edition because it had classic German typography [*laughter*]. I just wanted my pseudonym to be Sativa, as a reference to marijuana, but Girodias added Mary. I would never give myself the name Mary.

What was your involvement in the second Mary Sativa novel, The Lovers' Crusade?

After I got the money from *Acid Temple Ball*, I bought a VW bus. I had graduated from art school that year and went out to California. Girodias paid me regularly to write another book, which was a really rare thing in his business. So I had to start something. At this point I was pretty bored with writing about hippies having sex. I've always loved the Middle Ages and sort of set out to write [Ingmar Bergman's 1957 film] *The Seventh Seal* with sex scenes.

I think I had written the one erotic novel I had in me. The second one was unpleasant in that I became more violent with my characters. I was bored with them and wanted to kill them off. I didn't even know at the time whether the book had come out. I'm pretty sure that it was heavily edited and changed around.

How did you first become involved with underground newspapers? It seems like every town that was big enough to have a college or a head shop had one in the late 60s and early 70s.

Well, they really flowed out of the anti-war movement. It wasn't just publishing for fun. The first one I worked on was called *Take Over*. It was put together in a church basement underneath the offices of a left-wing anti-war group. This was in Madison, Wisconsin.

My husband and I had been to California and couldn't get any work. Eventually Girodias got sick of paying me, so we travelled to Madison because my husband, who I based a character on in *Acid Temple Ball*, got a scholarship. I ended up being an illustrator for the university but also worked on the underground paper.

Madison was a real hotbed for radicalism at the time. It was where the Army Math Research Center was blown up in 1970. SDS and the Weatherpeople were nearby in Chicago, and by this point the militancy of the movement had really amped up. I thought Wisconsin would be isolated, but there were

Sharon Rudahl in the late 1960s (above), and in the mid-70s (below)

Acid Temple Ball (Olympia, 1972)
Page from *Wimmen's Comix* #1 (1972)

always people travelling through from New York, California or Boston. The whole movement was very connected at that time.

There were different strands in the local scene. You had doctrinaire labour leftists, and feminists who were opposed to people wearing see-through clothes—I was censored once because I did a poster with naked people and men with erections. There was conflict, but when it came to the war or fighting the draft then everyone pulled together.

Whilst the paper covered a lot of politics it also had a lot of humour. It did a lot of things like [news satire organisation] *The Onion* does. Lots of stories about real figures which were basically nonsense. The *Take Over* line on reality was that there was no such thing. It was pretty extreme both artistically and politically.

When did you come to California and begin creating underground comix?

I had never thought about doing my own comics. When I moved to New York to study art it was at the height of the Op Art scene, and of people making all-white and all-black paintings. At the same time I would be coming home and reading *The East Village Other*, which had some early underground comix. I would think, "This is wonderful, I love this stuff, it makes me so happy", but it didn't occur to me until later that I could do my own comics. It just didn't seem to have anything to do with what people did in art school.

When I became involved with underground newspapers I got drafted into doing illustrations. With *Take Over* I was basically the whole art department. If we needed to do a fake ad for the marijuana dealers who had all been arrested, or put a photomontage together with a sausage machine grinding up left-wing students, then that was my job. I learned to draw straight lines and corners and do all this technical stuff I had never learnt in art school. I was only able to support myself later on as a technical artist because of that experience.

After my second or third winter in Wisconsin, where I was sleeping in an unheated attic and had a cold that wouldn't go away, I came to San Francisco and worked on *Good Times*. It was sort of similar to *Take Over*, but had lots of benefit concerts with people like Jefferson Airplane, and everyone lived in a commune. We shared cooking and childcare and put the paper together. We had a gay left-wing spiritualist commune as neighbours. It really was an experiment with a different way of living. *Good Times* was also oriented towards community organising and worked together with people like the Black Panthers. I tried to convince them that I was an artist, but they put me to work writing and taking photographs instead.

Then in San Francisco [underground comix artist] Trina Robbins recruited me to do work for *Wimmen's Comix*, and I took to it like a duck to water. There had always been this struggle between me wanting to use words and wanting to use pictures. At one point I had tried to sell Girodias a picture for a cover thinking maybe I could use my words to sell my pictures.

Trina had previously done a comic called *It Ain't Me, Babe* (1970) which I'd seen in Wisconsin. It's sad to say that even though it was exciting to see women finally doing comics, I felt it was all a bit too girly, with stuff about horses and women's romances. By the time it came to *Wimmen's Comix*, there was a little more range and more possibility to tell different stories. I loved it. It suited me perfectly.

You contributed to 12 issues of Wimmen's Comix, *which began in 1972; you also edited one. Was the series a reaction to the male dominance of the underground comix scene of the time?*
The roots of it weren't as political or feminist as people might think. A lot of it involved artists who hadn't had an opportunity to get published. There was a really wide range of opinions and backgrounds. There were mothers, there were very young women, there were lesbians, there were careerists who ended up working in animation, and so on.

Trina and I were roommates at that point, with another artist named Leslie Cabarga. We called ourselves Naturally Curly Studios. We did any work we could dredge up.

I was also doing a story for *Playgirl* magazine every month or so. One of my friends in the cartoon scene at the time, Lee Marrs, was in an airport and glancing through an issue when she read one of my stories. It was written under a pseudonym, but she immediately knew it was by me.

Once every year or two I would go to New York to try and sell work to *National Lampoon* or one of the other bigger publishers, but as far as getting published in the Bay Area, it was really a matter of who you knew. Trina has been quite right in pointing out that it was pretty much a boys' gang of buddies who printed each other.

Wimmen's Comix had a revolving editorship. Being editor involved asking lots of women to contribute and making tough decisions about what went in. In a way I didn't like being editor, because it meant turning down lots of people's work and that didn't suit me at all. I did it once and it was an interesting experience but I wouldn't want to do it again.

You've continued to create comics for the rest of your life, including contributing to publications such as Rip Off, Dope Comix, Tits & Clits, *and* Anarchy Comics, *as well as creating the graphic novel* A Most Dangerous Woman *in 2007, based on the life of pioneering anarchist Emma Goldman. What was it like being part of the San Francisco underground comix scene at the point at which it really took off in the early 70s?*
At one point we tried to have a union. I remember meeting at [underground artist] Spain Rodriguez's house. We were going to form the Cartoonists Union but it was like herding cats, no one could agree on anything. The one thing we did do together was order a whole lot of artist materials because it was meant to be cheaper, but they turned out to be incredibly shoddy and not usable at all. We did have someone talk to us about tax law, and I learnt some things that have been useful to this day. So I did learn something from the experience [*laughter*].

It was an exciting scene. Amongst the underground artists there would be parties and get-togethers. You could drop by the house of someone like Art Spiegelman, who later drew [Pulitzer Prize–winning graphic novel] *Maus*, and he would give you advice on drawing buildings or something. Everyone wandered in and out of everyone else's places checking out what they were working on. It was a great time and place to learn how to draw comics.

IAIN McINTYRE

144 Piccadilly—Samuel Fuller

(Richard W. Baron, 1971)

Samuel Fuller is primarily known as a filmmaker, but he also wrote a few books during his long career. *144 Piccadilly* is an account of a real-life event that occurred in September 1969, when members of the London Street Commune movement squatted the house named in the book's title, to the obvious consternation of the British press and establishment. Squatting in this affluent area—previous attempts had taken place in less salubrious locales—was a deliberate provocation, designed to raise the profile of the movement and their rather Marxist agenda.

Some of the events in the novel have a basis in fact. Skinheads were pictured outside the property and there was apparently a fracas when they fired airguns at the house. Some wannabe Hells Angels were in attendance and a free concert in Hyde Park took place during the period the house was occupied. However, the events that take place in the house, as well the characters, are fictitious. The key players in the action are a tough-guy American filmmaker Charley (an obvious avatar for Fuller), commune leader and pacifist Robert, his girl Molly, divisive lieutenant Peter, sexy lawyer Europa, and the Hell's Angel leader, Lover Boy, a man turned on by **weird clothes, soul food, heavy beat music and perversion**.

The falsest note in the novel is in fact Fuller's insertion of himself into the narrative in the character of Charley. A bystander when the original entry to the property was made, he joins in the squat, miraculously manages to bed the best looking girls and beat up several skinheads and Angels, all while proposing some fantastically strategic ideas to defeat the authorities on the squatting issue. Elsewhere, the drug scenes come across as unreal—Fuller seems confused about the effects of various illicit substances. The novel ends with a triumph of sorts as Charley and Robert escape the police crackdown through a back door and live to squat another day.

AUSTIN MATTHEWS

Mindblower (Olympia Press, 1972)
Memoirs of a Beatnik (Olympia Press, 1969)

144 Piccadilly (New English Library, 1972)

Suddenly a girl screamed. Two long-haired bearded youths had ripped off her clothes. When I trailed Robert through the squatters towards the scream we came upon them urinating on the panic-stricken girl. The two maniacs were dragged off.

Their false beards fell. Their long-haired wigs fell. They were bald youths.

"Skinheads!" shouted Peter.

The two Skinheads swung wildly, kicking out their feet.

"No violence!" cried Robert.

Peter and a number of burly longhairs seized and carried the two Skinheads across the drawbridge and deposited them outside the iron fence.

"You load of queers on the dole!" yelled a Skinhead.

"We'll see you run through!" shouted the second Skinhead. "We'll dust you up and put the boot in a bit!"

They vanished.

"What are Skinheads?" I said.

"Bastards," said Robert. "Bastards who enjoy beating up longhairs."

"I'd better get Lover Boy," said Peter, panting hard.

Robert turned white. "No!"

"I say we put it to a vote!" Peter insisted.

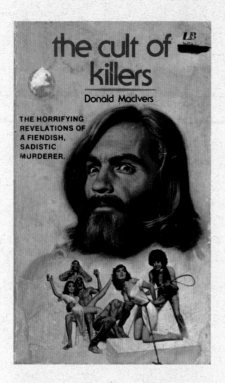

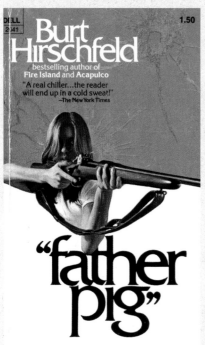

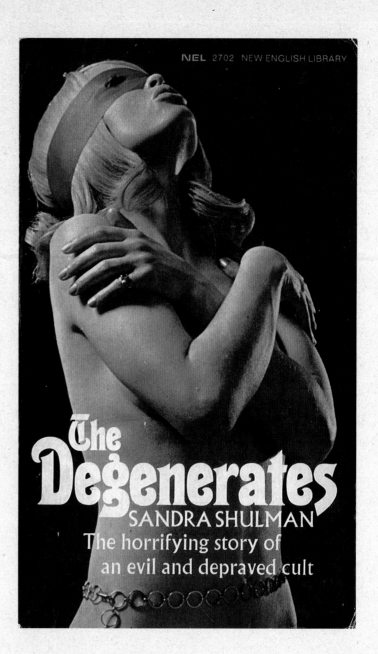

The Cult of Killers (Leisure Books, 1976)
The Degenerates (New English Library, 1970)
Father Pig (Dell, 1973)

SATANIC SLAVES AND HIPPIE DEATH CULTS
Charles Manson–Inspired Paperbacks

As happens with just about any moment when pop culture meets sudden tragedy, one of the aspects of the 1969 Tate/LaBianca murders that has always fascinated me is the way in which the case was portrayed—in either a quasi-factual or purely exploitational way—by lowbrow media.

From skid-row film producers to sleazy underground paperback publishers, the sensational aspects of the savage killings committed by members of the Manson Family—from its celebrity victims and the shattering of the 'peace and love' illusion to the LSD orgies and charisma of the Family's leader, Charles Manson—were a potent melting pot of ingredients ripe for exploitation. Low-budget movies like *The Love-Thrill Murders* (1971), *I Drink Your Blood* (1971) and *The Deathmaster* (1972) were clearly inspired by the Manson case and kept audiences in grindhouses and drive-ins entertained with lurid tales of violent, doped-up hippies on a murderous rampage.

The mass-market paperback industry also gladly fed the fear and paranoia being whipped up not just in middle-class America, but also among the rich and famous of Beverly Hills, who started electrifying their fences and arming themselves to the hilt after it was revealed that Manson kept a 'hit list' of potential celebrity targets. While mainstream books appeared covering almost every aspect of the Manson case and subsequent trial (helping to create and define the popular true crime literary genre in the process), the more salubrious publishers preferred to create fictional potboilers which used the news headlines as a springboard for an adventure far more raunchy and gaudy. The following is a selection of paperbacks that belong squarely, and quite proudly, in the latter category.

The Hippy Cult Murders—Ray Stanley
(MacFadden-Bartell, 1970)

> He was a saint to a 'family' of potheads. And he led them on a freaked-out sex-and-blood bath that picked up where the brutal Sharon Tate killings left off.

Published by MacFadden-Bartell in 1970 as a paperback original, *The Hippy Cult Murders* has as its demented saviour a psychotic guru who is somewhat prophetically known as Waco. Proclaiming himself to be the Son of Zember (the God of Fear), Waco and his long-suffering sidekick Whitey jump in their VW bus and split San Francisco for the more happening scene down in L.A., where Waco plans to recruit a family of followers while spreading the word of Zember and finding a pure young hippie chick to be his bride (not an easy task in the free-lovin' L.A. of 1969).

The physical and psychological similarities between Waco and Manson are obvious:

> Waco was aware of the power within himself. And he knew the key to it was his eyes. His voice was soft, his manner quiet. He had the ability to gather girls around him. He had once been told by a girl that he reminded her a lot of Jesus Christ, with that bushy beard, those piercing blue eyes and the way he acted—like tolerant, like everyone came to him for wisdom, like they wanted him to tell them some great truth. The girl had been young and easy to impress. She had offered no resistance when he told her to undress.

Likewise, the character of Whitey is clearly drawn from key Manson acolyte Charles 'Tex' Watson (though he is portrayed as a lot more flakey), and Waco's group of young followers are modelled on some of the more infamous members of the Manson Family, who became virtual household names during the trial, thanks to the obsessive media coverage which the case attracted.

Once in L.A., Waco funds the set-up of his family by killing a couple of young female groovers who are on their way home from a discotheque and taking off with their cash and checkbooks. He then hatches a plan to set up base on a large plot of land out in the San Fernando Valley, owned by an old widow (filling in for George Spahn, whose property hosted the Manson family) who is struggling to keep up with the payments (and who just happens to be looking after her innocent young granddaughter Debbie—the perfect virginal bride for the Son of Zember).

As expected, the big set piece in *The Hippy Cult Murders* occurs when the author stages his own version of the Cielo Drive killings. This comes

The Hippy Cult Murders (MacFadden-Bartell, 1970)

at the halfway point of the novel, after Waco dons a lavender robe and drives Whitey and a trio of his chicks to the house of a well-off couple whom he'd earlier discovered were planning a little key-swapping party that evening.

> Except for asking where they were going when he first came around, Whitey had remained silent. The girls, too, had not said much during the drive. In the front seat Marsha had gotten herself so worked up on pills and excitement that she had pulled her skin tight pants down and had pulled Waco's hand over to her. The rest of the girls were drowsily high on pills.

Although Waco puts his violent impulses and behaviour down to the will of Zember, it is really all about the bread, man. Specifically, the bread he needs to move his family and set up base on the plot of land out in the Valley. Naturally, since it is a swingers party he's invaded, Waco discovers the three couples inside stark naked and writhing around on mattresses laid out on the living-room floor. In what is perhaps a slight dig at the middle-agers who thought they were hip at the time, the victims here are not beautiful young fashionistas, but bland characters in their forties with sagging breasts and greying hair and names like Harold and Ruth. So in a sequence that stretches itself out to 30-plus pages, it's *Bob & Carol & Ted & Alice* meets *Helter Skelter* as Waco and his crew berate, extort, terrorise, rape and finally slaughter their captives.

With ten grand now lining his robe, Waco settles his family on widow Elsie's land and turns his attention to the virginal Debbie, who, after a drug-laden ritual reminiscent of the climax from Russ Meyer's *Beyond the Valley of the Dolls* (released the same year), is readied to accept Zember's seed. However, Whitey, frustrated at playing second fiddle and having to make do with Waco's sexual cast-offs, decides it's payback time and takes away Debbie's purity, sending Waco into a rage that doesn't end until a couple of L.A. cops on the Family's trail turn him into Swiss cheese (unlike Manson, this cult leader received swift and savage justice).

> Suddenly an avalanche of gunfire exploded along the street. Waco felt hundreds of tiny needles stabbing into him. But as the needles entered his body they widened to nails, then

to spikes, then to stakes and to shovels. His body twitched and jerked. He bounced against a railing of the porch. His body was on fire! It hurt. It hurt badly. He grabbed the rail for support. What was happening? He felt all bubbly inside. Something was pouring out of him. A part of him was leaving his body. When he touched his stomach his hand came away wet and sticky. He was bleeding! Those bright lights. They were hurting him. But they didn't seem as bright as they were before. They were becoming hazy.

Unfortunately, while its subject matter gives it some undeniable off-beat appeal, and the cover (credited simply to "O'Brien") is a great piece of psychedelic art, *The Hippy Cult Murders* is not a particularly re- markable or memorable piece of work. It has enough cheap visceral thrills peppered throughout to at least keep you turning the pages, but you also get the feeling that the author (about whom nothing is known) is afraid to get his hands really dirty and take full advantage of the potential he had at his fingertips. Regardless, it is still an intriguing piece of paperback pulp, and makes a nice addition to any collection of Manson-related literature.

The Man with Mad Eyes—Peter Hawkins
(New English Library, 1973)

He used his evil power for sensual satisfaction.

One of the things the mass media picked up on after the arrest of Manson was the madness that was apparently evident in his eyes (the infamous *Life* magazine cover of August 21, 1970, is a prime example). Journalists and television reporters who managed to get up close and personal to Manson often noted his intense, hypnotic eyes, which—along with his psychobabble rantings—were thought to explain the influence and power he wielded over his followers.

The Man with Mad Eyes plays up the 'hypnotism in the wrong hands' angle, with author Peter Hawkins delivering an uneven work that seems to have a bit of trouble deciding exactly what genre or style it wants to belong to. The book kicks off well enough, with a doctor giving us a brief rundown on a series of increasingly brutal slayings of young women, including an au-pair girl and a would-be film actress, in circumstances which lead authorities to believe

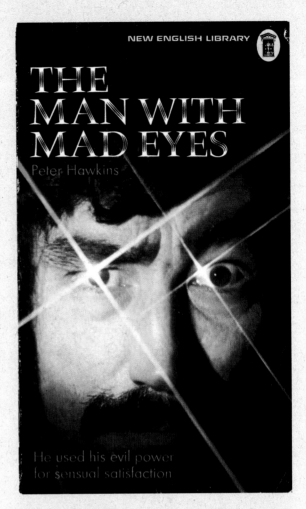

they were the work of one man. From here, the story deviates from an expected yarn about a modern-day Jack the Ripper and instead becomes a first-person account of the young perpetrator of the crimes, John Wilmot, who starts off as a trainee photographer with a self-flagellation fetish and a rather depraved boss who tries to do things to him in the darkroom.

After his boss is jailed (for committing **a crime that caused a crisis in one of our local boys associations**), Wilmot embarks on a series of comical sexual escapades that read like a draft for an unfilmed *Carry On* movie, before he finally meets a saucy nurse who shares his taste for the feel of leather lashes on bare skin.

Up to this point, there's been precious little mention of hypnotism, apart from Wilmot's fascination with a book on the subject titled *The Magic Eye*. When the book's author, Innes Farquharson, rolls into town to give a lecture, Wilmot attends and finds himself becoming the master's newest pupil. Despite Wilmot using his developing powers to land himself a prime job as a Fleet Street glamour photographer, the murder and mayhem promised in the opening pages (and on the book's back-cover blurb) only really makes itself visible during the last 20 pages of the book, as Wilmot tries to (unsuccessfully) resuscitate a French lady, whipped to death by an overzealous female model, by indulging in a spot of necrophilia.

Though its link is rather tenuous, the Manson Family are briefly referenced in *The Man with Mad Eyes*, and it seems clear that Hawkins was playing up the aura of evil influence which the Manson case generated, even if the face on the cover looks more like moustachioed 60s TV dandy Jason King than it does Charlie.

The Fear Dealers—Jack W. Thomas
(Bantam, 1975)

They came together in a five-person nude wedding orgy and vowed to take on the world of the 'straights'—to the death!

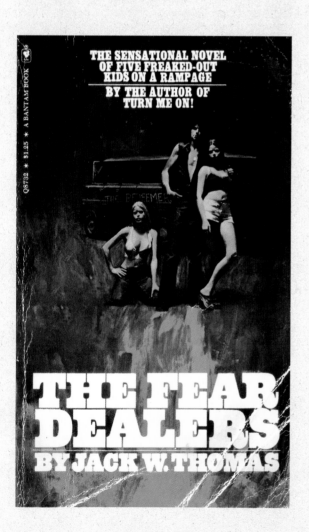

Jack W. Thomas is an author well overdue for reappraisal; his paperback novels read like lurid versions of the cheesy after-school television specials that were so popular in the 70s. No doubt influenced by a lot of the people he met, and situations he experienced as a deputy probation officer in Los Angeles between 1964 and 1970, Thomas's books revolved around the low-rent, soap-opera lives of America's lost teenagers, who seemed trapped in a perpetual world of cheap dope, pills, alcohol, disinterested parents, violence and sexual angst.

In *The Fear Dealers*, a disillusioned 25-year-old by the name of Jangle (so named because he works for a company that collects coins from public pay phones) gets picked up by foxy high school hippie Mallory. In the blink of an eye their lives are turned upside-down as they find themselves on the run from the girl's father, who arrives home in time to catch the couple making a wet mess (literally) on the water bed (which is adorned with a hand-painted illustration of a naked Burt Reynolds!).

Taking off in Jangle's work van, the pair are introduced to Fritz and his gal, Can, while trying to sell their spare tyre for cash, and just like that the quartet decide to scoot from Chicago and head for the more happenin' climes of Southern California. En route, they add free-lovin' Jessie to the mix (**Young and beautiful, she thought sex was the answer to everything**), indulge in orgies at a swinging roadside motel in Nevada (where they film their exploits courtesy of the motel's private video camera system), and get married to one other in a nude wedding out in the desert (though this isn't a marriage built for eternity, but **Just 'til our scene burns out**).

Calling themselves the Redeemers (**Redeemers are supposed to show other dudes how to groove**), our band of merry (but rather dim-witted) countercultural travellers roll into California. They quickly ingratiate themselves into the ultra-modern home of an upper middle class family, who seem only too happy to take in this scruffy rag-tag bunch of strangers, give them gasoline, let them use their swimming pool and shower, and provide them with a nice cooked meal. After having spent nearly half the book talking about suburban houses being little more than soul-destroying prisons, the Redeemers quickly decide they have stumbled upon quite a cosy set-up (**You ever see a crapper with a painting in it?**), and plan to extend their stay for a few days, nailing the doors shut, cutting the phone lines and keeping this typical

70s TV family hostage in their own home. Rape, beatings and psychological torture ensue, until the whole simmering cauldron eventually boils over into an explosive orgy of bloody violence that leaves very few people standing.

A pacey and easily digestible, if ultimately unexceptional, effort from Thomas, *The Fear Dealers* melds elements from the Manson case with Wes Craven's gritty 1971 grindhouse movie classic, *The Last House on the Left*. The lesson put forth in this book is simple: never trust a hippie, and never be trusting (or stupid) enough to let a bunch of them stay overnight in your button-down, plastic fantastic house.

The Man with the Power—Leslie Thomas
(Pan, 1975)

Best known as the author of the 1969 comic novel *The Virgin Soldiers*, Welsh writer Leslie Thomas offers us a unique look at America through the eyes of a foreigner in *The Man with the Power*. Young Willie Turpin travels from London to the United States in order to find his runaway wife Silvie, a striptease queen. On his flight to America, he meets a shonky South Wales minister, the Reverend John Properjohn, who makes note of Turpin's physical resemblance to Jesus Christ (the standard hippie image of long hair and beard). Before long, Turpin signs up with Properjohn and his followers (the Church of the Livid God) on a crusade from New York to Las Vegas, trying to save America before God destroys it all.

Written in the style of comic social commentary for which he is best known, Thomas keeps *The Man with the Power* from becoming too deep, dark or depressing, peppering it with pop culture references (*Deep Throat*, 1972, gets a brief mention) and giving the reader an entertaining view of America's dying counterculture, as seen through the eyes of a bemused and confused foreigner. Though of Welsh origin and in his mid-fifties, Properjohn is clearly created in the

Manson mould, described by Thomas as **a prince of vanities with a loud mouth, a power over people and the date of the end of the world in his pocket.**

Originally published by Eyre Methuen in 1973, the 1975 Pan paperback of *The Man with the Power* features a suitably lurid photo cover of a naked blonde kneeling in front of a man in a robe, suggestively tugging at his rope belt.

JOHN HARRISON

JANE GALLION/Authoress of BIKER

STONED

$1 95

0128

AN ESSEX HOUSE ORIGINAL

ADULTS ONLY

Stoned (Essex House, 1969)
Jane Gallion, photo courtesy of Amber Nichols

NOTHING TO LOSE
An Introduction to the Work of Jane Gallion

The counterculture of the late 60s and early 70s provided rich fodder for pulp writers. Just as they had done with juvenile delinquents and the beats, writers—some of them directly involved in the counterculture, the majority not—took its most sensationalist aspects—psychedelic drugs, free love and political radicalism—to use as material for their stories.

Many of these books are unmemorable. They were quickly produced, often highly formulaic, aimed at middle-aged white readers seeking a vicarious thrill from reading about the often-exaggerated sexual and drugged-out goings-on in the communes and 'happenings' of the alternative lifestyle movement that was sweeping much of the West. But, amid the dross, there are some gems that capture the zeitgeist of the time as well as, if not better, than some of the mainstream literary offerings of the period. Jane Gallion's *Stoned* is one of them.

Gallion wrote erotica or, as it was more commonly marketed, smut or porn. As she wrote in the accompanying letter to Harriet Emerson, which originally appeared in *Making Our Own Way: Rural West Virginia Women Artists*, Emerson's 1990 unpublished Master of Science in Journalism thesis: "I was the only woman smut writer in America for a good long while. There were others before me, Anaïs Nin and a few others in France, and plenty of them since. I don't think I was so much discriminated against as treated like a dancing dog . . . I loved the acclaim, but shrank from the conflict of being a woman smut writer, and from the spotlight that working in such a field turned on my private life."

Smut paperbacks sold in huge quantities in the US in the late 50s and the 60s through mail-order catalogues, adult stores, back-issue magazine parlours and newsstands. The publishers engaged in an ongoing cat and mouse game with the authorities, who tried various methods to close them down. By the late 60s the publishers were winning.

One of these publishers was Brandon House, set up by Milton Luros. According to *Sin-A-Rama: Sleaze Sex Paperbacks of the Sixties* (2005), Luros was born in the Bronx, New York, in 1911. Prior to entering the smut book trade, he illustrated covers for leading science fiction magazines. When the sci-fi magazine market collapsed in the mid to late 1950s, he shifted his focus to illustrating for men's magazines. He moved to Los Angeles, where he set up a publishing group called American Art Agency. He revolutionised nudist magazines by making them glossy and using attractive models. He then shifted into softcore publications, establishing his own printing operation, London Press and Oxford Bindery, and developing an efficient mail-order business to distribute his product. His operation eventually grew into one of the country's largest producers and distributors of smut books and adult magazines.

In 1966, Luros responded to retreating censorship laws by developing a line of books under Brandon House Library Editions, translations of vintage erotica, mainly from Europe, most of which had never appeared in English. He hired a jazz drummer and rare book dealer from Detroit called Brian Kirby to oversee the operation. According to *Sin-A-Rama*: "Kirby designed the covers, wrote the cover blurbs, supervised his team of translators, and hired novelists and poets to write introductions at a time when most industry intros were written by bogus PhDs to provide legally required redeeming social value, now matter how tenuous."

Under the imprint Essex House, Kirby was soon also publishing original erotic novels by bona fide poets and writers—no pseudonyms allowed—including Charles Bukowski and Philip José Farmer. Essex House also published Gallion.

There is no complete bibliography of Gallion's writing, and what little information is publicly available consists of snippets on the Internet. Copies of her books are hard to locate and the secondhand copies that occasionally become available command hefty prices. Some of her work is available digitally, mainly through a publisher called Renaissance E-Books, run by science-fiction writer and friend of Gallion, Jean Marie Stine.

It appears that she first started writing while active in the Los Angeles Science Fiction Society in the mid 60s. According to Amber Nichols, her youngest daughter, Gallion was married at the time to sci-fi author William Bert Ellern (her second husband), who wrote stories set in the universe of the Lensmen series originally created by Edward Elmer 'Doc' Smith. This marriage brought Gallion opportunities to attend parties with big name sci-fi authors and film people.

She remained in L.A. after the break-up of that marriage. "Things went financially unstable," says Nichols, "and she was scraping for 'a pot to piss in or a window to throw it out of' as she would say . . . poor during the mostly communal living situations in L.A."

She got a job writing for Luros's London Press. In an unfinished biography, Gallion describes her first day on the job:

London Press was a vast, ramifying empire of smut. The New Jerusalem of pornography. Its business offices, editorial suites, typesetting rooms, production and photography studios, darkrooms, warehouses and helipads clustered on the carcass of Fulton Avenue like a flock of turkey buzzards, flapping, squawking, proliferating. The parking lots were ponds, in which limos and ruinously expensive sports cars multiplied like bacteria. Forklifts buzzed and clanked as they trundled loads of paper into the warehouses from ranks of delivery trucks, and returned with steel-strapped bundles of books and magazines to load up other delivery trucks. Jaded photographers criss-crossed with camera straps hustled groups of tired-looking girls in and out of discreet side doors.

Were we in the right place? I wondered, clutching my firstborn manuscript to my chest. This was no dim redoubt where dirty old men squatted at dusty tables, scribbling "fuck" on underground walls. This was an industry, whose captains held meetings, commissioned market studies, attended conventions in corporation Lear jets attended by squads of yes-men, and maybe (probably) even chased busty, mini-skirted secretaries around the desks. I couldn't believe my eyes.

Through the front door, past a haughty receptionist whose expression suggested that she had now seen everything, I was towed, numb with shock, by a grimly striding Gene Henry. He stopped abruptly before an open office door and shoved me inside. When I came out again, I was a fuckbook writer.

Her first novel for Essex House, *Biker* (1969), was a dystopian porn story set in a future California ravaged by nuclear war and dominated by bikers, drifters and cults. The main character is a 'bikebroad' called Feather, a speed addict and prostitute for a local biker pack.

She decides she's finally had enough of being sexually abused, murders and castrates one of the bikers, and escapes into the desert on a stolen motorbike. Feather meets up with an ex-biker called Bear who appears to treat her well, but then trades her to an anonymous drifter in exchange for LSD. After the drifter sexually uses her, she kills him and Bear, and escapes back into the desert, where she eventually hooks up with a hippie commune led by Chris, a Christ-like figure who preaches that women should be feminine and bear children. Over the course of the book, Feather is transformed from a victim to a hardened survivor who has to exercise control of her own destiny, and she decides the commune is just another pack of men out to oppress her.

Biker is not for the faint-hearted. The book opens with a visceral gangbang scene and is packed with violence and graphic sex, both forced and consensual. Nonetheless, it earned a positive rap from sci-fi writer Theodore Sturgeon. Gallion wrote in the introduction to the 2001 digital edition of *Biker* that she ran the manuscript past the local biker chief in her neighbourhood, Baron, to see if it had authenticity, before submitting it to Essex House.

[*Biker*'s] sources were in the Vietnam era and the resistance and hostilities of the new women's movement. I'd been through three divorces, by that time, had three children and very few job skills apart from the obvious: keeping house, having babies, placating men. I had just recently encountered Women's Liberation and the fledgling drug culture, and was consequently so full of old rage newly recognised and new fury emerging as I watched that I just couldn't keep on being compliant as I was trained to be. There was a whole other world out there—terrifying, brutal, bewildering, full of danger and potential enemies. But also full of possibility, of odds against, of slim chances, and maybe even a few rewards. And I had—Feather had—not a whole lot to lose.

Her second book for Essex House, *Stoned*, was also published in 1969. Elaine Stuart and her husband, Randy, live in outer suburban Los Angeles. It's the late 60s but their lives are a world away from the hippie scene and the bright lights and fast times of L.A.'s infamous countercultural hub, the Sunset Strip. Elaine spends her days at home, chained to their two poorly behaved children. There's never enough money, and her sex life with Randy is in the toilet. Randy is equally frustrated. He loathes his job as a truck driver, hates his right-wing co-worker and spends much of his day fantasising about cheating on Elaine with other women.

One day Elaine's best friend gives her a joint to help her relax. Life seems more chilled when she is stoned, and dealing with the kids is easier. Randy turns on as well, and smoking marijuana and taking acid leads to a revolution in their sex life. At the same time, Randy finds the changes more difficult to deal with. Elaine's not surprised. **It was a great pity, she'd decided, that despite Randy being all mouth about the Now Generation, he was such a card carrying prude.**

One night they host a party. Randy has an unsuccessful coupling on the back lawn with a female neighbour he's desired for some time. Elaine has a rather more fulfilling encounter with Charley, a member of a local rock band considerably younger than she is. It's a pivotal moment, and Randy can tell things have changed when he comes to breakfast the next morning and Elaine is wearing a bronze medallion of a Cretan snake princess.

Charley's band move, in and Elaine and Randy's drug use and extramarital sex become more open. But has anything really changed? Elaine still seems to be doing all the cooking and housework, everyone's behind in paying the rent, and Randy is still sullen and just wants to get laid. He's also resentful of Elaine's successful relationship with Charley.

Barefoot, he went out to the kitchen for his coffee.

This mine? He indicated a full cup on the table next to Elaine's elbow. Elaine nodded, sipping from her own. Three strings of beads were around her neck along with a peace symbol strung on a rawhide thing. When she turned her head, he noticed that her long hair was braided with a length of green yarn ending in several orange pony beads and a bunch of feathers. Huh?

"What's all that garbage for?" Randy asked. Elaine looked up. "What garbage?"

"All that feather and bead hippyshit." Randy tried not to sound too amused. She was really going all out, it seemed. He hoped she wasn't going to embarrass him by wearing all that shit tonight with all the people here.

The book ends with Elaine unsure what to do.

JANE GALLION

BIKER

$1.95

AN ESSEX HOUSE ORIGINAL

0124

VA-ROOOOOOM!

Now there's this wild, sexy chick, see . . . her name's Feather. She rides a bike. The Great War is over, and the country is overrun by motorcycle gangs . . . grotty, lustful sex freaks! So Feather wants to escape! But she runs into this cat, Bear, and they make it! Oh, do they make it! But Feather, she's got other things cookin' for her . . . and other guys lookin' for her! What they want, she knows how to give . . . what they take, she takes back! Feather is a future chick, and BIKER is a future book. Sex? Full of it, like people, like Feather's people! Like life!

HEAVY!

Biker (Essex House, 1969)

Elaine slumped against the seat. She wished she had settled for what she had, never found out that all men were not like Randy. If she had met Charley a long time ago . . . but it probably wouldn't have made any difference. Charley was such a heavy looking, beautiful person that when he gained a little self-confidence, he was going to be shooing the chicks away like flies. The only thing she had to offer him was a temporary remedy.

Should she take Charley up on his offer to 'shack up' with him? Should she stay with Randy and the kids? Is a more radical departure from her old life needed? These questions are left hanging.

A slew of books and films depict middle-class America's attempts to deal with the shifting sexual and social mores of the late 60s and early 70s. These include Sue Kaufman's *Diary of a Mad Housewife* (1969), made into a movie in 1970, Jacqueline Susann's *Valley of the Dolls* (1966), released as a film following year, the 1966 film movie adaption of Mary McCarthy's 1963 book, *The Group*, and the 1969 comedy, *Bob & Ted & Carol & Alice*. It's easy to dismiss *Stoned* as a low-rent, smuttier version of these. It does indeed have some first-class sex scenes, including a couple of great descriptions of sex under the influence of various hallucinogens. But the book is unique in some other respects.

Stoned is about a working-class couple. Their decision to embrace aspects of the counterculture feels authentic, with a lot more at stake than there would be for an affluent, middle-class couple. *Stoned* never veers into the heavy-handed morality parable territory of later books exploring drug use, like *Go Ask Alice*. There's no sense Elaine is going to start taking smack and become a hooker to pay for her habit. Drugs open doors to new experiences, as well as throwing up challenges and questions. Elaine can fuck someone or have another joint, but she's still got to deal with the basic inequality between the sexes. While the book has an explicit feminist orientation, it avoids being didactic. Randy is not a particularly sympathetic character, but neither is he a caricature. He is as much a victim of their circumstances as she is.

In addition to *Biker* and *Stoned*, Gallion's letter mentions two other novels she did for Essex House: *The Phoenix Business* (publication date unknown) and an erotic science-fiction novel called *Going Down*, which was sold to them but which it appears they didn't publish (it is now available in digital format). In terms of payment, her daughter recalls it was "anywhere between six hundred to one thousand or twelve hundred per book. Depending on length. They always gave her a bump up front to buy things like typewriter paper and supplies, which were very expensive."

Gallion also worked as an in-house editor for Essex House and Brandon House from 1968 to 1971. In the late 60s she wrote a non-fiction feminist book entitled *The Woman as Nigger*, published by Weiss, Day and Lord in 1970. According to the back cover, the book REALLY TELLS WHAT INSIDE EVERY WOMAN'S HEAD . . . WHAT THEY ARE GOING TO DO AND WHAT THEY'RE NOT GOING TO DO ANY MORE.

"*The Woman as Nigger* was such a stupid title that the publisher chose and I believe it ruined her chances at a national audience with that great piece of work on feminism," says her daughter. Gallion's letter mentions numerous other books that she wrote, including a number of smut novels, but publication details about these are unavailable.

As the accompanying letter makes clear, she found writing smut hard. She expressed similar sentiments in her incomplete biography:

Nothing on earth could have prepared me for the smut industry. In our house, sex was discussed a lot but not above a whisper . . . What three marriages taught me about the joy of sex could have been inscribed on an eyelash in nanoseconds, and washed off just as fast with one good cry.

Gallion left L.A. with her children (her fourth, Amber, was born in 1972) in the early 70s. Her daughter says of the decision: "She told me that when the older kids saw three blades of grass and screamed 'Park, let's go to that park', she knew it was time to head for the hills."

They arrived in West Virginia in 1973 as part of what was called the back-to-the-land movement, which saw people leave the cities and move to rural areas to live in small communities and grow their own food. Paralleling the desire to get in touch with nature was the desire to reconnect with physical labour. Elements of the movement were captured in the 1969 movie, *Easy Rider*, when Wyatt and Billy visit a rural commune and witness former city-based hippies struggling to eke out a living in harsh conditions. The migration, which had peaked by the mid 1970s, was significant enough that it was identified in the American demographic statistics.

As Gallion put it in her biography:

> The Back-To-The-Land movement sprouted from the seed time of the Flower Children, sown in the 60s. America was still fighting the longest war in its history, the ghettos still burned with an unquenchable fire, and the few hippies remaining in the fabled Haight-Ashbury had staged a funeral for the corpse of the Movement. Hip was officially dead, and from where we stood, Amerika and maybe the whole planet might be following it. Apocalypse soon.
>
> I found myself waking up sweating and trembling a lot in those days. I was haunted, as so many were, by dreams of nuclear holocaust. Most often the Night Mare caught up with me knelen on my kne [sic] in a jumble and chaos of possessions, scrambling and sorting, gathering together and casting away, unable to decide what to take with me as I fled from the approaching terror. It was a time of immanent [sic] destruction, the time of the Change, and if I didn't get my act together pretty soon I was going to find myself understudying Lot's Wife, turned to a pillar of salt as she looked back over her shoulder regretting her new slipcovers. Independence, possibly bare survival, began to look like a couple of acres in the country somewhere—far out in the country—with a pocketful of garden seeds and half a dozen chickens. In addition to the looming specter of nuclear disaster, the sixty-mile by forty-mile sprawl of metropolitan Los Angeles had become a howling inferno, populated by four million monsters and me. Seeking a solution to all this, I ate a hit of acid one night and in the morning descended through the smog and sirens with a piece of inside information not even Gene Henry [one of her partners] could pick holes in. I'd gotten the solution to both spiritual and temporal entanglements in one knock.

Gallion and her daughters left West Virginia and moved to Austin, Texas, in 1988. She eventually ended up back in Los Angeles, where she died of cancer in July 2003, aged 65.

Gallion gave up fiction when she moved to West Virginia but took up writing poetry. "She was working our land, tending the gardens and livestock, keeping four kids fed, navigating her husband Peter's ego (he was trying to write to be published, too), another in a long string of who were jealous and got outraged if publishers liked her work," recalls her daughter. "I think all of this and working odd jobs (one at a diner doing dishes) and going to college to get to make ends meet finally snuffed out her passions but also prevented her from writing on a deadline. She worked in various print shops and for local publishers and newspapers and went back to college on and off in the 70s and early 80s. She amassed a huge student loan debt as well . . . using most of that money to supplement her incoming food stamps and welfare after last husband was gone [she was married four times]."

"Over time I think her cynicism was a byproduct of doing the best she could with a, many times over, broken and trampled heart," recalls her daughter. "I think she was also hugely disappointed with the 60s free love movement being pretty much a farce and full of mind games and sexual tension that she wished wasn't there. She felt lied to about the 'sexual revolution' and set on a path of her own liberation—which *should have* opened doors for many but her work was not taken seriously or didn't land in the right publishers' hands . . ."

The digital version of *Stoned* contains a short introduction by Jean Marie Stine, in which she makes the following observation:

> When Jane Gallion penned *Stoned* in the late 1960s, women's condition in Western society may not have been in the Stone Age, but it hadn't yet entered the Renaissance. *The Feminine Mystique* was only slowly beginning to affect the ideology of a handful of American women, and *Ms.* magazine and *Sexual Politics* were yet to be published. It seems likely that had Gallion's novel been issued by a major publisher, rather than a small West Coast publisher of erotica, it would have become a bestseller, taken to the hearts of millions of frustrated housewives . . . whose lives—in moments before the feminist revolution—she paints in such unflinching sexual detail.

ANDREW NETTE

The author would like to thank Weed, Harriet Emerson and Amber Nichols for generously providing much of the information used in this article.

"THE POWER OF THE WORD"
A Letter from Jane Gallion

Austin, Texas
June 23, 1990

Dear Harriet,

I sat right down the minute your letter arrived and answered it, but the fact is I'm half nuts, shell-shocked and crazy. I've spent the last three months pretending I'm perfectly okay and I'm not. The pretense has cost me.

It's doubly a bitch for a writer to get in this shape. When communication with your nearest—but not necessarily dearest—goes, writing goes too. It's bullshit, but that's how it is. In these times I read and read and read, getting next to the Art, but not being able to establish connection with Art either. I hope to Goddess I can get it up to print this letter and mail it. I have to, actually. Something's got to give.

All those questions on your list. No one asks me questions. I interpret this as: no one in my family is interested. Inside my family, what is wanted is Jolly Old Mom. This makes me nuts. There is a whole other Jane in here with Jolly Old Mom, and that one is losing it.

I was born and grew up in La Sierra, CA, a Seventh-Day Adventist college town, containing two grocery stores, a hardware store, a feed store and a blacksmith shop. You may object that this isn't the sort of town California is supposed to contain, but things were markedly different in the 40s. Outside of the businesses I mentioned, all there was to La Sierra was alfalfa fields and an Army base, which is now the burbs of a metropolis.

Suffice to say that I grew up in an utterly non-supportive environment. I was raised a Seventh-Day Adventist, and that group, at least while I was in it, considered writing sinful. They consider almost everything sinful, everything that pleases or contents. If it feels good, you can't do it. This is both the source of my fiction writing (because who wouldn't want to construct a more congenial ambiance?) and the source of my blocks (because my early training makes me feel as though anything that makes me feel better is wrong).

My professional name (maiden name) is Jane Gallion.

That's the name I've always written under except for a few bits and pieces and my astrology column, "Almanac," which I wrote for two years for the *Salem Herald*, the Doddridge County weekly, under the name Jane Martin. Come to think of it, I don't think I've ever mentioned the column to you.

If anything's West Virginia, that was. A short squib about country life to open the column and then the aspects for the day, taken day by day. It was unique among astrology columns, because I worked with the day itself instead of with people's sun signs. I gave planting and pulling weeds, baling hay, castrating pigs, all that country shit, and once in a while I'd get a psychic flash about one of my readers and print that too.

I had a great big following all over Doddridge County, but the Baptist minister didn't like me much. I kept encouraging people to carpe diem instead of hanging loose in prayer meetings.

I was thirty when I sold my first book. At that time, I had three children, two yard kids and one lap kid. Denise was nine months old when I began the first chapters of *Biker*, but the older two were living with their father for a time. It took me three months to complete that novel, and immediately afterward I started *Setups for the House*, which was published under the title *Stoned*.

Jill came back to live with me before *Biker* was finished, and William returned while I was writing *The Woman as Nigger*, a non-fiction piece commissioned by a rich asshole who wanted to capitalize on all the revolutionary shenanigans that were happening right then.

Why Get Married?, *The Phoenix Business*, and *Going Down* were written with all three kids underfoot, in various roosting places where the Mud Elephant Hippie-Trippie Peace, Love and Flower Commune bunked up before getting evicted/moving in the dead of the night/being run out of the neighborhood by rednecks.

Quickie and *Trailer Tramp*, the two collaborations I wrote with Brandon's brother Gil while we were living together, were written in a trailer park in Van Nuys, CA, and if writing a book in a tacky house trailer in Van Nuys, with or without help, doesn't qualify as Herculean, I don't know what does.

The biggest task involved with it was preventing the kids from hearing me switch on the typer. It was like shoving a can under an electric can opener and ducking back out of the way before the cats climb up your legs. Like Garfield when Jon locks a lip over a chocolate chip cookie. Don't matter if they're in the next COUNTY, they hear! The four novels, *Biker, Stoned, The Phoenix Business*, and *Going Down*, were all published by Essex House, a division of Brandon House, which was a vast smut publishing empire in the San Fernando Valley.

I worked in-house as an editor for a short while, editing a magazine called *Response*, which was aimed (they said, anyway) at women. From 1968 to 1971 or thereabouts I worked either for Essex House or Brandon House, or for a second smut publishing house called Panupubco, which did highly illustrated sex magazines.

I co-authored some 40–50 "guides" for Panupubco, variations on the "How to Fuck" theme. These were 55-page manuscripts on topics like "Multiple Orgasms for Men," sex toys, oral sex, etc., though one of them was called "Coito Ergo Sum," which translates (roughly, roughly) as "I fuck, therefore I am," with abject apologies to Descartes. These were all co-authored by Peter Martin, and we wrote under the names Cassandra White and Richard Santine. Eventually we put together a book for Brandon House called *The Pursuit of Pleasure*.

Essex House was modeled along the lines of Olympia Press and the French publishing houses of erotica who published Henry Miller, Anaïs Nin, Harriet Daimler, et al. It was not straight smut, but rather experimental, in that we were allowed (and sometimes even encouraged) to produce literature.

Theodore Sturgeon's novel *Godbody* was written for Essex House, but he balked big time at being paid $1,000 for it, the going price for Essex House books. Sturgeon was one of my culture heroes, and cost me some lumps by heaping me with praise in front of Gil. Poet David Meltzer also wrote several Essex House books, and novelist Michael Perkins, who wrote a fuckbook version of Dante's *Inferno* just to see if it could be done (it could). They (Essex House bunch) were not real happy with humor; American smut publishers were and are essentially humorless. I was summoned into The Presence one time and instructed not to write any humor. "Jane," he said grimly, "no satire. Ya can't laugh and keep a hard-on."

We did have one editor who understood where we were coming from. He cherished us, because we could always be counted on to turn out good, tight books in almost no time. Our record for a 225-pager was one week. That was *Trailer Tramp*, a prize piece of smut. So we dedicated it to him with a quote from D.H. Lawrence. "What is pornography to one man is the laughter of genius to another. For Larry Shaw, who laughs a lot."

He bought my last novel from me twice after Essex House folded. *Going Down* was written by taking the "do-not" list I'd been given by the publisher and including every one of the smut factory taboos. The book was also intensely political (it was the Nixon years, after all). Needless to say, even though I sold it three times it has never been published, but I consider it some of my best work.

My situation as a female artist is unique, I think, because I began my work as a writer in the field of erotica. I was the only woman smut writer in America for a good long while. There were others before me, Anaïs Nin and a few others in France, and plenty of them since. I don't think I was so much discriminated against as treated like a dancing dog. My mentor refused to allow me to use a pseudonym on my books, so I was precipitated into a spotlight that was agonizing for me. I loved the acclaim, but shrank from the conflict of being a woman smut writer, and from the spotlight that working in such a field turned on my private life.

Few genres are so merciless to women as porn. I was naive, shy, and pitifully ignorant on the topic of sex. It showed in my work, and after reading my work, everyone knew. It turned out that I was a much better writer than anyone, myself included, suspected. So my self-revelation was also merciless. If I had had less integrity, been more able to and more willing to be a bull-shitter, I'd have suffered less.

I came to West Virginia in 1973, at the crest of the back-to-the-land movement. From the middle of Hollywood, CA, I arrived in Glenville ahead of most of the wave of BTTL freaks. Hot on our heels came a million and a half scruffy, ignorant hippies without the least idea how to cope. I, however, was raised by displaced Okies, who had migrated to CA just after the "dust bowl" era. I knew all about scrubbing diapers on a rub-board, building fires, mulching the pot plants, and foraging. I'd done my homework before I arrived in WV, to the unending scorn of all the other hippies, who thought planning ahead was buying two packages of Zig Zags. I even planted and transplanted my pot by the Moon, and pruned it ditto, with the result that my plants were nine feet tall in August, while the hippies up-holler, who thought I was a superstitious if hyper-rational asshole, had scraggly plants two feet tall a body could hardly catch a buzz off.

I wrote about different things in a rural area than I did and do in the city. My settings were different, and my imagery was more organic in West Virginia than anywhere else. Rural West Virginia still appears in my poetic imagery, though being in Austin is beginning to show. There seems to be more fertility in the air in a rural environment than here in the city.

When I took Appalachian Culture at Glenville State College, I wrote a poem for my class project. We were supposed to produce an authentic Appalachian craft for our final project, and most of the other students made baskets, quilts, toys, etc. Stuff that you see at fairs and festivals. But I had been reading regional authors, and one poet, whose name I can't recall but I think it was Murial Somethingorother, wrote a poem called "I Am Appalachia." It was one of those gassy numbers about self-contained noble mountain people, and put down outsiders in careful verse. As poetry goes, it was a pretty good poem, but it made me angry and despairing.

After all, I wasn't born in West Virginia. My family hadn't squatted on the same hillside for generations. I was in Appalachia because I couldn't hack city life and wanted something more for myself and my children than slummy L.A. and cops and drugs. And here was this bitch, who had, from what I could see, everything necessary to be happy, and instead of being generous, here she was preening herself and coming on like some Appalachian Pharisee that she wasn't a Poor Immigrant. So I wrote "I Too Am Appalachia" and turned it in for my class project. I got an A in the class. I don't think my professor liked giving it to me, because he was a West Virginia bigot who thought us hippies were shit, but at least he possessed the integrity to do the right thing.

As it happened, I quit writing smut when I moved to West Virginia, because the topics I was being given to examine didn't seem relevant anymore. I could still write erotic fiction, but non-fiction was impossible. I never completed my last smut assignment, which was a 55-page piece about what bored housewives did with their free time—fuck the mailman, fuck the guy who mows the lawn, join a swappers' club, etc. I ask you, who can get it up to write about shit like that when you're living a couple miles up-holler from the hard road and cooking dinner for six to eleven hippies on a Coleman stove by lamplight?

Did I "choose" to be an artist? Oh, hell no. Who chooses? All I chose was whether to exercise the art and whether it would be good when I did. I can choose whether or not to publish, and I can choose not to be a hack. That's about it.

There are a whole lot of hard parts about writing books—running out of money and typing paper at the same time, having children in your hair, wondering if you really CAN do it again or if the one you just finished was a fluke—but the hardest, for me, anyway, was knowing that the man in my life would withdraw from me if it was good. This happened with my mentor (as soon as I sold *Biker*), with Gil (who beat the hell out of me frequently, but most often when I was working on a book and he wasn't, or when someone jokingly called him Mr. Jane Gallion), and with Peter, who worked on my self-confidence day and night, night and day for nine years, and would do stuff like appropriate my typewriter to keep me from using it although he had one of his own. The wrenching choice between my work and my emotional security is the hardest. All three of them would have forgiven me if it had not been good. It is not this way for men. Men can expect to be lionized, idolized, deferred to, cherished if they are good writers. It may be otherwise for other writers, although Erica Jong would know just what I'm talking about, and probably Marge Piercy, too, but for me it was a clear choice, so instead of writing *Time to Kill*, a manual of creative terrorism, or finishing *Crossworld Puzzle*, I had another baby, Amber, and retreated into the hills and hollows of West Virginia to try and be a Real Woman at last, one that would not threaten The Man.

Eighteen years later, having been unsuccessful at stifling the lifelong torch I've carried for the English Language, I am at work on *Any Friday*, a horror novel, and will eventually get back to work on *Crossworld Puzzle*. I am also putting together a volume of poetry called *Vegetable Matters*. I already have about 40 poems for the book, and am working on the design for it with a friend down here who is an artist.

The best part is feeling like god, knowing that you can take the raw material of people, events, imagination, extrapolation, and remold them all in your own image, make it like it should have been with the power of the Word. The best part is being there with the right tool for the right job in your own able hand, and setting to work at the task. Watching the people you have constructed out of three or four qualities, given names to, put in situations, and seeing them come alive under your hands. Feeling the skill come bubbling up out of the spring of your own subconscious and knowing that all you have to do is keep the leaves raked out and the groundhogs from drowning in it. Shit work, maintenance. So it's not hard, and anybody who tells you that the act of creation requires agony and justifies lousy manners is no writer. Well, but I feel that way making Chicken Kiev, though less so. The act of creation itself is the best part.

And yes, I feel alone. Even when I was a collaborating author I felt alone. Just the rock and the petroglyph. I wrote a poem about that once. Creativity is like life in that no one else is responsible for your integrity. And no one else can particularly do anything to help. It's nice, though, if someone is around to say "There, there" and "Wow" once in a while.

I was asked the other day, by someone I met at a friend's house, what my books were about. I said I wrote about love. That IS what I write about, and all that I write about. That is what I want to say to people through my work. My philosophy, if you can call it a philosophy, is that life—and love—has a structure of its own, and if you study that structure and cherish it, it will feed you and nourish you and make, no, encourage you, to grow. Love and creativity are one and the same, because creativity is the dynamic aspect of love. Love is, creativity does. So I feel that I won't stop creating till I'm dead, and possibly not then.

I left West Virginia because the economy collapsed and I couldn't find a job. If I could find one, I'd probably come back. Or maybe not. You can't, after all, go home again. I miss it, and I'm homesick a lot of the time, but there are compensations. After all, I'm writing this on my home computer, ain't I?

Love,
Jane

This letter, which has only been slightly edited for clarity, originally appeared in *Making Our Own Way: Rural West Virginia Women Artists* (1990) by Harriet Emerson, and is republished with her permission. Photo of Jane Gallion and daughter, West Virginia, early 1970s, courtesy of Amber Nichols.

Sappho in Absence, John Crosby (Collins, 1970)

I don't know how well known the name of John Crosby is nowadays, but for those who need a refresher, he first came to public attention as one of the founding fathers of TV criticism in the 1950s. Or as P.G. Wodehouse put it: "John Crosby is the fellow who watches television for the *New York Herald Tribune*, than which I can imagine no more appalling job—just think of having to watch television." Having established himself in American journalism, Crosby came to Britain in 1964 and the following year gave the world the concept of Swinging London with an article in the *Sunday Telegraph* colour supplement.

This first novel turned up a few years later, when Crosby was already 58, and opens in a London where preening peacocks are reaching a sartorial standard of rarefied heights:

> **He was dressed in flamboyantly pop style—an armless sheepskin waistcoat over a purple silk shirt with a mandarin collar on which were emblazoned in gold thread Etruscan horses and Greek nymphs. The trousers were burnt orange and the shoes were of orange patent leather with gold buckles.**

Frankly, I could have read a couple of hundred pages of this without any complaint whatsoever, but Crosby has another kettle of much bigger fish to fry, and before you know quite what's happening, the heroine—Sappho Constant—has left the social whirl of Chelsea far behind, seduced by the lure of the hippie trail. Soon we're in Istanbul, ready to make the 4,000-mile trek to Kathmandu in the company of a travelling circus of idealists, drug casualties and social misfits, such as **a bearded man with granny spectacles** called Nirvana Now who used to edit a poetry magazine titled *Fuck Them All*. And chasing on in their wake is Sappho's husband, and our narrator, Gerald.

The blurb on the hardback edition captures something of the atmosphere:

> **In Istanbul, a blonde teeny freak who was sixteen but used to be much older rapped on about the Oneness of the Universe; in Ankara, Hippetty Hotpants sold herself for thirty Turkish pounds to any passing Turk; the flying saucers were thick in Tabriz; in Darpa it was**

Sappho in Absence (Collins, 1970)
Sappho in Absence (Fontana, 1971)

> **fuzz; in Beshawa floods. And in the end, on a Himalayan mountain top, Gerald Constant found the answer to his riddle.**

Not just a period piece—though its evocation of the era is superb—this is also a genuinely fine novel of great charm. It is also great fun and a superbly observed bit of social satire. If the cover's claim that it's **THE FIRST TRULY MODERN LOVE STORY** is somewhat over-blown, it is at least a warm, nice kind of book to have around. I was particularly fond of the relationship between Gerald and his friend from childhood, Fiona, which features a lovely line in the sort of nonsense that takes a lifetime to establish.

ALWYN W. TURNER

SAPPHO IN ABSENCE

John Crosby

When a wife turns hippie . . .

"Amusing and very readable"
Sunday Express

"I had a full, rich childhood."

"I thought it was unhappy."

"Full, rich and unhappy. That's why I have this doomed look. You haven't noticed my doomed look."

"I have! I have! It's very becoming. You should wear it over one eye. Like this." I showed her.

"That was last year," said Fiona. "This year they're wearing the doomed look at the back of the head like this— and breasts are coming back."

"I didn't know they'd been away."

The Artist Type (Pan, 1969)
The Judas Freaks (New English Library, 1972)

Harris in Wonderland
—Philip Reid (Jonathan Cape, 1973)

Harris in Wonderland is a tight little potboiler in which a **brainy, but idle** investigative journo gets into a mess of bother after shooting his mouth off at a politician's dinner party. Stalked during a weekender in Amsterdam (**the city of the 70s**) he finds himself charged with drugs importation after a shady hippie claiming to be an acquaintance from the past plants a bottle of liquid LSD in his luggage. Thanks to his sideline in digging up dirt for The Maggot (an Oz-like underground paper replete with scurrilous Aussie editor), the novel's protagonist is able to conduct an investigation into his own frame-up. Following a path from decaying Kings Road head shops to Welsh communes, his adventures not only lead him into the arms of a bourgeois lady dropout, but also into the consumption of some fearsomely strong acid. After a Labour leadership contender and a number of other high-powered types come to his aid our hapless hack finds himself drawn into the murky world of high finance and political power plays. The case is eventually solved, but not before the reader encounters enough red herrings to make this a brief, but highly enjoyable read.

Harris in Wonderland, published in the US as Fun House, defies the tendency of political thrillers to bloat out to grandiose proportions, while also managing to deftly capture the feel of the British counterculture as it entered terminal decline. Written by Private Eye stalwarts Andrew Osmond and Richard Ingrams, the novel avoids the sometimes snide attitude of their magazine and succeeds as both mystery and spoof.

IAIN McINTYRE

HARRIS IN WONDERLAND

PHILIP REID

We drove up to Finchley and took in the show. The Barn is a disused Army riding school which has been converted into a theatre in the round. The show was called Sunburst and the programme described it as Tantric Rock. It cost us a pound to get in, but I didn't object because somebody said the money was for the Black Panthers and I felt I had a bond with outlaws everywhere.

Inside, the place was in darkness except for a cat's cradle of spotlights aimed from the gallery on to a central stage. The seats had been stripped away and the floor was crowded with freaks, hundreds of them, leaping about to the music. I say music, but it was really noise, raw undiluted decibels, filling every corner of that circular cavern. To walk towards it was like walking into a strong wind. When we reached the stage I saw that it was coming from a pair of house-sized speakers labelled DO NOT APPROACH WITHIN 20 FEET UNLESS PROTECTED and was mostly the work of a very fat freak in a solar toupee, shaking his hair and jumping up and bouncing in his seat as he punched with all ten fingers on the keys of an electric organ. The rest of the group had guitars and drums. On the edge of the danger zone Charlie shouted something which I couldn't hear and pointed to the other end of the stage. I followed the line of her finger to where a Negro in a loincloth was gyrating under a stroboscopic light. Suddenly a bunch of long haired whites rushed on with balletic movements, tied him to a chair and ran off again. He kicked and writhed, screaming soundlessly as the music rose to a crescendo. The chair fell over and he hit his head on the stage. After much simulated effort he broke his bonds and ran off, one fist raised in the Panther's salute. The music blared on.

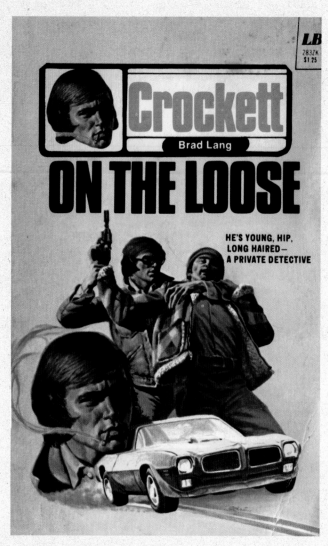

Brand of Fear (Leisure Books, 1976)

On the Loose (Leisure Books, 1975)

The Perdition Express (Leisure Books, 1976)

THE HARDBOILED HIPPIE
The Detective Fiction of Brad Lang

By the mid-1970s the countercultural scenes spawned during the previous decade had entered a period of stasis. In the US, left-wing movements had attained successes regarding civil rights and against conscription, but these either fell far short of the lofty and revolutionary goals to which radicals had aspired or served as big enough concessions to demobilise their support base. Although industrial militancy was peaking, the withdrawal of troops from Vietnam removed a major motivational and unifying force, and after years of intense activity and state repression many activists burned out, settled down to have families, or retreated into political sects or the Democratic Party. Coupled with severe economic downturn, generalised post-Watergate political exhaustion, and an influx of hard drugs into inner-city and alternative communities, radicals found themselves faced with increasing apathy and cynicism, as well as a right-wing backlash that would inflict severe reverses during the 1980s.

On a cultural level, much of the creativity and energy of the 1960s had also run its course. The counterculture's trappings—clothes, long hair, and rock music—remained, as did widespread drug consumption and a general anti-authoritarian attitude, but the artistic challenges of earlier times had largely been subsumed into the sale and production of an ever-widening array of consumer goods. Unconventionality became increasingly vapid as all manner of goods, from cars to cleaning products, were marketed as groundbreaking and 'groovy.'

Emerging from—and tapping into—this changing social atmosphere, Michigan author Brad Lang wrote three detective novels in the Crockett series—*On the Loose* (1975), *Perdition Express* (1976) and *Brand of Fear* (1976)—for paperback publisher Leisure Books. Featuring a long-haired, hip detective who takes on the cases the police can't solve, or don't care about, these politically and culturally astute mysteries transplanted the classic PI into a (then) modern setting. In keeping with the hardboiled tradition the novels engaged with the darker side of the counterculture while avoiding the standard 'marijuana leads directly to heroin' and 'all hippies are Manson-like murderers' clichés then rampant in pulp fiction.

In the following interview Lang expands on what inspired the series, as well as how he came to find a publisher during a period when crime novels and thrillers were dominated by vigilantes, cold-blooded assassins and disaster themes.

Tell us about your involvement in the 60s anti-war movement and counterculture.
I grew up near Michigan State University and started school in 1965. This was right at the beginning of the anti-war movement and there was a lot going on there in terms of [the national radical movement] Students for a Democratic Society (SDS). I became immediately involved in the student rights movement and a group of us were elected as student representatives in the late 1960s and made all sorts of trouble. By 1970 I was involved in [revolutionary group] Weatherman and had been arrested for inciting a riot, malicious destruction of property, and all that sort of thing. None of it was true, but it was during this militant period that I was involved.

How did you come to write crime novels?
To me the 60s in terms of the anti-war movement really ran from 1963 to 1972. By the end of that, I was still around the scene and had begun writing fiction. I began with a novel about the 60s which I have yet to finish. I started on the detective novel because someone suggested to me, "Why don't you start with something simpler than the great American novel?" Up to that point I hadn't read any detective novels so I began reading what was lying around my parents' house, things like Mickey Spillane and Shell Scott [aka Richard Prather]. Subsequently I spoke to somebody who knew the genre, and they put me on to Raymond Chandler, Dashiell Hammett and Ross MacDonald. That immediately inspired me.

Politically the early to mid 70s were a very desperate and frustrating time and it seemed to me that a character like that of Fred Crockett could emerge along the lines of Chandler's Phillip Marlowe. Somebody who could walk the mean streets, but was not in themselves mean.

The central character of Crockett is a man involved with the hippie scene but also a tad removed in that he is an ex-cop working as a private detective.
Originally his name was Keller and the title of the first book was *Keller On the Loose*. Unfortunately my pun was scrapped because the publishers realised somebody else had used a character called Keller, 'Keller the Killer Cop' or something. I chose Crockett,

and the first book became *Crockett on the Loose*, or simply *On the Loose*, because they used the Crockett name and logo above the title.

The character was based on some people I had met who were [military] veterans, as well as people like 'Dirty Harry', people who didn't get along well or play well with others. I never thought about making him a veteran, but the idea was that he was going to Michigan State and was in what was then known as the School of Police Administration, but later became Criminal Justice. Through being on campus he met people in the anti-war movement and so had a foot in each world. He graduated and became a cop, but didn't like it and wasn't cut out for it and subsequently moved on to become a private detective.

By the time of the novel he is 28. He's a big guy and knows a lot of people in the underground and moves easily in those circles. He has a crummy office and isn't making a lot of money. As the series goes on, he becomes increasingly involved with people on the seedy side of life. This was reflective of what happened in the movement. It had started out with civil rights and nonviolence, and as it ran into the reality of the war it became more dark and people began to fight back. This was the milieu that Crockett emerged from.

Unlike most writers working in the pulp field, your books show an understanding of where the counterculture was at by the mid-70s, as the hippie and radical scenes stalled.
There was still a lot of politics going on, but things were very fractured and much smaller than what they had been just a few years before. The scenes around the colleges nevertheless still gave me lots of material to work with, in terms of interesting conversations and characters, red herrings and so forth.

At their base the novels were still mysteries and were supposed to bring you along slowly by introducing possible suspects, and then end with a solution to the mystery. I tried to stay true to that while at the same time inserting some political issues. Some people who knew me were critical and felt the novels should have been more political, but I wanted them to be entertaining and didn't feel I could do both, even though I had written for the underground publications for years.

The first time I wrote a draft featuring Crockett it was terrible. I had him infiltrating a cult. It was very political and full of speeches, but none of it was very realistic. It just didn't work and I had to go away and read some more Chandler.

What made you decide to set the novels in a college town rather than a more typical big-city setting?
Because it was where I lived. Most people figured the books were set in Ann Arbor, which is where the University of Michigan is, but actually I was thinking more of East Lansing, which is where Michigan State is. Lansing is the capital of Michigan, so it's a big enough town to have the things that go on in the novels.

I purposely kept the location vague, other than it being a Midwestern college town. I wanted to do that because I wasn't familiar with any big cities other than Detroit. I wanted to set it somewhere that I was familiar with, where I could walk around and visualise things.

Tell us about the inspiration for Crockett's main hang-out, Ralph's Bar, as well as for his dope-dealing pal Big Eddie?
Big Eddie was a composite of various people. His main role was to serve as a foil for Crockett to bounce ideas off. Every detective also needs a buddy who can serve as a go-between to different parts of the culture. While I was writing these novels I was playing in bands as a guitarist and later a drummer, as well as a singer. Ralph's Bar is a reflection of a lot of places I was playing, not upscale obviously, a 'peanut shells on the floor' kind of place.

The Crockett series seems to have been quite different to most of what Leisure Books released. They did horror, disaster and soft-porn novels, but many of their books were series in which vigilante figures were either killing off the mafia or reacting against the changes wrought by the 60s.
Much of the detective and action fiction of the time was very right-wing. I thought it would be neat to create a different character, because progressives need heroes too and I figured it would be great to have a liberal character who carried a gun and took on the bad guys. At the same time I was very influenced by Chandler and people with a sense of humour. I wasn't aware of crime writer Robert B. Parker at that point, but I had a similar emphasis on dialogue and one-liners.

Did you have a particular audience in mind for the books?
No I didn't, and neither did the publishers, unfortunately. Most of their books were somewhat seamier in that they featured ultraviolent vigilantes or characters like [soft-porn heroine] Cherry Delight. I don't know why they thought my books would find an audience among their existing readership, and I don't think they ever really did find their audience. I did three of the

Brad Lang in the 1960s.
Courtesy of Brad Lang.

books, until the editor responsible for my series left the company, after which they promptly dropped it.

I wasn't aware of it at the time, but the only other person doing something like this was Roger L. Simon with his Moses Wine series. The first book was made into a film in 1978 with Richard Dreyfuss. The books were very different to mine in that they are they are steeped in Jewish culture, and not hardboiled at all. However, Wine is a detective who has come out of the hippie scene and is still around that, and his community is politically involved. I think Leisure thought this would be their version of that. Everything that publisher did was derivative.

Regardless of Leisure's intentions, I didn't come across the Wine books until after my first book was published. I saw a review which said, "Having read the Moses Wine series this is nothing new, but it's nice." Which I thought was unfair.

What was it like working with Leisure? Did they pay well? I notice that your novels, as with many Leisure titles, included tobacco advertising, in the form of a colour insert bound into the text pages.
Yes, I think they made a lot of their money from advertising cigarettes. They paid me an advance against royalties, but there were never any royalties, so I was going broke writing. They didn't promote the books. They just showed up in bookstores and airports. It was all very random. I think their approach was just to pump out as many different books as possible in single runs, so that they never had to pay royalties.

They never made any changes to the books. So far as I know, there was no actual editing. Maybe that was a tribute to my writing skills, but I have a feeling they just didn't do that sort of thing.

Did you have any input into the cover art?
I never had any input or gave them any information at all. That was Leisure Books, they just did what they wanted. They pulled quotes out of context and stuck them on the cover. At the time I had a part-time job and was working in a band and this was just something else I was doing, so really I was just happy to be published.

If you line the three books up, you can see the evolution in their art. With the first book the artist tried to make Crockett look like he did in the novel. He has long hair, a blue denim jacket and sunglasses, and is driving a Trans Am. The long hair is only Beatles-length, so it's probably more from another era, but the look is closer than later on. As the books went on, the logo with him smoking a cigarette disappeared and they put him in a leisure suit to try and appeal to their usual audience. Crockett never would've worn a leisure suit in his life, certainly not with a pink shirt.

The first Crockett novel, On the Loose, *was published in 1975 and concerns the search for a missing college student.*
Yes, the girl's father comes to Crockett via a recommendation and has trouble believing that this guy can be of any help at all. It opens with the line **He stood in the doorway, staring at me and the office like a man who'd walked into the Christian Science Reading Room and found himself witnessing an appendectomy.** There was definitely a culture clash.

Eventually Crockett takes the case, and in the process of looking for the girl uncovers a network of police involved in drug dealing, topless bars, etc. The starting premise was about broken family ties, but in the process of Crockett trying to track down the daughter to see if she wants to come home, he discovers she has fallen into a lot of things that are pretty dodgy.

The book had an early working title of *All the Crooked Cops,* but I decided that was a bit too obvious. However that's what it was about, Crockett and other people from the political movement running up against corrupt police. One of the things that had happened was that as people involved in the anti-war movement came up against the police, their focus shifted to things like police brutality. I tried to walk a very fine line here in that I wanted to avoid it becoming a political novel, while having elements of that in it.

With this first novel, I didn't plot everything out beforehand. I just began writing and saw where it took me. I don't think the debut was the best of the three because it rambles around a bit. I was trying to find the character and discover what he was capable of doing.

The second novel, Perdition Express, *came out in 1976. It concerns the murder of a bass player belonging to a band, and sees Crockett navigate intra-band sexual and religious struggles as well as conflicts with rival bands and managers. Where did you find the inspiration for all of this?*

The bar band scene in the mid-70s was very popular. There were half a dozen large venues in East Lansing alone, and I was lucky enough to play some of them regularly. Most college towns tended to have some pretty big venues that were more like nightclubs. During the period in which these novels were set the drinking age was 18 in our area, so bars were very popular with college students. East Lansing was dry for many years, but there were all these bars just outside the city limits, so eventually the authorities gave up.

While playing covers in these bars it occurred to me that someone could kill one of the musicians, particularly the bass player, who was often standing toward the back, and nobody would notice because the music was so loud. The first line of the book is: **The drummers' licks sounded like gunshots,** which it turns out they are. After this murder, which Crockett witnesses, the rest of the novel is an investigation into who committed the crime, including one band member who is into the occult and another who is a Jesus Freak. As with most crime novels, some of these served as red herrings, or were characters I thought it would be interesting to have Crockett, who was the ultimate cynic, run into.

It was only pointed out to me later on that the band depicted on the cover of the second book is directly based on a promotional photo of the New York Dolls. I certainly didn't have a band like that in mind. I was thinking more of a heavy-metal cover band.

Brand of Fear, *which was your third novel but the second to be published, in 1976, featured another original premise in that Crockett is hired by a gay computer programmer to deal with someone who is blackmailing him. Later on in the novel Crockett finds a second employer in the form of Gay Liberation activists who employ him to solve a murder related to the blackmail case. Given Leisure's presumably straight blue-collar audience it's perhaps not surprising to find there is no explicit mention of homosexuality on the book's cover or inside blurb. How did the publisher respond to you making the gay scene the focus of the book?*

As with the other books, there wasn't any discussion. I sent them the manuscript, and they said "Great" and published it. The cover image is interesting as it features a figure who looks vaguely professorial, but is not identifiably gay in the style of the time. The original title was 'Man in the Closet', in part because one of the plot points involves somebody literally hiding in a closet to take blackmail photos. That was the one thing they changed by making it *Brand of Fear*, which sounds like something they had left over from a western.

During the 60s I knew people who were gay and closeted, but nobody was out. The mid 70s was still a very homophobic period, but I was interested to set the book in the gay scene because people were just beginning to discuss those issues in Michigan. I wasn't particularly seeking to break new ground or be overtly political, but I thought this would be a great setting for a blackmail plot.

Why did the series come to an end?

I was working on a fourth book, but all I really had was an opening sentence: **I was playing dartboard baseball with a part-time pickpocket by the name of Flaherty when this 220-pound drunk started tearing up the bar.** The drunk had been in a poker game and lost a lot of money, so Crockett decides to check it out. This was another subculture that I knew something about, private poker games. There had been someone killed in a game in our town around the time I was writing. I had the novel all set to go, but then the deal with Leisure ended. I probably could have found a better publisher, but my agent had started out at Random House and worked their way down to Leisure, who were pretty much at the bottom. My agent was with the Scott Meredith agency, who had a pretty good reputation at that time, but once I had been published in paperback it was considered very difficult to break out of that world.

Also around this time I got married and was looking at raising a family. I wasn't making much money writing short stories and novels and playing in a band, so I answered an ad that was looking for a copywriter. I told them I was a novelist and hadn't done copywriting before but thought I could do it. Oddly enough they agreed and that became my career for the next 20 years. I was kind of a reverse Elmore Leonard in that I wrote books first and then went into advertising.

IAIN McINTYRE

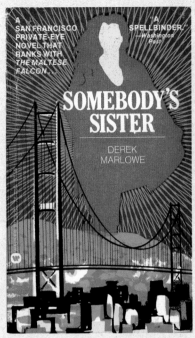

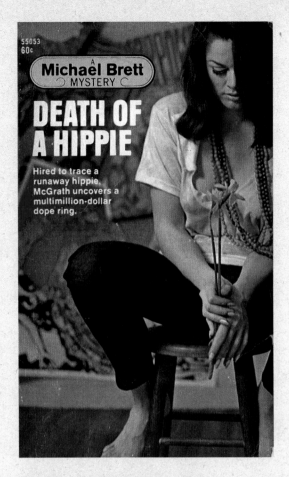

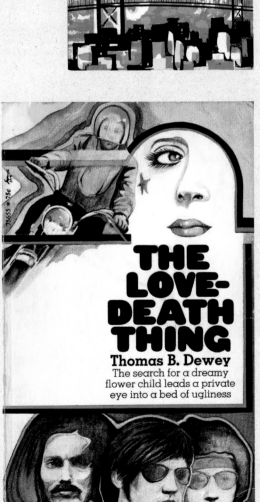

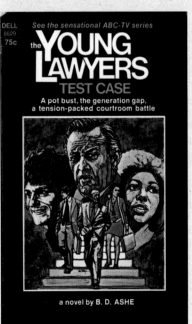

Somebody's Sister (Warner Books, 1975)

Death of a Hippie (Pocket Books, 1968)

The Young Lawyers Test Case (Dell, 1970)

The Love-Death Thing (Pocket Books, 1971)

Pulp Fiction Music Novels

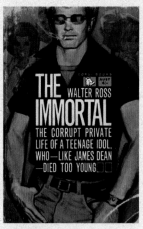

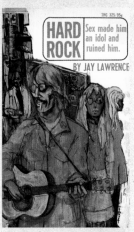

Rock'n'Roll Gal (Beacon, 1957), *The Immortal* (Corgi, 1960), *Jazzman in Nudetown* (Gaslight Books, 1964), *Johnny Staccato* (Consul Books, 1964), *The Big Blues* (Digit Books, 1963), *Hard Rock* (Triumph, 1968), *Sex-a-Reenos* (P.E.C, 1966), *Second-Hand Family* (Bobbs-Merrill, 1965), *King Jude* (New English Library, 1971), *Queens of Deliria* (Star, 1977), *Why Not Join the Giraffes?* (Dell, 1970), *Soul City Downstairs* (Pyramid, 1969)

The Big Scene
(New English Library, 1969)

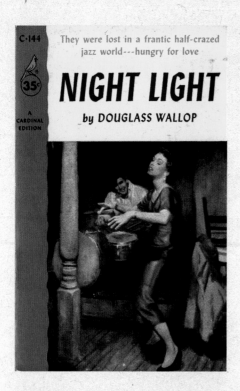

Night Light (Cardinal, 1954)
The Jazz Sinner (Leisure Books, 1966)

Hot Lips—Jack Hanley
(Designs Publishing, 1952)

If only the titles and cover copy of pulp novels lived up to the often fervid expectations they provoke . . . But, as every latter day reader of these books knows, they seldom do. *Hot Lips* is no exception. The cover depicts a voluptuous babe in the midst of a torrid dance while, to her left, another sexy woman plays hot licks on sax, her lips sensually caressing the mouthpiece. Behind the dancer sits a man, tie askew, transfixed by booze and lust (one assumes) and appearing ready to initiate some serious erotic activity. The painting of a nude sits serenely in its frame just above his head. Cover copy proclaims SHE MADE HOT MUSIC—AND TORRID LOVE. And: THIS ORCHESTRA GIRL KNEW RAPTUROUS NIGHTS . . . WILD REVELS . . . FLAMING RHYTHMS AND BURNING DESIRES . . . The reader of such a book today would be excused for expecting to find a scene in which the three principals ended up in bed together—an old-fashioned ménage à trois or new-fashioned threesome—which would give the title considerably more resonance and accuracy than the novel does.

The narrative contains no such scene. Rather, it relates the story of an all-girl vagabond (i.e. traveling) orchestra, the Musical Queens, hoping to make it to the big time. But when the lead soloist Ethelda suffers DTs and is forced into rehab, the mood of the orchestra turns decidedly dour. Before the reader can turn the page, however, a younger, prettier, infinitely more talented musician magically appears on the scene to take Ethelda's place and reinvigorate the band's aspirations. Althea Allen is just 19 and desperate to elude the clutches of her stepfather, who was determined **to fiddle with her** (in keeping with the musical motif). The band publicist, Pete Dwyer, and fellow musician Mona Storm take the gifted, virginal Althea under wing. While ostensibly looking out for the young woman, both fall in love with her. Through some rather creaky exposition we learn that Pete had been briefly married to a Hollywood starlet—until he found her in bed with another woman. And Mona had soured on men when her second husband absconded with cherished items from her wardrobe in order to enter a drag-queen contest. Pete's distrust of women, Mona's desire to get even with men, and Althea's naiveté and fear of rough, sexually aggressive men make for a combustible denouement—followed, fortuitously, by a happily-ever-after ending.

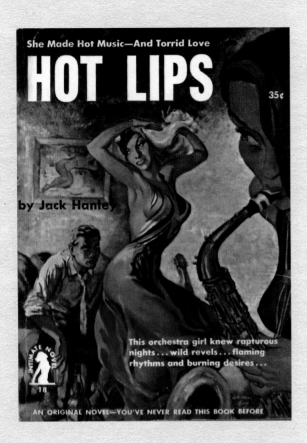

Hot Lips provides an early manifestation of the still rare fictional response to the women's bands that proliferated in the years around World War Two. The novel does a fair job of dramatizing life on the road, the drudgery of rehearsals, and the degrading extent to which the female musicians were subjected to the mercy of clothing and make-up, like the stewardesses of the same era. It is probably redundant to add that the story also contains frequent references to booze, weed, and sex—especially lesbianism. Passages like the one on this page must have challenged the boundaries of censorship for 1952, even while earning the work's status as **INTIMATE BOOK 18**.

DAVID RIFE

"You are a darling," Mona said softly and her hand holding Althea's drew her close, gently Althea could feel the sharp prominences of Mona's breasts through the thin gown, pressing against her own while Mona's left arm encircled her waist.

Althea was a little dazed, yet not displeased at the affectionate gesture. She was slightly ill at ease on the one hand, being unaccustomed to physical evidences of affection, on the other, her natural hunger for love responded to the closeness and warmth of Mona's embrace, the low, soothing sound of Mona's voice . . .

"You're quite the loveliest bit of a girl I've ever seen," she purred, "and with it all you're gentle and modest . . . it would be hard not to be fond of you, Althea dear." Her hand cupped Althea's chin, lifting her face until the clear, gentian eyes were looking into her own burning gray ones, then before Althea realized her intent, Mona's head moved lower and her mouth was soft and warm against Althea's . . . The warmth of Mona's body next to her and the fragrant softness of Mona's arms set up a feeling of deep content, of exciting warmth. Without realizing it, her own lips responded, trembled against Mona's until she pulled away to take a deep breath.

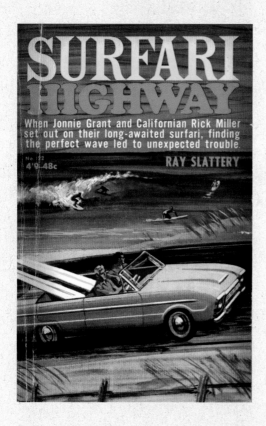

The Restless Ones (Horwitz, 1960)

Surfie (Horwitz, 1966)

The Sound Mixers (Widescope, 1977)

Surfari Highway (Horwitz, 1965)

WILD BEATS
Australian Rock Pulps

The point about pulp is speed. Write it fast, read it fast, don't dwell on it. But that doesn't mean to say its rapid currents don't run deep.

In keeping with these noble traditions, I'm going to quickly consider here a clutch of Australian pulps that could double under the 'rock book' subset. That is, mainly novels like Bill Sheridan's *My Boy George Rivers* (1963), Joanne Joyce's *It's All Right, Ma, I'm Only Sighing* (1968), *Surfari Highway* (Ray Slattery, 1966), *The Groupies* (Ricki Francis, 1972), Pete Draffin's *Pop* (1967, with illustrations by Martin Sharpe), *The Sound Mixers* (Eric Scott, 1977) and two by Carl Ruhen, both from 1967, *The Rebels* and *Wild Beat*.

As far back as 1886, Fergus Hume's famous *The Mystery of a Hansom Cab* provided a vivid picture of the popular music people enjoyed in Melbourne at the time—not dissimilar, in a way, to the virtual soundtrack someone like George Pelecanos evokes in his more recent Washington, DC, crime novels. Louis Stone's *Jonah* (1911) could be Australia's first JD novel in the way it portrays Sydney's larrikin pushes at the turn of the century, complete with their attendant sort of dance-hall fever. Since then, music-infused fiction in Australia has stumbled forward.

Bringing up the rear are a number of other pulp titles that don't quite make the first rank because music only passes through them tangentially at best, or they are non-fiction. Among the latter are Charles Higham's two groundbreaking 1961 books on rock and roll, *Teen Beat* and *The Big Beat*, Jim Oram's *The Business of Pop* (1966), James Holledge's *The Flower People* (1967) and Ken Taylor's *Rock Generation* (1970). In other pulp fiction, like the clutch of local 'bodgie' novels from the early 60s, music is only incidental. But I will briefly note some these books along the way, as part of the larger shift that pulps underwent in the 1960s.

Rock books were born, as both fiction and non-fiction, at the turn-out of the 1950s. The rock novel actually predates rock journalism, whose birth date is usually given as the mid-60s, when the counterculture underground press swelled up and New Journalism, which accepted the new cultural primacy of rock and roll, began to infiltrate the mainstream media. If Ernie Weatherall's *Rock'n'Roll Gal* of 1957 wasn't the first rock novel, it was Harlan Ellison's *Rockabilly* (1961).

Rockabilly (later retitled *Spider Kiss*) is a good book, establishing at least one of the major tropes that would recur throughout so much rock fiction to follow: the overnight sensation chewed up and spat out by the music business, usually courtesy of an exploitative manager.

The broader bibliography of rock books begins with another couple of standard genres, the star biography and the pseudo-serious sociological study (the juvenile delinquency—JD—book writ scientific). Australia in the 50s produced a rich lode of pulp: war stories, westerns, crime, adventure, romance, a little science fiction and horror. The youth/gang/juvenile delinquent genre would become a staple in the US in the 50s, with its extensions to hot rods and rock and roll—and all underpinned by sex and violence—but Australia produced little in this vein until the 60s, when the JD novel was transformed locally into the bodgie novel, and to a lesser extent the 'surfie' novel. As the 1960s progressed, the sex and violence set against an increasing amount of rock music in these books was tweaked, in the hippie era, into sex and drugs and rock and roll. The morality tales themselves didn't change much, just the backgrounds.

The first Australian rock book, *Teen Beat*, by Charles Higham, was published by Horwitz in 1961. It was followed the same year by Higham's *The Big Beat*, also from Horwitz. Both followed the model set by Englishman Royston Ellis's contemporaneous *The Big Beat Scene* and American Steve Kahn's *Tops in Pops*, as a gallery of star profiles. Horwitz was Australia's pulp merchant supreme, and if Australian rock books had to begin anywhere, it was appropriate they began here. The cover of *Teen Beat* is gorgeous, and the content is pretty good too—a series of well-written pen-portraits of Johnny O'Keefe, Col Joye and all the rest of them. Higham, an Englishman who wrote on pop for the Australian magazine *Bulletin*, went on to edit a couple of anthologies of horror stories for Horwitz before moving to Los Angeles and writing a string of very successful Hollywood biographies, including controversial ones of Errol Flynn and Howard Hughes.

Horwitz published Australia's first rock novel proper in 1963, Bill Sheridan's *My Boy, George Rivers*. Music had been coming to the fore in fiction, but don't be deceived by Ru Pullan's *The Restless Ones*, which Horwitz published in 1960. It was essentially a JD novel, the story of spoiled kids on Sydney's North Shore who are let down by their parents. Their kicks—driving fast and crashing oldies' parties—are pretty tame and astonishingly exclude sex, drugs, and rock and roll. Rupert Pullan was a playwright who touched equally superficially on emerging youth culture in other Horwitz titles like *The Hardskins* (1960), as promising yet disappointing as *The Restless Ones*, and *Bird with a Medal* (1960), whose change of scenery to the beach doesn't help it to be much better.

My Boy George Rivers was a novel about a rock star, set in the music business, **THE HILARIOUS STORY OF A SWINGIN' SINGER AND HIS SEXY FAN CLUB PRESIDENT.** Bill Sheridan's name doesn't otherwise crop up in bibliographies, but he was presumably Australian—the book's content certainly is. It's the light-hearted, mildly cynical story of manager Sam Young, who discovers young George Rivers singing with a band called the Ding Dings. Signing to Rialto Records, they have a hit single that goes gold (160,000 sales) with a song called 'Rooty Rooty Chip'. The nature of this song is never explained. George then falls in with his fan club president Millicent Pringle, who turns out to be a Yoko Ono figure. She is a politicised vegetarian who writes his next single, the anti-smoking 'Nicotine Jane', which is a hit until it's pulled from the market due to pressure from tobacco companies. George ends up with his own national TV show singing the pregnant Millicent's latest composition 'One Day I Was a Girl, the Next Day a Mother' (with the gender switched, of course). There is no comeuppance for anyone, not even Sam Young.

In 1964, everything changed. The big stars, Elvis, Cliff Richard, Tommy Steele, had spawned virtual publishing industries in their own right, but when the Beatles came along, it was a whole new ballgame again. That year there were about a dozen notionally 'rock books' published around the world, and nearly every one was about the Beatles.

The Australian bodgie novel was a variation on the standard pulp JD novel, in which sex, violence, fast cars, crime, and rock and roll were all intertwined to varying degrees. The best remembered include William Dick's *A Bunch of Ratbags* and Colin Johnson's *Wild Cat Falling*, both from 1965, along with Criena Rohan's *The Delinquents* (1962), and Gunther Bahnemann's *Hoodlum* (1963). Ru Pullan's characters in *The Restless Ones* and *The Hardskins* were never rough enough (too middle-class) to be mistaken for real bodgies. *The Delinquents*, of course, even

as it cited such specific songs as 'Rock Around the Clock' and 'St. Louis Blues', had a lot more rock and roll about it when it eventually reached the screen in 1989, starring Kylie Minogue. There was a soundtrack album to sell now, after all. But still, the music was only present as something that was assigned partial responsibility for bodgies' waywardness.

That *The Delinquents* ever became a film at all is an indication of its renown. But its author Rohan was a one-hit wonder; she published only one more book before dying young. William Dick was a similar story. *A Bunch of Ratbags* (1965) was a hit, the story of a young bodgie in Melbourne's working-class suburb of Footscray, laced with sex and crime. But again, it was only when it was translated into another medium—as early as 1966, when it was produced as a stage musical which was revived as recently as 2005—that it took on much rock and roll. William Dick aspired briefly to a literary career—he published a second book, *Naked Prodigal*, in 1969 (which told essentially the same story over again)—but after that never returned to print.

In 1966, Horwitz published Ray Slattery's *Surfari Highway*, which was matched in the Horwitz catalogue by Roger Carr's contemporaneous *Surfie*, which also appeared in 1966. *Surfari Highway*'s author, Ray Slattery, otherwise specialized in war stories, though he also wrote *Love Me in Ecstasy* (1963) and the horse-racing yarn *The Tip* (1965).

Surfari Highway has American visitor Rick Miller driving along the NSW north coast in a Ford Falcon. Up around Angowrie he gets a job singing at some café. He's supposed to be a folk singer, though he doesn't seem to be carrying a guitar and uses the local piano player to perform 'Go Tell It on the Mountain'. Then Cab Trewman shows up, a rock star escaping from pressure with his girlfriend, and of course he has a sing—Beatles songs—and upstages Miller. The days are spent surfing and the nights singing. **Folk songs appealed to the majority of older people rather than the young.** There are some eyes between Ricky and Cab's girlfriend, and some madness on Cab's part, a stealing incident, and in the end everyone goes along on their way. No real sex or violence, just a bit of music.

Another Horwitz release from 1966 was *Cross Section*, by Julian Spencer, which crosses over with arguably the most unique Australian pulp genre of them all, the Kings Cross book. In *Cross Section*, Spencer has Dezzo run away from home (Moonee Ponds) and fall in with the fast set up the Cross. He

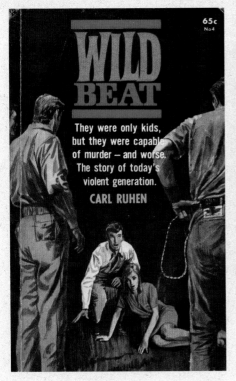

Wild Beat (Scripts 1967)
A Bunch of Ratbags (Ure Smith, 1968)
A Bunch of Ratbags (Gold Star Publications, 1972)

falls for 'rich girl slumming it' art student Melinda, and narrowly escapes the cops when delivering a package to the infamous George Hotel (what does it contain—pot, heroin?). Then the couple moves in with a band called the Emotions before they run off together up the coast to Byron Bay, where they join Melinda's MG-driving surfie ex-boyfriend. There's a showdown for her affections that Dezzo loses, and they part, but he will not go back to Moonee Ponds. *Cross Section* features an ever-increasing amount of alcohol consumption, and drugs, mainly pot, and the persistent presence of music, especially Dylan and the Beatles. And then there are the Emotions. Spencer went on to publish several more titles including the Kings Cross pulp, *The Spungers* (1967).

By 1967 the Summer of Love was in full effect in the UK and US, and new kinds of pop novels were emerging, such as Nik Cohn's *I Am Still the Greatest Says Johnny Angelo* (1967) and movie novelizations like *Privilege* (1967) and *Wild in the Streets* (1968). New kinds of pulp publishing were also emerging along with the rise of the underground press. The new novels reset the plot trajectory from the earlier evil-manager-exploits-naive-star to the star-who-falls-from-grace, an arc that would also inform later exercises like the film *Stardust* (1974) and the rock operas *Tommy* (1969) and *The Rise and Fall of Ziggy Stardust and the Spiders from Mars* (1972).

Rock culture became such a fact of life that even the Australian serial detectives could no longer avoid it, from Carter Brown's *Death on a Downbeat* and *Hi-Fi Fadeout* (both 1958) to Larry Kent's *The Weirdos* (1978) and *How Far to the Top?* (1979). But it was a clutch of novels from 1967 that are the most intriguing. Books like *Wild Beat*, *The Rebels*, *Pop*, and *It's All Right, Ma, I'm Only Sighing*, most of which were published by Scripts, an imprint of Horwitz.

Wild Beat and *The Rebels* were both by Carl Ruhen, who went on to become the master noveliser of 70s films and TV shows. The *Rebels* is about a Brylcreemed bodgie called Bernie who gets caught up in a cycle of crime. Does it qualify as a bodgie novel with longhairs on the cover? Certainly, music—rock and roll—is Bernie's constant companion. As the story opens, Bernie is bored at a Kings Cross club called Michelangelos. He describes the scene at the club where the kids are grooving to the music, **Good music too. Locky Drefus up from Melbourne and the Charioteers** and **Bobo Adams**. Bernie hangs out at another club called the Dancing Bear, where the house band is the Sheikhs, who play their hit song 'Surf City Socrates'. Bernie and his gang boost cars and like fighting. His parents smother him. His gang rapes some girls they pick up at Luna Park, then beats up a north shore mod, and their exhilaration is matched by the song on the car radio that has that **good solid meaty rock beat.**

In Ruhen's *Wild Beat*, the setting shifts to Melbourne—the same western suburbs depicted in *A Bunch of Ratbags*—where cynical, aging radio DJ Earl Klaxon is trying to bring peace to the warring gangs, the mods and the sharpies, although the latter fit the description of bodgies more closely. But then Ruhen gets his subcultural details even more confused. **It was the kids who were Klaxon's bread and butter, and he hated them. Punks.**

Wild Beat is about Alex Brittle, 18, a sharpie, which can only be understood now, in its 60s sense, before the classic 70s definition came in, as a sort of rougher, more working-class version of a mod, although at no point does the author offer any definition of either a sharpie or the mods with whom the sharpies are at war. Basement coffee shops like April's, off St Kilda Road, all have chromium jukeboxes in the corner. **The music bellowed out and rocked the small dark room, great solid slabs of sound that bore down on them.** The Mecca dancehall in Footscray is a sharpie stronghold. Mods invade and one is killed. Klaxon, whose musical diet is never described, appoints himself public peacemaker. The police solve the crime. There's plenty of violence and a little sex, but no drugs apart from drink, only a little actual music, and not a lot of plot.

Pete Draffin's *Pop*, also published by Scripts in 1967, is a novel, more or less. Its format is unusual, a square-shaped paperback with black-and-white cover art as well as line illustrations by Martin Sharp. Less a novel because it is not so much plotted as an atmospheric account of a party, or 'happening'. The illustrations, needless to say, are terrific, and as an artifact, a period piece, this is one of Australia's lovely lost ones. The party, thrown by an artist at his studio, has the very strong presence of a band, **a wild rhythm and blues group**, not to mention includes cameos by characters like devil-worshipper Alistair Black. It becomes a bad trip, which is eventually broken up by a gang of bodgies who bash everyone in sight. Bummer.

After penning *The Swingers* for Scripts in 1967, Joanne Joyce wrote *It's All Right, Ma, I'm Only Sigh-ing* for Horwitz in 1968. As befits a book named after a line from Bob Dylan, it is a coming-of-age story infused with music and the mood of the times. The book opens with Mardie at a party at which they're listening to Jefferson Airplane's *Surrealistic Pillow*.

Later, lying here in the darkness, she had realised it was really beaut, the kind of record that worked both ways—it could turn you on as it had at the party, or it could give you something to think about when you were on your own.

Mardie meets Mike, who is careful with his stereo gear when he plays his Hendrix LPs. They hang at a club called Bach's, popping purple hearts, listening to a band called the Serpents **really belting it out**. One big Saturday night is a love-in at Paddington Town Hall, headlined by the Rainbow Tarantula. They listen to 'Itchycoo Park' and the **new BGs' LP**. It's all rather a hoot, and leaves author Joyce with a perfectly formed two-book legacy.

By the end of the 1960s, pulps were changing again. With their very life threatened by the rise of television, transistor radios and record players—not to mention the underground press—and with the codification/relaxation of censorship laws, pulps in the 1970s became predominantly about sleaze. One exception that ventures into rock territory is Ricki Francis's *The Groupies* (Scripts, 1972). Francis was extremely prolific in the early 70s, churning out titles such as *96 Kings Cross* (1972), which must have been the inspiration for the racy Australian TV show *Number 96*, *Queen Rat* (1974), *Sex Farm* (1972), and *Teenage Jailbait* (1974). *The Groupies* has as its centerpiece a rock festival in Barrona, the original hometown of rock star Judd Morrow, who is dissatisfied with sleeping with his manager, and returns home to encounter the mother-daughter love-interest team of Grace and Dora. It's a fair read that might benefit from a bit more sleaze!

Eric Scott's quite impressive *The Sound Mixers* (1977) features a classic cover illustration whose models uncannily resemble singers Daryl Braithwaite and Renée Geyer, and tells the story of an ambitious young rock promoter who has an office romance with his Girl Friday as they try to get the biggest band in the world, Andromeda, to come and tour Australia. It has a ring of authenticity to it, and Scott was well qualified: an English show-business reporter, he migrated to Australia in 1970, where he worked for *TV Times* and briefly edited the teenybopper rag *Spunky*.

GIRL GANGS, BIKER BOYS, AND REAL COOL CATS

When he found himself jobless in 1976, he set to writing *The Sound Mixers*, drawing on experience that included going out on the road with Daddy Cool, Ted Mulry, and Sherbet. Scott says he based Andromeda loosely on the Bay City Rollers, who toured Australia twice in 1975/76, while the book's climactic concert scene was virtually a piece of straight reportage on a Neil Diamond show in Melbourne. *The Sound Mixers* was published by Widescope, who in their short lifespan most notably also published Esben Storm's novelization of his 1978 film *In Search of Anna*. *The Sound Mixers* was mooted as a TV movie, and Scott also wrote a stageplay version, but it was never produced in either medium, and the book was soon forgotten, although when Paul Goldman's film about Frank Sinatra's controversial 1974 Australian tour, *The Night We Called It a Day*, came out in 2003, its plot seemed to have been lifted directly from *The Sound Mixers*. Scott went on to publish a number of other novels (mostly for children, and none set in the music scene); *The Sound Mixers* is now available as an e-book, as is Scott's appealing memoir, *I Could Have Been a Contender*.

Remarkably, even though Stuart Hall churned out Australian bikie novels in the early 70s, and even after Richard Allen in the UK had made the skinhead novel a staple, no one in Australia wrote about 1970s sharpies, who would surely have been ripe for exploitation, until much more recently. But then, much of the impetus behind the pulps was in the process of shifting over to films, and specifically B-movie exploitation, at the time. Surfers and bikies alike graduated to the big screen, complete with rock soundtracks, and the Australian car opera—a sort of cross between the road movie and a western—became a unique local genre that hit its first peak with the *Mad Max* trilogy, starting in the late 1970s, and is still alive today.

The rock novel, too, remains alive: after going through a highbrow rite of passage—David Foster's *Plumbum* (1983)—it has in some sense ended up back where it started, in a state of suspended hysteria, with books like Linda Jaivin's *Rock'n'Roll Babes from Outer Space* (1996); with JD transmogrifying into YA; with music and crime continuing to crossfertilise in Peter Doyle's and Dave Warner's novels; and with the sex, drugs and music mix remixed in Christos Tsiolkas's *Loaded* (1995), Fiona McGregor's *Chemical Palace* (2002) and Venero Armano's *The Dirty Beat* (2007).

CLINTON WALKER

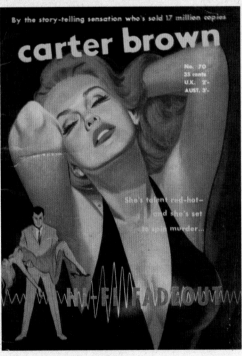

The Groupies (Scripts, 1972)
Hi-Fi Fadeout (Horwitz, 1958)

A Sad Song Singing—Thomas B. Dewey (Schuster, 1963)

Folk singers and private eyes are not the most likely of combinations. What's so criminal about the 1960s coffee-house scene and long-haired guitar strumming entertainers singing ancient songs of doomed love? The closest you'd get to danger is if someone sang a song with a strong anti-government theme, like a pacifist's paean to the end of the Vietnam war. But Thomas Dewey manages to tell a story of a missing folk singer, his grief-stricken girlfriend, and the mysterious contents of a suitcase she's been entrusted with, and come up with a fast moving, action-packed tale that is basically a pursuit thriller.

The plot is fairly straightforward. Cresentia Fanio seeks out the help of Mac, Dewey's world-weary Chicago PI, and asks him to locate her missing boyfriend, singer Richie Darden. She claims she's been followed, has just managed to lose the men on her tail, and needs Mac's help to hide a suitcase and find Richie soon. He's skeptical about the whole thing, especially about the suitcase Richie has given Cress to watch over. She refuses to open it as she promised Richie she wouldn't. When thugs burst into his office, and Mac only just manages to beat them off and escape with Cress and her suitcase, his mind is pretty much made up. He'll do his best to find Richie and get to the bottom of why the thugs want the suitcase so badly.

Detective-novel elements are at a minimum here. It's the story of Cress and her complete immersion in the folk-singing scene that makes for a fascinating read. Dewey creates a variety of coffee-house locations, from swank carpeted establishments that serve meals and alcohol to the dingiest dive offering only regular coffee and apologies for the broken espresso machine from a waitress in a leotard, while college boys play chess and turtleneck-wearing beatniks strum their guitars on a wobbly wooden stage. The atmosphere feels oddly old-fashioned, almost clichéd yet wholly authentic. Dewey even dreams up a few folk songs with haunting lyrics. You can practically hear the music wafting off the pages. Mac can't help but succumb to the lure of the music and discovers that Cress herself has an unmined talent for singing just waiting to be unleashed on a welcome audience.

We rarely see the teens and college-age kids through their own eyes; rather, they're shown from the point of view of Mac (who, like any good PI, is the first-person narrator) or other adults. He does a good job of seeing people as they are, but is fascinated especially by Cress and her music world. The music has an almost mystical power, captivating not just Mac but all the adults in the story, as in this exchange between Mac and the owner of a music venue who finds their music to be unique to the youth culture:

"Is he good? Special?"

"Well—they liked him. . . ."

"Does it take a musician to judge?"

"Oh no—you see, it doesn't have much to do with music. I think what you have to be is seventeen, eighteen years old—at heart, anyway. It's the song, you see, and how you come by it and how you sing it, how much heart you put into it. That's how I see it, anyway. Leave it to them—the kids know the difference. We get along fine. I tell you—some of these kids they can break your heart."

At each new gig Mac gathers up bits of vital information about the missing singer. He begins to wonder if Darden may have been involved in a robbery. When he gets a chance to handle the mysterious suitcase and finds it suspiciously light, he suspects the worst, fearing that Cress is being exploited as a decoy while Darden makes his escape. But it's more than just another case. By the end of the book, Mac has come to respect not only the subculture of the coffeehouse scene and the talented musicians who make it unique, but all young people just like Cress.

Mac is not your typical private eye. Sure he's great in a fistfight, and though he carries a gun with a legal license he's reluctant to pull the trigger. This case that forces him on a road trip through the folk-singing world with a teenage girl also puts him in the role of surrogate father. We see a tender side to him as he comes to care for her not only as his client, but as a lost girl too much in love with a fantasy. At one point he seems utterly lost himself. No longer able to reach her with his compassionate talk, yet knowing he needs to convince her that Darden's disappearance may have very dangerous consequences, he dissolves into frustrated silence. His lament is summed up in a simple painful sentence: "If only I could sing, I thought."

J.F. NORRIS

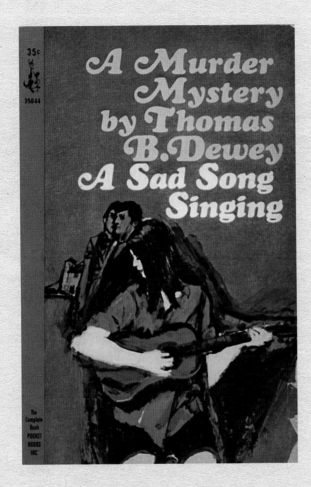

The boy sang another tune and this one went over somewhat better. He got a nice reception when he finished, except for Cress.

"That's a good song," she said. "Too bad he has to ruin it."

"Well," I said, "he seems to know all the words to it."

She gave me a look, then her shoulder. The waitress brought the Negro a cup of coffee and lingered, talking to him in a low voice. His white teeth flashed at her.

"Jocko!" the guitar player said loudly, "sing something!"

Everyone turned and looked at the Negro, who had stopped smiling, disconcerted by the sudden attention. Applause broke out and I heard the waitress say:

"Go ahead, Jocko."

The guitar player stepped down, offering his instrument. With what seemed to be honest reluctance, the Negro got up and accepted it

"Now . . . !" Cress said under her breath.

Two bright spots of color glowed in her long, pale face.

"You've heard him before?" I said.

She gave me another look.

"He's bound to have something to sing about," she said.

I had to agree on general principle, but I didn't see how she could know merely by looking at him that he would be able to deliver it.

Surely, I thought, in stubborn skepticism, there are Negroes who can't sing with unusual distinction.

As it turned out , this boy sang with a lot of power and style. I had never heard the songs before. They were original and gusty and he sang them as near as I could judge, from the heart.

All Night Stand (Mayflower, 1967)
Myself for Fame (Consul, 1967)
All Night Stand (Ballantine, 1969)

SIR OR MADAM, WILL YOU READ MY BOOK?
British Beat Group and Rock Fiction of the 1960s

By 1964 Beatlemania had most of the civilized world in its grip. Its impact and style swept across our culture, its influence felt not just in music, but in film, the visual arts, and of course literature. The hedonistic world of the beat groups was ripe for exploitation by paperback writers and hardcover scribes alike. Sex, drugs, sensation and scandal sell books. Stir in a little social commentary and some inter-generational friction and, as the Beatles postulated in 'Paperback Writer', it might just "make a million for you overnight".

Rock fiction sprouted in several countries in the 60s, but it was from Britain that its most defining works emerged. Some of the best of these are examined here in more or less chronological order, to give the reader a sense of the genre's evolution.

Myself for Fame—Royston Ellis (Consul, 1964)

Dating from 1964, *Myself for Fame* is the first British beat group–themed novel. Dubbed "King of the Beatniks" by the press, Royston Ellis was one of the most recognizable figures on the UK beatnik scene, having published several volumes of poetry, most notably *Jiving to Gyp* (1959) and *Rave* (1960). He'd also performed recitations of his poetry—'Rocketry,' he called it—backed by early rock groups like the Shadows, the Red Caps, and the embryonic Beatles, then still a quintet with Stu Sutcliffe on bass. It was Ellis, in fact, who suggested the group amend their name from Beetles to Beatles. He also introduced the Liverpool lads to the pleasures of chewing Benzedrine-soaked strips torn from the inside of asthma inhalers.

Ellis's interaction with the pre-fame Beatles informed *Myself for Fame*, which he wrote in 1963. "The Beatles appear as the Rhythmettes in that book," he told me in 2013. "A lot of material was also drawn from my time with the Red Caps and also the beat lifestyle—and drinking—of bass guitarist Jet Harris of the Drifters/Shadows." The Red Caps, a London rock-and-roll group featuring singer Chris Tidmarsh (aka Neil Christian) and teenage lead guitarist Jimmy Page, provided backing music for several of Royston's Rocketry readings in late 1960 and early 1961, and were the inspiration for the fictitious rock-and-roll combo in the opening chapter of Ellis's 1961 book, *The Big Beat Scene*, an otherwise factual overview of the worldwide teenage rock and pop scene of the

day. The opening chapter of that book, with the Red Caps recast as Tavy Tender & His Teensters, was in many ways a dry run for *Myself for Fame*, which appeared a couple of years later.

Myself for Fame is an especially gritty, cynical portrayal of the pop music world as experienced by a young pop singer called Danny Gabriel. **I'm a bastard, it begins. Not in the literal sense, as it happens, but in the slang sense, which is far worse. I'm perverted, deceitful, vicious, immature, narcissistic, gonorrheal, depraved, unprincipled, dissolute, and a slag. I'm also a teenage idol.** The cracked idol narrates his own story from a hospital bed, where he is convalescing after a breakdown. It's a tale of innocence corrupted, how a fresh-faced lad from a small rural village is lured away to the big city where he is exploited by managers, agents and other music business bastards, each of them extracting some kind of toll on the road to fame. Much like Cliff Richard, until recently, Gabriel's public image is one of purity and innocence, but, like Cliff's band mate Jet Harris, he soon succumbs to the temptations of alcohol, sex and drugs, and the succor they provide for his emotionally scarred self-image. Gabriel's story also mirrors that of other doomed English rockers of the era like Vince Taylor and Terry Dene—and many others yet to come.

While the book's unwavering cynicism is overplayed at times, the story itself is compellingly told, and the characters feel authentic, because most if not all of them were based on real people Ellis had spent time with in the music industry. *Myself for Fame* created the template for rock music fiction, establishing the themes that would run through much of what followed.

All Night Stand—Thom Keyes (W.H. Allen, 1966)

Myself for Fame may have been the first, but *All Night Stand* is the best-known and most commercially successful beat group novel of the 1960s. It was published in several different countries in different editions.

Thom Keyes was born in California, but moved to Britain as a young child. Educated at the exclusive Malvern College and then at Oxford, he arrived in Liverpool in 1961, where he befriended Johnny Byrne, an Irish-born beatnik type and art gallery manager who just happened to live downstairs from John Lennon and Stu Sutcliffe. Keyes's tenure on Merseyside and proximity to the early Beatles helped provide the impetus for *All Night Stand*, which he wrote in 1965 after he and Byrne had relocated to London. With Beatlemania at full pitch, the time was ripe for a novel based around a Beatles-type group, and Keyes was perfectly positioned to provide it. Keyes's fictitious beat group (the Rack in the first UK hardcover edition, W.H. Allen, 1966, the Pack in the UK paperback, Mayflower, 1967) is a quartet from Liverpool who cut their teeth in the clubs of Hamburg, but any resemblance to the Beatles ends there. *All Night Stand* charts the Rack/Pack's ascent from the club scene to international superstardom, then their gradual disconnect from reality culminating in the possible—or perhaps imminent—suicide of rhythm guitarist Gerry.

The book's unconventional structure has each of the band members narrating a section of the story, which makes for an interesting rotation of perspectives. Keyes devotes more time to describing the band's sexual escapades than their musical activities, so one never really gets a sense of what the group sounds like or why they are so popular. Nevertheless the book is well written, the dialogue reasonably believable, and a couple of unexpected dark turns give it some depth.

Interestingly, the US edition (Ballantine, 1966) is substantially different. The band, renamed the Score, starts out with a fifth member, lead singer Roy, whose quirkily naive perspective adds another 20 pages not found in the UK editions.

Record producer Shel Talmy (the Kinks, the Who, the Creation) helped Keyes place the book with a publisher (initially W.H. Allen in the UK), netting Keyes a handsome advance, and soon afterwards 20th Century Fox purchased the film rights. Talmy also persuaded Ray Davies to write a song of the same name, which the producer cut with the Thoughts and released on his Planet label in October 1966.

The movie never eventuated, but Keyes lived large on the proceeds for several years. He and Byrne leased a huge house in Kensington, Cranley Mansions, which became a haven for artists, poets, painters, musicians, inventors, druggies and assorted freaks. "A lot of people went there 'cause it was really a constant party," underground journalist and musician Mick Farren recalled in conversation with me. "It would be perfectly on the cards that Jimi Hendrix might turn up there after the Speakeasy. That sort of place. It was very luxurious and there was a lot of money temporarily flying around through Keyes. He thought he was going to make a million dollars—he didn't—out of *All Night Stand*. There were movie deals and stuff, and he bought a Rolls. He'd go down the Kings Road and pick up girls in his Rolls."

Keyes's Cranley Mansions milieu would later give birth to another well-regarded work of 1960s rock fiction, Jenny Fabian's *Groupie*, co-written by Keyes's friend Johnny Byrne. More on that later.

Give Me Money—John Love (Corgi, 1966)

No information seems to be available about John Love, who wrote this beat group-themed saga for Corgi in 1966. The story is told from the point of view of a band manager. Peter Seymour runs the Hendon Palais, a London ballroom that caters to the teenage pop crowd. His life changes when he discovers a group called the Saddlers, who play an unusual Country & Western flavored brand of beat music. He signs on as their manager and through hard work and dogged determination takes them all the way to the top. They have records in the charts, specials on television and successful tours of America. Along the way though, they cross paths with the inevitable parade

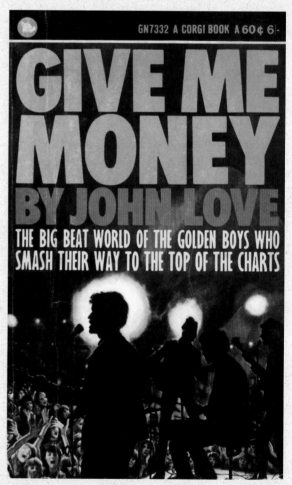

GIRL GANGS, BIKER BOYS, AND REAL COOL CATS

of groupies, backstabbers, muckrakers, rip-off merchants and dope peddlers. Harmonica player 'Spud' gets mixed up with drugs and collapses onstage after mainlining cocaine (pretty out there for 1966). The group's songwriter and guitarist, Lenny, has a prison conviction hidden in his past, and their trusted road manager sells out the band to the tabloids. After Lenny is forced to leave the group, the hits start to dry up. The band's popularity slips and by the end of the book it all comes crashing down.

Seymour is an admirable protagonist who only wants the best for his boys—a heterosexual Brian Epstein—but his good intentions are overrun by bad luck and the corrupting forces of the entertainment business. The competitiveness and underhanded dealings of the music industry are realistically described. The plot plods along in places, but continues to sustain interest, especially when the wheels start to fall off.

Cry for a Shadow—Chrys Paul Fletcher
(Barker, 1967)

Although not strictly a beat-group novel, Cry for a Shadow plays out in approximately the same 1960s youth landscape as the other books covered in this chapter and touches upon many of the same themes. Nineteen-year-old Chris Plater is a successful folk singer in the early Donovan beatnik mode; he travels around the country playing his earnest, poetic songs and making the scene, sometimes ditching the comforts of the tour van to hitchhike and sleep rough. Chris is obsessed with finding the true meaning of the song 'Mr. Tambourine Man,' and, oh yeah, he's a serious manic-depressive.

He's also had problems with the law.

> **When he was seventeen there had been a fight with a policeman on Clacton beach. Chris had been there somewhere in the middle of the fight. When everyone had been caught, Chris was accused of the policeman's murder. Three weeks after the trial he had made his first record.**

A lot of existentialist angst is thrown around in these pages as poor Chris flounders around the scene contemplating the futility of his existence. His songs have lyrics like: **No one is real / Nothing is real / It's—just a void / Just a void.** The author clearly wants to make the point that the **mod/rocker generation** of Chris Plater and his friends lacks any underlying morality or

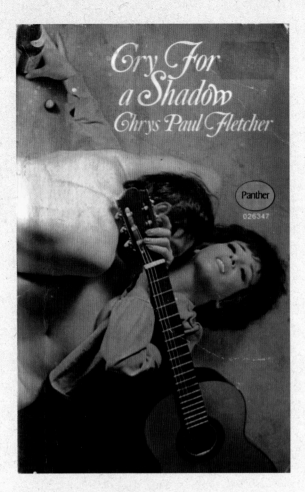

sense of purpose. They shun the stale conventions of the older generation—faith and religion, monogamy and marriage—but beyond vague notions of 'freedom' have nothing substantive to offer in their place. Chris and his girlfriend Lorraine love each other, but they have an open relationship: **"If Chris sleeps with some girl he picks up after a concert or someone he meets in a bar, then what's wrong with that?"**, asserts Lorraine. **"I don't care about it. And he wouldn't care if I went to bed with some other boy."**

Inevitably though, things start to get complicated. Chris gets another girl pregnant; she's only 15. His friend Pete—who plays guitar in a fading beat group called the Representative—commits suicide by taking an overdose of aspirin. A hypnotic-eyed cult leader-type tries to get inside his head, and Chris starts to lose his mind. **"This small hint of madness, of insanity, in me, is it just mine of is it a reflection of the general insanity of a whole generation?"** he asks himself, summing up the main theme of the story.

By the end of the book, much like Myself for Fame's Danny Gabriel, Chris is confined to a hospital bed—

but *Cry for a Shadow* goes one better because Chris is locked up in a mental asylum. His fans wait loyally outside the gates waving placards reading **"CHRIS PLATER IS SANE."** Maybe in madness he found some kind of paradise after all.

The melodrama may be laid on a little thick at times, but *Cry for a Shadow* remains a memorable and engaging portrayal of the grimier side of mid-60s Britain. According to copyright records, Chrys Paul Fletcher was a pseudonym for one Robert Mills, but beyond that the identity of the author is something of a mystery. Whoever he was, he left behind one of rock fiction's most provocative and serious-minded works.

Square One [aka *The Big Scene*]—Robin Squire (W.H. Allen, 1968)

Robin Squire wrote *Square One* in 1966, the same year *All Night Stand* was published, but its publication was delayed until August 1968, by which time the beat group boom had subsided, which may explain its relative obscurity compared to Keyes's book. "I was aware of Thom Keyes's *All Night Stand*," Squire told me, "but I deliberately didn't read it at the time because of not wanting to be influenced by it." Sure enough, although *Square One* also follows the fortunes of a British beat group, Squire's book takes an entirely different trajectory. His invented band, the Fancy Free, labor on a much lower strata of the pop scene, traveling the country in a beat-up van, playing small town gigs for very little pay, getting into fights with provincial louts, and of course screwing lots of teenage girls. It's a much grittier, more authentic take on the British beat scene of the day, one that digs deep into the day-to-day machinations of beat-group life: the traveling, the gigs, the rehearsals, the recording sessions, the interactions with booking agents, record company people and publicists, and the financial hardships.

The book's authenticity was a result of some smart research on the part of the author. "It was the 'Swinging Sixties' and the pop scene fascinated me," relates Squire. "In the summer of 1965 I hitchhiked from London down to the South of France, chancing to meet another English lad en route. A couple of American girls rambling around Europe in a Citroën 2CV picked us up at the roadside, and we were in Nice when the Beatles appeared there. So I knew Beatlemania at first hand, in a huge auditorium when the entire audience went mad with screams. So when, during the following year, I was renting the top room in a house in Bayswater, and found that one of the other tenants used

to manage a pop group, I wanted to see if I could write a book about the scene. But I didn't want to do a cosmetic version, here was my chance to discover the nitty-gritty realities, and that's what attracted me."

The tenant was David Booth, a professional photographer who had once managed a group called the Cyan Three; they'd had one unsuccessful single released on Decca earlier that year. "My research was to buy a reel-to-reel tape recorder plus several large cans of beer, and interview my ex-pop group manager fellow tenant intensively of an evening after work," explains Squire. "This went on for a couple weeks . . . So just about all the information came from my interviewee, and I had no reason to doubt it was genuine. It took a while to transcribe the words on the tape to my typewriter, but in the end I had quite a manuscript, which Dave checked, double-checked and verified for accuracy, and where I'd misunderstood or put something that didn't vibe with reality, I was duly corrected. In the end he was happy that everything I'd written was essentially correct."

Having soaked up the real-life story of the Cyan Three, the author then set about creating his own fictional band, the Fancy Free, and photographer-turned-manager Tim Staines. The story is told from Staines's perspective, his discovery of the group and his efforts to launch them toward fame. The book charts their struggles, playing one-nighters for little or no pay, writing their own songs, recording a demo, getting signed to a record deal and a booking agency, only to be mishandled and sidelined, their first record delayed, setback after setback but always seemingly inching closer to their goal. Their song 'The Sighing Game' appears to have all the ingredients to become a huge hit, but the record company wants to bury it on the B-side. The various complications of Tim's love life add another layer to the plot line, and there's some real suspense as the calendar counts down to the band's first record release, on which their whole future seems to ride. With 'The Sighing Game' they seem poised for big-time success. Or total failure. Which will it be? By the end of the book you're invested in the characters enough to care.

The book got good reviews (*Time Out* called it "one of the better books about the pop scene"), and there was even serious talk of a film adaptation, not to mention the possible involvement of a bona fide Beatle. "Soon after publication I was approached by film director Val Guest [whose credits included *Expresso Bongo* in 1959 and the 1961 science-fiction movie, *The Day the Earth Caught Fire*] who expressed a wish to make a film of the book," recounts Squire. "I was invited to his home in St John's Wood, London, to talk about it. Here I met his wife, Yolande Donlan, who had starred in *Expresso Bongo* a few years earlier, and their teenage son—who said he'd loved the book and so did his pals. Youth had spoken! Paul McCartney lived just round the corner from Val on Cavendish Avenue, and had already been provisionally asked to write the pivotal song 'The Sighing Game'. This was wonderful news for me, especially given that I'd had McCartney's 'Yesterday' and 'Here, There and Everywhere' in mind when I imagined how the song would sound. But then fate stepped in when a certain director, who was to have shot a film titled *Toomorrow* (1970) with Olivia Newton-John, was injured in a car crash and Val Guest was called in to helm the film. Not wanting to make more than one film with a pop theme, he decided to shelve *Square One* and make *Toomorrow* instead."

That turn of events doomed *Square One* to undeserved obscurity and leaves us with a tantalizing 'what if?' to ponder. "In the book I wanted 'The Sighing Game' to be a potential world-beater of a song which nonetheless gets overlooked for lack of sufficient exposure to the buying public who could have sent it to the top of the charts," reflects Squire. "Had McCartney written that song and the film been made by Val Guest, I like to think the song would have topped the charts and created a paradox: in the book it flops through lack of exposure, in reality it does all that Tim Staines and the Fancy Free dreamed it might."

In 1969, *Square One* was repackaged in paperback by New English Library as *The Big Scene*, emphasizing the groupie content. "I didn't know New English Library had changed the title till it came out in paperback," says Robin, "so I wasn't consulted at all about the new cover design. Although the groupies were incidental to the main story, they were clearly seen as an important sales focus by NEL's marketing people." Indeed, by 1969, groupies appear to have exceeded the importance of groups, at least when it came to selling paperbacks.

Groupie—Jenny Fabian & Johnny Byrne
(Mayflower, 1969)

A direct line can be drawn between *All Night Stand* and *Groupie*. Jenny Fabian and co-writer Johnny Byrne were part of Thom Keyes's circle of friends at his infamous house in Kensington, Cranley Mansions (Byrne lived there for some time, and Fabian was a regular visitor). However, *Groupie* flips the angle of the standard rock-band exploitation work exemplified by books like *All Night Stand*. Instead of horny, devious rock musicians taking advantage of their gullible and/or promiscuous admirers, *Groupie* is told from the perspective of a young woman, Katie, who gets her kicks sleeping with band members. But Katie isn't some empty-headed dolly bird surrendering her innocence to the savages; she's a strong-willed, intelligent young woman living life on her own terms and making her own choices—good or bad. *Groupie* isn't a tale of sexual exploitation; it's a tale of sexual liberation.

The book is based on Jenny Fabian's real-life encounters and relationships with various musicians on the British underground rock scene in 1967–1968. Although the names of most of the musicians and bands have been changed, it's relatively simple to figure out who many of them are. So . . . Pink Floyd's Syd Barrett becomes Ben, the withdrawn guitarist and songwriter of the Satin Odyssey: **his eyes had the polished look I'd seen in other people who had taken too many trips in too short a time.** Davey of the Transfer Project (**this incredible group Zach Franks formed from his Big Sound Bank since he took acid**) is future Police guitarist Andy Summers of Dantalian's Chariot (the incredible group Zoot Money formed from his Big Roll Band after he took acid). Davey soon leaves for the States to play with the Savage (the Animals), while Joe, who plays bass in Relation is based on Rick Grech of Family. The Nice, Soft Machine, Aynsley Dunbar Retaliation, Spooky Tooth, and the Fugs also make appearances in various guises. Thom Keyes is here, too, as Theo, a speed-addled writer struggling for focus, juggling schemes, a prisoner in his own mansion, his powers slowly being drained by the deadbeats and parasites with whom he surrounds himself.

A fog of malaise was beginning to roll in as the decade stumbled towards its closure, and *Groupie* captures something of its essence.

Remember Jack Hoxie—Jon Cleary
(Collins, 1969)

A view of the 1960s rock world from an unusual vantage point—that of a pop star's parent. Jon Cleary (1917–2010) was one of Australia's most popular writers, best known for his crime and adventure novels. His most commercially successful work was *The Sundowners* (1952), set in the Australian Outback in the 1920s, so *Remember Jack Hoxie* was a departure for him in terms of both setting and style.

Cleary was inspired to write the book after watching a pop star leaving Sydney Airport for London. "He was surrounded by hundreds of squealing fans, reporters, photographers, and TV cameras," Cleary explained in 1969. "The TV kept zooming on to the faces of his parents, who stood a little away, looking totally bewildered by the whole thing. This intrigued me. How did ordinary parents feel when their son was caught up in a world far beyond their understanding?"

For his research, the author travelled to England to spend several weeks on the road with an unnamed pop group. The bewilderment Cleary apparently experienced was transferred to the book's main character, Patrick Norval, a 41-year-old widower and insurance adjuster whose son Bob is suddenly thrust into the pop spotlight by an eccentric Australian talent spotter, who envisions wholesome, boy-next-door Bob as the next big thing. **"Clean, well-brushed Christian sensuality is what I'm looking for,"** he explains to Patrick. Some kind of pop paradox, perhaps?

Patrick takes leave from his job to accompany Bob and his band, the New Type, on tour, and the expected laundry list of fan hysteria, shady characters, promiscuous sex, and dishearteningly loud music is duly unfurled. Patrick's efforts to navigate this alien world and shield his son from unsavory influences are described with the kind of detached humor and cynicism often found in Kingsley Amis's work at the time.

Cleary obviously didn't 'get' rock music so some of his observations are wide of the mark (he likens the experience of attending a recording session to **standing in a subway tunnel with a musical train going by**, for example), but he's a skilled writer with a good sense of pacing, so it's easy to overlook these shortcomings and just enjoy the story.

Patrick is a likable character who is trying to bring up his son as best he can while struggling to overcome the loss of his wife. His introduction to the world of pop coincides with the arrival of a new love interest, Suzanne Locke, Bob's manager's secretary. But is Patrick ready for a new relationship? Things start to get even more complicated when the band tours the United States in the summer of 1968. Robert Kennedy is assassinated and the book takes a more serious turn—racism, drug use, religion, and abortion all factor into the plot. Upon their return to England, there's an unexpected twist when Patrick takes the rap for his son on a pot-smuggling charge. But all turns

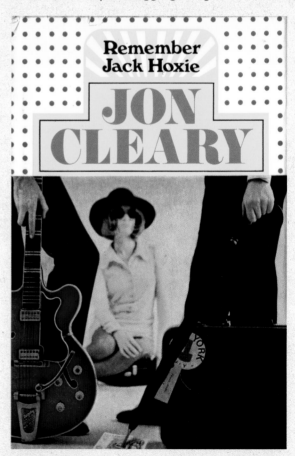

out well in the end, all things considered. A rarity in this genre.

The Tale of Willy's Rats—Mick Farren
(Mayflower, 1974)

Although its publication postdated the era it describes, Mick Farren's *The Tale of Willy's Rats* is one of the 1960s rock fiction's pinnacles. Because Farren was able to draw directly from his own experiences as a lead singer with a British underground band, the Deviants, the book has an authenticity that is often lacking in some of the other works I've described. The book's protagonist and narrator, Lou Francis, is basically an idealized version of Farren himself, while the band, Willy's Rats, are a more musically together version of the Deviants, synthesized with various elements of the Stones, the Doors, and the MC5.

The book follows Francis's musical journey from the early 1960s Cliff and the Shadows-era through the nascent British R&B scene and into the psychedelic era. This section of the book is especially vibrant, with an evocative account of seeing the early Pink Floyd at the UFO club and one of the most enjoyable and realistic evocations of an LSD trip I've read—refreshingly free and clear of all the standard *Alice in Wonderland* or jump-out-the-window tropes. As befitting a self-described **bedtime story for degenerates** about **the most demoniac rock band ever**, there are plenty of lurid sex scenes to accompany all the rampant drug use, but Farren always keeps the rock music plot line rolling along.

The band's self-consciously dark, depraved image begins to envelope them, and they seem to be heading for a terrifying day of reckoning that would eclipse even Altamont. A series of chilling death threats suggests a sniper may take one of them out onstage, a scenario that may have provided some inspiration for [*Game of Thrones* creator] George R.R. Martin's 1983 novel *The Armageddon Rag*, a story about an even more demoniac fictitious 1960s rock band, the Nazgul. That ongoing sense of danger, stoked throughout by a series of jump-cuts, ensures there's a thread of tension running through the entirety of *The Tale of Willy's Rats*, making it one of the genre's standouts.

"It had a certain charm," admitted Farren. "It came in a very unpleasant cover with a woman who looked like Marsha Hunt on it. It got passed by rather quickly and it's incredibly rare now."

Other latecomers to the 60s rock fiction field include Ray Connolly's *That'll Be the Day* (1973) and *Stardust*

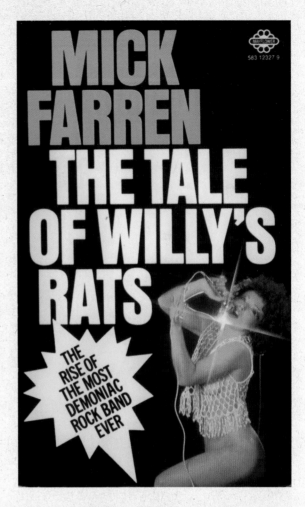

(1974), both adapted from his own movie screenplays. Set in the late 1950s and early 1960s, *That'll Be the Day* tells the story of an up and coming young rocker called Ray MacLaine and his beat group, the Stray Cats, while the sequel, *Stardust*, takes MacLaine's story from the late 1960s into the even more decadent 1970s. *Flame*, John Pidgeon's 1975 novelization of Andrew Birkin's screenplay of the Slade movie of the same name, is also well worth reading, a pleasingly seedy and cynical trawl through the world of 60s pop in Britain that captures much of the dark realism of the movie itself.

Honorable mentions should also go to *Privilege* by John Burke (1967) and *Sexton Blake: Death in the Top Twenty* by Wilfred McNeilly, but it's the eight titles covered in more detail above that, between them, capture something of the zeitgeist of this tumultuous era.

MIKE STAX

Give Me Money (Corgi, 1966), *Cry for a Shadow* (Panther, 1969), *Square One* (W.H. Allen, 1968), *Remember Jack Hoxie* (Collins, 1969), *The Tale of Willy's Rats* (Mayflower, 1975)

The Time of the Hawklords (Star, 1977)

I Am Still the Greatest Says Johnny Angelo (Penguin, 1970)

Cold Iron—Robert Stone Pryor
(Modern Promotions, 1970)

Written for a quick buck by historical novelist Cecelia Holland, this cool little novel was issued under a pseudonym because the author was contracted to another publisher. *Cold Iron* is a retelling of Jim Morrison's life up to 1970, taking in the Doors front man's outrageous onstage antics and adding in a rather fanciful fictional backdrop, where the hippies always outsmart the cops despite being stoned to the gills on enough hallucinogenics to fry two Syd Barretts.

Renamed in the book as Jim O'Leary, the Lizard King is given a proto-feminist lover called Woody Hagen. She has her own legal troubles, though still manages to keep up with his crazed dope and mescaline intake while speeding round L.A. in an open-top Lotus. Events for O'Leary's band, Cold Iron, quickly spin out of control as the singer uses all of his dangerous sexual charisma to instigate a riot at an open-air love-in, much as Morrison was alleged to have done in 1967 at the New Haven Arena. O'Leary later goes on the run from the cops after exposing himself at a gig in Wisconsin, again echoing Morrison's actions at the Dinner Key auditorium in Miami in March '69. One could hardly miss the Doors parallels, however. Their lyrics are quoted on the back and inside cover of the book.

A dedication to the police and narcotics departments of the United States of America opens this cheeky paperback. Full of bogus druggie argot and improbable scenes, this is no classic, but has a certain naive charm to it. When contacted recently about the novel, author Cecelia Holland responded, "I had a massive crush on Jim Morrison at the time. The book is a nonstop indulgence in Morrisonia—it was a glorification of hippiedom. We never had any money or big houses or fancy cars. We were always stoned all the time." Pushed for her thoughts on *Cold Iron* she said, "I think the book sucks. I hope I never hear of it again."

AUSTIN MATTHEWS

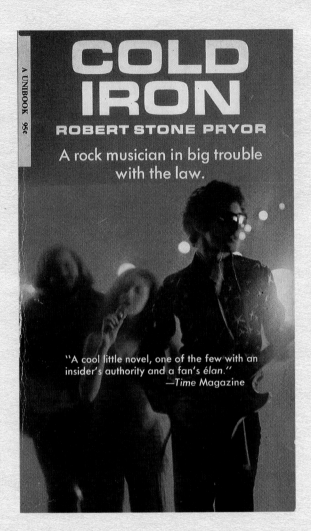

COLD IRON

ROBERT STONE PRYOR

A rock musician in big trouble
with the law.

"A cool little novel, one of the few with an
insider's authority and a fan's *élan*."
—*Time* Magazine

O'Leary was dancing, his feet
planted still, and around the
stage the swarm of kids waved
their arms and swayed and shouted
wordlessly. The straights had pulled
back and were staring at them, and the
cops, more interested in the kids than
in O'Leary, pushed in, encircling them.
O'Leary wound himself around the
mikestand and crooned, "Fuck, fuck,
fuck," stroking the stand with both
hands. Sam walked around keeping out
of his way, cool and watchful. Hitting off
crush rolls in a blur of sticks, Dogfoot
managed to knock over his cymbal, and
a road crew kid leapt onto the stage to
set it up again.

The cops spread around the tangle of
people, keeping them contained, but the
rippling motion of the crowd changed;
it started to thrust towards the cops,
and somebody screamed, "Liberate the
park!" Woody flung her arms out and
laughed, and O'Leary saw her, waved,
and stepped back, his eyes flickering
like a snake's tongue over the scene. He
drifted up the mike and whispered, "Pig,
pig, pig."

Drummer—Richard Carlile (Tandem, 1971)

A future world dominated by vast discrepancies in wealth and power, shaped by sex, drugs and rock and roll, with lashings of violence, riots and revolution, not to mention transvestites and deviant sex. It's a hell of a ride in Richard Carlile's *Drummer*. There's barely a pulp-fiction button left unpressed.

Yet this is no straightforward exploitation novel of the kind churned out by Carlile's contemporaries over at the New English Library. You notice the difference from the outset: no one else writing paperback originals in Britain in the early 1970s was likely to use the word 'mnesic' in their opening paragraph.

Carlile had left St Andrew's University in 1969, where he had studied English literature and philosophy. Disillusioned with literary fiction, and feeling that "things had turned bad" with the counterculture, he threw himself into producing a lurid vision of the future that would be deliberately unliterary. Written at speed, and published exactly as written with no editorial input, *Drummer* was one of the first works to articulate the comedown from the cultural high of the 1960s.

The story is of Ariston, an erstwhile drummer eking out an existence on the rubbish dumps of **a city without a name**, who gets recruited into Satiety Incorporated, a small-time band just about to break big. When they do, it's to the accompaniment of a **civic war** that almost brings society to its knees. Ariston, however, is removed from these wider concerns. During his starving, scavenging days he had resorted to eating the liquefying pulp of the city's garbage, an unidentifiable substance somewhere between Viagra and Larry Cohen's *The Stuff* [a 1985 horror film involving a delectable organic substance which turns its consumers into zombies], that keeps him just about alive and gives him enormous sexual staying power. Consequently, he finds himself adopted as a lover by the sex-starved wife of a movie producer. And then the story starts to go weird, as Ariston descends into a world of horror, murder, sadism and biker gangs.

Actually, the narrative pretty much defies rational analysis. It's an impressionistic collage of scenes and images that makes as much sense as a nightmare, and has the same lingering, haunting power. The closest parallel is probably David Bowie's *Diamond Dogs* album from 1974, another fragmentary dystopia that documents the decline of the progressive dream. And the proto-glam of *Drummer* also prefigures the

Brilliant and thought-provoking: a hallucinatory trip into a savage, amoral, rock-horror nightmare

Richard Carlile

transgender fixation of glitter rock, with its depiction of the Doll People, a youth tribe composed of boys brought up as girls so they can be sold into marriage to wealthy, decadent pederasts. When those relationships inevitably collapse, the Doll People drift into the streets, a collection of **subtly merging heteroclites** whose erratic, unpredictable behaviour symbolises the instability of a society that is careering out of control.

Despite its post-Altamont origins, *Drummer* isn't fixed in time, largely because Carlile had the good sense not to attempt any description of the music played by Satiety Incorporated. I first read it in the late 1970s, when punk was at its peak, and it made perfect sense then in the context of the Sex Pistols and Derek Jarman's film *Jubilee* (1978). In a world of transglobal corporations and growing economic inequality, it still does.

ALWYN W. TURNER

A novel more sensational than 'Groupie'

Drummer

Richard Carlile

The scene is everywhere and nowhere,
Drummer is everyone and no one,
living is vision and nightmare

Drummer (Tandem, 1971)
Drummer, alternate cover (Tandem, 1971)

O f all the gangs of motorcycle creeps the most infamous was the Naughty Nihilists, an amalgam of hell-bent Neanderthals numbering over two hundred members who rode and roared under the leadership of Suchandsuch Smith. I speak of the Suchandsuch Smith, unlucky seventh son of a seventh unlucky son, born under inauspicious signs in the year of the Howling Wolf. Six feet six, with eyes of piercing blue, his blonde hair grown shoulder-length, he was striking enough to have been a film star . . .

The Nihilists rode four abreast, keeping in close formation, and their long hair flowed back in the slipstream. Of society's misfits they were the aristocracy. Their filthy, grease-smeared clothing was decorated with occult emblems and weird signs and symbols—the haphazard devices of their heraldry—and on the backs of their leather jackets, set in chrome studs, were the gang mottoes, *Per Ardua Ad Nihil* or the more straightforward, *Fuck Everything*.

The Destroyer #13: Acid Rock—Warren Murphy and Richard Sapir

(Pinnacle, 1973)

The Destroyer series got off to a bumpy start—the debut novel was not published until eight years after it was written, and only because Richard Sapir's father, a dentist, pushed it onto a patient who worked at Pinnacle books—but it has since proved to be as hardy as its protagonists, with a variety of authors having by now pumped out more than 150 volumes.

The Destroyer novels are very much in keeping with other products in the 70s/80s vigilante genre, combining a thinly veiled knockoff of the the TV series *Kung Fu* with Mickey Spillane–style ultra-violence and bigotry, albeit with a healthy dollop of humour. Its key characters are employed by shadowy government agencies to do the extrajudicial black-ops work that namby-pamby politicians and liberal courts won't allow the police and official intelligence services to carry out. Over the years the daring duo of Remo Williams, a former cop wrongly sent to the death chamber only to be reborn as a government killer, and Master Chuin, a North Korean assassin whose only loves are his deadly work, daytime soap operas, and picking on Remo, have fought everyone from the Mafia to Chinese vampires and angry white postal workers.

The series has a certain goofy charm, particularly in the hammy relationship of master and apprentice, but its poisonous delight in having its protagonists stomp on and revile hippies, black militants, unionists and other progressive targets tends to leave a bad taste in the mouth. And any suspense the novels try to generate is immediately lost, since Remo and Chuin's super skills mean that any adversary is turned into a gory mess before the reader can make it to the next page.

Written at a time when originators Sapir and Warren Murphy were still collaborating—even if they each wrote half of each book and exchanged manuscripts via their shared business agent in order to avoid any personal interaction—*Acid Rock* sees Remo and Chuin assigned by the president and their bosses at CURE to act as bodyguards for a spoiled hippie commerce student Vicky Stoner who has fallen out with her father and threatened to spill the beans on the latter's questionable business practices. Poppa is none too pleased and in turn has issued an open contract on her—anyone who can confirm a hit on his not-so-dutiful daughter will receive a million-dollar fee.

Unfortunately for Chuin and Remo this witness is no ordinary socialite stoolie; she's a stock market-obsessed dilettante who combines her passion for profit with copious drug use and the conquest of rock deities. No flamboyant front man is bigger or more desirable than Maggot (lead singer of the Dead Meat Lice), who regales festival crowds with such lyrical pearls as **"Dirt waits in the fields."** Determined to conquer the aforementioned singer, the supergroupie winds up dragging her protectors across the country as she hitchhikes to a massive outdoor rock festival. Upon arrival Chuin finds himself stunned by the volume and Remo is forced to kill a bunch of Altamont-style bikers after knocking over their choppers. The descriptions of the Alice Cooper–style shock rock and the overall festival scene elicit numerous chuckles—as does the corny ending, in which Dirt and Stoner find true love through their mutual devotion to the futures market.

Acid Rock is probably the most enjoyable of the 1970s-era Destroyer novels, if only because the authors' piss-taking is generally quite funny here, rather than, as so often in the series, prickly and hateful.

IAIN McINTYRE

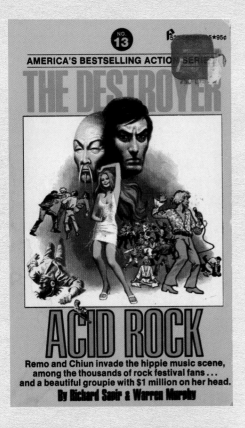

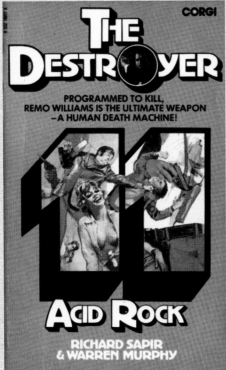

Acid Rock (Pinnacle, 1973)
Acid Rock (Corgi, 1975)

The Dead Meat Lice crawled and tumbled onto the stage. There was a drummer who doubled as the beater of the gong. In a round enclosure from stage right rose a piano, organ and clavichord, with another Dead Meat Louse seated in the middle. A frowzy-headed man with two wind instruments pulled himself onstage. The crowd cheered the arrival of all three Lice.

Maggot waved his arm and they sang. They sang what Remo made out to be "Bedred, mother-racking, tortoise, humpanny, rah, rah, humpanny, mother-racking, bedstead, rackluck." "Bitchen", screamed Vickie Stoner in Remo's ear, and then the tower to their left gave a wiggle with an explosive pop, then another pop, and people were falling from it and it was coming down like a sledgehammer right where Vickie Stoner was jumping up and down, screaming with everyone else.

The crowd would hamper free movement so Remo grabbed Vickie like a loaf of bread and drove his way through bodies to what he felt would be the safest place. The tower came whoomphing down, eight tons of it, crushing a ten-yard-wide stretch of people with a heavy dull splat. Remo and Vickie were safe. They were at the base of the tower where it had been blown off its foundations head high, just where a big man with a scarred face had been casually moving his hands around.

"Bedred, mother-racking, tortoise humpanny, rah, rah, rah, humpanny, bedstead rackluck." "They're going on", someone shrieked, "They're going on." "Dead Meat Lice go on and on. Rule forever Dead Meat Lice", yelled Maggot, and this was met by cheers blanketing the moans of the victims of the tower. "Rule forever, Dead Meat Lice", yelled Vickie Stoner.

The Drop Out—Hugh Miller (New English Library, 1973)

A pacey tale of the music industry, groupies, sex and disaffected youth, all *The Drop Out* would need is a gang of vicious bikers in order to push every single hot button of 70s British pulp fiction.

The central character, Terry, is a 17-year-old woman adrift in the miasma of early 70s London. The story opens with her waiting in the local youth employment centre:

> **The paint on the walls always let you know what you were in for. Terry had been inside police stations, a couple of juvenile courts and a clinic for the treatment of venereal diseases. The walls were always green and cream. The green was the colour of decay rather than budding and the cream looked like pus.**

The employment counsellor directs Terry to an opening for a waitress at a groovy Earl's Court café called 'The Chicken Hot Spot', the walls of which are covered with expensive litho blow-ups, depicting famous generals from British military history.

She bombs out as a waitress but catches the eye of Ike Rabin, the **brooding handsome** drummer of progressive rock band Ectoplasm. Ike tells her the band is looking for dancers to perform as part of their new mini rock opera, *Credo*, which they are about to perform on a UK tour. Ectoplasm is Terry's favourite band. As a friend of hers puts it, listening to their songs is **like having your own soul set to music**. She jumps at the opportunity.

The tour involves abundant drug use and casual sex. There's a riot at one of the concerts, and a lot of Machiavellian scheming amongst the various members of the band and its entourage. The most difficult personality is Gary Kirk, Ectoplasm's messianic lead singer (who Terry discovers in the course of one of the band's orgies is a closeted gay). He believes **Ectoplasm is more than a group or a band, we're a movement, something that fills the role of God for a hell of a lot of people.**

Terry also has to fend off the unwanted carnal attention of Chick Taylor, Ectoplasm's sleazy predatory agent, and a sanctimonious Vicar, Stanley Wilson, who is determined to save Terry from her sinful life of sex, drugs, and rock and roll. Although it's only one scene in the book, Wilson's encounter with the Reverend Archie Elliot, who runs a radical church drop-in centre, and wears a leather jacket and a dog collar, is priceless.

The constant exposure to Ectoplasm's antics cools Terry's ardour for the band and the music business generally. Vicar Wilson, who she initially trusts, turns out to be just another adult phoney (and a voyeur, to boot). Taylor, nervous about the challenge Terry presents to his authority, pays the members of a previous music act he used to manage to sexually humiliate her. The book ends with Terry back with her parents and at the employment centre.

While *The Drop Out* is straight out NEL exploitation pulp, Terry's character is surprisingly well drawn. She is smart and makes decisions as much as possible on her own terms. The author makes no attempt to judge her actions and implies her cynicism is more than justified, given what she goes through.

The Drop Out was Scottish author Miller's debut novel and the first of several books he did for NEL. His second, *Kingpin* (1974), was also set within the music industry (**BEHIND THE GLAMOUR OF THE POP BUSINESS IS A SLEAZY WORLD OF EASY EXCHANGE**, read the front cover blurb). *The Open City* (1974) had as its subject a young man who moves to London and becomes involved with a corrupt disc jockey. Miller went on to to write a total of 27 books, as well as novelizations of the *EastEnders* series and *Ballykissangel*. He also authored ten books on forensic medicine.

ANDREW NETTE

THE
DROP
OUT
Hugh Miller

A shocking and detailed
portrait of an amoral
eighteen-year-old.

The Drop Out
(New English Library, 1973)

Kingpin
(New English Library, 1975)

"Let me explain. We're going to perform a piece called Credo. It lasts, as you've been told, for an hour. No breaks. It is a punishing piece, the most ambitious Ectoplasm has ever devised. It tells a story, and here and there, words are used to get the story across. When the message goes beyond the words, the music takes over totally. The first vocal is called Rock Garden, it paints the picture of an idea turning to a solid fact. The idea is the kind of hot rock that mirrors the ecstasy end of the human soul, and the solid fact is Ectoplasm. Even our name is loaded with the essence of what we are. An ectoplasm is two things: it's the emanation of from the heart and soul of a medium, the stuff of the spirit. But it also means the shell, the outer skin of a living cell, the visible component at the source of life. You have to know this to know what we are, why we are. We take every frustration, every joy, each and everything that happens, every item that totals life, and we celebrate them with a sound that rejoices in and hallows this stage of grace we call life."

The girls were spellbound. Nobody was bothering with her companions' reactions, they each felt the power of Gary Kirk's conviction and that alone. Terry had never realised he could talk like that. It was shattering. He was saying things she could only have felt mistily, guessed at, and he was living proof of his statements.

Pulp Biker and Motorcycle Gangs

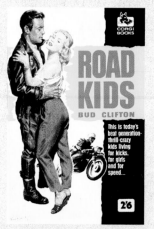

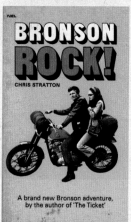

Road Kids (Corgi, 1960), *The Hellcats* (Holloway House, 1968), *The Death Cycle* (Frederick Muller, 1963), *Run Tough, Run Hard* (Monarch Books, 1964), *Girls on the Loose* (Stag, 1964), *Avenging Angel* (New English Library, 1975), *Girl Gangs* (Classics Library, 1968), *Bronson Rock!* (New English Library, 1971), *Saddle Tramps* (Scripts, 1977), *Dynamite Monster Boogie Concert* (Popular Library, 1975), *Jail Bait* (Castle Books, 1980), *The Blood Circus* (Gold Medal, 1968)

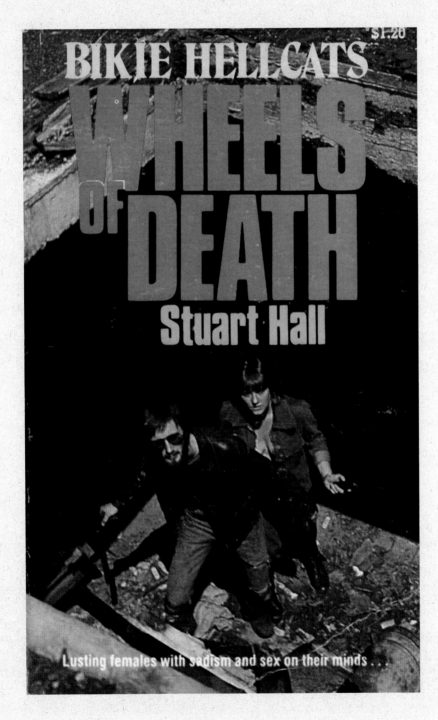

Wheels of Death
(Scripts, 1975)

The Leather Boys—Eliot George [Gillian Freeman]

(Anthony Blond Ltd, 1961)

In 1957 Lord Wolfenden's committee reported to Parliament, recommending that male homosexuality should be legalised in Britain (albeit within heavily restricted parameters). A mere ten years, later the Sexual Offences Act finally implemented its proposals. In the interim, British popular culture took a few tentative steps towards a more liberal world. There was a gay character in Shelagh Delaney's play *A Taste of Honey* (1958), Dirk Bogarde starred in Basil Dearden's film *Victim* (1961), and Gillian Freeman wrote this novel.

First published under a pseudonym (because of Freeman's contractual obligations to another publisher), *The Leather Boys* was a tale of gay love amongst working-class youth. Sidney J. Furie filmed it in 1963 with a cast that included Colin Campbell, Dudley Sutton, and Rita Tushingham, at which point Freeman put her name to the screenplay ("adapted from the novel by Eliot George"). The 1966 New English Library paperback edition that followed the movie is also credited to Freeman, but you'll notice that the photo on the cover is not a still from the film, nor does it even hint at the fact that the story within concerns male homosexuality—indeed, you may think that the depiction of a young blond woman clad in black leather, the swell of her breast partially revealed, has been chosen deliberately to mislead the casual browser. And despite NEL's cover and sleeve notes (**THEY'RE BRITAIN'S 'WILD ONES'—THE MOTORCYCLE COWBOYS WHO LIVE FOR GAS MACHINES AND FASTER GIRLS**), the book has little to do with bikers either. One of our heroes does have a motorbike, but that's hardly definitive of the character. Quite different from later portrayals of the biker world, there are in fact nods here towards a nascent mod culture:

> **One didn't only dress up for girls . . . His appearance mattered to himself. The time he spent on it was entirely for his own satisfaction. Well, perhaps not his entirely. Some was for the other boys, in peacock competition. They were the ones who judged and criticized and appraised.**

The story is terribly slight, but that's hardly unusual for this sort of work: it locates itself within the longstanding tradition of the English male gay novel—from E.M. Forster's *Maurice* to George Moor's *The Pole and Whistle* (the entire storyline of which is: man falls in love with another man). There may be the odd variation where things go wrong, because of the need for the characters to keep their love hidden, but essentially gay novels were so rare that this was considered sufficient material for a plot—which turns out to be a perfectly reasonable assumption.

But even though it's only a thin book, Freeman's faultless eye for the trivial reality of life on the dingy fringes of decent society is always a joy. She's back in the working-class world that formed the setting for many of her early works, articulating the voices of the inarticulate.

ALWYN W. TURNER

   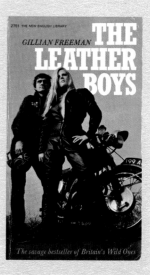

GIRL GANGS, BIKER BOYS, AND REAL COOL CATS

There was so much in his mind that he hadn't the ability to express. He wanted to ask Reggie if he loved him, but it was embarrassing to talk about love, although he watched it in films and sang about it.

The dance was ending as they burst into the hall. They stood silently, staring, not moving, yet somehow on the point of moving like preying animals, fifteen or twenty boys wearing motor-cycle kit. Their hair was greased and combed into styles called College Cut and Latin Cut and Campus Cut and Perry Como. Their expressions were contemptuous and excited. A record of 'Good Night, Sweetheart', sung by Vera Lynn, was being amplified by the loudspeaker equipment attached to the wall above the door.

Someone shouted derisively, "Call that dancing?"

"My mum could do better."

"Come on, Dad, move your fat arse."

One of them, the boy who owned the car, suddenly seemed to become the leader. He was nearly six foot, heavily built, with a fleshy white face. His jacket had a tiger's head painted on the back, his black leather jeans were stuffed into ex-army dispatch-rider's boots. He moved swiftly to the radiogram and, swinging his leg back, brought his boot crashing into the fan-shaped grill, splintering the wood and tearing the beige canvas material behind it.

The other boys surged forward on to the floor. Six of them paired and started to jive. Another used the paneling of the door as a sounding board to beat out a rhythm.

"Come on," yelled the leader, Les. "Let's do it over."

He picked up a folding wooden chair and brought it down on top of the gramophone. The Vicar advanced with his palms outstretched as if to calm them down.

"Boys, boys. Please. Let's not have any of this rough stuff."

"Want to dance, then?" Les shouted. He seized the outstretched hands and forced the Vicar into a grotesque parody of rock-an'-roll.

Dick and Reggie ran from one side of the hall to the other, seizing the chairs and swinging them against the wall. Then, breathless, they ran side-by-side into the little room which was used as a kitchen and began to hurl the crockery on to the floor.

The Vicar followed them, protesting. Somebody grabbed him by the collar of his jacket and pulled him round.

"'Ere, Vicar, 'ave a drink," he shouted, and emptied a milk bottle over his head. The milk cascaded down his forehead and over the lenses of his glasses, and for a moment his eyes were obscured by two opaque white screens.

"Please, please, boys," he pleaded ineffectually. He was scarcely heard through the jeering and the din of smashing cups.

Louder and more effective came the shout of "Law!" from the hall. Immediately they abandoned their destruction. Some made a dive for the door. Two climbed up and lifted the sash of the window and scrambled out into the darkness. Reggie grabbed Dick's arm. "Come on, on the bike."

The Leather Boys (Ballantine, 1961)
The Leather Boys (Four Square, 1963)
The Leather Boys (Four Square, 1966)
The Leather Boys (New English Library, 1975)

A ROCK-AND-ROLL *LORD OF THE FLIES*

Davis Wallis's *Only Lovers Left Alive*

"So, in any average year about five thousand inhabitants of the United Kingdom of Great Britain and Northern Ireland commit suicide," **said Mr. Oliver to his class half an hour before he killed himself.**

Thus opens one of the darker and better-written youth culture-oriented novels of the 1960s, Dave Wallis's *Only Lovers Left Alive*. As the inside blurb for the original 1964 British edition put it: IMAGINE THE COUNTRY TAKEN OVER BY TEENAGERS . . . FREE TO SMASH, LOOT AND LOVE AS THEY LIKE, THE GANGS ROAR, ON THEIR BRAND-NEW EXPENDABLE MOTORBIKES, THROUGH THE LITTERED STREETS. BY NOW, THE CURRENCY IS BAKED BEANS, LIPSTICK AND PETROL. THEY BEGIN TO RUN OUT. SHORTAGE LEADS TO WARFARE.

Mainstream society's fear of out-of-control youth was always a dominant strand in pulp fiction. But the idea of what would happen if young people were *actually* in control, the brutal flip side of their energy and naivety, has only been explored a few times in literature and film. The earliest example is William Golding's 1954 classic dystopian novel, *Lord of the Flies*, about a group of British schoolboys stranded on an uninhabited tropical island and the savagery that erupts as they try to rule themselves.

The theme was given greater prominence as the counterculture gathered steam in the late 60s. *Wild in the Streets* (a 1968 movie and paperback tie-in) told the story of Max Frost, a mysterious 24-year-old millionaire rock star who teams up with an ambitious California politician to get the voting age lowered to 14. Frost becomes president and creates a bizarre youth-controlled authoritarian state in which older people are interred in camps, permanently dosed with psychedelic drugs. The army is disbanded, free grain is shipped to poorer countries, and Frost's pro-youth movement starts to spread across the globe. Another movie example, *Gas-s-s-s* (aka *Gas! or It Became Necessary to Destroy the World in Order to Save It*), was a 1970 black comedy about a post-apocalyptic world in which the accidental leaking of an experimental military gas kills everyone on earth over the age of 25.

But the best take on this topic is *Only Lovers Left Alive*. As a reviewer in the *Observer* said of the book when it was published, Wallace was the first writer to directly pose the question: "What would happen if all the adults committed suicide tomorrow?"

A rock-and-roll *Lord of the Flies*, the book vividly conveys the feel of early-60s England. World War Two was long over, and rationing had ended in 1954. But the torpor that characterized the 50s still hung heavily over everything. A general anti-establishment discontent was brewing but the Swinging Sixties were still a long way off. Life for many—like Wallace, born in 1917 and working as a teacher in north London while he wrote the book—must have seemed dull and uneventful. One can well imagine a scenario in which one almost feels like killing oneself to relieve the boredom.

That Wallace's book is remembered at all nowadays owes much to the striking wraparound black-and-white photo cover of anarchic, machine gun-toting youths that graced the 1964 UK and US hardback editions. It was taken by British photographer, Bruce Fleming, best known as Jim Hendrix's personal photographer in 1967 and 1968. While less arresting, Pat Owen's illustration for the cover of the 1966 Pan paperback, a sneering leather-coated youth brandishing a Sten gun, nonetheless exudes hardboiled menace. Updating the theme, the cover of the ultra-rare 1970 US Bantam paperback edition features an illustration of two hippies, a woman and a man, holding a baby; both the adults are armed.

The book's major claim to fame derives, however, from its place in the canon of great unmade movies. No doubt influenced by the phenomenal success of the Beatles' 1964 film, *A Hard Day's Night*, the Rolling Stones announced in March 1966 that they would make their film debut in *Only Lovers Left Alive*. Their mercenary business manager Allen Klein was set to co-produce with their producer/mentor Andrew Loog Oldham. Oldham said in a May 2001 piece for *Gadfly Online*: "I first tried to get the rights for *A Clockwork Orange*, but Anthony Burgess had been, very prematurely, told he was dying and had sold the movie rights to Stanley Kubrick for a tawdry five grand, and Mr. Kubrick didn't reckon Mick. We settled for a second-best novel called *Only Lovers Left Alive*."

As is the case with all unmade films, what was rumoured to be in the pipeline and what would have happened had the film actually been made, will remain the subject of conjecture. The Rolling Stones

Only Lovers Left Alive
(Anthony Blond, 1964)
Cover photo by
Bruce Fleming

and Marianne Faithfull were to play the various members of the gang that is the focus of the story, and create the soundtrack. According to the website *Existential Ennui*, the screenplay was to have been written by Gillian Freeman, who also penned the screenplay for the film of her novel, *The Leather Boys* (reviewed elsewhere in this book). The aging Nicholas Ray, who oversaw such classics as *In a Lonely Place* (1950), *Johnny Guitar* (1954), and *Rebel Without a Cause* (1955), was approached to direct. But aside from a few meetings and a press release, nothing eventuated.*

Only Lovers Left Alive deserves recognition as a compelling novel in its own right, however. It is well written, and Wallis displays a surprising grasp of youth culture, perhaps because of his experience as a teacher. The story is told in three parts. The first depicts the creeping birth of the new young-people-only society. At first, it's just a few 'oldies' who decide to do themselves in. The young people who make up the Steely Street Gang, including Ernie Wilson, their leader, Charlie Burroughs and top girl, Kathy Williams, sit around in their local café, Tropic Night, and hardly notice the change at first. They have other things on their mind, like dress:

Ernie Wilson favoured the leather-grained black plastic jacket act. Above the waist he dressed for the Arctic Circle and below it, with thin, tight jeans, nylon socks and pointed pliable shows, for the Tropics.

And their motorbikes:

They had an unformed trace of the trained fighter squadron's sense of manoeuvre, in any case their mood corresponded. When they felt like stopping no signal was needed. Above the orange lights a street-long airliner loomed low, flashed its lamps as if it were a car about to turn left. The column thought, "Let's stop at London Airport and watch the planes".

A tabloid columnist visits the café to try to get a story on Mr. Oliver, their recently deceased teacher. The young people treat him with low-key rebellious disdain. The attitude of the young characters is contrasted with the desperate efforts of the authorities to hide the magnitude of what is occurring from the general population (the inference is that it is a global problem). They shunt the bodies around, spreading the load so no one will get suspicious. Medical authorities are told to keep their mouths shut so as not

* Jim Jarmusch's 2014 vampire movie, which is also called *Only Lovers Left Alive*, has no thematic connection with Wallis's book, but Jarmusch reportedly knew of it and deliberately borrowed Wallis's title for his film.

to spread panic. Media outlets are leaned on to print positive stories. But things only get worse.

"I think they've just given up all around, now," says Charlie, one night at the Tropic. **"They gave up trying to boss us around any more . . . They couldn't be bothered to try and get with it. Now they can't be bothered with anything at all."**

There is the occasional mention of a parent, but for the most part, youth bravado won't allow them to be mourned in public. It is not until Kathy's mum kills herself, having previously sworn she wouldn't take the easy way out, that Kathy and the reader realise the enormity of what is occurring. In her suicide note, the mother apologies to her daughter but she is just **"so sick and tired of it all"**.

Supplies start to run out. Coffee and sugar become rare **and the cakes were always stale**. A black market grows up around petrol, nylon stockings, leather shoes and tyres. The roads empty in the evenings **Whole stretches of highway came to be taken over for scooter and motorbike races between organised gangs.** The authorities start distributing so-called Easyway suicide pills. Soon whole groups of older people are killing themselves. The streets become full of garbage. There are no teachers, so no school. A barter economy replaces money and the National Bingo Governing Council (NATBINGO) takes control of all remaining assets and forms its own militia. The Steely Street Gang rummage for food and party in abandoned flats. Then the lights go out in London for the last time.

These were like the golden days, forever after to be remembered like a dream of childhood, but they came with squabbles for a greater share of plenty, begins part two. **The supply of food and petrol seemed endless. The problem was not how to grab it but how to best enjoy yourself at the same time. All central government ceased with the collapse of the NATBINGO barter system. Faced with the Board's ultimate sanction of a cutting off of supplies and an exclusion from the Bingo Halls, defaulters have simply shrugged or wept and then done it. Apart from a few madmen and hermits, it was now a teenage world.**

The Steely Street gang establishes its headquarters in an old cinema. They go on raids to get food and petrol, pouring over maps **in their best war-film style**. They even adopt an emblem, a tiger, as the symbol of their group. London becomes a patchwork of gangs. There's one at London Airport and another is rumoured to have its base in the vast kitchens and wards of a large hospital. But the most powerful gang is the Kings, formed out of the remnants of the old NATBINGO militia, who wear leather jackets with the insignia of an upside-down crown. They have taken over Windsor Castle and are reportedly hoarding supplies.

The first cases of typhoid occur. Tinned food, nylons, lipstick and petrol for motorbikes become scarcer. Packs of wild dogs roam parts of the city and there are rumours some of the gangs are running slave farms. Ernie realises they need to get out of London, but they need supplies. The best possibility of securing these is to attack Windsor Castle.

Bob, the gang's 'head of intelligence' is sent to reconnoitre the Kings' territory. He finds a group of orphaned young children who take it in turns each night pretending to be the adult parent. He sleeps with a woman, Julia, whose job, when she is not prostituting herself, is to train the women of the Kings' 'home comforts department' and perform abortions. She tells him the Kings have guns and trucks and food, left over when the royal family **"either did it or hopped over to Canada or Australia"**. They have based their organisation on what they have read in history books. **"Then they got the worst things out of *The Scourge of the Swastika* and the Eichmann trial books and did them . . ."** Julia continues, **"Well, it's just that everyone's scared of the Kings and it makes it all, well, I know it sounds a funny thing to say, but it makes it almost like it was when the oldies and squares were running everything."**

Bob reports back and the Steely Street Gang plan their attack. They hold a party the night before.

This led them back to earlier memories, of puerile investigations between the legs behind the lavatories. Their talk had no inhibitions, "not like the oldies" as they kept putting it. But in all this the fear of the immediate battles of the next day and the terror of revealing that tears had once wet their cheeks as they had tidied the lolling heads and stiffening arms and fingers of parents, found on scullery floors, and with engines running in cars and garages or just lying in the two armchairs of the three piece with a gas tube in their gaping mouths, were not mentioned. Such memories were only whispered, lover to lover, in the drugged mo-

ments after coitus but were never brought out in public. New sets of conventions were slowly forming to take the place of the old.

The Steely Street Gang vanquishes the Kings in a brutal battle. The majority of the Kings are killed in a petrol blaze. Their former slaves castrate the survivors as an act of revenge.

In the third part of the novel, disease has forced what is left of the Steely Street Gang to flee London and head north. **It became dangerous and then impossible to remain in the vast decaying, collapsing honey-combs of the cities.** It appears to have taken two years for this to occur. They set off with ten people in a couple of battered vans, with **only a faint trace of the old bravado.**

The population of the north is sparse and suspicious and better adapted to a harsh environment than the people from the city. The non-sentimental, youthful attitude on display when the first old people killed themselves is gone, replaced by the imperative to survive. Soon the gang is whittled down to three couples; male/female relations evolve and become more permanent. The last of their petrol eventually runs out and they have to find and look after cattle and sheep, train dogs and make bread. Kathy becomes pregnant and they have to learn how to deliver a child from an old manual. At the conclusion of the book, a gathering is held of various gangs or 'tribes' as they are now known; at which the decision is taken to head back south to face whatever awaits them there.

Wallis was a member of the Young Communist League in the 1930s. He trained for the Royal Signals and was posted to Egypt in March 1941, wounded in 1942 and hospitalised in Cairo. Towards the end of the war he was posted in Germany. He carried on his political activity throughout the war, including using internal military networks to distribute communist propaganda. He drifted away from communism after 1945, joined the Labour Party and began working as a teacher.

Only Lovers Left Alive was his third book. His first, *Tram-Stop by the Nile* (1958), was set in Cairo and drew on his wartime experiences. His second, *Paved with Gold* (1959) was described in the *Observer* as a shrewd, funny story of young lovers, "both hauling themselves up the social ladder by way of big business, whose affair is mangled by a takeover bid." Wallis's fourth book, *The Bad Luck Girl*, was published by Macmillan in 1971

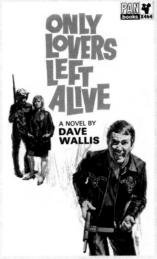

Only Lovers Left Alive (Pan, 1966)
The Bad Luck Girl (Mayflower, 1973)

and reprinted in paperback by Mayflower in 1973. He died in June 1990 aged 72.

Only Lovers Left Alive was out of print for nearly half a century until it was reissued by Valancourt in 2015. During that time, the only faint cultural resonance the book had was in a short-lived series called 'Kids Rule OK' in the controversial British comic book *Action*, published by IPC Magazines in the mid 70s. It was set in the then-future year of 1986, after all adults had been wiped out by a plague and society had degenerated into anarchy as youth gangs, including a gang of young police cadets, fought each other.

A major fan of *Action* as a teen, I remember reading the series, which along with 'Probationer', about a kid in trouble with the law, and 'Look out for Lefty', about a football player, led to the magazine being banned for several months in October 1976. Although 'Kids Rule OK' never acknowledged the influence of *Only Lovers Left Alive*, the parallels are striking. *Action* also had a reputation for what its editor Pat Mills called "dead cribs"—producing comic series that were variations on popular films and books. 'Hook Jaw', a blood-soaked story featuring a giant white shark with a harpoon embedded in it, was an obvious nod to *Jaws*, and 'Death Game 1999' was a thinly disguised and ultraviolent take on the 1975 movie, *Rollerball*.

ANDREW NETTE

The author would like to acknowledge information used in this article that first appeared in posts by Nick James on the site, Existential Ennui, and Steve Holland at Bear Alley.

Bonnie—Oscar Bessie (Domino/Lancer, 1965)

American writer Burt Hirschfeld produced dozens of books between the mid 60s and the early 90s. He specialised in elite epics in the style of Harold Robbins and Jacqueline Susann—*Fire Island* (1970) was the highest seller—often referencing the high times of the period with plenty of drugs, sex and rock and roll going down from New York to Acapulco.

His trashiest fare was published under pseudonyms. In the early to mid 60s he wrote as Oscar Bessie, producing titles such as *The Queer Frenzy* (1962) and *Angela, Be Bad* (1965). In the late 60s and early 1970s he wrote as Hugh Barron. A true journeyman, his work ran the gamut from TV tie-ins for the popular soap opera *Dallas*, including *The Women of Dallas* (1980) and *The Man of Dallas* (1981), to non-fiction historical titles on topics as varied as the Boxer Rebellion, McCarthyism, and the Alamo.

During the early 1970s UK pulp publisher New English Library issued a half-dozen or so of Hirschfeld's Barron novels including a reprint of *Bonnie*, which had originally been published in the US as an Oscar Bessie title by Domino/Lancer in 1965. The tale of a petulant child of the ruling class who turns to biker mayhem, *Bonnie* opens with the protagonist urging her staid fiancé to satisfy her sexual needs; when he fails to do so, she takes to skinny dipping at the beach. After a dangerous encounter with members of the local Apaches gang she decides to quit the bourgeois life and join the crew in mugging locals. Rising through the ranks she makes a bid for the gang presidency by leading a horrific attack upon their sworn enemies, the Monarchs.

A precursor of the glut of biker novels that hit the market in the years that followed, the book captures a time in which bike gangs were still essentially local conflagrations of juvenile delinquents on motorcycles. As much sexploitation as wild-child-gone-wrong biker fare, *Bonnie* manages to squeeze in such unlikely scenarios as our heroine's gang initiation, which involves being bathed by handmaidens prior to an auction in which she is sold off to a leather-clad S&M mistress. But *Bonnie* is a mainstream pulp novel of the mid 60s, so the numerous lesbian and heterosexual sex scenes are not exactly what you'd call hardcore. Exploding stars and similar metaphors fill in the gaps where thrusting organs, etc. would do service five to ten years later.

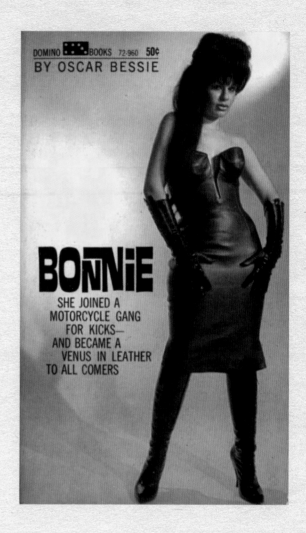

Despite being republished at a time when the biker scene had grown up and coalesced into a definitive subculture, the 1970 British edition of *Bonnie* fitted into the NEL canon rather better than many similar reissues, which stuck a contemporary photo on the cover in order to pass off kitchen-sink novels such as *The Leather Boys* as genuine members of the Hell's Angel set. Putting aside its purple prose and ridiculously conventional ending, *Bonnie* can stake a claim to uniqueness, and current-day interest, given that its central protagonist is not only a woman, but a bisexual member of a mixed gender gang to boot.

IAIN McINTYRE

Bonnie (Lancer Domino, 1965)
Bonnie (New English Library, 1974)

"**I**'ve been doing a lot of thinking since the Monarchs jumped three of our people. I, for one, don't intend to allow that to pass unavenged. Do you feel the same way?"

"Yes!" the answer came back loud and clear.

Bonnie smiled tightly. "That's more like it. All right, then. Here's the way it's going to be. You all know that Whitmore mansion up the beach on the point. Well, the Whitmores are away now, and the house is empty. Leo knows how to get inside, and that is exactly what we are going to do. We are going to throw the biggest, wildest party that house has ever seen."

"A party!" Mike exploded. "Is that your idea of a way to get back at the Monarchs?"

"Patience," she said evenly. "Yes, we are going to throw a party and the guests of honor are going to be the Monarchs."

"Oh, no!"

"Oh, yes" she went on. "And we are going to ply them with liquor, all they want, and beer, and food. And our squaws are going to be nice to their men, very nice, and our warriors will flirt with their girl's auxiliary."

"Why are we going to do this?" someone called.

"Yes, why?"

"Because we are going to invite the Monarchs to sign a treaty with us. A peace treaty."

"A surrender, you mean!" Mike broke in. "I'm against it."

She retorted quickly. "That's exactly the implication I want them to get. I hope they believe we intend to cop a plea, asked them to take it easy with us. I want them to come to our party full of smugness and confidence, sure of themselves, certain of their strength, their power, their victory and our weakness."

"What's the point?" Paula asked weakly.

"The point, dear Paula," Bonnie said slowly, choosing each word with utmost care, "is to take the Monarchs apart, to shred their ranks, to bust them up finally, to murder them."

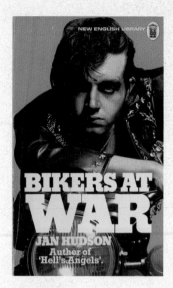

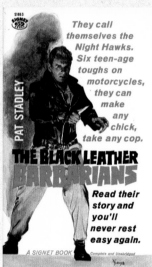

Bikers at War (New English Library, 1976)

Chopper (New English Library, 1971)

The Black Leather Barbarians (New English Library, 1974)

The Black Leather Barbarians (Signet, 1960)

BLACK LEATHER BARBARIANS
The Biker Pulp of New English Library

The heyday of British youthspoitation novels was certainly the first half of the 1970s, and the publisher at the centre of it all was New English Library. NEL produced a constant stream of youth-centred novels typically 50–60,000 words long, with eye-catching photographic covers that left no doubt about the books' subject matter. Amongst the most popular products of this publishing phenomenon were the Hells Angels novels written to order by NEL's stable of professional writers.

New English Library was formed on September 1, 1961, when New American Library acquired the British paperback publisher Four Square and renamed the company. By the early 70s a group of young, innovative editors at NEL—Peter Haining (later to become a prolific anthologist), Mark Howell, and Laurence James—were looking to extend NEL's list in order to appeal to a youth readership that had been largely ignored until then. The NEL editorial team would meet regularly to discuss the latest popular movements and trends with a view to commissioning novels that focused on those subjects. The books needed to be written and published quickly to catch these markets before the trend changed or disappeared. Professional writers were approached to churn them out, including James Moffat (1922–1993), who wrote a series of bestselling skinhead novels under the name Richard Allen.

As early as 1967, NEL had reprinted Jan Hudson's *The Sex and Savagery of Hell's Angels*, first published in 1966 by US soft-porn paperback publisher Greenleaf to cash in on the success of Hunter S. Thompson's *Hell's Angels: The Strange and Terrible Saga of the Outlawed Motorcycle Gangs* (1966). Jan Hudson was the pseudonym of George H. Smith (1922–1996), an American writer of second-rate science fiction novels and softcore erotica who would go on to write two more biker books for NEL, *The New Barbarians* (1973) and *Bikers at War* (1976).

The repackaged *Sex and Savagery* sold well in the UK, and NEL promptly reprinted other biker novels and purported exposés, such as *Freewheelin' Frank* (1969) by Frank Reynolds and Michael McClure, Gillian Freeman's *The Leather Boys* (1969), H.R. Kay's *A Place in Hell* (1970) and Hugh Barron's *Bonnie* (1970). Between 1970 and 1971 NEL also reprinted three novelisations of the NBC TV series *Then Came Bronson*—about a drifter who rides a Harley-Davidson—which were packaged as biker novels.

It wasn't until 1971, with the publication of Peter Cave's seminal novel, *Chopper*, that NEL's Hells Angels line really took off. Cave was a young British science-fiction writer and freelance editor of men's magazines who was contracted by NEL to write a Hells Angels novel in six weeks. *Chopper* was published in April 1971 and immediately began to ring up big sales, eventually selling about three-quarters of a million copies over seven reprints. The youth market was lured by the photographic cover depicting a nasty-looking biker with jet-black shades, homemade swastikas burnt into his cheeks, and a studded German military helmet secured to his chin by a length of metal chain. The quote on the back made it clear that the Hells Angels were in a different league from the other gangs and cults of the time:

> Chopper moved into position. The skinhead was still bent double. Bringing up his knee, Chopper felt with satisfaction the scrunch of broken bone as the kid's nose made contact. The kid went down, while blows from boots rained upon his body. He lay groaning, spitting out gouts of deep red blood and pieces of broken teeth.
>
> "Don't ever pull a blade on an Angel," snapped Freaky before they left the kid. "It's not friendly."

Here is someone to be reckoned with. Indeed, Chopper Harris is a man on a mission—he aims to wrest control of the London chapter of the Hells Angels from Marty Gresham (aka Big M) and take his beautiful but dangerous girlfriend, Elaine Willsman (aka Mama), for himself. *Chopper* features the indiscriminate mix of sex, violence, and drugs typical of youthsploitation novels. In one scene Chopper and the Angels beat up and rob a junkie of his fix in a public toilet, which they use to tempt a hapless girl addict outside a 24-hour pharmacy; they take her back to her squalid bedsit in a rundown part of London, where she is used and abused. This is a bleak, nihilistic world that resonated with Britain's disaffected youth, who were still four years away from the no-future punk movement that gave them a voice. Chopper eventually triumphs and relieves Big M of his position, his girl, and his coveted bike. But he is brought down by his own devices, killed while riding Big M's Harley, which he had ordered to be sabotaged. The poetic irony—Chopper is destroyed by the thing he covets most—is consistent with Cave's epic Shakespearean theme: he even has Elaine allude to the Ides of March.

He thought he was writing a single, stand-alone novel, so Peter Cave didn't think twice about killing off Chopper, but the success of the novel had NEL clamouring for a sequel. The result was *Mama* (1972). With Big M no longer in the picture, and Chopper dead, it is up to Elaine to grab control of the chapter from Danny the Deathlover. Sporting a one-piece leather cat suit with 'Big Mama' emblazoned on the back, she restores the Harley-Davidson that was the instrument of Chopper's downfall and takes control of the directionless Angels chapter. Continuing his epic theme, Cave associates Elaine with England's Virgin Queen, Elizabeth I, having her embrace celibacy and rule without a consort:

> **She had sworn herself to celibacy when she made her great decision. Apart from her unfortunate, but necessary encounter with Bernie, there had been no other man near her.**
>
> **Elaine was determined that no Angel should know her, and aware of her own sexuality to realise that a moment of weakness could drag her down.**
>
> **Sexless, she was Queen of the Angels—an undisputed leader. Just one indiscretion and she could be dragged down to the level of an ordinary woman . . . another one of the mindless bitches who opened their legs like coin operated sex machines. . . .**
>
> **But the animal lust was still there under the aloof exterior. It came upon her with ever-increasing frequency, and it made her body scream out for release.**

She worships the image of Chopper, turning her bedroom into a shrine to his memory, and even masturbates in front of his photograph. But Mama is also a ruthless and successful leader, and her Angels brutally subdue a gang of suedeheads (an offshoot of the skinhead subculture and, significantly, the name of the Richard Allen sequel to *Skinhead*) and a group

of Pakistanis in a race-motivated attack that recalls the worst excesses of the skinhead novels (the only black member of Mama's gang is called 'Superspade'). Elaine wants to fund a move to America through an armed heist, but ambition gets the better of her and she is captured and sentenced to 12 years in the nick, leaving Juice, an amphetamine-addicted sociopath, in charge.

More sequels followed with *The Run* (1972), in which Juice has to deal with an invasion of American Hells Angels, *Rogue Angels* (1972), in which the London Angels renew their conflict with the rejuvenated suedeheads as well as facing an incursion from the north by the Glasgow Angels, and *Speed Freaks* (1973), which chronicles the ill-fated efforts of a filmmaker to make a documentary about the Angels.

Peter Cave's editor was Laurence James (1943–2000) who had joined NEL in 1971, edited Richard Allen's skinhead books, and was a guiding hand in NEL's phenomenally successful western series, Edge. When Cave moved on to other writing projects for NEL James tried his hand at writing a Hell's Angel novel himself; the result was *Angels from Hell* (1973), written under the pseudonym Mick Norman, for which he received the standard NEL deal of £150 and four per cent royalties. But *Angels from Hell* is more than just hack work. James lifted the genre to a new level with his subversive themes, futuristic dystopian settings and counterculture allusions.

Set in a hazy late-70s Britain in which motorcycle gangs have been outlawed and repressive laws have been introduced by the Big Brother–like home secretary, George Hayes, *Angels from Hell* traces the efforts of ex-soldier and Northern Ireland veteran, Gerry Vincent, and his anarchist girlfriend, Brenda, to assume control of London gang, the Last Heroes, and take the fight to the reactionary government. James alternates the narrative chapters of the book with pastiche TV reports, newspaper columns, extracts from academic texts and counterculture sources; he quotes classic authors like Jane Austen and Shakespeare and even chapter headings are drawn from popular elements of youth culture (e.g., **The Order Is Rapidly Fading**).

The novel is peopled with outrageous characters: the gang leader Vincent, who like his artist namesake has only one ear, the deranged, sadistic Priest, the rampant bisexual filmmaker, Donn Simon, the wise old head, Kafka, and Harlequin, who comes to a nasty end when his head is impaled on a metal spike that falls off a speeding lorry on a motorway (a scene

Mama
(New English Library, 1972)

Speed Freaks
(New English Library, 1973)

perhaps inspired by the Rolling Stones' 'Jumpin' Jack Flash').

Angels from Hell ends with a violent pitched battle between the police and the Hells Angels; the second book in the series, *Angel Challenge* (1973), takes up the story a few years later, when the British public's disgust at the bloody conflict has seen George Hayes's repressive regime replaced by a more liberal, progressive government. As a result, the youth cults have been decriminalised and are flourishing again, but they have become a law unto themselves and murder and mayhem is the order of the day. The Skulls are futuristic skinheads, a cross between the recognisable skinheads and mods of the 60s and early 70s and Anthony Burgess's Droogs, whose gang leaders, like the malevolent Charlie Marvell, attire themselves in glam fashionwear:

> He wore tight, faded jeans, white shirt with a ruffled front, an elegant embroidered waistcoat and black ankle boots with platform soles nearly four inches thick. His hair was cropped almost painfully short, his skull gleaming bone-white through the stubble. He had long curling sideboards.

In a prescient nod to reality television, the rival motorcycle gangs, the Last Heroes and the Ghouls, are manipulated into a televised competition by tabloid hack Melvyn Molineaux. Just for something different, the Ghouls are a chapter of gay Hells Angels who dress in satins and platform shoes and are harder than the straight Angels in leathers. *Angel Challenge* continues the innovative narrative structure James pioneered in *Angels from Hell*—the story is developed through interviews from invented rock magazines, song lyrics, official memos and investigative reports, and for good measure the apocalyptic finale takes place in the offices of Molineaux's salacious rag, *The Daily Leader*.

James reached new heights in self-referential satire with his third novel in the series, *Guardian Angels* (1974). Taking his cue from the infamous Rolling Stones concert at Altamont in 1969, *Guardian Angels* has Gerry Vincent's Last Heroes employed to act as security for a huge rock tour of the UK by the top American bands. This is a time when groupies have become dangerous, knife-wielding celebrity-stalkers, and the previous security staff have been killed by the audience at a gig. Throw in a violent feud with the Skulls, and a rival Hells Angels chapter from the States who have been jetted in from California to beef up security, and we have all the ingredients for a typically blood-drenched riot at the final gig, which ends with Brenda being killed when she takes a bullet for her man.

The third of the triumvirate of biker novelists referenced by James in *Guardian Angels* is Alex R Stuart, the pseudonym of Richard Alexander Stuart Gordon (1947–2009), who published five biker novels for NEL between 1971 and 1973. Stuart's books are replete with counterculture references—Jerry Cornelius, *Siddhartha*, the Fabulous Furry Freak Brothers, *The Lord of the Rings*, Alistair Crowley, Jung, LSD, underground bands, rock festivals—and are written in a crazed, baroque, steam-of-consciousness style that recalls the Gonzo journalism of Hunter S. Thompson:

They clear aside for his hog satisfyingly fast, dozens of shaded stoned wondering dreaming ice-filmed calculating frightening eyes flicking across his face, down to his claws, stepping carefully. A lot of them are like a hip fashion parade; they believe in freedom of expression, while plenty more of them like padding around the countryside barefoot because it feels better that way.

In *The Bikers* (1971), Stuart introduces Little Billy, the iconic NEL biker, never seen without his black shades, who is built like a Mexican wrestler with a taste for meat pies and sports a *Fuck the Cops* tattoo on his chest and a claw hand to replace the one that was hacked off by a rival biker. He's the president of the Shoreditch chapter of the Apostles From Hell, a breakaway faction of the East London Angels. Little Billy has been away in the US, on a research trip to the Oakland chapter, and returns to find that his second-in-command, Larry the Lamb, notable for his massive puffball of multi-coloured hair, has taken over the chapter, as well as and Billy's woman, the pale, vampiric Linda. Events culminate in yet another riot at a music festival, with gas-masked soldiers called in to control the mayhem: approaching dimly out of the dark, these goggle-eyed, pig-snouted, gas-masked creatures are straight out of Mordor.

The Outlaws (1972) sees Billy on the run from the authorities while pursuing the instigator of the riot, the psychotic working-class lad turned conservative MP, Sir Frank Rutledge. Rutledge has been developing the Uric Acid Regulator, a device that, when perfected, will stimulate compulsive-aggressive or tranquil behaviour in any human being, making it an ideal device for the robot consumer age of potted philosophy, packaged politics, and power-mad control addicts. Billy gets his revenge and escapes the carnage that follows.

In *The Last Trip* (1972), Billy, now a celebrity anti-hero, is pursued by the police and the media; he takes off to Scotland and in a final act of defiance throws himself off a cliff as the authorities close in, giving them the two-finger salute:

The past is forgotten.
The future is not worth consideration.
There's just the NOW that he approaches.
The one, high, final, NOW.

Alex Stuart's last two biker novels, *The Devil's Rider* (1973) and *The Bike from Hell* (1973), fuse the genre with occult horror, which had become a lucrative theme after the success of Ira Levin's *Rosemary's Baby* (1967) and William Peter Blatty's *The Exorcist* (1971). They feature a motorcycle gang, the Sons of Baal, that practices black-magic rituals and sacrifices at pagan sites like Stonehenge and Glastonbury.

In the late 60s and early 70s a new popular culture centered on Britain's disaffected youth was emerging, which mass-market paperback publishers like New English Library were quick to identify and exploit. The biker novels were published in quick succession to cash in on the notoriety of the Hells Angels and to appeal to the anti-establishment sentiment and nihilistic world-view of a generation of young people fed up with conservative governments, growing unemployment and a world order that seemed on the verge of collapse. The 'fuck you' attitude of characters like Chopper, Gerry Vincent, and Little Billy were a short-lived expression of popular opinion.

JAMES DOIG

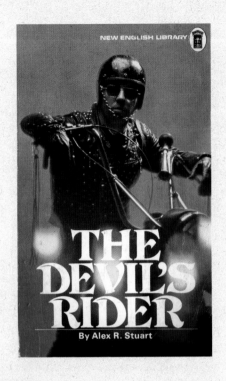

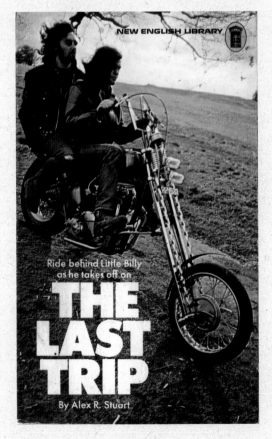

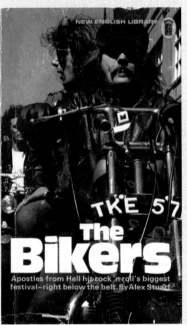

The Devil's Rider (New English Library, 1975)

The Outlaws (New English Library, 1975)

The Bikers (New English Library, 1973)

The Last Trip (New English Library, 1972)

all in paperback
The World of Hell's Angels

Get these eight great NEL paperbacks at booksellers and newsagents everywhere. Or direct by post (add 5p per volume for post and packing) from: NEL, P.O. Box 11, Falmouth, Cornwall.

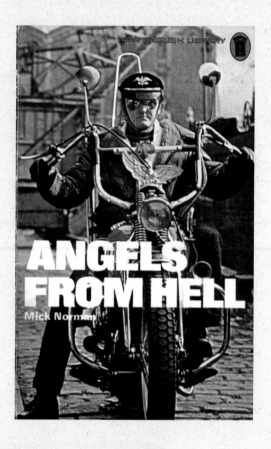

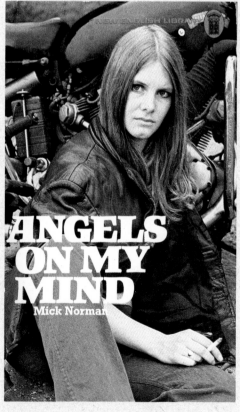

'The World of Hells Angels': early-70s ad for New English Library's extensive range of biker-themed novels

Angels from Hell (New English Library, 1973)

Angels on My Mind (New English Library, 1974)

Angel Challenge (New English Library, 1973)

BIKE BOYS, SKINHEADS AND DRUNKEN HACKS

Laurence James Interviewed

Among other things, Laurence James is the author of the legendary 'Mick Norman' Hells Angels books, which rank among the best English-language youthsploitation novels of all time. Before becoming a full-time writer, James worked at New English Library, where he edited the early Richard Allen books and a lot else to boot. The four Mick Norman novels—*Angels from Hell* (1973), *Angel Challenge* (1973), *Guardian Angels* (1974) and *Angels on My Mind* (1974)—were very successfully republished in an omnibus edition by Creation Books in 1994.

I talked to Laurence James shortly after the Mick Norman books were reissued, but the disappearance of the tapes prevented me from doing anything with the interview. By the time Simon Strong returned the two 90-minute cassettes to me six months later, I'd missed my deadline for *The Modern Review* and was in no rush to transcribe them. Instead, I consoled myself with the thought that at least Simon had satiated his curiosity about the author of his favourite Hells Angels novels. Later, I stumbled across an analysis of the 'Mick Norman' output in *British Low Culture: From Safari Suits to Sexploitation* by Leon Hunt (1998) and decided it was time to dust down the Laurence James interview tapes.

Shortly after this interview, Laurence's health collapsed. He was taken into hospital in Oxford, where he then lived, with chronic renal failure. This was diagnosed as being linked to terminal myeloma, or bone cancer, and he was given a prognosis of no more than a couple of years to live. During this period he finished off existing contracts but took on no new work. In the autumn of 1997, well past his literal deadline, his specialists told him that he didn't have terminal cancer, and indeed never had. It had been confused with an extremely rare condition called light chain deposition disease. In the late 90s Laurence was hoping to be put on the waiting list for a kidney transplant. He was looking forward to resuming writing, concentrating this time on children's books. Very sadly, Laurence died in February 2000, leaving an extraordinary body of work with us.

Where did you grow up?
In the Midlands. I was born in West Bromwich and I spent my first 18 years in Birmingham, which is why quite a chunk of the Angels quartet is set in and around Birmingham. I went to a minor public school there.

Which one?
King Edward's.

It's notorious because Tory racist Enoch Powell was an ex-pupil.
It's a place that always finishes at number two or number three in the league tables for state scholarships to Oxford and Cambridge. It's a great scholarship school. I wasn't very successful. Rather than going on to Oxford or Cambridge, I finished up training as a PE teacher at Goldsmith's in New Cross, cuz I didn't have the Latin, which was a shame. After a year, I decided teaching was not for me and I went to work in Foyles bookshop.

So when was it that you came to London?
I came down to London at the beginning of the 60s and dropped out of college about '62. Then I worked in Foyles and Harrods, that was in my short-hair days. After that I worked in publishing for ten years off and on, till about 1970 when I went to New English Library and ran the editorial side of NEL for three years.

So where were you working before NEL?
Before NEL I was working for a firm called Leslie Frewin.

What sort of operation was it?
It started off as a small publisher and was very successful, but then, as time went by, every year there'd be slightly more. Six books, then 12 books, then 24 books. There's a point at which you're not getting good product in at all—Leslie reached that point and carried on publishing. I was really sorry he went bust.

You were in London in the 1960s, rumour has it there was a lot happening.
There wasn't a lot happening in Hither Green. Not down in south London. I hung around with a lot of friends living down in New Cross. I had a girlfriend down there at the time. I don't think very much was happening outside the centre. It wasn't a drug-crazed heaven at all.

But presumably every now and then you were going down some of the clubs in the West End.
Not very much. We tended to stay local. We tended not to go to the West End a lot. I had friends in Chelsea, so I used to go and play around there. I was playing rugby at the time as well. I was kind of rough trade for these friends in Chelsea. They had a flat just off the King's Road and they were all very nobby, and I was kind of rough trade, you know what I mean. We used to play a game called Indians where you gave everybody one

card face down, you pick it up and you hold it against your head and you can see everybody's card, but you can't see your own. We used to make money out of these people. We used to cheat by working together. They were terribly upper-class.

Did you know any of the beat-related writers, like Alexander Trocchi?
No, though I met him in a bookshop just off Charing Cross Road, Indica. Miles used to work there.*

Did you feel part of that scene?
No, it was a small literary scene. People like Ginsberg would come over, Burroughs would come over, you know, and read, but it was a very tiny clique. Wholly Communion at the Albert Hall was an amazing one-off. It was a good thing to go to because suddenly you realised that actually there were two and a half thousand other people in London who liked the same things as you.

So this is the kind of stuff you were reading, American beats.
Yeah, I was working for Foyles and my predecessor was the post manager there. I was at Foyles for three months. I'd been there for three weeks as a post clerk [when] the post manager was sacked. So the shop manager came and said, "Has anybody got a degree?" and nobody had. He said, "Has anybody got A levels?" and I said, "Yes, I've got A levels". He said, "Right, you're post manager", and so I took over that department. And in the desk I found a copy of *Kaddish*. That was the first thing I read by Ginsberg. That was about '62 and that's when I really started reading. At NEL I got to edit a book called *Electric Underground* (1973), which was a best of City Lights anthology, all the beats were in it. That was a great book to do.

Right, so another question about the 60s is: did you have any run-ins with motorcycle gangs?
Absolutely none, not at all. I mean what really started the motorcycle thing was Hunter S. Thompson's *Hell's Angels* book. It was very successful and then at New English Library we published Jim Moffat's skinhead books, which were very successful, so we looked for another area of youth culture and the motorcycle gangs were an obvious area for that. I think Peter Cave did the first ones, and also a guy called Stuart Gordon, who wrote some bike books under the name Alex R. Stuart.

At the time I was getting disillusioned with publishing. I was not quite 30, and there wasn't really anywhere higher

*Author Barry Miles, co-owner of the influential countercultural bookshop.

to go. In a sense, I was almost at the top of my profession and I thought, "Christ, another 35 years. This is tedious." And I'd take guys out to lunch and give them ideas for books, and they'd go and write them and they'd make £150, £200 out of these books, and I thought, I could do that. So I wrote the first Angels book and sent it in through a friend anonymously to the other editor, so I actually never touched it. NEL bought it and after that I did three more. They all did well, they sold about 70,000 copies each, which was good sales even then.

Could you tell me about James Moffat, who wrote the Richard Allen skinhead books?
I inherited him as an author cuz the guy who ran NEL was Peter Haining and Moffat had written for him. In fact, the first book I was ever involved in at NEL was a book called *Satan's Slaves* (1970).

Moffat's highly collectible Manson cash-in.
That's right, the Manson book. I'd either just started at NEL or I was about to start, and Peter Haining and his wife were round having supper at our house and we were talking about Manson, and Peter said: "We'll get Jim Moffat to do a book on the murders". So Peter got me to ring Jim, who was living in Cheltenham at the time and I said: "Do you fancy doing a book about Manson?" That was all I had to say and then four days later the manuscript arrived on my desk.

It's an extraordinary production because the first two chapters are about Manson and then he goes on about [American pre-war Christian evangelist] Amie Semple MacPherson and other people like that for most of the book.
That was my fault. I think he was inadequately briefed for that one. You know his research methods. The research he did for the skinhead books was like two hours in one pub talking to half a dozen skinheads. He hated skinheads, he hated kids. He was not a youth-oriented man, Jim really wasn't. I can't remember now who had the idea for the skinhead series, it may have been Peter Haining. It may have been mine, it may have been Jim himself, but the first skinhead book came out and sold extremely well.

The story Moffat always told about it was that some Chelsea fan had been commissioned to do the first book and hadn't come up with the goods, and so he got in at the last minute. I've no idea if this is true, but this is his story about how he got to do the book.
I have no recollection of that at all. I'm not saying it's not true. But I can't remember how it did actually come up, where it came from. I can't remember the catalyst for

the skinhead books, but Jim started doing them, and he was a terrible old man. He was unreliable, extremely right-wing, a terrible drunk, a liar, he hated kids. What more can I tell you about Jim Moffat?

He was a talented hack with reactionary political views and a drink problem.
In his early days he was an *extremely* talented hack, a really good hack writer, but unfortunately, as it went on, he began to believe that he was in touch with youth culture. And youth culture to him was fascist skinheads. He started putting masses of terrible racism in his books. His manuscripts were just completely racist. And I was labouring away trying to get rid of all this from his prose and saying, "Jim, sorry, you can't keep kicking the heads of Asians, no, sorry Jim". And in the end, after *Skinhead Girls* (1972) I actually refused to deal with him anymore because of his drink problem. He'd ring me up and say, "Have you got the manuscript?" and I'd say, "No" and he'd say, "Well I posted it yesterday. I'll post you another copy." And I actually knew that all the time he was sleeping on the floor of his agent's office in Bloomsbury in Great Russell Street writing the books. He hadn't even started some of these books. He became terribly unreliable, and in the end I wouldn't have anything to do with him. I had him moved to another editor. I'd had enough of Jim. One of the worst things for an editor is to have an author who lies to you. I mean if an author says, "Look, I'm really in the shit here. Can we meet? I'm going to be three weeks late, or I'm going to be six weeks late or whatever." As long as he gives you warning, it's okay. But when you get an author who says, "Yeah, nearly finished it, it'll go in the post tomorrow", and this isn't true, and you're bound by a production schedule for the book, and you've got your slot at the printer's, and if you miss that slot there isn't another slot. The next slot's probably down along here. And that was a terrible problem.

Do you know anything about Moffat's father, who was supposedly a serious literary writer?
No, he never talked about his father. I met his wife because his wife did a bit of writing as well. Jim did a lot of books apart from the skinhead series. He did *The Gold Cup Murder* (1973), set at the Cheltenham races. There was *The Sleeping Bomb* (1970), which has one of the great covers of all time. That's one of Dick Clifton Dey's first covers for NEL. The cover was wonderful. Jim did *The Marathon Murder* (1972), which was the book he supposedly wrote in a week.

I've heard some interesting stories about that book because it is the one where he went on BBC2's Late Night Line-Up and was given a plot outline, then had to go back a week later with the completed manuscript. I think it was Jim's idea to pretend to do a book under great pressure, as a media stunt.

I think as far as the TV audience were concerned, Jim went on the show one week and was given a plot outline and then wrote the book in a week and then NEL got it out the week after that. I've been told that the book was written and ready for the printer before Jim was given the outline on air.
Yes. He cheated slightly, because the brief he had was very loose and sloppy, and so Jim just fitted in something he was going to write anyway.

How did the book actually do?
It was a total disaster, an utter disaster. I think we probably printed something like 100,000 and sold about 20,000. It seemed a good idea. Jim fulfilled his part perfectly well. He wrote a perfectly acceptable book, but it had a very dull cover. It's a perfectly competent piece of writing, but Jim did get worse and worse as he went on.

There are a few other figures I'd like to ask you about. Did you have anything to do with the Sam Fuller book 144 Piccadilly (1971)?
That was mine. I bought that book. It didn't do very well. I thought it was a smashing book. I bought it really cuz I thought I'd get a chance to meet Sam Fuller and I never did. It was a lovely book.

So how did you get offered it?
It was published in the States and it was sent by an agent in a big box of stuff. I fought very hard to do it because I thought it was a great idea and there was talk of a movie as well. Sam Fuller was going to make a movie from it, which he never did, and he was going to come to London, which he didn't. It's a good book, an interesting book. It's clearly an American's book looking at the London situation, so in some sense, it's slightly flawed. If I wrote about Los Angeles gangs I would obviously make some mistakes and Fuller does this occasionally, he's not always quite on the ball.

How many books were NEL publishing a year?
Probably something like 60 or 70 hardbacks and 150 to 200 paperbacks. And there were only two of us. I was working much of the time with a bloke called Mark Howell, who's now editing a newspaper in Key West. We had a good time at NEL, we were doing all the commissioning, we were doing all the contracting, we were writing all the blurbs, doing any editing, proofreading

that went on, as well. It was good. An astronomical amount of work.

For what was supposed to have been a hack operation, you had a few writers who are now quite well respected by the literary establishment. You had Chris Priest . . .
That's right. Chris was doing hack writing all the time under a variety of names and I bought him as a serious writer, books like *Fugue for a Darkening Island* (1972).

Who wrote the NEL horror books?
I think they were mostly bought in from America. An agent called Singer used to handle a lot of stuff like that. Horror generally wasn't selling all that well. Not as well as science fiction in those days. We did things like republishing the Asimov juveniles, which weren't actually great literature, but they were quite fun. They'd never been done before in England and you could sell 40,000 of them effortlessly. We did Heinlein juveniles as well.

Also, you had Peter Haining at NEL, who edited some very impressive horror anthologies.
Yes, he's a great anthologist, a brilliant anthologist. He included the first story I ever had published in one of his anthologies, a story called 'Mercy'; it's in *The Unspeakable People* (1969) that he did for Leslie Frewin.

So that was in the 60s.
That would have been in the late 60s. It was the first story I had published. Then I had stories published in *New Worlds* and in Corgi *New Writing* series, I had short stories published. Then I more or less gave up short-story writing.

Another person I wanted to ask you about was Tony Lopez, who wrote a gangster series called The Hoods *and is now a well-respected academic poet.*
He was after my time. There was a very hectic period during the early 70s when the *Los Angeles Times Mirror*, who owned New English Library and New American Library as well, they came over intending to close down New English Library because it was a loss-making operation. Bob Tanner had just been managing director there and he'd come from wholesale newsagenting and he brought Peter Haining in as the editor. Anthony Cheatham worked there for a time as well, and it was such an incredibly low-budget operation that year after year it made money. Very few of the books I bought lost money. There's a book by Mervyn Peake's widow, Maeve Gilmore, that probably lost money, but it was still a nice book. We published [morals campaigner] Mary Whitehouse as well. To have Mary Whitehouse on the

same list as the skinhead books and Harold Robbins, I thought was quite cool.

You reprinted The Hell-Fire Club *(1959) and* The History of Torture *(1963) by Daniel P. Mannix.*
I love Mannix.

Did you ever have any direct contact with him?
No. Mannix wrote a book called *Memoirs of a Sword Swallower* (1951). That was one of my great seminal books when I was about 14, and it was a time when they were bringing out books like Stetson Kennedy's *I Rode with the Ku Klux Klan* (1954), these really weird American pulp non-fiction books, and *Memoirs of a Sword Swallower* is a classic of the genre. But I don't know anything about Mannix, or if he is still alive.

You were involved in producing jacket copy, have you got any particular favourites that you wrote?
At the time, because there were only two of us, we would have to do as many as 20 or 25 blurbs a month. You were supposed to spread them out over the month and in fact you had the big production meeting on the last Friday of every month, so normally on the last Thursday of each month, after lunch, Mark Howard and I would do all the blurbs, which would be about 25 blurbs between us. We would pass them backwards and forwards to come up with minimalist copy which would say things like, "Two men, a town, the gold. They'll come together at rainbow's end". That would be it.

NEL blurbs often took a paragraph out of a novel and stuck it on the back cover.
That still goes on. English publishers don't use it all that much, but at NEL we'd try to find a nice paragraph to stick at the top of the back cover and that was a third of the blurb done.

I think NEL had more in common with American pulp publishing than a traditional English approach.
Mark Howell was an English public schoolboy who came from a background in American mass circulation journalism, and I'd not been involved in paperback publishing before. The traditional paperback end of publishing was simply to publish hardback books in softcovers. You'd go to publishers like Michael Joseph or whoever, and they'd send you their hardbacks and you'd buy them and put them out in paperback. That was the traditional way it was done, but that was too expensive for NEL, so we originated an enormous amount of material in-house. We had people like Alex R. Stuart, Peter Cave, Chris Priest, Terry Harknett—who did the Edge western series—and

Guardian Angels (New English Library, 1974)

her ideas are incredibly extreme, but she is inherently a decent person. I can't mock Mary Whitehouse, because she has decent beliefs, although she carries them too far. Her ideas about censorship I can't agree with at all, but her basic ideas of protecting young children, you can't really argue against it. As I say, she took her ideas too far. But she was good, we got a Foyles literary luncheon for her. The only Foyles literary luncheon NEL ever had in those days. Lord Longford was there, it was good.

To move on to your own writing, how did you get the idea for the first Angels book?
I thought I could write, I wanted to try it. I always think the great trick about writing is: you can either do it or you can't. Creative writing courses seem to me a waste of time, because I genuinely believe you either have the talent or you don't. You can improve that talent, you can hone it a bit, but if you can't do it, you can't do it. I didn't know whether I could do a novel or not. I'd done short stories and I thought I'd try a novel. The Angels books were about 50,000 words, and so I did the first one, which as I say was bought and was successful, and then I did the other three which followed, and they were all successful, they all did well.

So how did you actually set about writing the first one? It was your first novel. What was your actual modus operandi for its production?
It was triggered by the opening episode at Hither Green station, where there's this long tunnel. I lived in Hither Green for a time, and I always thought it was really creepy, this pedestrian tunnel that ran under the railway. The tunnel was only about five or six feet wide and I always had this nightmare that you'd be walking along late at night and some guy on a motorbike would come thundering down the other way. That was what triggered the opening scene in the book. Everything else came from that. As I say, I'd read Hunter Thompson's book and I'd seen some of the Angels movies. We also wrote two Hells Angels magazines in-house at NEL. Mark Howell and I wrote those.

I understand you actually made up the interviews with the bikers and Angels.
Yes [*laughter*], yes. I'm sorry, yes I did, this is true.

No, no, I admire that approach.
We started off by doing a Johnny Cash magazine. That was the first magazine we ever did in-house, cuz Johnny Cash was booked for a big tour. So we wrote this magazine and it had lots of personal messages to his fans from Johnny. We made all that up, and in the end he didn't come over, but we still sold a lot of magazines,

they were extremely successful. In the end even the authors made some money out of it, they earned royalties. Even Mary Whitehouse made money. Mary Whitehouse's great skill was she'd give talks, and authors, as you know, are allowed to buy copies at trade price. Most authors now and again might buy about three copies of one of their books to give to their relatives or whatever, but Mary Whitehouse used to send for about 1,200 copies of her books at trade price and then she'd sell them at her talks and lectures. She did very well out of it.

Was publishing Mary Whitehouse your idea?
Yes. My idea originally had been to do a biography of Mary Whitehouse because I thought it would be really interesting to see what the lady was really about. I thought I'd write to her first and ask if she wanted to do an autobiography, and when she said no, I'd then go ahead and get a journalist to do a biography. To my amazement she agreed to do an autobiography. She was a very enthusiastic, very nice lady. I think a lot of

which was really interesting. The Hells Angels magazines sold extremely well—I mean, very, very well.

The Angels magazines are very straight fake reportage; your Angels novels are much more interesting.
What I wanted to do was shift the genre a little bit, kind of move the genre sideways from just the straight Hells Angels narrative to something that was, in a sense, subversive, slightly more political. That was why I set it in the future. A much more reactionary future, which now, I mean, a lot of the things in that did come true in terms of the [UK's repressive 1994] Criminal Justice Act. That's the kind of act that is imagined by making the Hells Angels actually outlaws. I mean, genuine outlaws—not just disliked, but actually illegal. In the same way the Criminal Justice Act hit at raves and that kind of thing.

So to go back to the first book, you said you got the idea from the opening scene. Before you wrote the book did you know how it was going to end?
It wasn't actually going to be a series. I didn't see it being a series of books. I thought there was always a chance. As far as possible, you keep your hero alive. By the time I'd finished the first book and they'd bought it, it then seemed to me there was a strong possibility I could do at least another two. Events that were happening then find their way into the books. Particularly the police . . . the increasing power of the police. It was nice to be able to use the Angels.

I think the thing about the Hells Angels is that they are uniquely tribal. There were probably no more than 1,000 serious registered members of the Hells Angels in America, even in their heyday. In England there was only a tiny handful, but what they represented was this incredibly close knit, Samurai-like closed warrior cult, with their own laws, their own rules, their own ideas of chivalry in the sense of protecting each other. The nearest parallel is probably the Masons. A Masonic order is a closed order whose members mainly help each other, help themselves, and they have their own rules and their own rituals as well. Masonic rituals are actually no more arcane than the rituals of Hells Angels marriage. I think that's what attracted me, the idea of an outlaw group operating on the very fringes of society.

You allude to the Angry Brigade in the books and say that the anarchists had once been a beacon of hope, but now the Angels represented the only hope for freedom.
That was never a realistic thought, it was an image. I think tiny fringe groups are a political hope because they're not leaned upon by other large organisations.

Groups like the Angry Brigade [who carried out a series of bombings and attacks on embassies, banks and other establishment targets in the early 1970s].

You had no contact with that Notting Hill/Stoke Newington radical scene?
No. Obviously I was aware of it through newspapers and television, but not directly. They were no real influence on the books in that sense at all. One of the things that I enjoyed in the Angels books was putting the small chapters in-between, which are kind of media parodies of television, film, newspaper interviews.

I thought that was one of the nice things about those novels.
Yes. One straight chapter and then the little chapters which I would cut in. I enjoyed doing that. I always enjoy pastiche and parody. You can actually have fake government documents saying really extreme things, and you could get away with that and it would work within the structure of the books.

I really like the poem supposedly written by a schoolboy.
Funnily enough, last night I was reading through the end of the last book again and I really got quite moist-eyed at the end of it. And I thought, I like that, because that of course was Brian Jones's death and Jagger reading Shelley at Hyde Park and releasing butterflies. Most of them were dead and they just fell out of the boxes onto the floor, but the idea was nice. That was what triggered that poem in the last Angels book.

I understand you were going to do a fifth Angels book, but it was never written.
Yes, John Harvey did a couple, because by then I'd gone full time. I quit publishing and decided I wanted to be a full-time writer and I got contracts to do books for Mayflower and another series for NEL. The NEL series was Wolf's Head, which was the Saxon and Norman series I did with Ken Bulmer, and I did another series for Mayflower called The Killers under the name Klaus Netzen, and I did a series for Mayflower about gladiators, which was The Eagles, and that was written [under the name] Andrew Quiller, which is a nice pun producing 'aquila', the Latin for eagle.

When I was at school, after I read your books I read the two Harvey novels, which were published under the name Thom Ryder. Harvey's prose was much softer than your writing. One of the things I noticed on rereading them when I was older were things like the T.S. Eliot references. For example, Thom Ryder has a character called J. Arthur Prunefork who'd say things like, "That was not what I intended".

Yes, John had been a schoolteacher. I've had a crack at a similar kind of thing, in this series I'm currently doing [1994], this American male action adventure series called Deathlands. I'm constantly putting in references and my American editors love it when I put in a little bit of Schiller or a bit of Eliot, bits of Robert Frost and, you know, "The woods are silent, dark and deep, I have promises to keep". The editors just love this, and I love doing it. I can't resist putting in quotes and pastiches. I put a Mervyn Peake pastiche in the last Deathlands book. It's a nice self-indulgent thing to do, but it mustn't ever intrude. You mustn't ever have the reader thinking, "Christ, what's going on here, I don't understand this bit, this doesn't make sense". It's got to be part of the book, it's got to work within the structure of the book. So, if people get the joke, that's fine, and if they don't, it doesn't matter.

To go back to your Angels books, there's the obvious Stones reference with the Angels doing the security at gigs, but are the bands actually based on anyone in particular?
I think the glam band was probably based on the Sweet because they were very heavy glam rock, lots of glitter at the time, but the main band wasn't really based on anybody at all. It was a totally fabricated band. In fact the band has loads of private jokes in it.

Isn't the drummer called Chris Rees?
Chris Priest. I've got a feeling he is, if I remember rightly. And some of the band tracks have family references, things like that. I think one of the bands is Matt David and my two sons are Matthew and David. It's full of stuff like that. Obviously, there are a lot of Dylan references as well.

One of the other things I think is very impressive in your Angels books is the sex. I could imagine you having problems with people at NEL with the levels of sadism in some of the sex. The scene that always stuck in my mind was the young girls who tried to sneak into a pop concert and after getting caught by the Angels they are punished by being shaved, covered in glitter and marched naked onto the stage with a whip swishing behind them.
Yes, that in a sense spins off from stories like the Plaster Casters [US groupies who made casts of musicians' penises] and *Groupie*. Jenny Fabian's book *Groupie* (1969) was one of the great books of the time. I read a lot of books about Stones tours and what goes on, but I think,

in a sense, that's the defence. If people criticise, you say, Yeah, but at least I haven't got anybody fucking a dead fish [as members of Led Zeppelin reportedly had a female fan do]. I mean, this is really quite moderate compared to what really goes on.

You had an MP stroking a dog while being beaten by a prostitute.
That's utterly realistic.

You never had any criticism over that?
No, none at all.

There's quite a lot of cunnilingus in the books, and a lot of homoerotic material, was that a problem at NEL?
Bob Tanner found gay sex quite a problem and we always had to slip that through. The Angels books weren't read by the senior directors. I consciously put in things like the oral sex. People were much more worried about the violence.

What actually gave you the idea for having a chapter of gay Angels in satins who were harder than the straight Angels in leathers?
One of the things I always try and do in all my writing is actually to subvert expectations. I thought gay Angels would do that.

You've written a lot of novels since you did the Hells Angels books.
I've done a lot, 165 books in 20 years. At times I was doing 14 books a year, westerns, they're only about 50,000 words. Currently, with the Deathlands series, this post–nuclear holocaust series set about 90 years after the world has gone, civilisation has vanished—which is really just a futuristic western series—I'm on number 28. These are much longer, 125,000 words, so I'm doing 6 a year, which is actually more than when I was doing 14 westerns a year. It's all relative. I did 12 Confessions books—fun to start with, but it got very tedious. A lot of westerns, children's books, some with my younger son Matthew that did very well, some horror books, women's fiction under pseudonyms. Altogether, over 150 books under about 20 pseudonyms. Whatever the publishers wanted. Westerns when the publishers wanted westerns, then I moved on when they wanted something else. Films were always a big influence, I'd extrapolate scenes from stuff I'd seen and liked in movies.

STEWART HOME

The High Side—Max Ehrlich (Gold Medal, 1970)

Launched in 1950, Fawcett's Gold Medal imprint helped pioneer the publication of original stories in mass paperback format. Over the next two decades, many of the company's writers would sell millions of books, and a handful, such as David Goodis, Kurt Vonnegut, Jim Thompson and Richard Stark (aka Donald E. Westlake), produced works that are now considered classics.

By the late 1960s the glory days of the company had largely passed. Whilst retaining stalwarts such as John D. MacDonald, Donald Hamilton and Dan J. Marlowe the publisher was clearly struggling to stay relevant amid the growing popularity of TV and the emergence of a new breed of writers producing best-selling men's adventure and vigilante series for other companies. Staying the course with detective novels and westerns, Gold Medal also experimented with genres that were in the process of being reinvented, such as mafia novels and horror tales, or tackling relatively new subgenres, such as rogue vigilantes and bikers. *The High Side*, a novel dealing with a Hells Angels–style gang named Satan's Outlaws, falls into the latter category.

As with many of the books published by Gold Medal, *The High Side* was the product of an experienced hand. Max Ehrlich only produced this one book for Gold Medal, but he had worked as a journalist and writer for TV, radio and paperbacks since the mid-40s, having previously turned his hand to subjects ranging from medical dramas to crime and sci-fi (including a 1967 episode of *Star Trek*).

Torn between his love for the young hippie runaway who is to bear his child and his deep bond to the gorgeous, golden-maned *Übermensch* biker leader known as Beautiful Brad, the main character of *The High Side*, Cal McCue, agonises his way through a series of bacchanalian romps, violent brawls and deadly betrayals. Lacking the padding and philosophizing of many a pulp effort, Ehrlich's dramatic plot ploughs at breakneck speed through the usual sensational elements lifted from Z-grade biker films, tabloid newspapers and the work of Hunter S. Thompson. Drug binges, beat-downs of citizens and lawmakers, misogynistic attacks on women, denouncements of both straight society and the unpatriotic counterculture, and filthy initiation rites all abound, although unusually there is nary a rock festival to be found.

The homoerotic, but never consummated, relationship between Brad and McCue allows the book an original twist. The pair rocket down a winding mountain together on a Methedrine-fuelled ride. Following this escapade, Brad buys Cal a fancy watch before the pair tattoo each other's names on their chests. They have sex with the same woman, but never manage to have sex with each other.

Ehrlich also has the Outlaws frequently relieving themselves on all and sundry as part of rites and actions alternately denoting humiliation and comradeship. Even a cop gets in on the act while taking revenge on a biker who had previously urinated on him. Who knows whether the device was a fetish of the author, or merely a device to further excoriate already beyond-the-pale biker customs?

The High Side, which featured cover art by fantasy master Frank Frazetta, was Ehrlich's sole biker effort and one of only a few books Gold Medal produced in the field. The author continued to regularly produce books until just before his death in 1983. His fiction increasingly focused on supernatural themes, following the 1974 success of *The Reincarnation of Peter Proud*, which was made into a film starring Margot Kidder the following year.

IAIN McINTYRE

A Fawcett Gold Medal Book

R2207
60¢

Satan's Outlaws — hellbent
for kicks, they played tag with death
and took all their curves on

THE HIGH SIDE

A BRUTAL, BATTERING NOVEL OF REBELS ON WHEELS
BY MAX EHRLICH

"Tell you something, Cal. People like us could never make it in squaresville. You ever try it with this chick, and you ought to have your head examined." Cal wondered why Brad was making such a point of all of this. "You see, Charger, you're already a fuckup like the rest of us, in a certain way. But this way is good for you. How long do you think you'd last in the straight world? The people in it look upon you as some kind of animal, a dirty, disgusting, violent punk. Okay, let them think so. But you know, and I know, it's all our own put-on, our special way of telling the Establishment to go screw itself. You don't fit into its plans. It'll put you down every chance it gets. You're the one-percenter who won't conform to the whole lousy, money-grubbing, ulcer-producing routine because you value things like freedom, like being a man. With them, you're nobody. The only place you fit is here with us. How about another beer?"

"Fine."

Cal watched Brad as he sipped his beer, and again he thought, what a beautiful man.

WHEELS OF DEATH

Bikie Birds—Stuart Hall (Scripts Publications, 1976)

Bikie Birds takes a key trope of outlaw motorcycle pulp, the vicious female gang, and gives it an Australian makeover. 'Bikie' is the Australian equivalent of 'biker' and 'bird' is a slang term for a young woman. The gang in *Bikie Birds* has four members: Ursula, the leader, who wields control through brute force and a set of knuckle-dusters; Irene, the slightly aloof, intellectual member of the posse; Melina; and Rose, whose hair-lip (the result of a bungled childhood operation) has left her with a permanent chip on her shoulder and homicidal tendencies. All four have suffered at the hands of various men: fathers, husbands, boyfriends, and male bikies who they've been attached to at stages in their lives. All are outsiders who had few friends until they joined together.

Bikie Birds opens with the gang robbing a rural post office. They subdue the elderly husband and wife owners, beating the husband to death and seriously injuring the woman. With the proceeds of the job, they ride to the nearest town, commandeer a couple of rooms in the local pub and try to find a male for the night. The only eligible prospect is Hugh Salisbury, an ex-Vietnam veteran working his way around rural Australia. The women kidnap Salisbury, transport him to a secluded camping spot, and take turns forcing themselves on him—all except Irene, who declines to take advantage of the prisoner.

When the rest of the gang ride off to find food (a raid on an isolated farmhouse in which the gang members physically and sexually abuse the woman unlucky enough to be home at the time), Irene confides to Salisbury that she is pregnant and wants out of the gang. She allows him to escape but he is torn between going to the police and returning to the bikie birds' camp to take Irene away before the rest of the gang returns.

A couple of local coppers are indeed following the trail of carnage left by the bikie birds, but their investigation is hamstrung by their disbelief that such brutal acts could be committed by females. Meanwhile, discovering Salisbury gone, Ursula, Melina and Rose head back into town to locate a replacement. They kidnap a young man, his girlfriend, and a bar maid from the local pub who they fear will be able to identify them to the police. The books concludes with a high-speed chase along a deserted country road, in which all the gang members except Irene meet a

bloody end, clearing the way for Salisbury and the sole surviving bikie bird and her unborn child to live a 'normal' life.

Bikie Birds has none of the genre flourishes or dystopian themes evinced by some of the New English Library motorcycle pulp produced in the UK at the time—the book is more soft porn with a bit of motorcycle action sprinkled through it. Hall focuses his descriptive talents, such as they are, on the often semi-undressed female characters, particularly their breasts.

Bikie Birds may be completely out of step with contemporary tastes in popular literature, but in the 70s and 80s the exploits of violent, sex-crazed motorcycle gangs were a mainstay of pulp publishing in Australia as well as the US and the UK. Motorcycle gangs originated in America after World War Two and grew in popularity after the release of the phenomenally successful film *The Wild One*, starring Marlon Brando, in 1953. By the late 60s, Hunter S. Thompson's book *Hell's Angels* (1966), the movie *Easy Rider* (1966), the 1969 Rolling Stones concert at Altamont, at which Hells Angels working as bouncers killed an audience member, and the growing involvement of outlaw biker gangs (as opposed to recreational motorcycle clubs) in crime, particularly drug trafficking, saw mainstream interest in the subculture reach fever pitch.

Influenced by British Rockers (particularly their widely reported beachside clashes with rival Mods in 1964) and the US Hells Angels, motorcycle gangs grew in popularity in Australia, too. Local interest was further piqued by movies like *Stone* (1974) and *Mad Max* (1979). Sydney-based pulp publisher Horwitz had published some motorcycle-themed stories in the 60s, then starting in the early 70s it released a string of local bikie pulps under its adult-oriented Stag and Scripts imprints.

The authors of these books included Peter Brand (a pseudonym for Carl Ruhen, mentioned earlier) and Gordon Kurtis. But the most prolific was Stuart Hall, who wrote over a dozen titles, starting with *Wheelie* in 1973 and culminating in *Jail Bait* in 1980. The plots usually took place in and around rural towns, and involved the plight of citizens (particularly females) and local police who drift into the predatory orbit of bloodthirsty biker gangs. First published in 1973, *Bikie Birds* was re-released in 1976 and again in 1983.

They used men only to satisfy their insatiable appetite for sex & thrills

*$1.20

BIKIE BIRDS

STUART HALL author of
BIKIE RUMBLE, WHEELIE, BIKIE'S LUST

Hall followed it up with *Bikie Hellcats* (1975), about a ruthless woman called Flower who builds up an all-female bikie mob who go to war against a male bikie gang. Remnants of the Hellcats would reassemble in *Fatal Females* (1978). The concept of the female bikie gang also appeared in his book *Birds of Destruction* (first published 1973 and reprinted in 1983) and *Saddle Tramps* (1977). Hall also wrote numerous softcore porn books, with such titles as *Sex Resort* and *Sin Convention* (1974), *Exotic Island* (1976), *Swinging Couples* (1977) and *Summer of Sin* (1984), to name a few.

ANDREW NETTE

Then she felt one hand slip from her shoulder and slide down her side, across her hip to the hem of her skirt, where it hesitated, awaiting resistance. When she didn't give any, it became bolder, and slipped beneath her skirt, moving along her bare leg to the ridge of her panties, where it hesitated again, and Irene felt the excitement working through her, moistening the material near his finger-tips.

She opened her eyes, and over her shoulder, saw Ursula creeping towards them across the grass, her knuckle-duster glinting in the moonlight, and to hold the big man's attention, she allowed her thighs to fall open a fraction, as though innocently, and taking the invitation, his fingertips slipped beneath the material of her pants, feeling the curling pubic hairs there, and became even bolder.

His hands were exciting her terribly, when Ursula's knuckle-duster swung downwards in a gleaming arc, and cracked solidly behind his left ear. With a soft grunt, he fell across Irene, his straying hand falling limp, then rolled in her lap, and flopped onto the white gravel of the pathway, where he lay still, his arms spread eagled. Irene dropped to her knees beside him and turned his head to study the small, bleeding wound on his head. She looked at Ursula, seeing that she had changed back to her jeans and shirt.

"He'll live," she stated. "Now let's get onto a bike and find a place to hide out for a while."

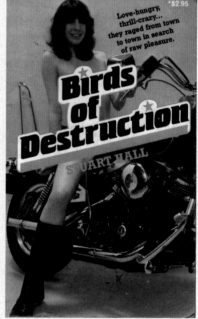

Bikie Rumble
(Scripts, 1975)

Birds of Destruction
(Stag, 1973)

Birds of Destruction
(Scripts, 1983)

Bikie Hellcats
(Scripts, 1983)

Ruthless gangs on a terror ride of rape, murder and destruction.

Bikie's Lust

PETER BRAND

*90c

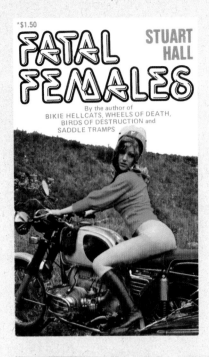

*$1.50

FATAL FEMALES

STUART HALL

By the author of
BIKIE HELLCATS, WHEELS OF DEATH,
BIRDS OF DESTRUCTION and
SADDLE TRAMPS

Brutality, hate and savage death
as half a dozen bikie gangs
embark on a violent trail
of revenge . . .

*$1.30

REQUIEM FOR A BIKIE

GORDON KURTIS

Bikie's Lust
(Scripts, 1974)

Fatal Females
(Stag, 1978)

Requiem for a Bikie
(Stag, 1977)

Bikie Girl
(Scripts, 1975)

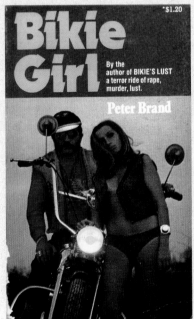

*$1.20

Bikie Girl

By the
author of BIKIE'S LUST
a terror ride of rape,
murder, lust.

Peter Brand

1960s British Youthsploitation Novels

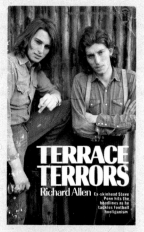

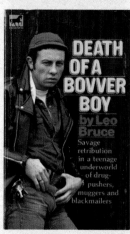

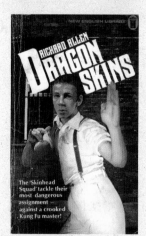

Trouble for Skinhead (New English Library, 1973), *Mod Rule* (New English Library, 1980), *Death of a Bovver Boy* (W.H. Allen, 1974), *Terrace Terrors* (New English Library, 1975), *Death of a Bovver Boy* (Mews Books, 1976), *This Right Soft Lot* (Panther 1971), *Skinhead Farewell* (New English Library, 1974), *The Kids* (New English Library, 1976), *Up the City Road* (New English Library, 1969), *Quadrophenia* (Corgi, 1979), *Dragon Skins* (New English Library, 1975), *Punk Rock* (New English Library, 1977).

Skinhead
(New English Library, 1970)

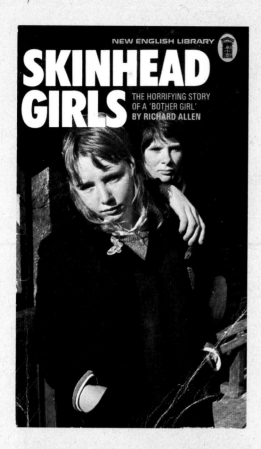

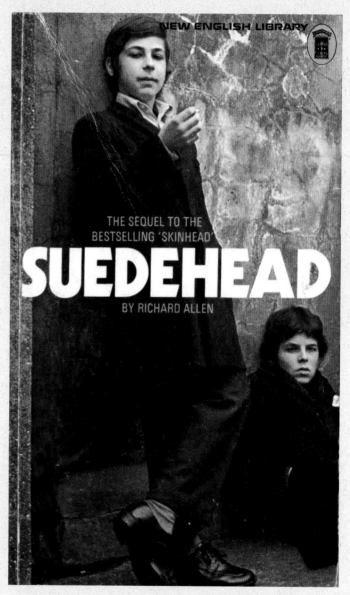

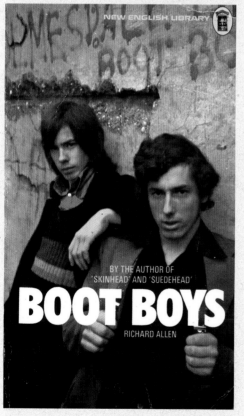

Skinhead Girls (New English Library, 1972)
Suedehead (New English Library, 1971)
Boot Boys (New English Library, 1972)

THE BEST OF BRITISH BOVVER
Richard Allen and New English Library

> Joe's cosh lashed out, striking the hapless guard across the cheek. The crunch of breaking bone was a glorious sound for Joe's mob. Like a pack of wolves they swarmed forward, bent on the kill. Boots found their target, 'tools' slashed viciously, fists landed with dull, sickening thuds.

This brutal vignette is typical of *Skinhead*, Richard Allen's visceral novel chronicling the exploits of East End skinhead, Joe Hawkins, and his belligerent lifestyle of racism, misogyny and casual violence (or, in the street vernacular of 1970s Britain, 'agro' and 'bovver'). The book was a publishing phenomenon. First issued in 1970, *Skinhead* sold over a million copies, reaching its tenth pressing within two years and spawning six *Skinhead* sequels, all written by Allen.

Many readers fondly imagined Allen to be one of their own; a young thug stalking Britain's back alleys and football terraces. In reality, 'Richard Allen' was one of countless *noms de plume* used by James Moffat, a Canadian-born middle-aged hack who hated kids and lived quietly in a seafront cottage in Sidmouth, a picturesque town on Britain's southwest coast. Yet Moffat found his métier in the series of terse, violent youth novels he penned for publisher NEL throughout the 1970s. After the success of his Joe Hawkins skinhead stories, Moffat followed up with such truculent fare as *Boot Boys* (1972), *Terrace Terrors* (1974), *Knuckle Girls* (1977) and *Punk Rock* (1977). All taut, punchy tales that grandstanded the headline-grabbing hooligan subcultures of the day, they were a parade of pugnacious paperbacks that made NEL the home of British 'bovver books', with 'Richard Allen' the genre's unrivalled master.

THE 'KING OF SKINHEADS'

NEL started life in 1961 following the takeover of two small paperback companies—Ace Books and Four Square Books—by US publishing giant the Times-Mirror Company. In 1960 Times-Mirror had acquired New American Library, a New York publisher originally founded in 1948 and known for producing affordable paperback reprints of classics and scholarly works, as well as popular, pulp and 'hardboiled' fiction by authors such as Mickey Spillane and Jim Thompson.

With NEL, Times-Mirror sought to develop a similar strategy in the UK, tapping into Britain's expanding paperback market. During the 1960s NEL had some success with science fiction, mystery and suspense stories, and boasted a few major writers, but struggled nonetheless. But under Bob Tanner, managing director throughout the 1970s, NEL discovered a new market niche. Tanner steered the company towards a younger readership as NEL carved out new territory in horror, action, and erotica titles. Relaxation of UK censorship laws enabled NEL's cheap, skinny books to explore new horizons of sex and violence, while developments in printing technology made it possible to have lurid photographic covers that leered provocatively from the bookracks.

Alongside sex, action and horror novels, NEL came up with sensationalised depictions of 70s subcultures as a means of hooking younger readers—children, teenagers and young adults—with the bait of streetwise grit. As Peter Haining, a former editor at NEL later recalled in a TV interview:

> There seemed to be this youth market out there [who] were interested in contemporary things that were happening. Not just literary, fantasy worlds, but what was happening on the streets . . . We used to have these brainstorming sessions, members of the editorial department, when we'd see what was making headlines in the newspapers. What people were discussing, where the young people were going, where their interests lay. And . . . use that as the background and the basis for commissioning books on those subjects.

One of the authors commissioned for NEL's new direction was James Moffat. Born in Canada in 1922, Moffat had lived in America during the 50s and early 60s, earning a living as a hack writer for pulp magazines and churning out at least six western, spy and gangster stories a week. By the mid-60s Moffat had moved to Britain and was rattling off paperback westerns, thrillers and romances under an array of pseudonyms—Johnny Canuck, Shirl Astley, Hilary Brand, Roy Court, Hank Janson, Derry London, Trudi Marsh and innumerable others. His first work for NEL appeared at the beginning of 1970. Writing as James

Taylor, Moffat knocked out *Satan's Slaves*, a sensationalist 'exposé' that cashed in on the Charles Manson murders of the previous year. But when NEL began casting around for an author to produce a book about the burgeoning skinhead phenomenon, Moffat hardly seemed an obvious choice. As Victor Briggs, Moffat's agent, later recollected:

I jokingly said to him that NEL wanted a skinhead book. And he said, 'I'll write you a skinhead book'. And I said, 'You can't do that. It's ridiculous'. And he said, 'No, I'll do it'. I mean, here we're talking about a 55-year-old man at the time, who looked no more like a skinhead than Greta Garbo. But he could apply himself. Which he did. And he produced this skinhead book. I took it into NEL, and I don't know if they were delighted or what. But it was what they wanted and they published it.

Moffat finished the manuscript for *Skinhead* in six days. NEL editors concocted the name 'Richard Allen' for the author, and the novel duly hit the shops. The story follows the exploits of 16-year-old docker's son and incorrigible soccer hooligan Joe Hawkins. Alienated and angry, Joe hates his parents and loathes his job as a coal deliveryman, but finds identity in the violence and thrills of the skinhead subculture:

Union shirt—collarless and identical with those thousand others worn by his kind throughout the country, army trousers and braces; and boots! The boots were the most important item. Without his boots he was part of the common-herd—like his dad, a working man devoid of identity. Joe was proud of his boots. Most of his mates wore new boots bought for a high price in a High Street shop. But not Joe's. His were genuine army-disposal boots; thick soled, studded, heavy to wear and heavy to feel if slammed against a rib.

Against a backdrop of London's grubby back streets, 'greasy spoon' caffs and East End 'boozers', the book is a chronicle of sadism and sleaze. Joe and his skinhead mob molest passengers on the underground (**Joe grinned, feeling his cosh bounce off the man's temple, seeing blood spurt**), they attack rival soccer fans (**His cosh curved across the kid's tender check, smashing bone. Then it slammed down, busting the skull**) and assault an Asian student ('**Bloody wog!**' Joe snapped, kicking the Pakistani in the face, knocking him backwards across the pavement). Travelling to Brighton, the skinheads hunt down a group of hippies (**Joe felt his boot sink deep into the tall one's groin**) and gang-rape their girlfriend ('**Me next mate,**' he yelled, watching Billy penetrate the half-stupefied girl hippie), before returning home to wreck a church youth club, beating up the vicar and his virtuous flock (**Albert sank to his knees as Joe's boot found his stomach**). In a brief interlude Joe has sex with a 14-year-old girl (**Her body flowed through his greedy hands, her thighs straddling him**), and treats her outraged mother with contempt (**When you want what Sally likes be sure an' let me know, Mrs. Morris . . .** '). Reunited, Joe and his pals batter an army sergeant (**They swarmed over him, knocking him to the ground, kicking and gouging and slashing with all the ferocity of their ugly minds**), run riot in a nightclub (**Like automatons, the mob erupted . . . slashing, kicking, hitting**), and finally boot a policeman into insensibility (**He felt the second boot crash against his temple and the night became inky black**).

In the book's last two pages, Joe is ultimately brought to justice, but remains defiant to the end:

Once he paid his fine—which Social Security would fork over anyway once he pleaded 'compassionate circumstances'—he would be free; free to continue as he always had; free to rule with an iron fist over his mob . . . Oh, the stupid bastards—didn't they ever learn! Didn't they know that his crime being publicized would make him a king of skinheads . . .

BADFELLAS: THE SKINHEAD SEQUELS

Published just after *Skinhead* in 1970, *Demo* saw Moffat/Allen turn his attention to other headline stories of the day. *Demo* centres on student radicalism and what the book describes as **the threat of a young people's global uprising . . . [that] grows more real every day**. The novel focuses on 'Network Seventy', a counter-espionage force of young hipsters tasked with foiling Igor Gruginshof, a Soviet agent whose nefarious master-plan is to destabilise the West by **fomenting student unrest and the youth revolution**. Compared to *Skinhead*, *Demo* throttled back on the violence, but boosted its sexual quotient, with a procession of scenarios that painted the counterculture as a font of carnal debauchery:

At nineteen she had experienced every perversion, every sensation a woman three times her age should have sampled. Her own mother had never been treated to such orgiastic splendours as Jean had managed in two years at Essex University.

Demo's sales paled in comparison to the success of Joe Hawkins, however, and Moffat/Allen quickly knocked out a *Skinhead* sequel. *Suedehead* (1971) begins with Joe leaving prison, having served 18 months for assault. But times and styles have changed since Joe was sentenced, and back on the street he adapts to the new, more spruce brand of skinhead style. As a suedehead, Joe's hair is slightly longer, and his boots and braces are swapped for a more flamboyant élan—smooth, elite, expensive—but he has lost none of his self-assured swagger:

In his City suit, the Crombie coat with velvet collar, his furled umbrella and the new bowler perched cockily on his head he was enough to make silly little birds take a second glance and get their hormones working overtime.

This time, however, Joe is set on bettering himself. He cons his way into a job with a firm of City stockbrokers and secures a swank, West End flat, enjoying a taste of the good life. But he has lost none of his wicked ways. Robbing and beating a gay passenger on the tube, Joe adds homophobia to his malevolent repertoire (all the hatred went into those vicious fists), while his razor-tipped umbrella is put to merciless use in a fracas with Chelsea soccer fans (his weapon slashed and jabbed . . . bury[ing] itself in a soft buttock). Along the way, he relishes 'deflowering' a haughty socialite (his fingers curled into her tights and panties as her legs came up to facilitate the completion of her abandonment) and ravishes a sexually frustrated spinster (Willingly, she flung herself down on him, her hands as eager, as intimate as his), before beating her to a bloody pulp (Like a prize-fighter gone berserk he attacked, slamming her back against the wall, hitting, bruising, battering as she slowly sank to her knees). Brandishing his malicious brolly, Joe's sadistic spree reaches a crescendo as he attacks an African orator in Hyde Park (Cracking bone increased Joe's desire to inflict pain . . . Blood spurted from the man's throat as the vicious tip pierced his windpipe). The young anti-hero is captured and caged on the novel's final page but, once again, he remains resolutely defiant—They could say whatever they wanted but Joe Hawkins would always remain Joe Hawkins.

The success of *Skinhead* and *Suedehead* spurred NEL's publishing rivals to imitate the 'bovver book' formula. Sphere, for example, waded in with *Soccer Thug* (1973, A VIOLENT, SHOCKING INDICTMENT OF THE VIOLENT WORLD OF THE TERRACE TEARAWAYS), while Mayflower stood its ground with *Agro* (1975, A NOVEL OF VIOLENCE—AND THE KIDS THAT LIVE BY IT). But nobody equalled Moffat/Allen's preeminence or his prolificacy, and he quickly followed up *Suedehead* with more hooligan tales for NEL. For example, 1972's *Boot Boys* portrays the bloodthirsty world of Arsenal soccer thugs 'the Crackers' and their rancorous leader, Tom Walsh (Even his father had to admit that Tom Walsh was a rotten bastard). As before, *Boot Boys* is a pageant of tawdry sex (Tom removed his briefs and presented her with a vision of nymphomaniacal pleasure) and extreme violence (Tom unleashed a mighty blow and caught the kid across the nose. He felt sick as cartilage gave way and snot flowed through the nostrils). The same year also saw the release of *Skinhead Girls*. Touted as the horrifying story of a 'bother girl', the book's teenage protagonist, Joan Marshall, escapes from her down-at-heel life by running with the skinhead and suedehead gangs of East London, as Moffat/Allen returned to his familiar territory of sex and violence (Nora's sigh of pleasure turned to one of outraged anger as Joan's toe slammed into her arse).

The theme continued in 1973's *Sorts*, Moffat/Allen's tale of a teenage runaway's quest for thrills among folk festival dropouts, while Joan Marshall put in a second appearance in *Smoothies*. Deserting her husband, Joan takes up with Dazzler Black, a hooligan leader who would give even Joe Hawkins a run for his money:

The guy was a menace, a skinhead turned suede who'd forgotten how many Pakis he'd bashed, how many fuzz he'd kicked during a football match, how many girls he'd raped when his urges got beyond control.

But Joe Hawkins himself was not away for long. Moffat/Allen had intended to retire the character following his incarceration, but Joe was soon let loose. A flood of letters, the author informed his readers, had made it patently clear that Joe is an 'established' favourite. Almost without exception, he explained, these letters request—no, insist—on another 'Joe' book. Hence 1972's *Skinhead Escapes* sees Joe bust out of prison, raping a young woman (**'Cut that out, you teasing bitch! You're going to get screwed . . .'**) and embarking on a binge of armed robbery and cop-killing, punctuated by the occasional foray into soccer violence (**As the kid paled and doubled, Joe smashed him in the face**).

At the denouement of *Skinhead Escapes*, Joe once again has his collar felt, but as before Moffat/Allen gave way to 'a **clamour . . . too great to be denied'**. Joe's fans, the author related, 'insist that he continues to entertain them in paperback format'. Accordingly, 1973's *Trouble for Skinhead* recounted Joe's exploits in prison, interspersed with gloating flashbacks to his vicious glory days (**The cosh whistled viciously. Blood spurted from the thick black hair greasily matting the skull. The Paki slumped, fell when Joe released him**).

With the success of the Moffat/Allen novels, NEL sought additional spins on the 'bovver book' theme. Motorcycle gangs became a particular NEL speciality. In 1971 NEL published two *Hells Angels* magazines, featuring interviews and pictures of American biker gangs, the content subsequently re-released as a colour hardback, *Barbarians on Wheels*, in 1977. An array of American fiction and 'non-fiction' dealing with biker gangs, meanwhile, was picked up by NEL and republished in the UK, but the publisher also sired its own stable of authors. Leading the way was Peter Cave, formerly a writer for softcore porn magazines, who was recruited to write *Chopper*, the story of a Hells Angels gang leader who **gravitated towards the nearest possible fight, or the quickest possible sex like a moth to a naked electric light bulb, or a junkie to his nearest 'fix'**.

Like *Skinhead*, *Chopper*'s mix of sex and violence was a commercial coup. Hitting the bookshops in 1971, the novel went into seven reprints and prompted a succession of biker follow-ups for Cave. Alex Stuart and Thom Ryder (an alias for top crime writer, John Harvey) also produced a series of bone-breaking biker books for NEL, but the posse was led by Mick Norman (a pseudonym for Laurence James, a NEL staff editor). Norman's 'Angels from Hell' quartet—*Angels from Hell* (1973), *Angel Challenge* (1973), *Guardian Angels* (1974) and *Angels on My Mind* (1974)—intercuts imaginary news reports, press cuttings and sociological extracts with tightly written narratives of underground biker gangs pitched against an oppressive police state in an apocalyptic vision of Britain in the not-too-distant future.

The front covers of NEL's 'bovver books' underscored their uncompromising themes. Garish and dramatic, *all* NEL's books had enormous visual appeal, but the covers to their 'bovver books' were especially iconic. Featuring photographs of 'real' subcultural members—skinheads, soccer hooligans and bikers—the subjects have a raw, stark quality, and stare out at the reader with brazen defiance.

'STRAIGHT FROM TODAY'S HEADLINES'

Bleak, downbeat and relentlessly brutal, NEL's 'bovver books' crystallised the mood of 1970s Britain. Rising unemployment, spiralling inflation, a global recession, a terrorist bombing campaign, industrial conflict and urban disorder made it seem as if the country was slipping into crisis. And, amid the chaos, youth subcultures were routinely cited by the press and politicians as the most sinister examples of the national plight. The tabloid press regularly conjured images of feral motorcycle gangs wreaking carnage in sprees of wanton violence and pillage, while a welter of headlines cast skinheads as the prime culprits in a wave of soccer hooliganism and violent racism.

NEL's novels were permeated by the same sense of catastrophe. As Moffat/Allen himself explained in the introduction to *Suedehead*, his books **faithfully represented Joe Hawkins as the epitome of society's menace. Youth**, the author averred, **has always 'had its fling' but never more blatantly, more unconcerned with adverse publicity than today . . . this instantaneous explosion now places the nation as a whole in jeopardy. Britain**, Moffat/Allen gravely averred, **cannot survive long in a climate of anarchy**. The back-cover blurb of *Skinhead* explained the grim reality more succinctly: **SKINHEAD IS A STORY STRAIGHT FROM TODAY'S HEADLINES—PORTRAYING WITH HORRIFYING VIVIDNESS ALL THE TERROR AND BRUTALITY THAT HAS BECOME THE TRADEMARK OF THESE VICIOUS TEENAGE MALCONTENTS.**

Indeed, it is easy to see characters such as Joe Hawkins, Tom Walsh and Dazzler Black as embodiments of the 1970s 'crisis'. Immoral, vicious and running amok through decaying cityscapes, they seem to encapsulate notions of a society sliding into dissolute anarchy. The motif culminates in Moffat/Allen's portrayal of **the Brass**—a paramilitary gang of über-skinheads

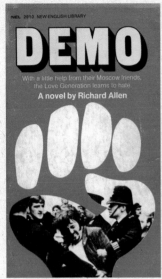  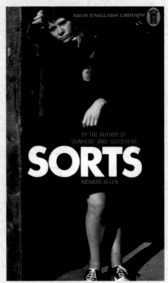

Demo (New English Library, 1970); *Smoothies* (New English Library, 1973); *Sorts* (New English Library, 1974)

featured in 1973's *Smoothies*. Explicitly compared to contemporary terrorist groups, the Brass are **Dedicated to violence, terror and everything touching on the televised portrayal of IRA and UDA thuggery in Ireland.** Even fellow hooligans regard the Brass as excessive in their malice, while the police are helpless before their lawless brutality:

> **Like a swarm of irate wasps the other four Brass attacked . . . Nero felt sick. Vomit almost strangled him. He didn't mind a bit of agro, a bloody punch-up, a soccer scrap. But this was bestial. He couldn't tear his gaze from the four Brass working over the unconscious coppers. There was nothing impersonal in their bone-breaking, flesh-battering assault. Just sheer hate. And a desperate need to inflict pain, serious injury.**

Smoothies exemplifies the way NEL's 'bovver books' ransacked the 1970s tabloids for stories of shocking sensation and boiled them down into exaggerated narratives of subcultural mayhem. But Moffat/Allen's novels did more than simply trade on the mood of crisis. The author also contributed his own belligerent viewpoint. A cantankerous right-wing populism permeates his novels, with recurring allusions to what he sees as the baleful consequences of 'permissiveness', the greed of trade unionists, the indolence of welfare 'freeloaders' and the malevolent influence of 'namby-pamby' liberals and Lefties. Calls for tougher 'law 'n' order' are writ particularly large. In *Skinhead* for,

example, a police officer at the scene of one of Joe's attacks **didn't believe in countering violence with more violence. He believed, as his superiors had taught him to believe, in the British policemen's duty to temper violence with understanding**. Describing the officer's thoughts allows Moffat/Allen to intervene with his own judgment:

> **And therein lay the problem. He could not reason that consideration for these thugs gave them a feeling of confidence. He could not see where tolerance was taking him and the public. He could not see that the teenage hoodlums needed strict measures and stricter punishment when caught in the act.**

The sexual politics of Moffat/Allen's novels are also relentlessly misogynistic. The countless sex scenes are written as male pornographic fantasies, while rape is frequently configured as a source of female sexual pleasure—not least in 1972's *Skinhead Girls*:

> **Toby grinned and bored deeper. Nobody had to write him a letter to state that this bird was getting the fullest pleasure from his rape. Her every panted exhortation spoke highly of his ability to please.**

Virulent racism is also a recurring theme, exemplified by Joe Hawkins's repugnant views expounded in *Skinhead*:

He leant against the bar between two huge co-loured men. The stink of the blacks made him sick. He hated 'spades'—wished they'd wash more often or get the hell back where they came from. This was his London—not some-where for London Transport's African troops to live. He enjoyed the occasional agro in Brixton. Smashing a few wog heads open always gave him greater satisfaction than bashing those bleeding Chelsea supporters.

Moffat himself firmly denied any sympathy with the far Right. Indeed, writing in the skinhead fanzine *Skinhead Times* in 1992, the author claimed that during the 1970s he had been contacted by the National Front (NF), a neo-fascist political party with a reputation for racism and violence. Moffat recounted how the NF were "very interested in getting [his] characters involved in their dubious activities" and related how, on meeting with NF leaders, he "was told exactly how skinheads should be portrayed—like anti-everythings determined to put the boot into everybody not in tune with the Front's undemocratic ideals". According to Moffat, the meeting was part of a media sting he helped engineer to reveal the NF "for the rats they were", but the scam petered out following a reshuffle of the party's leader-ship. Yet, while Moffat may have regarded the NF with contempt, the bellicose nationalism underpinning his books is still unmistakable, and it is made explicit in his introduction to the 1992 reissue of *Skinhead*:

Joe Hawkins and his ilk were, essentially, patri-ots fighting for a heritage. The battle was lost, though, when many in high places yielded to pressures from beyond our shores. And these wishy-washy types celebrated what they believed was the end of a bothersome cult. As in every war, when the overpowering might of an enemy appeared to have crushed the opposing force, underground armies regrouped and prepared to regain their rightful place in a homeland they had never relinquished. It has happened. Is still happening. Skinheads are everywhere.

A WALK ON THE WILD SIDE

Moffat/Allen's 'bovver books' are bigoted and jingoistic; riddled with prejudice and conservative moralising. At the same time, however, their sensa-tionalistic narratives and salacious delivery gives them an open-ended ambivalence. Superficially, the novels

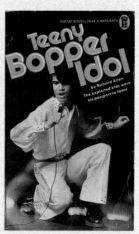

Glam (New English Library, 1973)
Teeny Bopper Idol (New English Library, 1973)

feign righteous indignation, bewailing skinheads as the **epitome of society's menace**. But beneath their moralistic façade there bubbles an enthusiasm for the wild and the wanton. In this respect Joe Hawkins reigns as the Lord of Misrule. An eruption of physical excess, he rides rough-shod over conventional sensi-bilities, revelling in a world of illicit havoc where, as *Suedehead* makes clear, he defers to none:

Nobody was going to say that Joe Hawkins ever knuckled down to authority. He was a law unto himself.

This anti-authoritarian streak is also a staple of NEL's biker books—especially Norman/James's Angels from Hell series. Set in a dystopic 1997, where a dictatorial home secretary has outlawed all youth cults, only four Hells Angels gangs remain as a beacon of freedom. Pre-eminent are the 'Last Heroes', whose leader—ex-soldier Gerry 'Wolf' Vinson—flirts with a series of anarchist guerrilla groups before turning the bikers into an army of subcultural freedom-fighters:

The Angels had become the first true Under-ground in Britain for centuries. For the dilet-tante scribblers of the early 70s the name had been a collective affectation—for the bikers it was a necessity of existence.

As an oppressive police state grinds down a spine-less population, freedom's only hope lies with 'Wolf' Vinson and the 'Last Heroes':

Screaming like demons from the seventh circle of hell, the surviving Angels, led by Gerry, hurtled out of the quarry into the confused ranks of the police. Any attempt to stop them was futile . . .

It was these thrills of defiance and transgression that gave the 1970s 'bovver books' much of their appeal. For young readers they offered a beguiling taste of forbidden freedoms. As (**real life**) Hells Angels leader, Maz Harris, explains in his introduction to the republished (1995) edition of *Chopper*, NEL's biker classic:

Look at the covers. Look at the impact they must have had on young, impressionable minds—mine included. Sure the characters are far-fetched. Sure their exploits are exaggerated beyond belief. But, back then, that was what we wanted . . . We didn't want to be told that the rest of our lives would be taken up with trying to make ends meet; that marriage, mortgage and middle age would follow in swift succession. We wanted to make an impact. We wanted to walk on the wild side. We wanted to take the world by the balls and twist it until it begged for mercy. And if we couldn't break through the barrier, between us and our aspiration, well we'd read about others who had, even if it was mostly a myth.

NEL's 'bovver books', then, were shot-through with contradictions. Undoubtedly, many were racist and chauvinistic. But, alongside their bigotry and misogyny, they also tapped into an avowedly anti-authoritarian sensibility. Revelling in their anti-heroes' thirst for defiance, the books won a hip cachet with young, rebellious-minded readers who had a taste for the riotous, the outrageous and the taboo.

SKINHEAD FAREWELL

By the mid-1970s, however, the 'bovver books' formula was wearing thin. In 1974 Moffat/Allen killed off Joe Hawkins in *Skinhead Farewell*. Freshly escaped from prison, Joe hightails it to Australia to hunt down a longtime foe. Arrested and extradited, his plane crashes on the journey home and Joe is presumed dead. In his place, the author attempted a new spin on the 'bovver books' blueprint, with a series of 'good guy' skinheads—every bit as tough as Joe, but walking on the right side of the line. Hot on the heels of *Skinhead Farewell*, for example, *Top-Gear Skin* (1974)

introduced the heroic Ray Baird, an American stock-car racer turned skinhead gang leader. In *Terrace Terrors*, meanwhile, Steve Penn is an ex-skinhead recruited to police football grounds plagued by a new generation of violent yobs:

"Look, boys," Steve spoke with authority. "We're legal now. That means acting responsibly. Think of yourselves as fuzz without the uniform. We don't act as skins or boot-boys. We try to bring decency back onto the terraces".

Steve returned in 1975's *Dragon Skins*, which cashed in on a craze for martial arts by pitting the hero against a gang of kung fu villains. Two years later, meanwhile, *Knuckle Girls* saw Moffat/Allen introduce Ina Murray, virtually a female clone of Joe Hawkins (**before the blonde bitch knew she was a target Ina's knuckles bounced off her front teeth. Ina blew on her closed fist, smiled sweetly**). Under various aliases Moffat also continued writing horror novels and thrillers for NEL and, under the Richard Allen moniker, produced a series of novels based on the machinations of the pop music industry. *Teeny Bopper Idol* (1973), *Glam* (1973) and *Punk Rock* (1977) all presented an acerbic view of youngsters being manipulated by scheming pop moguls. But Moffat's work for NEL came to an end with *Mod Rule* in 1980.

Mod Rule cashed-in on the renaissance of mod style that followed the box-office success of 1979's *Quadrophenia*, a silver screen homage to the mods' 1960s heyday. *Mod Rule* sought to ride the tide of the mod revival. Moffat/Allen's novel chronicled the lurid adventures of teenager Joe Watson—bastard son of the original Joe Hawkins—and the book's back-cover blurb promised the usual ingredients of subcultural thuggery (**LONDON MODS IN HASTINGS RIOT!**). By then, however, Moffat was 60 and a life of chain-smoking and heavy drinking had taken its toll. Sordid sex and knuckle-bruising violence still punctuated the text, but the writing lacked the pace of the original books and the few passing references to mods, scooters and seaside brawls seemed at best half-hearted. Consequently, *Mod Rule* failed to scrape into a second edition and the Richard Allen oeuvre drew to a close. NEL also slid into decline. Like other publishers, NEL was hit hard by the recession of the late 1970s and the firm increasingly shifted away from the youth market in search of more lucrative mainstream pastures. A succession of takeovers during the 1980s and 1990s saw NEL continue as a mass-market imprint for the publishing conglomerate Hodder Headline, focusing on thrillers and horror, but the brand's heyday was over, and the NEL name was finally retired in 2004.

SKINHEAD RETURN

Joe Hawkins was gone, but not forgotten; the 1970s 'bovver books' genre helped shape a generation of British writers. Authors Julie Burchill and Tony Parsons have both cited the NEL novels as part of their youthful reading and an influence on their subsequent work, while Victor Headley's acclaimed 1992 gangster novel, *Yardie*, was widely seen as following in Richard Allen's footsteps. Avant-garde writer and artist Stewart Home, meanwhile, distances himself from Moffat/Allen's reactionary politics, but cites the cynicism and "grinding pessimism" of the Richard Allen novels as a crucial influence on the development of British punk; and Home himself consciously pastiches their prose style in his own agitprop series of low-life fiction.

The Moffat/Allen novels also won iconic status in skinhead subculture. According to Scottish skinhead aficionado George Marshall, "skinhead literature virtually begins and ends with Richard Allen" and "most skinheads have at least one or two of his books tucked away in their collection". Indeed, the novels' subcultural standing prompted Marshall to acquire their publishing rights in the early 1990s, subsequently repackaging the Allen opus in a series of six omnibus collections, issued between 1992 and 1997. Marshall also recruited Moffat for a projected series of articles for *Skinhead Times*, Marshall's 1990s fanzine dedicated to skinhead style and music. Even a new 'Richard Allen' skinhead novel was in the offing. *Skinhead Return* was to tell how Joe Hawkins had, in fact, survived the Australian plane crash, saving his police escort's life and returning to Britain to be pardoned. But the plans were cut short by Moffat's death in 1993. The author produced just one final coda to the Richard Allen saga—an article for *Skinhead Times* that saw the king of 'bovver books' thank and salute all his fans.

BILL OSGERBY

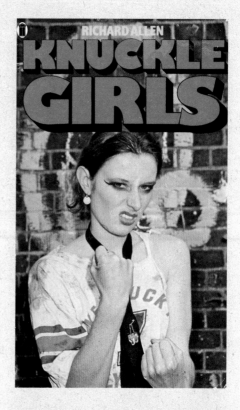

Knuckle Girls (New English Library, 1977)
Top-Gear Skin (New English Library, 1974)

GIRL GANGS, BIKER BOYS, AND REAL COOL CATS

GENDER, SEXUALITY AND CONTROL
in New English Library Youthsploitation Novels of the 1970s

Tom grinned, bringing his fist down with a chopping motion on the back of the United fan's neck. He felt the blow jar his muscles. He kicked as the man slumped. Then the boots went in hard. Muffled moans lost themselves in the frantic chanting from the terraces. Boot Boys! Boot Boys!

So reads the copy on the back of Richard Allen's *Boot Boys* (1972). Beneath this blurb the covers of two of Allen's earlier novels are reproduced—*Skinhead* (1970) and *Suedehead* (1971). The promotional copy for all Allen's books focuses on their depiction of violence. But although violence plays a major role in Allen's novels, it was by no means the only element crucial to his bestselling success. Allen's audience were obviously interested in reading about violence, but this violence was not simply 'soccer aggro,' it is extended into the realm of general social relations and sex. And it is a violence with a dualistic nature. It is simultaneously mechanical and mystical. It is beyond the control of those who vent it, but it is destined to be neutralised by some outside authority, usually the police, at the conclusion of each story. Parents and social workers also play important roles in the exercise of discipline and punishment. Some of these qualities surface in the following extract from *Boot Boys*:

Basically, Tom had a 'feeling' for violence. It had not been something thrust upon him through environment, poverty, the necessity of fighting to stay alive. He had been given more opportunities than most to further his education, forge a career. Yet he had rejected all decency in his lonely search for power through brutality. His venture into skinhead-ism had been choice, not following a trend. His association with 'The Crackers' came from the inborn desire to command, to know that he was capable of ordering total destruction on the heads of those daring to stand up and be counted against his way of life. He was hard, had never backed away from bother, enjoyed proving how tough he was. Yet, deep down inside, there was a spark of fear when it came to any showdown with his father.

Do-gooders would, no doubt, strive to prove some childhood moment when Tom had been victimised by his parents. But Tom knew different. His father had invariably come to him offering the hand of friendship, comradeship, man-to-man relationship. That every gesture had been skillfully rejected by the growing boy was not parental fault. It was that intangible something which compelled him to repel all those who hoped to gain his affection.

Allen's books were not the only series that his publishers, NEL, issued which gave expression to, and simultaneously depicted the containment of, youth violence and sexuality. There were Hells Angels novels by Peter Cave, Alex R. Stuart, Mick Norman and Thom Ryder, which although targeted at the adherents of a different subculture, also focused on the issue of youthful deviance. In the following extract from Mick Norman's *Guardian Angels* (1974), it can be seen that these books, too, were concerned with a mystical, perhaps genetic, aspect in the nature of their protagonists:

These were not men of the nineteen-eighties, used to slick suits and the soft answer. There was a primitive violence and strength in the Angels.

However, there are major differences between Allen's depiction of deviance and its control, and that of the Angel novelists. Allen's characters tend to be teenage, whereas the heroes of the bike books are usually in their early or middle twenties. The Angels have a far greater emotional investment in the concept of freedom. Whereas Allen's characters tend to end up before the courts, the Angels neutralisation as a threat to authority is far likelier to be achieved through violent death. And even this neutralisation is more often than not the result of feuding between deviant youth groups, in contrast to Allen's protagonists, who are often subject to control by representatives of authority. Norman's *Guardian Angels* is clearly marked by these differences, as well as providing examples of those elements which were crucial to the success of both genres:

The offices of the *Daily Leader* had erupted in a plume of death, and many had breathed their last. Again, the premier chapter of Hells Angels in Britain the Last Heroes, linked with the Wolves, affiliated by charter to the great chapter of Oakland in California went underground. But, times changed. Many of the dead had been members of a rival chapter—the Ghouls—and the public were not that concerned. Of far more interest was the news, only three days after the Holborn cataclysm, that a Minister of the Crown had paid a high-class prostitute to beat him with bunches of thistles, while he stroked her Alsatian. Not only had he admitted this absurd perversion, but a leading paper actually had photographs of him taking his pleasure. And the lady was reputedly of foreign extraction.

It is the combination of sex and violence, and their linking to those in authority, and the process of control that accounts for the success of these books. This is a theme that occurs over and over again. For another example we will turn to one of Allen's last novels, the 1977 epic *Knuckle Girls*:

Already displaying signs of rebellion against parental authority, Ina suffered at her father's hands while her mother weepingly shut herself in the bedroom. From an age when memory registered events, Ina associated violence with her father. Yet, she also found pleasure in this painful relationship. The pleasure and pain were synonymous in her mind; inseparables creating an interweaving confusion marked by a noted adrenal rise.

This extract also demonstrates another crucial aspect of these books, that of gender differentiation. Allen, in particular, is obsessed with reinforcing both sexual and racial stereotypes. While his male characters are simply sadistic, his female characters often have a masochistic aspect in their personal make-up. This viewpoint reaches a particularly obnoxious level of fantasy in Allen's depiction of rape. There are rape scenes in a number of his books, such as *Skinhead* and *Skinhead Escapes* (1974), but his most offensive use of this theme is to be found in *Boot Boys*:

"I haven't mentioned this before because I wasn't sure how you'd take it but," and she closed her eyes, sat down with hands clasped in her lap, "the night those boys raped me I suddenly realised a very basic feature of a woman's make-up Wilf, she is not that far removed from the jungle. I mean it Wilf . . ." and her gaze pierced his with a power he had not known her to possess. "At first, I was so frightened I could have died. Then, the pleasure became intolerable."

"You mean," and he hesitated before placing words in her mouth . . . "you mean you actually began to enjoy it?"

She nodded, unashamedly now. "I did! Is that so bad?"

Allen skillfully builds up the recollections of the rape, intercutting them with other scenes. The recollections continue as the rape victim is making love to a journalist who is supposedly preparing a news report on her assault:

She couldn't rid her mind of that night. It had been terrible—yet pleasurable. The four whose breath had stank had been worth less than nothing for a woman. But the fifth one . . . She remembered how he had whispered to her. The foul words falling on her delicate ears . . . Then the heightening of union as his movements brought her to that beautiful pinnacle from which man and woman can never jointly return. She climbed back down the steep cliffs alone, conscious of his youthful body rising from hers. It had ended so suddenly, so dramatically. His final spoken encouragement still burned her ears.

Taken out of context it is hard to believe that this is purportedly a recollection of a rape. It reads more like a piece of sheaf-busting romantic fiction. And Allen's treatment of race is as inaccurate and offensive as his treatment of female sexuality, as the following extract from *Top-Gear Skin* (1974) demonstrates:

Thick Irish voices spoke of pints to be consumed and wages paid for goofing-off. Some even wore union buttons proudly in their caps. What a laugh, Roy mused. Always shouting that the English are a nation of lazy bastards. Crying for their rights as trade unionists and striking for higher pay. And what do they offer in return? Contributions to the IRA so that British soldiers could get shot in the back.

But if Allen's depiction of Wimmin, Irish, Blacks and Jews are no more than bigoted stereotypes, his depiction of those he and his readers identify with are also caricatured, as the following extract from *Terrace Terrors* (1975) demonstrates:

> "A wild one," Debbie admitted. "She's married and got three kids now" . . . "I don't believe that," Steve said and went to the door. "No man in his sane mind would have undertaken to make a mother out of Myrtle."
>
> "One did—a cop called Lew Rickman. Apparently he arrested Myrtle for shoplifting but didn't press the charges. She was so relieved she took his advice and swopped her skingirl gear for a dress and settled down in a cashiers job."
>
> "Well, I never . . ." Steve was still shaking his head as he left the office. It made him feel proud of the majority of ex-skins and suedes. They'd sown their oats, but they'd always been workers, too. Not like hippies and other drop-outs.

It is in the depiction of gender, and sexuality, that major differences begin to emerge between the various series of teen cult novels. In Peter Cave's *Mama* (1972), a **motorcycle groupie becomes queen of the Hells Angels** by sacrificing any expression of her sexuality:

> She had sworn herself to celibacy when she made her great decision. Apart from her unfortunate, but necessary encounter with Bernie, there had been no other man near her. Elaine was determined that no Angel should know her, and aware of her own sexuality to realise that a moment of weakness could drag her down.
>
> Sexless, she was Queen of the Angels—an undisputed leader. Just one indiscretion and she could be dragged down to the level of an ordinary woman . . . another one of the mindless bitches who opened their legs like coin operated sex machines . . .
>
> But the animal lust was still there under the aloof exterior. It came upon her with ever-increasing frequency, and it made her body scream out for release.

As this extract shows, sexual stereotyping, while still a feature of the Peter Cave novels, is something individual protagonists may overcome. *Mama* depicts Elaine Willsman breaking free from her heterosexist conditioning, but only by reducing her sensual expression to auto-sexuality. Mick Norman's Gerry Vinson series allows for the expression of a far more liberated sexuality. In these novels two female characters, Holly and Lady, reject patriarchal sexualities and become lovers. However it is wrong to jump from this, to claiming that Norman represents an anti-heterosexist praxis. In many ways Norman's books are similar to those of Allen, Stuart, Ryder and Cave. For example, all these authors associate sex with humiliation and pain. One of the 'explanations' of Ina Murray's vicious behaviour in *Knuckle Girls* is a sense of (sexual) inferiority:

> Regardless of what the others said about group sex, Ina had still to indulge in that kick. She joined in every other activity, but strongly rejected Terry's urging to be a sport and gangbang. She knew why this one enjoyment was not for her. Looking in her wardrobe mirror told its story. She appealed to Terry but what if the blokes found her too skinny, too lacking in the knocker department. No, she could not afford to be ridiculed in front of Terry. And would not!

Norman, too, associates sex with humiliation, as the following extract from *Guardian Angels* shows:

> The rope ran to the neck of the first girl, then onto the necks of the others. The spotlights gleamed off their heads. Off their bald heads. Their hair had been brutally shorn by Holly and Lady, and the scalps coated with thick gold paint. Sequins had been scattered on top to give the glittery effect. They were totally naked, and even their body hair had been shaved. Hands were bound behind them, and ankles were hobbled so that they could only mince along in steps of not more than eight inches. Strips of sticking plaster sealed their mouths. Some of the brothers had spent an enjoyable time finger-painting all manner of bright, jolly designs on their bodies, during the afternoon.
>
> Bringing up the end of the line was Brenda, in her colours, with a short riding crop in her hand, which she swished with alarming vigour and carelessness in the region of the girls' na-

ked backs. When all four were roughly in the centre of the stage, Brenda made them turn to face the audience, then kneel awkwardly down, and bow till their heads nearly reached the floor.

Despite, or perhaps because of, this linking of pleasure and pain, Norman's depiction of sexuality is polymorphous. It is not limited by the rigid heterosexist definitions to which Allen adheres. Norman even brings out the latent homosexuality in Angel rites. For example, in this extract from *Guardian Angels*:

Gerry, who had been drinking heavily ready to play his part, stepped up first and took the honours as president. He unzipped his trousers and urinated over the prospect's back, shoulders and legs, reserving a little for the last to spray into Shelob's hair.

Norman had already gone further than this in his previous novel, *Angel Challenge* (1973), which concerns a rivalry between a traditional chapter of macho Angels, and a gang of satin-clad gay Angels. And not even the heterosexuals in this novel are exempt from homoerotic urges:

Gerry smiled to himself at the silence. It amused him to hear the sage words of advice of Sergeant Newman coming from the lips of an attractive girl. The old instructor would have considered it sacrilege. Girls was for screwing, and nothing else. Though Newman had once, when drunk at an NCO's party, admitted that "the best fuck I ever had was a young Arab boy. Lovely arse, Vinson. Lovely." Then he'd passed out cold.

It is at points such as this that we discover the real value of these books. Although more often than not they reinforce sexual and racial stereotypes, they do, at points, break them down. Their readers were mostly schoolchildren, and since the books were published with the intention of making a profit, they had to reflect the desires of adolescent readers, as well as trying to mould them. Thus while most of Allen's discourse on sexuality is no more than fascism dressed up as common sense, he doesn't give any credence to the liberal fallacy that those below the age of consent don't have a sexuality, as the following extract from *Top-Gear Skin* demonstrates:

Jeanette didn't mind older men paying attention to her. In school—when the rest of the class left—she frequently was asked to stay behind. Not for extra lessons unless one took sex as a vital part of education. Mr. Thompson had a thoroughly modern approach to everything—including the business of adulthood. Like when they were alone, her standing by his desk and his hand up her clothes doing such wonderful things. Things like she did at night, alone in her little bed. Things to make her appreciate the subtle change from childhood into womanhood.

And she couldn't ever forget that day when he showed her the difference between them! Actually showed her . . . but only fleetingly. Ever since, she had yearned for another man—a more courageous man—to complete her education!

The heterosexist manner in which Allen depicts adolescent sexuality *is* objectionable, but the fact that such sexuality gets depicted at all *is* worthy of note. Even the youngest of babies has a sexuality, and a sexual curiosity, a fact which the liberal discourse on sex has tried to suppress with its creation of the category of childhood and its 'romantic' notions of innocence. It should be stressed that pre-pubescent and adolescent sexualities are completely different to the sexualities of adults, but they nevertheless exist. It should also be stressed that power differentials between adults and children are such that kids cannot freely consent to sex with grown-ups, and since acceptable sexuality is necessarily consensual, there are logical and completely non-moral reasons for treating paedophilia as a thoroughly unacceptable and abusive practice. Returning to the New English Library novels under discussion, when dealing with them it is important to remember they were chiefly read, and in great quantities, by children aged 11 to 16. The concerns of the books make this clear, parental conflicts appear again and again, for example in *Skinhead*:

"I arsked you to fetch me bread this mornin'." his mother snarled. She waved a loaf before his face. "'And over the money . . . this is stale!"

Joe grinned: "It was all they had."

"The money!" Mrs. Hawkins said again, hand outstretched. Joe didn't frighten her. She was one of those heavy women with mas-

Skinhead Escapes (New English Library, 1972)
Rogue Angels (New English Library, 1973)

sive forearms and a determination to match her girth. She had been born in Plaistow and fought for everything she had. All her life, Thelma Hawkins had known poverty and hardship. Unlike her husband Roy, Thelma did not have cause to trust her neighbours nor to believe in anything except herself. Even her son was an object of suspicion when it came to money.

"I ain't got it." Joe sulked. Thelma's hefty hand swung, catching the lad across his cheek.

"Joe," and she breathed heavily, "I'm not arskin' a second time."

The boy's hand dipped into his pocket and handed over a coin. Thelma sighed, fingered the coin as a priest would a statue of the infant Jesus. "Next time I arsk you . . ."

"I won't bleedin' go!" Returning to his room Joe contemplated his face in the mirror. Her hand-marks showed red. "The old cow!" he muttered, fondling his cosh, wishing to hell

he could get enough courage to use it on her. Pleasant dreams flooded his mind and he saw his hand streaking down, the cosh a blur as it slashed across her cheek, the sound of cracking bone a satisfactory end to the fleeting wish.

The major characters in these books are always slightly older than the intended audience. This reflects the desire of the readers to leave behind the unwanted childhood they've had foisted on them by liberal humanists and enter the world of adulthood, where inequities are not as stark as the oppressive domination of adults over children. However, the freedom of adulthood brings with it a loss of security, and the ultimate triumph of the representatives of authority in Allen's books marks the dialectical resolution of these tensions. In this way, youths who are crossing the boundary between 'childhood' and 'adult life' can momentarily assert their 'individuality', before swapping one set of oppressions for the more subtle, but equally severe, restrictions of adult life. There is a temporary loss of control, when the child who has always been treated as an object, is asked to behave as a responsible adult subject. It is at this moment that the norms of the teenage peer group come to replace those of class society. Class society is simultaneously rendered universal in the Skinhead series, and explained away through metaphors of inheritance and genetics. Allen offers the following description in *Suedehead:*

> Basically, Joe Hawkins had a feeling for violence. Regardless of what the do-gooders and the sociologists and psychiatrists claimed some people had an instinctive bent for creating havoc and resorting to jungle savagery. Joe was one of these. Being part of a club which tried to foster a live-and-let-live fellowship did not weaken his desire to unleash brutal assaults on innocent folk. The club was a front to cover his deep, dark nature. A requirement for his suedehead cultism.

Finding everything about capitalist society unnatural, the deviant youth attempts to return to more primitive values. Rather than treating sexuality dialectically, that is to say, as something which is experienced as real, but which is actually socially constructed, such youth reject the dominant values and replace them with a taste for bother and promiscuous heterosexuality, which they invest with a mythical naturalness. *Boot Boys* contains this description:

> Coming—as he did—from Golders Green, Tom should have recognised that the way to success was by diligent pursuit of the Almighty Quid. He didn't. His pleasures in life were bashing heads, kicking the shit out of anyone too weak to defend himself, and laying anything from twelve to sixty that captured his passing fancy.
>
> During the skinhead era, Tom had geared up with a Ben Sherman shirt, Levis, Doctor Martens boots and a sheepskin. Somewhere at home he still had his bovver boots.
>
> That had been then. No longer. The fuzz crackdown on soccer crowds wearing skinhead uniforms had been the camel-breaking straw that started the rot. Personally, Tom did not mourn the 'passing' of skinheadism. He enjoyed being individualistic. At least when dress was concerned.

However, despite impressions they might like to give to the contrary, the readers of these books were not vicious psychopaths who had broken free of all control. They were searching for an authority they could believe in, rather than attempting to overthrow all forms of hierarchy. This manifests itself in an obsession with authenticity which occurs again and again in both the Skinhead and Hells Angels books. For example, Richard Allen includes the following description of author 'Dick Arlen' in *Skinhead Farewell:*

> Arlen grunted, sipped his tall drink. Personally he didn't give a damn about Lily Wright and her biased campaign against his books. He had been attacked often and by better antagonists than the ex–Sunday School teacher. But at the moment he could not afford to have his royalties cut by even a fraction. Of late, his outgoings had soared. This house with its acres of ground and a disastrous investment which had seen the loss of five thousand pounds had left him in dire financial difficulties.
>
> "It's all my fault." Emmett mentioned, lighting another cigarette. "I believed I was just stirring up a bit of newspaper dirt when I wrote those bloody articles . . ."
>
> A pretty blonde woman entered the room. Nodded to the reporter and opened a bookcase, extracting a volume before making a dignified exit.
>
> "The wife," Arlen announced casually. "She's in the middle of a romance. One of those dot-dot-dot affairs," and he laughed. "No free feels. No gropes. No bad language. Not like my stuff, eh?"
>
> Emmett had to admire the author. Ever since he'd been admitted to the Georgian mansion the feeling of frankness had permeated their conversation. Arlen, like his books, spoke in clipped terminology. Used whatever language suited the description.
>
> "This Wright bitch—is she hiding any skeletons in her cupboard?" Arlen asked.
>
> "If she is nobody knows about them."
>
> "And her kids—do they read my material?"
>
> Emmett sat upright, eyes blazing fanatically. "There's a thought," he murmured.
>
> Arlen smiled broadly, stretching his six-two frame. In open-neck shirt and slacks he looked every inch the country squire. Completely at

home in the surrounds. Part of the Cotswold background he loved so much. "When the opposition plays dirty you've got to find shit in their nest," he said. "It's been my belief that the 'Prissy Lil' brigade always have something nasty to hide. Nobody goes through this life without committing one sin and one is enough to get me off the hook. Don't you agree?"

Emmett slapped his thigh. "Nothing would bring me greater pleasure than to nail Lil to her cross."

Pouring himself a second drink as against Emmett's five, Arlen refrained from bringing up a poignant topic—the original articles. All writers had to make a living. Even journalists, he allowed generously. He'd been in the profession some ten years now and until he hit on the idea of doing a series about teenage antics his efforts had been strictly bread-and-butter. Run of the mill paperback material. No longer, though. Every book under his real name sold out first, second and third printings. Money he desperately required to maintain the standard he'd set for himself.

The inference is that Allen's novels are authentic—indeed, rather than being fiction, they are fact. Allen is obviously the author he is describing (the one letter difference in the spelling of his name might even be a typesetting error). The average reader with no knowledge—and probably little interest—in the author's actual identity is unlikely to realise that this passage is one of the most cynical in the entire novel. Richard Allen was actually the pen name of NEL hack James Moffat. This obsession with the authentic—or at least a cynical pandering to the readers demand for it—surfaces most vividly in Allen's introductions to his books, and on some of the cover blurbs. For instance, the copy on the back cover of *Demo* (1971) claims: RICHARD ALLEN HAS WRITTEN A MASTERFULLY RESEARCHED NOVEL THAT PROBES BEHIND THE SCENES OF TODAY'S UNIVERSITY UNREST. The fraudulence of such a claim is demonstrated by the front cover copy which boasts: WITH A LITTLE HELP FROM THEIR MOSCOW FRIENDS THE LOVE GENERATION LEARNS TO HATE.

Similar obsessions with authenticity are found in the Hells Angels books. For instance, Mick Norman includes the following passage in *Guardian Angels*:

Brenda: There are plenty of books about what we do. They're all old—written in the early 70s, most of them, but you might still find a copy around of one of them. Some of the brothers have copies, but they look like Dead Sea Scrolls. There are pages missing and what's left is held together by tape and glue. Try and read anything by either Stuart, Cave, or Norman. They all knew what it was all about.

Although these books could never be taken to constitute a 'radical project', their progression is still depressing. While Allen's views had always been reactionary, his earlier books at least depicted youth in conflict with authority. By the time of *Terrace Terrors* and *Dragon Skins* (1975), he was writing about Steve Penn's squad of ex-skinheads who had abandoned 'bovver' and become a private agency tackling hooliganism and crime. The following extract from *Dragon Skins* is typical:

Steve Penn sat back in his chair and studied Boots Welling. He liked what he saw. As an ex-skinhead he trusted Boot's admission that he'd had his share of aggro but wanted to break free of all taints. They had a lot in common, right down to the marriage bit . . .

Peter Cave turned to soft porn such as *West Coast Wildcatting* (1975) when the bottom dropped out of the market for Hells Angels books. After the fearsome Little Billy series, Alex R. Stuart wrote a couple of books, *The Bike from Hell* (1973) and *The Devil's Rider* (1975), which were nominally about Hells Angels, but actually had more to do with the occult. Most disappointing of all was Mick Norman's *Angels on My Mind* (1974), his fourth and final book about Gerry Vinson. In it Vinson is kidnapped by a crazed cop and then subjected to therapy by the cop's psychiatrist girlfriend. It is here that the Angel and Skinhead novels meet. The police feature in all the books, but the soft edge of authority (parents, teachers, social workers, psychiatrists) had, until this point, only found substantial depiction in Allen's novels.

STEWART HOME

Soccer Thug—Frank Clegg (Sphere, 1973)

Harold 'Striker' Richards is the self-proclaimed **king of the terrace tearaways**, a violent, anti-social young man interested in two things: football, in particular his beloved 'United Football Team', and agro, mainly bashing supporters of rival clubs. One could, at a stretch, add sex to those interests, but it seems a pretty distant third in Striker's priorities.

Striker is in jail after being nabbed by the 'bules' [police] for his latest bit of biff, and plotting revenge on the owner of the tea shack who shopped him to the cops. Upon release, he finds things have gone downhill. He catches his mum having sex with the television repairman while his sick father is in hospital, and a new guy, a sadistic sociopath called Rantic, is challenging him for the position as head of his gang and making a move on his 'bird', Lynn.

Striker and his gang demolish the tea shack but Rantic goes too far and nearly kills the owner. The ensuring confrontation between the two wannabe top dogs splits the gang. To console himself, Striker and a mate pinch a Ferrari and pick up a couple of women. They drive around and Striker ends up having sex with one of women on the Ferrari's bonnet.

The following Saturday, Striker gets into another fight at the football and only evades capture by taking a bus to a posh part of town. He crashes an upper class party where the hostess, who obviously likes a bit of rough, seduces him. But his heart isn't in it. It's unclear whether his lack of performance is related to the feeling he can't keep acting like he is, or whether he's just upset by the declining fortunes of his football team.

The owner of the garage where he works as a mechanic lets him have a motorbike on credit, a lovely old Triumph Bonneville. The gesture of kindness gets Striker thinking about going straight. But before he can act on the impulse, Rantic sabotages the motorbike, sending Striker to hospital. By the time he's out, his dad is dead, Rantic is living with Lynn, and his job at the garage is gone. Striker is determined to get his own back. The final confrontation between Rantic and Striker is a rather atmospheric scene, the two men stalking each other in a midweek friendly with a visiting Hungarian side during a downpour in mostly empty stadium.

Frank Clegg was the pseudonym used by Christopher Wood, an English screenwriter and novelist, best known for the Confessions series of novels he wrote under the name Timothy Lea. He also adapted two James Bond novels for the screen, *The Spy Who Loved Me* (1977) and *Moonraker* (1979).

Soccer Thug is a kitchen-sink description of working-class life, violence, casual racism, bad food and even worse sex in a bleak northern British satellite town. It was obviously written to take advantage of the media's obsession with soccer hooliganism in the early 70s. No doubt the publisher also had one eye firmly on the rival publisher New English Library's success in cashing in on youth subcultures.

Wood doesn't waste any words on faux-sociological analysis of football hooliganism. The only exploration is on the back cover, which describes the book as a **VIOLENT, SHOCKING INDICTMENT OF THE VIOLENT WORLD OF THE TERRACE TEARAWAYS**. The economy is a mess and everyone is bent, including the coppers, who seem to enjoy violence as much as Striker. If you want to go deeper, there's a bit of speculation about repressed male sexuality. Rantic is keen on Lynn but one of Striker's mates, Bazza, speculates that he might really be gay. Then there's Striker's love for United's flamboyant Irish superstar, Donnell. There are also some great descriptions of football.

ANDREW NETTE

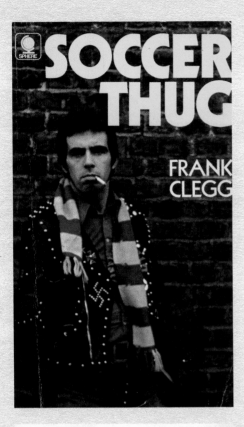

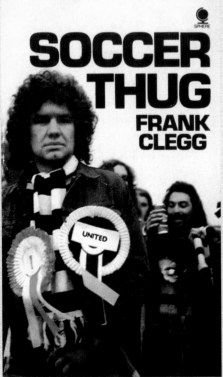

Soccer Thug (Sphere, 1973)
Soccer Thug (Sphere, 1975)

"Jesus Christ. Who let that little jerk in here?" said a voice that he recognised with a pang of excitement. "He can't think of what to say until he's drunk and then he throws up half way through his first sentence." Suzie Rayburn was standing in the doorway next to an equally striking black-haired girl wearing a brown velvet knicker-bocker suit the like of which Striker had not imagined in his most depraved fantasies. Both girls peered at Striker. "Oh. It's that lovely Ted I was telling you about," said Suzie. "Or are you a Greaser, or a Rocker? You can't be a skinhead because you've got too much hair."

Agro—**Michael Parry** (Mayflower, 1975)

Given the huge sales of Richard Allen's *Skinhead* series, it is surprising that the field of 'youthsploitation' was almost entirely left to its originator. Allen's books for New English Library—on skinheads, mods, punks, glam and any other subculture that emerged in the UK during the 1970s—sold in the millions, but only a handful of books exist by other novelists that deal with these groups. Leo Bruce's *Death of a Bovver Boy* (1974) featured appropriately eye-catching covers in hardback and paperback but was a rather plodding and unsuccessful attempt to restart the long-running Death series of "cozy" headmaster detective novels, with a completely confused take on subcultures (skinheads riding motorbikes, etc.). Tony Parsons, later to become a loudmouth newspaper columnist and bestselling novelist for ageing lads, kicked off his career with an unremarkable tome named *The Kids* (1975) for NEL about a bunch of young tearaways belonging to no particular subculture, getting into trouble before succumbing to heroin, criminality and suburban monotony. Punk, the scene Parsons would do his bit to popularise as a journalist at the *New Musical Express* (while popularising himself in the process), only resulted in two imaginatively titled 1977 novels: Richard Allen's *Punk Rock*, and 15-year-old Gideon Sam's *The Punk*, even though the scene was tailor-made for exploitation.

Another entry in the shallow pool of British youth exploitation fiction was Michael Parry's *Agro* (1975), which matched skinheads against NEL's other big subcultural seller, bikers. Along with his kung-fu westerns *Sloane: Fastest Fist in the West* and *Sloane: Fistful of Hate* (both 1974), *Agro* represented a rare detour for its author. Having worked in London as a junior editor for schlock-film outfit American Independent Pictures (AIP) in the late 1960s, Parry went on to specialise in writing and anthologising horror stories, producing more than 30 collections during the 1970s. He also dabbled in scriptwriting, bringing together an interest in horror and the feline in 1977's supernatural cat thriller *The Uncanny*, starring Donald Pleasance and Peter Cushing.

Given his connection to the studio that inaugurated the biker genre and maintained a steady slew of motorcycle movies thereafter, it is predictable that Parry's *Agro* started out as a film treatment for AIP. Once rejected, he turned it into a novel for Sphere in 1971. Released under the pseudonym of Nick Fury the novel was soon pulped, supposedly in response to libel action from the Hells Angels. Regardless of the veracity of that tale, the book reappeared in a second incarnation—this time with Parry's real name attached to it—in 1975.

Agro opens with a raid by a posse of skinheads on a pretentious countercultural dive, adorned with a vagina-like eye, known as the Erogenous Zone (EZ). The first to go down in the one-sided battle is a hard-working dealer named Barnaby, who—only a few sales away from heading home to a dinner of warm lentil soup—meets with the fury of ultra-sharp Steve McQueen fan Terry Staines. Staines's boot boys subsequently career through the club, bringing an avant-garde performance of *Hamlet* to a close and gaining the attention of a Machiavellian far-right politician who recruits them in the hope of creating his very own brownshirts.

Amidst the escalating attacks on hippies, gays and immigrants, Cisco and Speedy, two members of a US biker gang called Satan's Saints, arrive in London. No strangers to violence and patriotism, the pair nevertheless line up with the EZ crowd due to a shared interest in drugs and connections forged through the Californian freak scene. Ostensibly in the UK to score a large amount of hash, the Americans soon whip Britain's sad-sack wannabe bikers into fighting shape via the usual orgy of group sex, initiation ceremonies and brutality, before heading into a final confrontation with Staines's skinheads at a multi-media Happening.

Like Mick Norman in his Angel Chronicles, Parry clearly had a lot of fun writing this book. At times he succumbs to the genre's excesses, but he avoids the hateful moralism and pseudo-realism of the Allen novels. Writing at times in the whimsical style of the era, the author largely succeeds in simultaneously celebrating and satirising Britain's subcultures as well as the books that had cashed in on them.

IAIN McINTYRE

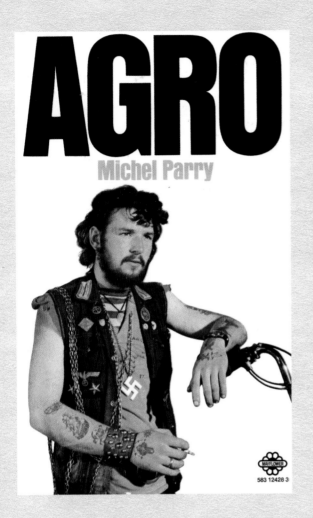

AGRO

Michel Parry

MAYFLOWER
583 12428 3

He used to get on well with his brother, really look up to him, the flash Mod in the latest gear, taking purple hearts, watching *Ready Steady Go!*, spending the weekends up Tiles dancing to the T-Bones, or tooling off down to the coast with the rest of the scooter-boys in their furry parkas. He remembers how his brother was one of the huge mob that stormed across Brighton beach, hunting down the remaining Rockers like the first men trapping the brutish Neanderthals. It was the dawning of a New Age and Terry felt the excitement of being part of it. Then the novelty died away and so did the excitement and it became a waste of money being a Mod, keeping up with 'In' shirts and the 'In' shoes and everything else that changed week by week. So Terry's brother sold his scooter and got married and found a council flat down the road and now he works in an office and has a squalling brat—one of them.

Terry felt the Excitement again when the Skinheads appeared—less flashy than the Mods, tougher than the stupid hippies. He knew this was it, feeling again the thrill of belonging to a powerful group, one that outraged everybody, that ruled London with steel combs and thumping boots. And he's one of the Leaders! A king! But suddenly, his sovereignty feels threatened. The streets are full of kids who have grown their hair into spiky corkscrew halos, who wear satin jackets and velvet loons and bouncey shoes in colours that hurt Terry's eyes. They sparkle in the sun as if sprinkled with stardust and glitter and behind them floats the fragrance of flowers. Terry can't understand it. A few months ago these self-same kids were skinheads and proud of it. Now they look as soft as the hippies, like a bunch of bleedin' fairies. Don't they know being a Skinhead is it?

The Punk—**Gideon Sams** (Polytantric Press, 1977)

Billed on its cover as **ROMEO AND JULIET WITH SAFETY PINS** this 62-page novella was also originally marketed as **THE FIRST PUNK NOVEL**. Apart from an obligatory effort from New English Library's ever reliable Richard Allen (*Punk Rock*, 1977), *The Punk* was one of the few fictional takes to emerge from the first wave of punk, even though the scene received heavy coverage in the media and spawned scores of writers of its own via fanzines and the music press.

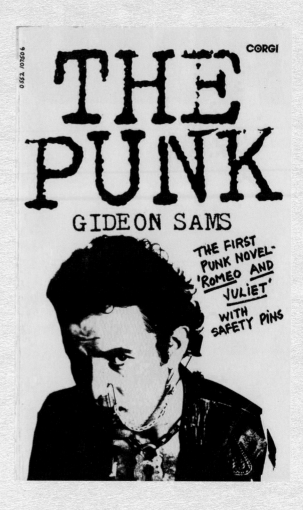

The Punk chronicles the misadventures of young Adolph Sphitz, the son of a policeman who lives in high-rise hell out near the iconic Westway [a section of elevated highway built through West London in the 1960s]. Sphitz whiles away his days arguing with his parents, drinking Special Brew, listening to the Clash and reggae on the stereo, and attending interviews for the dead-end, menial jobs foisted upon him by the Employment Exchange. He also spends an inordinate amount of time avoiding the attentions of faux Edwardian-clad, conservative retro-rocker teddy boys who are out to slice up any punk rocker they can get their hands on. In keeping with the ennui of post-boom, late-70s Britain—the very source of punk's rejectionist attitude—things appear pretty grim. Until, that is, Adolph meets Thelma, a young teddy girl who saves him from a beating at the hands of her boyfriend Ned. In the time it takes for the Damned to rip through 'Stab Yor Back', Thelma has crossed over to the punk side and the star-crossed lovers' very lives are under threat.

Slim in both size and content, the novel's rudimentary style and naive feel almost too cartoonish, leading the reader to suspect that an older, more sussed hand than the supposedly 14-year-old author was behind it. But the claim that Sams wrote the book as a school project, only to see it rejected by his teacher and then retrieved from the bin by his mum, is true. The salvaged manuscript was passed along to his parents' friend Jay Landesman, whose Polytantric Press published 500 copies with a cover featuring an image of the Sex Pistols' Johnny Rotten and an actual safety pin thrust into it. Sold on to Corgi, the book wound up shifting tens of thousands of copies and provided the basis for the 1993 film *The Punk and the Princess*. Sams never wrote another novel and lived a short, reportedly troubled, life—he died in New York in 1989, aged only 26.

IAIN McINTYRE

"No, Ned, please leave him, he's done nothing to you. Besides, if you get nicked by the Old Bill again, you'll be in Wormwood Scrubs before you can say, "Where's my Brylcream?"
Some punks played with safety pins; others paid with their lives ......
ADOLPH SPHITZ was just another 'nobody' until he met Thelma... In spite of the violence surrounding their relationship, together they explored the very heart of hard Punk and felt like 'somebody'.
They knew they had no future and didn't give a damn. Neither did anyone else.

THE PUNK, the first novel on this subject, was written by a 14 year old closet punk. Now his ambition is to become a brain surgeon.

THE PUNK
the first Punk novel

A Corgi/ Polytantric Press Book

UK..75p
Australia.....................*$2.15
New Zealand.............$2.35
Canada.......................$1.95
*RECOMMENDED PRICE ONLY

A roar of appreciation rose from the crowd and John Rotten staggered to the front of the tiny stage. He was wearing a black torn boiler suit. Around his neck he wore a dog's collar, and his legs were joined by a chain about two feet long. In one hand he held a large can of lager. He was bleary eyed and his fair hair was dark with sweat and grease.

"I don't know why you stupid snots waited, 'cause we ain't gonna play with all you morons fighting, now get up and move."

Johnny looked up the balcony, he saw a few familiar faces in the audience up there.

"Wot's this. Old farts gathering day?"

Mick Jagger and the others of his entourage blushed a deep purple under their Californian suntans. Johnny Rotten turned and looked out into the crowd with his usual demented stare. He brushed the hair from his eye and said, "The BBC won't play it, Woolworths won't stock it, but it ain't gonna stop you from buying it."

Then the Pistols blasted into 'God Save The Queen'. The song had everyone in the Roxy pogoing, and when it was finally finishing the crowd joined in the chant of "No Future."

Sid Vicious wiped his face with the sleeve of his leather jacket. "If a Mr. M.P. Jagger would like to meet me outside the Roxy later on, he might get a good kicking."

Gang Girls—Maisie Mosco (New English Library, 1978)

By the late 1970s the best of New English Library's pulp days were well and truly behind them. The formula that had worked in so many of its youth exploitation novels felt tired. Perhaps not unconnected to this, Britain was also changing.

Maisie Mosco's *Gang Girls* illustrates these trends. Set in the northern town of Manchester, *Gang Girls* concerns the exploits of an all-female gang of juvenile delinquents who call themselves the Wallopers. While the front cover is typical NEL, combining a grim, semi-documentary feel with a dash of lurid sexuality, the contents only nod faintly in the direction of the foul-mouthed, violent, kinetic energy of the publisher's earlier efforts. Indeed, *Gang Girls* reads as if the author was torn between wanting to write a gritty tale of out-of-control young females and providing an ideological justification for the tough on crime policies of the Tory government of Margaret Thatcher that would sweep to power the year after it was published.

The book opens with two unemployed teenagers, Gina and Karen, hanging out at the local social security office, wondering how they can get their hands on more 'lolly' [money]. Gina may have been named after one of her movie-mad mother's favourite actresses, Gina Lollobrigida, but any resemblance ends there. **Six foot tall, with a suet pudding face and marmalade hair, she looked like a mass of blubber poured into a sweater and jeans.** Karen, by contrast, **is blonde and petite, seemed like a tiny doll standing beside her.** Karen also has a major anger management problem.

Gina is pissed-off at being unemployed and overweight. Karen hates living in a tiny public-housing flat, which she shares with her mother, her ex-skinhead brother Stan, and Stan's pregnant, nagging wife.

Enter Di, who hails from a comfortable middle-class background but detests the secretarial college she is attending and is angry that her parents think she is a failure and compare her unfavourably to her old sister Lyn and Lyn's fiancé Jeremy, a self-satisfied right-wing lawyer.

Di meets Gina and Karen in a café. They get talking and bond over helping out a Caribbean woman called Seraphina, who is being abused in public by the racist café owner, and subsequently becomes the fourth member of their soon-to-be gang.

The four women start hanging out and one night, in need of petrol money, they rob a drunk. Soon they're knocking over petrol stations. One night the four young women are hanging out in a local park when the groundskeeper tries to chase them away. They beat him to within an inch of his life, blinding him. The attack makes the local papers, giving Gina and Karen a major kick. It also alerts the police to the existence of the Wallopers and underlines the dangerous nature of the gang.

As is par for the course in NEL youth exploitation pulp, the teenage characters view most of the adults as failures who have spent their lives working dead-end jobs for little gain, or sleazy, authoritarian types out to control them. The only exception is Di's Aunt Nell, a doctor, who makes an effort to understand what her niece is going through.

Another major subplot involves a young tough called Chuck, on whom Karen has a major crush. He sleeps with Karen, then dumps her, adding insult to injury by taking up with a green-haired punk girl, meaning Karen can no longer listen to her punk records without being reminded she's been spurned. A little later in the book, Chuck rapes Karen and carves his initials into one of her breasts. This triggers an interesting rape-revenge trope, as the Wallopers track Chuck down and castrate him.

There's a not very strong theme about the power being in a gang gives the girls to stand up their families and some discussion about law and order, including an argument in which Jeremy tells Di, **"People who commit robbery and violence aren't human"**.

In response to their combined disappointments and family tensions, the Wallopers decide to leave Manchester and head to London. But first, they need money. The fastest and easiest source is Di's Aunt Nell. But when they break into her apartment, Nell catches them in mid-act, and Gina overreacts and kills her.

Gang Girls would seem to be one of the few youth exploitation novels published by NEL in the 70s that was not written by the prolific Richard Allen (aka James Moffat). Maisie Mosco was born Maisie Gottlieb in Manchester. After World War Two, she edited the local Jewish newspaper and went on to write radio plays for the BBC. She wrote 16 novels, including a series of bestselling books for NEL about a Jewish family who fled anti-Jewish pogroms in Russia at the turn of the last century and immigrated to Manchester, which reportedly drew on her own family history.

ANDREW NETTE

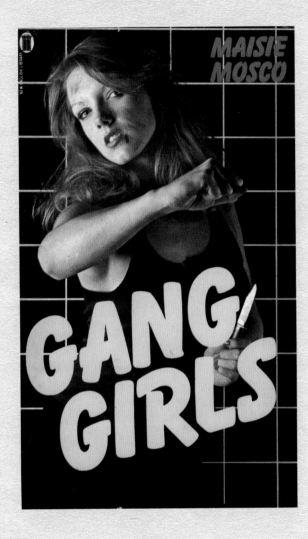

MAISIE MOSCO

GANG GIRLS

"Ow about some action?" Gina said as soon as she joined them at the table. They could see the teach-someone-a-lesson gleam in her eyes and Karen and Di felt the familiar excited anticipation setting them alight.

They let rip that night like a ship's crew who hadn't been ashore for months. What they intended to do wasn't put into words, it didn't have to be, they could read each other's thoughts. Di put her foot down hard on the accelerator and they zoomed through the darkness to a wealthy suburb. It was as if they had to make up for lost time, and the cash they took from their victims was the least important part of it. Six different women were relieved of the contents of their wallets and beaten up. In six different avenues. One after the other, Di, Karen and Gina, had the time of their lives, experiencing an orgasm of violence like never before, kicking, punching and laughing. Seraphina thought they'd gone mad and knew she would if they didn't let up.

"Don't use the knuckle-duster on anyone's 'ead, Gina," she kept imploring and Gina didn't. Not that night.

When Gina got home, Arthur had gone and her mother was waiting up for her.

"I've sacrificed me 'ole life for you," she said. "But you can't expect me to do it forever. I've me own life to live. Arthur's asked me to marry him."

Gina let out a howl that was part fury, part anguish, like an animal caught in a trap, and socked her on the jaw, but they didn't stop Mam from marrying Arthur.

Late-60s and Early-70s American Pulp
and the Rise of the Teen Novel

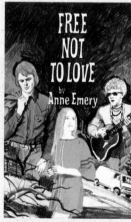
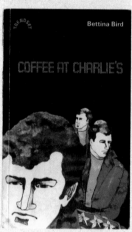

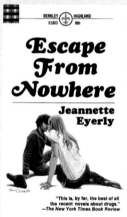

Don't Play Dead Before You Have To (Dell, 1972), *Heavy Number* (Bantam, 1976), *The Electric Grass Company* (Crown, 1974), *Think Wild!* (Pocket Books, 1970), *Escape from Nowhere* (Berkley Highland, 1970), *Coffee at Charlie's* (Trendset, 1971), *The Mod Squad* (Whitman, 1969), *Gaye Lizzie* (Trendset, 1971), *Free Not to Love* (Westminster, 1975), *The Peter Pan Bag* (Dell, 1971), *The Room* (Dell, 1977), *The Kid Was Last Seen Hanging Ten* (Paperback Library, 1971)

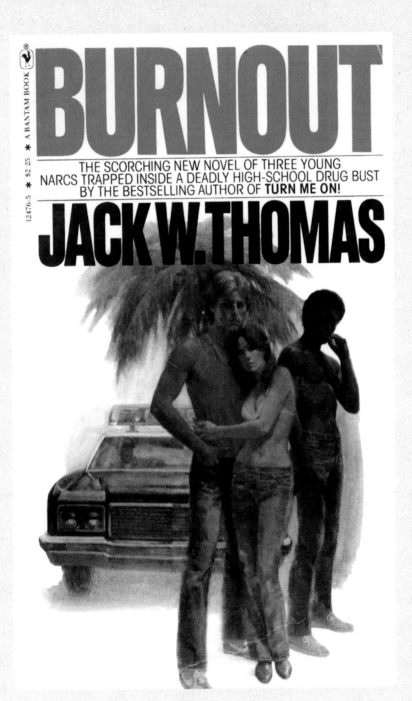

Burnout (Bantam, 1979)

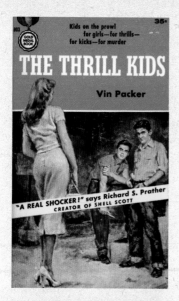

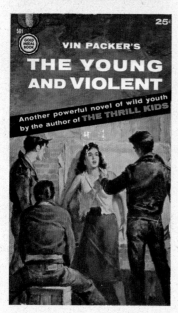

The Thrill Kids (Gold Medal, 1959)

Spring Fire (Gold Medal, 1952)

The Young and Violent (Gold Medal, 1956)

The Twisted Ones (Gold Medal, 1959)

GIRL GANGS, BIKER BOYS, AND REAL COOL CATS

SOMETHING IN THE SHADOWS
An Interview with Marijane Meaker

Marijane Meaker is the author of over 60 books spanning a myriad of topics and genres. Her debut, *Spring Fire* (1952), published under the pen name Vin Packer, effectively launched the American lesbian pulp novel, selling over 1.5 million copies. Under the pseudonym Ann Aldrich, Meaker wrote and edited non-fiction titles about lesbian life, while her Packer persona focused on crime, juvenile delinquency (JD) and romance paperbacks throughout the 1950s and 60s. The following interview covers this period as well as her transition to writing Young Adult fiction, for which she has won numerous awards since the success of her 1972 YA novel *Dinky Hocker Shoots Smack!*

How did you come to start writing for Gold Medal in 1952?
I came to New York from the University of Missouri with some sorority sisters, and one of them got a job at Fawcett Publications. She was raving about this new series they were starting of paperback originals. She was very enthusiastic about a man who had come from Hollywood to head up the imprint, Dick Carroll. She introduced me to Dick, who knew I wanted to be a writer, and he said, "Let's see something you can write." So I wrote an outline about homosexuality in a boarding school. He said, "That subject doesn't sell very well, and you can't put it in a boarding school"—because the characters would be underage, and the Post Office would object, because in those days they were responsible for censorship. So I set it in the sorority I had just left.

From a young age I knew that I was gay. Nobody ever talked about it, so I began to go to the library to look up things. In one book I read that homosexuality was rampant in boarding schools. So I immediately told my mother and father, "I hope I can go to boarding school." I didn't tell them why, but my father said, "That would probably be good, you will get a little taste of the world." And I certainly did [*laughter*].

The boarding school lived up to what the library promised: there were an awful lot of gay people there, including the teachers, who were always having fights and ripping up notes from each other. I had a little affair with a girl in boarding school—well, I didn't think it was little at the time, I thought it was tremendous—and my book *Spring Fire* was about that. Dick told me

to shift it to a college setting and that I could not have a happy ending, because the Post Office wouldn't accept that either. When the book was reprinted by Cleis Press [in 2004], I did a foreword explaining what life was like when the book first came out.

The title Spring Fire *wasn't your first choice, was it?*
No, it was *Sorority Girl*. Dick, who was very interested in sales, told me that there was a book called *Fires of Spring*, by James Michener, and that if I called the book *Spring Fire* people might mix the two up and I could gain some readers. I said, "C'mon", and he said, "No, I'm serious. Let's call it *Spring Fire*."

They didn't expect any big sales because of the subject matter. Little did they know that it would outsell the paperback of Erskine Caldwell's *God's Little Acre* (1933), which was a massive seller. Fawcett, who were the publishers of Gold Medal Books, just couldn't believe it. This was how Fawcett first became aware of a lesbian readership and that they could sell books on the subject matter.

Where did your pen name come from?
I was having lunch with a man named Vincent and a woman whose last name was Packer. I had no idea that writing would become a career, so I just randomly chose Vin Packer. I chose a male name because Dick had told me male names sold better in paperback.

How did the success of Spring Fire *change your life?*
It made me richer than I ever would have been at that age. I never made as much with a book on a new subject as with *Spring Fire*. I was able to get my own apartment and take a trip to Europe.

You would go on to write 20 books during the 1950s and 60s under the name Vin Packer, including a number of mysteries and romances. What dictated the genre you wrote in at different times?
The first mystery I wrote was inspired by an actress named Geraldine Page. She played strange women, dizzy and absent-minded types. I thought she would make a wonderful character, so I based a character on her in my fourth novel, *Come Destroy Me* (1954). Once again this was not my title. Dick had a much more dramatic viewpoint than I.

This was the first time that the *New York Times* crime critic, Anthony Boucher, reviewed one of my books. Hardbacks completely dominated the newspaper reviews of the time, so I decided I would write crime novels from then on, because there was the opportunity to be mentioned in the *Times*. That, and my friendship with Boucher, meant that I stayed with crime a lot longer than I otherwise would have.

A lot of your books concerned controversial topics such as racism, matricide and suicide. How much was your choice of topics driven by your publisher, and how much by your own interests?
The publisher never suggested anything to me about what I should write, because they knew they didn't have to. I always had ideas. The interest in suicide and other outlandish ideas was all my responsibility. I was responsible for everything that came out of my typewriter [*laughter*].

Where were the books sold and in what sort of numbers?
Wherever they sold magazines, they sold these paperbacks. They usually printed 300,000 or 400,000 copies. They paid a penny a copy. Because my books were very successful they often did 500,000 so I would get $5,000 a book and when they reprinted it I got the same amount again. That was very good money. I had a friend who wrote a hardcover crime novel for HarperCollins, then called Harper & Row, and she got $1,500 a book. She hated it that I was getting so much for paperbacks.

The paperback industry hadn't grown up yet; it was just getting there in the early to mid 50s. Previously paperbacks had usually been reprints of a hardcover, but Fawcett Gold Medal were unusual in that they were publishing original stories.

Did Gold Medal require you to conform to a particular word count?
It wasn't a matter of conforming because it worked for me. With the first book, the required length worked for me and I quickly became used to creating books that were about 200 pages in paperback.

I didn't have to conform to any particular rules, except concerning sex. I didn't write good sex scenes anyway so that didn't bother me. It bothered a lot of the males who liked to write hot sex scenes and had to be wary of the Post Office.

Homosexuality was a big issue. Gore Vidal's *The City and the Pillar* [1949] was not advertised in or reviewed by the *New York Times*, and every time he wrote about homosexuality this occurred. It took them a very long time to review anything with homosexuality in it, or to even use the word 'gay'.

Were there many other women writing for Gold Medal at this time?
There were two. One of them, Rona Jaffe, became quite famous. She was Dick's secretary for a while, but really wanted to write and eventually wrote some big bestsellers. She was clever and wealthy enough to establish a prize in her name.

Then there was a young woman who wrote to me, who lived in Pennsylvania and was married with two children. She wanted to write and I introduced her to Dick, who subsequently published her under the name of Ann Bannon.

A lot of men wrote under women's names too.

Tell us about your work for magazines.
I had an interesting career as a literary agent. When I first came to New York I couldn't get an agent. I would send my stories out, and they would come straight back like boomerangs—so I decided to become an agent. I had stationery printed and all of my clients, Vin Packer and the rest, were me.

Once I set that up, I began writing for what were called the slicks. These were good magazines printed on slick paper. These were things like *Ladies' Home Journal*, *Good Housekeeping*, *Redbook*, *Seventeen*. I did short stories for them and they paid about $1,000–$1,500.

I also wrote some 'confessions'. I was very good at them, because all you had to do was think of an interesting title that would pull the reader in, and then make sure that the story did not live up to the title. For example, the first story I sold was called 'I Lost My Baby at a Pot Party'. It was a story in which a woman had the Teflon pot people come to her house for a demonstration, and while this was going on her little child ran out the door.

The confession magazines like *True Romances* and *True Confessions* just loved that sort of thing, because they weren't printing anything they had to defend yet were pulling in readers with those titles.

The magazines very much wanted to meet the authors, but I claimed that a very old couple named Edgar and Mimi Stone, who lived in Maine, were writing them and could not travel. For the confessions you got about $250 a story, which was less than for the short stories, but they bought them more often. I wrote everything and was the agent for all those 'writers'.

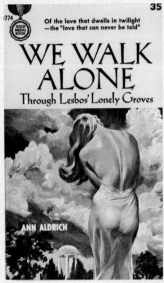

Monaco 1952

Marijane Meaker, 1952
We Walk Alone (Gold Medal, 1958)
3 Day Terror (Gold Medal, 1957)

After the success of Spring Fire *you continued to write books with lesbian themes, but most of these were non-fiction titles under the name of Ann Aldrich.*

There wasn't anything about lesbians anywhere. A man named Donald Webster Corey wrote a book called *The Homosexual in America* (1951). He covered the men and wrote about their bars, their habits and everything. It was very interesting and wasn't tawdry, so I copied the idea for women. I wrote about the bars, which were the only place where they could meet each other, the differences between those who lived Uptown and the ones who live down in the Village.

When I told Dick I wanted to do these books, Bianca Bligh was the name I came up with. He said, "No, no, no, stop. That's like Captain Bligh. Pick an all-American name like Henry Aldrich." This came from a radio series that was very popular about the Aldrich family. So I picked Ann Aldrich for all my books about lesbian life.

They sold really well because there was a great curiosity. Everything was banned and forbidden so anyone who wanted to know about it couldn't find anything out. This included a lot of men. My mail came in cartons, and about a third of it was from men, most of whom wanted to know how they could hook up with lesbians. I never paid much attention to them.

There were changes over time in how I approached the subject. When I was in boarding school, I thought I was committing sin and felt very guilty about all. I brought that into some of my early Aldrich books. The first one was called *We Walk Alone* (1955), the second was *We, Too, Must Love* (1958) and the third, *We Two Won't Last* (1963). The final one was called *Take a Lesbian to Lunch* (1972), so you can see that by then I had cheered up about the subject. This reflected changes in my own attitude as I lightened up and society changed.

All the books reported on what I was seeing in New York. In the 1950s the only place you could meet women was in bars. You would get the cab driver to drop you off a block away so that you wouldn't be seen walking straight in.

There was an Uptown [Upper Manhattan, above 59th Street] and a Downtown [Lower Manhattan, below 14th Street] scene. The Uptown women were the more successful ones and this was reflected in their dress. There was no role-playing in the Uptown bars. They were not all feminine in their bent, but they all looked feminine. Most of the female bars were on the east side of Uptown and the male ones were on the West Side.

Downtown there were the butch/femme bars. When I first came to New York, if you were in a bar you would see two women come in and one would be dressed very masculine and one very feminine. By the time of the last book this role-playing was dying out.

Nearly all of the Downtown bars were run by the Mafia. There were a few nice bars that were trying to copy what was going on Uptown. A few of the smaller ones were run by women, but they would usually get taken over by the Mafia. They also had a harder

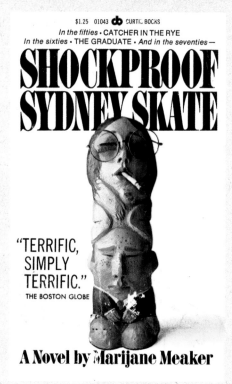

time keeping men out. The Mafia bars would have a big man at the door—they always had little-finger diamond rings and wore double-breasted suits, and were very stern. As the gatekeeper they would collect the three-dollar entry fee.

The police were paid off by the Mafia, because these bars were against the law. Any time the Mafia didn't like what was going on, they weren't getting enough money or whatever, then the girls were hauled off. The police would humiliate them by taking them to the police station and stripping them, examining them, and all that sort of thing. I never heard of an Uptown bar being raided, but it was always a possibility in a Downtown bar.

Two of your crime novels, Whisper His Sin *(1954) and* The Evil Friendship *(1958) involved gay and lesbian characters. Can you tell us about those?*
It began with my interest in the Fredan-Wepman case. They were two young male college students who murdered one of the men's mother. I wanted to call the book *One to Destroy,* because 'one to destroy' is the legal definition of murder, but of course Dick said, "That won't sell. Let's call it *Whisper His Sin.*" There was very little information beyond what the newspapers had written, so I imagined a lot of what had happened.

Once again this put me in touch with Anthony Boucher. He wrote me a letter asking if I was aware of the Parker-Hulme case, in which two young lesbians had murdered one of their mothers in New Zealand. I don't know how he got them, but he was kind enough to send me the whole proceedings of the trial. I followed these very closely in writing my book, *The Evil Friendship.* [The events also provided the basis for Peter Jackson's 1994 film *Heavenly Creatures.*] The girls deliberately both held the stone so that neither would be the sole murderer. One of them later grew up to be quite a famous writer, Anne Perry.

Your books often involved young people, even when you were writing for adult audiences in the 1950s and 60s. Amongst them are two juvenile delinquent novels, The Thrill Kids *(1955) and* The Young and the Violent *(1956). Were these based at all on personal observations?*
I lived on East 94th Street, which was far from what they called Spanish Harlem. Spanish Harlem was a whole world of its own, and very few people who lived in the East 90s ever visited there. The area had a mix of black and Latino culture. I was a little scared when I went there, because everything seemed so different; they had shops selling amulets and the like. I was also

Dinky Hocker Shoots Smack! (Dell, 1972)
Shockproof Sydney Skate (Curtis, 1973)

a victim of the idea that black kids were dangerous. Being so close to Spanish Harlem inspired me to write about juvenile gangs.

I spent time there, but I also did a lot of research looking at newspaper reports. I stopped at two novels because I was bored of the subject, I could only get so much out of Spanish Harlem.

Can you tell us about your writing process during the 1950s and 60s?
I used a typewriter and wrote every day except for Sundays. Usually I was living with somebody and I had to take a day off, but I loved writing. Sometimes I was inspired by the locale. For instance, I'm from Auburn, upstate New York, which has a big prison in the centre of town. If you go to that town there's this huge prison with guards walking right on top. We kids were always told we'd end up there if we didn't straighten up.

It was a strange town, because you had to go to Syracuse to get there, and when you were on the train there were always men manacled to other men. If you were leaving town, there were men in shiny blue suits leaving jail with bird cages, because those were their pets. I've worked elements of that place into novels, as well as Virginia, where I went to boarding school.

How did you get started writing Young Adult novels in the early 1970s?
There was a gay woman in my neighbourhood, Louise Fitzhugh, who was known for writing for children. She wrote *Harriet the Spy* (1964), which is now a classic. I was known as a murder writer, and when we would have lunch she would always tell me that she wanted to write murders. I wanted to write for young kids, so I copied everything she told me and even used her editor, Ursula Norsen, when I submitted my first book in the field.

It was great writing for young people. I could use my experiences from boarding school and growing up as well as things around me. It allowed me a new identity—literally, in that I became M.E. Kerr. I later wrote as Mary James when I created four books for Scholastic Publications. Those were fantasy novels for kids who were younger.

The name of your first YA book, Dinky Hocker Shoots Smack! *(1972), is reminiscent of your 'true confessions' titles, since it's about inter-generational emotional conflict and neglect rather than drugs.*
Harper & Row were very much against the title. They said, "This is terrible. You can't write that, she doesn't

shoot smack!" They wanted to call it *Inside Dinky Hocker,* on the basis that inside every fat person is a thin one trying to come out. However, my agent said, "*Inside Dinky Hocker* is not going to sell anything. Keep your title, since she doesn't shoot smack, how can anyone complain?" People did complain, but the book is still selling today [*laughter*].

I first got the idea around the time Martin Luther King was killed [1968]. They were asking writers—free of charge, of course—to go into schools and conduct writing classes. I went to a school near Harlem, and there was one African American kid who wrote really, really well. She wrote very bizarre stories, and her mother came to me one day and said, "You're encouraging my child to be strange." This mother spent most of her time looking after dope addicts through her church, and her teenage daughter felt very lonely because she also had no father. That situation provided me with the inspiration for this first Young Adult novel.

It's a funny book. It's got a moral to it, in that parents sometimes pay attention to people in need and ignore their own children, but I had fun writing it.

1972 seems to have been a very big year for you, because both Take a Lesbian to Lunch *and the novel* Shockproof Sydney Skate *were published.*
For *Shockproof Sydney Skate* I used my own name for the first time. I had written a book about suicide and I had wanted to write it as Marijane Meaker, but my editor thought it would be best to use the name M.J. Kerr for a book on that topic. With *Shockproof*, because it was so gay and because it was a hardcover, I wanted that under my own name so that people wouldn't think I was hiding. This was a funny book, too, as it was about a mother and her son being in love with the same girl.

Do you think there has been a thread running between your novels from the 1950s until today?
I've always been interested in the underdog. There is a German word for 'underdog lover' and a man I knew always used to call me that. I remember when I was writing *Little, Little* (1981), which is about a dwarf who came from a wealthy family and had all kinds of privileges except for her size. I was wondering how I would come up with dialogue for her, when I realised that we had much in common. In my younger years, young gay people didn't have peers, didn't grow up with their parents saying, "Oh that happened to me too."

IAIN McINTYRE

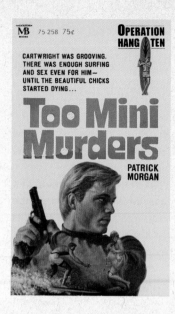

CARTWRIGHT WAS GROOVING.
THERE WAS ENOUGH SURFING
AND SEX EVEN FOR HIM—
UNTIL THE BEAUTIFUL CHICKS
STARTED DYING...

Too Mini Murders

PATRICK MORGAN

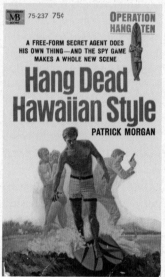

A FREE-FORM SECRET AGENT DOES
HIS OWN THING—AND THE SPY GAME
MAKES A WHOLE NEW SCENE

Hang Dead Hawaiian Style

PATRICK MORGAN

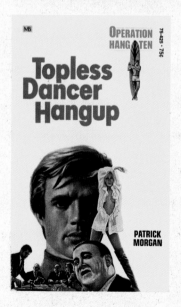

Topless Dancer Hangup

PATRICK MORGAN

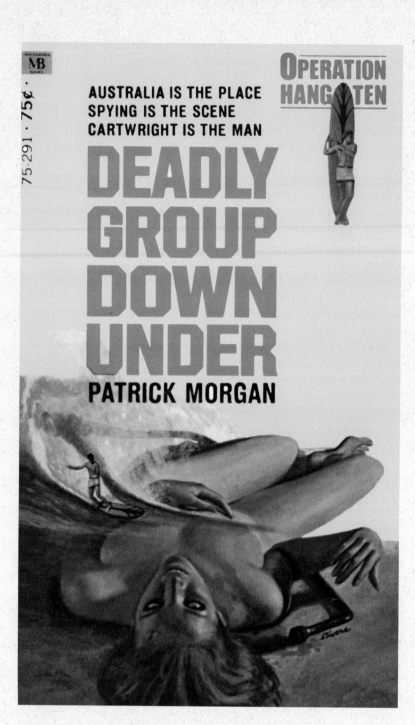

AUSTRALIA IS THE PLACE
SPYING IS THE SCENE
CARTWRIGHT IS THE MAN

DEADLY GROUP DOWN UNDER

PATRICK MORGAN

Too Mini Murders (MacFadden, 1969)

Deadly Group Down Under (MacFadden 1970)

Topless Dancer Hangup (MacFadden, 1971)

Hang Dead Hawaiian Style (MacFadden, 1969)

JAMES BOND NEVER SURFED
The Surfer Spy Pulp of Patrick Morgan

One of the hallmarks of the counterculture movement was to reject the old and live for the new. When it came to spy fiction, the personification of *old* was none other than James Bond. So how do you reject Bond? You create a spy who isn't 'a suit' and definitely not a part of the system, who lives an alternative lifestyle. You make your hero a hip, young, sandy-haired surfer. Or at least that appears to be what author George Snyder—writing as Patrick Morgan—did when he created the character William (Bill) Cartwright. Cartwright's attitude to life is summed up best by the blurb on the back cover of the first book in the series, *Hang Dead Hawaiian Style* (1969), as: SURFING, WOMEN AND WHENEVER POSSIBLE POKING A CROOKED FINGER IN THE HAIRY EYEBALL OF THE ESTABLISHMENT.

The character is as far removed from Bond as you could get. His backstory is that as a child he was a surf brat, spending time in California, Hawaii and Australia. When he was 17, his parents died in a car crash, leaving him ten million dollars. He's now in his early twenties, and if he chose to, he could just follow the sun, traversing the globe, living the carefree life of a full-time surfer. Instead, he works for a top-secret spy organisation called Operation Hang Ten, an ill-defined spy organisation loosely affiliated to the CIA and devoted to fighting the ever-present menace of beach crime. Why does he do the work? As he explains in *Deadly Group Down Under* (1970):

> He enjoyed the hunt, the uncovering, the pursuit, the kill. There was a primitive jungle streak in him he could never explain. Neither money nor position could take it out of him. The world was made up of the eaters and the eaten. He went for the eaters, maybe because he himself was an eater of sorts. He enjoyed the hunt. It had nothing to do with mother, country, or church, he wasn't the patriotic kind. It was a personal thing with him. He wanted to pit his ability against all the bastards of the world, all those who raped land and people. It had nothing to do with carrying flags for lost causes. It was him and them. And in that way he was using Hang Ten.

Cartwright may not fight for Queen and country like James Bond, or for the red, white and blue, as the case may be, but like Bond, Cartwright is a womaniser. Whereas Bond was depicted as a man who indulged in life's pleasures because he lived on the edge, Cartwright is presented more as somewhat of a cad, a user and abuser of women, as the following passage in *Hang Dead Hawaiian Style* attests:

> Criminal Record: Paternity suits filed—1961, 1962, 1963, 1964. Cartwright acquitted all cases for lack of evidence. Breach of promise suits filed—1963, 1965, 1966. Cartwright acquitted all cases for lack of evidence.

Cartwright's irresponsible sexual dalliances seem at odds with the sexual revolution that was happening when the books were written, but note the years of his indiscretions (1961–1964). The pill had only been introduced in 1960 (1961 in England and Australia), and further to that, the pill was banned in eight US States until 1965. The first book in the series was released at the height of the Summer of Love—and while Cartwright's alleged paternity suits could be viewed as being outdated, in some ways they are possibly an accurate time capsule of changing attitudes towards sex and contraception.

As for the surfing, James Bond never surfed—at least, not until 2002 in the film *Die Another Day*. But a lot of movie stars in the mid to late 60s did. Elvis Presley was still popular at the box office and his 1966 hit movie was called *Paradise Hawaiian Style*. The other big movie hit with the kids were the 'beach party' or 'surf party' movies with Frankie Avalon and Annette Funicello. The most popular of the series, *Beach Blanket Bingo*, was released in 1965. That is not to suggest that the Operation Hang Ten books were a parody of the beach party or Presley's rock-a-hula films, but their popularity undoubtedly inspired the publishers to consider a surf-themed series. And rumour has it that in 1973 the American television networks ABC and Viacom attempted to get an Operation Hang Ten series off the ground. A 30-minute pilot was reportedly produced but not sold, starring Christopher Stone, an American actor who went on to star in early 80s horror films *The Howling* and *Cujo*, as Cartwright.

Ten Operation Hang Ten books were turned out between 1969 to 1973. *Too Mini Murders* was published in 1969, the same year as *Hang Dead Hawaiian Style*. The third book in the series, *Deadly Group Down Under* dragged Cartwright across the globe to Australia. The story concerns an Australian surfer/pop singer, named Lisa Dane, known as 'Queen of the Surfers'. It is all image—she doesn't surf at all, but to maintain the fiction she is constantly surrounded by blond-headed surfers. Or people who look like surfers, at least. Why does Bill Cartwright get mixed up with her? Because one of her many acolytes is selling secrets to the Communist China. After three CIA agents are killed, the case is sent to Operation Hang Ten to crack. Cartwright is assigned to find out who the spy is.

Tapping into the 60s notion of being true to yourself and doing what you want to do, this story is essentially a battle of the phonies versus the 'realies' (the term used in the book, as in 'keeping it real'). It's a battle against the pseudo-surfers, the ones who don't go in the water, who are content to stay on the sand with a beach-bunny on their lap and pretend to live the life. Cartwright is a surfer, and looks down his nose at such types. But there is a strange hypocrisy in Cartwright. In some sense, he is just as fake as the people he is investigating.

So who did he think he was, setting himself up to judge moviemakers and Lisa Danes as phoneys? Just what the hell was he? A surfer, playing at being a private detective, who in turn played at being an agent for Operation Hang Ten. The only real thing was the shadow of death that followed you from day to day.

Cartwright seduces Lisa Dane and becomes part of her scene, traveling with her to Australia, where she is set to make a movie. The usual hijinks ensue, with Cartwright seducing several other women on the mission, and ultimately uncovering the spy. Astute readers will have worked out who the enemy spy is within the first 20 pages.

The fourth title in the series, *Cute and Deadly Surf Twins* (1970), begins with Cartwright searching for a man named Moon. His search takes him to the club of a neo-Nazi motorcycle gang called the Diablos. Bikers don't like surfers, so they beat seven shades of tar out of him and kick him off a cliff to what should be certain death. As this happens, the story flashes back

to Cartwright's mission briefing and his assignment, to discover who is behind a plot to ship money out of the country to the People's Republic of China. The link is a pair of female twins, one who may be good and the other bad. Of course, Cartwright survives the fall and picks up the trail, leading him to a swinging topless disco, before heading to Malibu and finally Mexico.

The Hang Ten adventures kept coming at a steady pace. *Scarlet Surf at Makana* appeared in 1970, followed by *The Girl in the Telltale Bikini* (1971), which found Cartwright back in Australia and framed for stealing Navy secrets. Also published in 1971 were *Topless Dancer Hangup* and *Beach Queen Blowout*, the latter of which saw Cartwright take on a California-based youth sex cult responsible for sabotaging oil rigs.

In the second-to-last title, *Death Car Surfside* (1972), Cartwright is out on his own. The book starts in the early hours of the morning, with him surfing near the Hermosa Beach pier in Southern California. The quiet is shattered when a Mustang shoots off the end of the pier into the sea. As the car goes over the edge, Cartwright makes out a woman behind the wheel of the vehicle. However, something appears to be wrong with her face, as if she were asleep. Cartwright doesn't want to get involved but knows he must act. He dives down to the vehicle and drags the unconscious girl out, but not before noticing that someone had rigged a mop handle to the accelerator to make the car continue off the pier.

On the beach, Cartwright examines the girl's possessions and discovers her name is Charlene Morris. Furthermore, the track marks on her arms and the tin of heroin in her pocket suggest she is a junkie. Just as Charlene regains consciousness, and before Cartwright can question her, he is rendered unconscious from a blow from behind. When he wakes up, Charlene is dead—stabbed eight times—and the police are on the scene. Naturally enough, the police believe Cartwright is the number one suspect. And to make things worse, Cartwright can't get hold of his Hang Ten boss, Jim Dana, to clear him. Instead, Cartwright busts out of the police station and takes matters into his own hands.

The series ended with *Freaked Out Strangler* (1973), but it was hardly Snyder's sole occupation. While he was writing the Operation Hang Ten series, he also penned seven Nick Carter adventures (and co-wrote an eighth). Nick Carter may not be a household name these days, but he is one of modern literature's longest-surviving characters. He started life in dime-

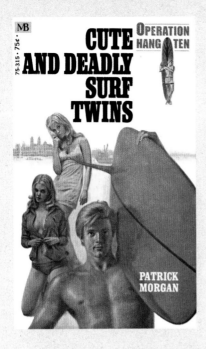

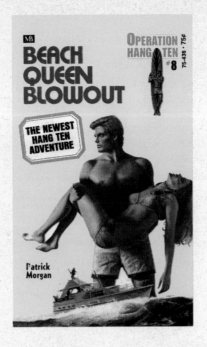

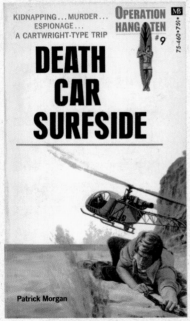

Cute and Deadly Surf Twins
(MacFadden, 1970)

Beach Queen Blowout
(MacFadden, 1971)

Freaked Out Strangler
(Manor Books, 1973)

Death Car Surfside
(MacFadden, 1972)

store sleuth-detective magazine stories penned by John Russell Coryell in 1886, fell out of favour and was reborn at the height of spy mania in the early 60s as 'the Killmaster', a secret agent working for AXE, a fictional US government spy agency, mainly dealing in assassination. Although the capital letters would imply that it's an acronym, like SPECTRE (Special Executive for Counter-intelligence, Terrorism, Revenge and Extortion), or UNCLE (United Network Command for Law and Enforcement), the name exists as a somewhat of an enigma.

A staggering 261 Nick Carter spy novels were published between 1964 and 1990. Snyder also co-wrote two of the short-lived Grant Fowler Hotline series, *Our Spacecraft Is Missing* (1970), with Jon Messman, and *The President Has Been Kidnapped* (1971), with Dan Streib. There were only three books total in the Fowler espionage series. They were poorly received and are now largely forgotten.

DAVID JAMES FOSTER

OPERATION HANG TEN
An Interview with George Snyder

The nature and tone of espionage fiction changed dramatically during the 1960s. At the beginning of the decade, Ian Fleming, and his creation, James Bond cast a large shadow over the spy literature landscape. In a March 1961 article in *Life* magazine, President John F. Kennedy listed Fleming's 1957 Bond novel, *From Russia, with Love* as one of his ten favourite books. The presidential endorsement certainly raised the profile and popularity of the Bond series, and many other spy writers emerged in the early 60s—John Le Carré and Len Deighton, for example—each of them eager to capture a slice of the lucrative spy market.

While Kennedy's endorsement helped popularise the Bond series, his assassination in Dallas on November 22, 1963, helped change the direction of spy literature. As the countless books, television specials and movies on the subject showed, a great many people thought the US government was lying about the about the real facts behind Kennedy's death, and that the Warren Commission—the investigative body set up by President Lyndon Johnson to investigate Kennedy's assassination—was a sham.

This distrust of authority became a key part of the counterculture movement. People were no longer prepared to blindly accept the word of governments. So too in spy fiction and film, an increasing number of spy heroes no longer worked for government-run bureaus or agencies, and if they did, were blackmailed into it, including characters such as Peter O'Donnell's Modesty Blaise and Adam Diment's Philip McAlpine.

One of the more interesting characters to emerge out of the shift away from staid authoritarian spy characters, such as Bond, was William (Bill) Cartwright, hero of the Operation Hang Ten, one of the most offbeat subcultural spy series ever written. The man behind the Patrick Morgan pen name was George Snyder. Snyder is still at work today, writing hard-boiled crime stories under his own name. But there was a time when counterculture espionage novels were his bread and butter.

How old were you when you wrote your first Operation Hang Ten book?
Twenty-six. At twenty-four, married with a couple young kids, we had just bought our house. I'd been hitting the men's short-story market with 50 to 60 per cent of the stories I wrote and the editor of *Best for Men*, who had contact with a Las Vegas paperback publisher, suggested I try writing something longer. I wrote a surfer novel that got me hooked up with the Nick Carter books that led to the Hang Ten series.

Where did the idea for Operation Hang Ten come from?
The original title of *my* surfer book was *The Surfer Killers*, a mystery about a surfer who gets his 'woodie' [a type of car once popular with surfers, so called because the rear bodywork is partly made of wood] stolen and this involves him in the gang run by his girlfriend's father. Neva Paperbacks paid a $500 advance and brought it out as *Surfside Sex* (1966). I never made another nickel on it.

A New York publisher, I think Merit or McFadden-Bartell, was bringing out a paperback series based on the old 30s Smith and Street Publications private eye, Nick Carter, but making him into an American James Bond. The books were assigned by country to different writers and handled by a New York huckster named Lyle Kenyon Engel [who among many novels also wrote the countercultural *Chopper Cop* series]. He put out a call to writers, but in order to eliminate most, he required they already have a book published of their own. I bundled up my little *Surfside Sex* and sent it off. I got a call from the publisher saying they loved my surfer book and when could I start?

My first Nick Carter was *The Defector* (1969), which went into four printings and was translated into French and Japanese. Once the publisher approved the first three chapters and outline, I was off and running with six weeks to finish a 60,000-word-long book. These were the days before computers, with carbon paper and clackety typing, banging away on a manual typewriter that my neighbor said sounded like a machine gun going off. A Sears Tower portable lasted about a year (the L went first). When I was heavily into the Nick Carter series, now divorced to never remarry (one marriage per lifetime is plenty) and travelling around, I wrote car-racing articles for several magazines Lyle operated besides his deal with the Nick Carter publisher.

Lyle asked me to do something with my surfer book, maybe make the guy a spy, dead parents leaving him

George Snyder today

hippie-type beautiful girls who smelled good and were eager for liberation and experience.

Another big battle came when women took over publisher reader and editing jobs. I got notes that the books were too sexist, and maybe we should tone it down by giving Bill a girl-match for some of his twisted ideas. I pointed out the covers (some of the greatest in book publishing) and told them to just look at that guy. What healthy bikini-clad, deep breathing, swivel-hipped surfer gal wouldn't get her thighs quivering to get some of that. The guy was a cool good-looking stud. The sexist street ran both ways. It didn't quiet the editors, and although I won battles, I was slowly losing the war. They also wanted me to tone down what they called snippets of philosophy the books carried. I didn't get that one.

Today I consider the series juvenile and badly written compared to what I write now. They were published pretty much as they peeled out of the typewriter; other than proofing, they had no real editing or polish. And to me, they read like it. But I still meet people who loved them and are sorry I stopped writing the series.

Did the counterculture themes, such as not working for the establishment and being your own person come from you? Or did the publisher shoehorn these elements into the story to appeal to a youth market?
When I turned 30, divorced, living in Newport Beach, California, I was part of a youngish culture. I sailed to Catalina Island for scuba and parties. The Newport Beach *South Bay Club* singles-only complex had enough partying for a lifetime. I bodysurfed the California coast but preferred diving; the diving community itself partied hard and hearty. I had no job to go to, for several years I lived on my writing. Gorgeous women were friendly, the scotch flowed easy and every night was either Friday or Saturday. I did uppers and downers and smoked a ton of pot. There was little the publisher could add to that kind of lifestyle. I felt they were a stuffy East Coast bunch anyway. It went three years until I moved out, much of that time a blur.

What market were the books aimed at? Were they written for the surfing crowd? Or were they simply an alternative to the staid authoritarian tone prevalent in other spy fiction of the era?
I have no idea. We writers of that time just cared about cranking the books out. Marketing was left to

rich, lots of contact with Chinese communists (popular bad guys at the time). If he got publisher approval, my advance would be $1500 a book for as many as I could write, same deal, 60,000 words in six weeks. Unlike now, in those days even small publishers gave some kind of advance. He chose the writer name, Patrick Morgan. I fought against Cartwright (sounded like *Bonanza*) but lost. Another thing I almost lost to the publisher was titles. They had the first title, *Too Mini Murders*, that I thought was dumb. The others I suggested they thought were too long: *Hang Dead Hawaiian Style, Cute and Deadly Surf Twins*, etc. But I dug in and fought it out, and won. Although written first, *Too Mini Murders* was released after *Hang Dead Hawaiian Style* (both appeared in 1969), which was also translated into Japanese and French. I titled all the other books.

The publisher also wanted more computer stuff, more than temperature and drink mixes and a rotating bed. I fought that too, because I didn't want to get bogged down in technology with a lot of tech babble I really didn't know. These books were to be fun romps, lots of sex with happy girls who liked giving themselves to my cool guy, and vicious villainous Chi-Com bad guys. At the time I lived in a singles-only apartment complex and was the resident bartender Friday and Saturday nights. Often tough getting out those ten finished pages every day, five days a week. The world was filled with free-thinking long-haired,

others. Not like today when the writer has to do it all. Surfers I've talked to liked the books. Tavern-drinking buddies who read them still think they were the wildest, raunchiest stuff I ever wrote. The James Bond types weren't too interested. There were many spy paperbacks out at the time, and PIs like Shell Scott and Travis McGee; books by Donald Hamilton, Don Pendleton, Mack Bolan. The field became crowded. The Hang Ten books were loudly laughed at by the literary crowd, as were the Nick Carters. Real-life surfers at the time were likely too busy with each other to do much reading.

The series presents the perfect, dare I say it, 'surfer' lifestyle. Cartwright is a character who follows the sun and the surf around the globe. How much of yourself is in the character of Bill Cartwright? Were you a subcultural rebel? Do you surf?

At the time I body surfed, seldom got on a board. Again, at the time, Cartwright acted and thought a lot as I did. I've always had a healthy disregard for what others say and think, specifically about my writing, because opinions are so subjective. The example being fighting with publishers; writers don't fight with publishers, they are god. Yet even today when I know how I want something in my book, I'll fight for it. I have always written what I like. If others like it enough to spend money so they can read it, I'm happy. But I don't write what I think will be popular or jump on the back of the latest trend, probably why I've never made a lot of money with my books.

My lifestyle was established then. Now, I live aboard a small sailboat. I've solo-sailed Puget Sound to Alaska and spent a year solo cruising Mexico. I've motorcycle toured more than 250,000 miles through five western states, Canada and Mexico, and have scuba-dived the California coast, Puget Sound, the Texas Gulf, the Gulf of Thailand, the Sea of Cortez, the Florida Keys. I took three months to camp-tour in my Honda Civic around the US living in a one-man tent. I've travelled the Far East and still intend to finish up the rest of the world. In travel, I'm not fond of two-week or packaged tours. I go at it several months or more, with no set itinerary. I've published 32 books, the last five hardboiled crime noir novels, in the past two years. I'm not sure how ordinary all this is.

In the late 60s, one character cast a large shadow over all spy fiction, and that was James Bond. What traits

Surfside Sex (Playtime Books, 1966)
Hang Dead Hawaiian Style (Eclipse, 1970)

GIRL GANGS, BIKER BOYS, AND REAL COOL CATS

did you take from Ian Fleming's famous creation? And what did you deliberately leave out?

Nick Carter was supposed to be an American James Bond. I always considered his books just spy entertainment. Federal penitentiary prisoners love them. I wrote several of the almost 200 titles out there, having sold millions of copies. Nick Carter books are closer to Bond than Hang Ten. Where Bond was slick in his philosophy, Cartwright was blue-collar; instead of brilliant deduction he used dogged determination; he moved along the fast food, beach shack, beach babes, burger and beers trail; he liked his scotch, but he'd never say, "Stirred, not shaken." Nick Carter might. Even today, I tend to write blue-collar guys because that's how I am.

Was it hard to juggle writing the Operation Hang Ten and Nick Carter series?

I was dealing with two opposite personalities: the well-dressed, calculating Nick Carter and the rich surf bum, Bill Cartwright (I still hate that name; my original name was Cody Falcon but no dice, sounded too much like a bird). Where I took my time was in putting together the first three chapters and outline. My outlines sometimes ran 25–30 pages. I wanted that to be my main labor, the hardest part, so I could buzz through writing the novel in the required six weeks. Once the publisher approved the three-chapters-and-outline, the gun was to my head and I had to hit the deck running. Maybe that wasn't such a big deal. These days they have a contest to write a 50,000-word novel in a month, and I guess several enter. It isn't anything I'd ever be interested in.

I alternated between Hang Ten and Nick Carter. This was the early 70s, crap was going on in Vietnam, the government we had was more corrupt than those previous—or at least we knew more about it. Everybody had a bitch about something: the war, no gas, the race card, immigration, burning bras, a free-love fantasy (it's never free), communes, back-to-the-land—mostly, folks did a lot of whining and demonstrating, made noise.

Besides writing those two series, I still occasionally knocked off a short story, and wrote some sailing articles, I'd gotten heavy into sailing and intended to go around the world (who didn't?). I bugged the publishers. I wanted my own series guy in my own name, controlled solely by me. All they replied, "More books, give us more books." While I enjoyed the lifestyle the books paid for, I'd grown weary of the battles. What

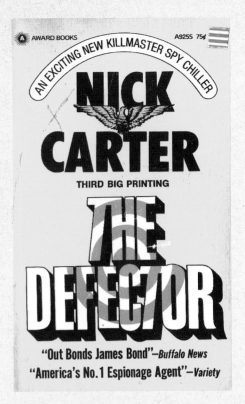

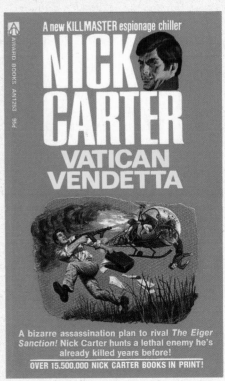

The Defector (Award, 1972)
Vatican Vendetta (Award, 1974)

editors wanted was woman empowerment and they wanted at least traces of that in every book published. I was ready for change.

What would you say were the main differences between Bill Cartwright and Nick Carter?
Nick Carter was closer to James Bond, closer in attitude, working style, gathering clues and how he handled action. I think of Bond and Carter I think sophistication. When I think of Hang Ten, I think beach or alley fight. It's like Nick Carter worked at being James Bond, the agent life was most important. Bill Cartwright lived his life, enjoyed the surf girls, travel, parties, and was a reluctant agent. He didn't need the money; he did it for the action.

Is there a place for either Carter or Cartwright in today's world?
With editing dominated by women, probably not. The books are sexist. It would be difficult to use them for woman empowerment without losing their masculine zing. Men actually did read those books. Today, with 80 per cent of readers being women, few care what men like to read. I recently learned 65 per cent of guys who graduate college never read another book. My take on that is there are few books out there men can get interested in. And most families don't read as a pastime. I'd say three-quarters of my tavern buddies haven't held a book in decades. While many books today are being published and read, especially now with digital and independent publishing, they all must satisfy current attitudes about the role of women in them. The blatant sexism of 60s and 70s paperbacks would be unacceptable. There are a few independents who defy custom. Editors won't accept what they write so they won't write what editors accept. In queries, when I suggest my novels are similar to Elmore Leonard, Richard Stark, John D. MacDonald, Richard Prather and some Lawrence Block, the claws come out and I'm informed those writers are immediately dismissed because of how they treat women in their books. Popular, modern writers like Dennis Lehane and Lee Child make sure the women in their books reflect standards set to show women equal men in every way. Even the James Bond movies have succumbed.

*A major part of the counterculture was, of course, the sexual revolution, and spy books written at that time really cranked up the sexual shenanigans of their he-*roes—*and heroines for that matter. This is even more apparent in the Nick Carter novels than the Hang Ten series. Nick certainly loved the ladies. Although, possibly considered tame by today's standard, were you comfortable with writing the sex scenes? Was a high sexual content a prerequisite when writing in that era, and for that market?*
Here's the thing about sex scenes. In the 60s and 70s and through the mid 80s, paperback publishers required three sex scenes in every book: one toward the beginning, one in the middle, one toward the end. It was a rule writers fought because the scene often had little or nothing to do with the story. The loudest critic of the practice was John D. MacDonald, because even lofty Fawcett Publications carried the silly rule.

In the scene, no intimate body part could be described, nothing about how it felt, or juices, or tightness, or the actual act itself; no grunts, groans, squeals or words and phrases like "harder" or "faster", or "Oh my God!" or "Here it comes!" The scene was supposed to be like syrupy movies when the camera shows fluttering curtains or bird-tweeting while the couple—out of sight—humped each other on the bed, or table or couch, or car seat, or phone booth, or hanging from a chandelier. The act was supposed to be about lovemaking not fucking, nothing clinical. I had no heartburn writing those scenes. At the time I was getting more sex than I ever wrote about, more than at any time in my life, including when I was married. It was easy to recall one of my personal events and write it, toning down the description. Editors didn't complain about my sex scenes, though they did send a Nick Carter manuscript back because my middle sex scene had been too light. Whatever the hell that meant. I jazzed it up but they ended up toning it back down a little.

These days I don't write sex scenes, I write sensuous innuendo, more about the build-up than the clinical act. Dialog is a wonderful invention for that. A man and a woman can get the reader breathing heavy before touching each other.

Your output at the time was rather prodigious, releasing by my count, eight books in 1970, and six in 1971. Were there other projects that you were working on besides the two spy series?
During some evenings I did write a science-fiction novel about the war between men and women. It was eventually published 30 years later as *Beyond Gender Wars* (2011) after very heavy editing. I now

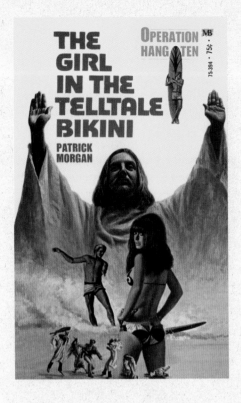

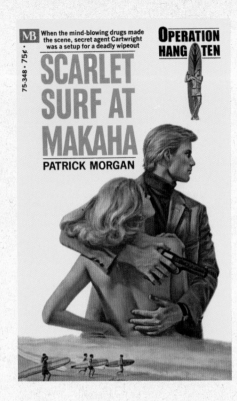

The Girl in the Telltale Bikini (MacFadden, 1971)

Scarlet Surf at Makaha (MacFadden, 1970)

have the rights again and will revise it back closer to the original and then release the revised edition. Not all editors are good editors.

My own series character finally did emerge: Baylor 'Bay' Rumble, a guy sailing the world on his self-designed, self-built catamaran where he runs into murder and treachery. The fourth novel in the series, *Baja Bullets*, was just released.

One area that may need clarification: In the old days, my writing day started at 6 am, Monday through Friday, going after the ten pages a day, however long it took. I didn't do any screwing around until Friday afternoon. While writing I was serious as a monk. I wrote on a punishment/reward basis. Typing away, I allowed myself all the coffee I could drink but I could not eat anything until the ten finished pages were complete. It sometimes made for a long-hungry day. During that block of time, I slammed the door on visitors and disconnected the phone, and shouted for people to stop bothering me and get lost, no doubt grumpy because I couldn't eat. Women and friends who knew me, and liked what they knew, respected that. I didn't care about anyone else. I usually had my ten pages around noon or one. Then I was free to hug the girls and raise hell. But like Hemingway, I got to bed before midnight because the work waited for me at six. Weekends, I went a little apeshit.

When I moved out of the singles apartment complex (they started letting married couples in, then couples with kids) and stopped writing the Hang Ten books, my life slowed. While I travelled there was less food, drink, and making merry. Over time, I stopped drinking and gave up the happy smoke. Years later I eased back to occasional beers and Captain Morgan Spiced Rum. I never went back to dope.

I've always continued to write. My guy Bay has been joined by two others: Logan Sand, an ex-fighter Northwest private eye with two books written. And my newest creation, a tough PI gal out in the desert who lives in the fictional town of Lakeshore just north of Lake Havasu, Arizona.

Every now and then I get contacted about the old Hang Ten series. I think I'm the only one alive who was connected to it. Those were happy writing days and happy living days. I'm kind of old and beat-up now and not of much significance. Sometimes I still attract a good-looking woman but women don't smile at me like they used to. I still enjoy their intimate company and how they look. I only wish they moved a little slower when they pass by me. I still travel and backpack and sail and ride my motorcycle . . . and write.

DAVID JAMES FOSTER

The Grass Pipe—Robert Coles (Dell, 1969)

Author Robert Coles is a Harvard-affiliated child psychiatrist, best known for his Pulitzer Prize–winning non-fiction series *Children of Crisis* (1966–1977), as well as *Dead End School* (1968), a novel about the racial integration of a school district through bussing, which was illustrated by Norman Rockwell.

However, in 1969, he just wanted to awkwardly rap with the young people about marijuana. While *The Grass Pipe* takes the standard tactic of conflating the effects of marijuana with LSD, cocaine and heroin in the service of scaring teens straight, Coles also aims to bore his young readers to death before they have had a chance to try it.

The book is narrated by Paul, a high school freshman, who admits that he's heard about 'trips' and 'pot' and 'grass', but hasn't really given the matter any serious thought. But as the products of neglectful middle-class parenting, Paul and his friends Tom and Charlie are ripe for corruption.

Tom's older brother has been **taking marijuana for two years, ever since he got to college**, which piques the boys' curiosity, but Paul tries to play it cool, confessing that he **knew all the words—marijuana, pot, grass.** (Reefer! The Devil's Oregano! Acapulco Gold! Texas Tea!)

Paul and Charlie are skeptical about their friend's ability to lay his hands on some of this marijuana, but Tom proves them wrong when he reveals that he has been going on 'marijuana-trips' for some time, courtesy of his hippie brother and his college friends. Paul and Charlie hurry over to his house, where he shows them his stash over the course of a six-page reefer striptease.

After all that build-up, Paul and Charlie are less than impressed by the actual marijuana, which sends Tom into a defensive, jive-talking rage. Coles's approximation of hippie vernacular is the highlight of the book:

"You don't know what gives. Well, now's your moment. This here stuff is pot, boys, real pot—grass, good strong pure grass, Acapulco Gold, my brother says. I'm still not registering? You're fighting me. Yes, you are. You don't get me. In Hicksville it's called marijuana—by the squares who don't want it. They have laws, lots of them, to make sure no one gets started. Because if they did let people use drugs, all the phonies and fakes around would be seen for what they are and people would say, 'No dice, boys, no dice, we want out.'"

The next day they gather at Tom's house, where he is still in full-on jive mode. Paul and Charlie agree that they would like to **try a smoke**.

So, they all pass around a corncob pipe. Yes, when titular appliance finally makes an appearance, it is an honest-to-God corncob pipe!

In order to drive home the point that 'Drugs are unpredictable and affect everyone differently', the drugs are unpredictable and affect everyone differently. Paul can see through time! Charlie gets the munchies. Tom won't stop yammering about how high he is.

But the next morning, Paul wakes up with a hangover and a serious case of the paranoids, and he gets into a fight with his sister, whom he thinks is going to narc him out.

He seeks guidance on the matter, and Tom tells him he should eat some ice cream. But he and Charlie decide that they should all go have a talk with Charlie's physician father about marijuana, and when they learn the real dirt on drugs, they quickly decide they will not be taking any more marijuana trips with Tom.

MOLLY GRATTAN

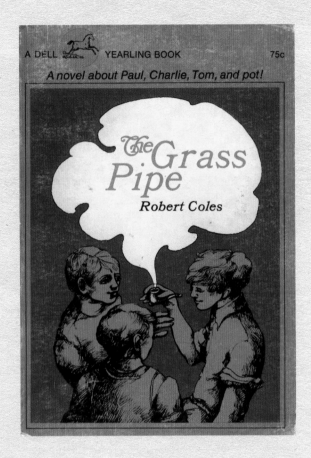

A DELL YEARLING BOOK 75c

A novel about Paul, Charlie, Tom, and pot!

The Grass Pipe

Robert Coles

Maybe all I can do is just tell you what I know, and then we can talk as long as you want. So far as I know marijuana comes from a plant, the hemp plant. What people call pot or grass is the dried-up top of that plant, the leaves and the flower. It's called all sorts of names around the world, like 'hashish' or 'bhang'. It can be smoked or chewed or sniffed—and I think cigarettes or a pipe are favored in the western world.

No one knows what he's taking when he uses marijuana. It's an illegal drug and much of it is distributed by gangsters and racketeers—men who control gambling and engage in all sorts of shakedowns, payoffs and bribes.

I'm no drug taker, but I know the term—they say it's 'laced', the marijuana is laced with other things. And if one of them is LSD—well, I can tell you as a physician that you're in bad danger.

What is dangerous about LSD is that it can take effect hours, even days after you've tried it—so you never quite know when or how it will work—and it even seems to affect your genes, through which we transmit ourselves from one generation to another. In other words, LSD can injure the body and really linger in it—and strike when unexpected.

Most students, I notice, are staying away from LSD, even a lot of hippies. They're right to be scared.

The Outsiders—S.E. Hinton (Viking Press, 1967)

Susan Eloise Hinton began work on *The Outsiders* as a high school sophomore, aiming to create a story about "real teenagers" based on her observations of student life at Tulsa's Will Rogers High School. When the book was published two years later (using her initials on the advice of her publisher to disguise her gender), it was a revelatory take on the JD genre. While the sensitive and introspective 14-year-old narrator, Ponyboy Curtis, speaks candidly about the casual violence that is a part of his everyday life, he differentiates his friends from common 'hoods' and rejects the theory that his troubles stem from his family being **economically disadvantaged**.

Orphaned Ponyboy and his older brothers, put-upon Darrel (Darry) and handsome and charming Sodapop, consider themselves a part of a loosely affiliated gang of 'greasers'—East Tulsa's poverty-stricken and parentally neglected teenagers. With a particularly teenaged insistence, Hinton introduces a huge cast of supporting characters, some of whom are more relevant to the plot than others. Ponyboy's narration also fills the reader in on the ongoing feuding between the greasers and the wealthy west-side students, the 'Socs', short for 'Socials'. While the two groups have a long history of violence between them, the incident that lights the powder keg of the plot occurs when Ponyboy and his friends innocuously strike up a conversation at the local drive-in with Cherry and Marcia, a couple of Soc girlfriends. Later that night the Socs retaliate against Ponyboy and his anxious, high-strung friend Johnny, who kills Cherry's boyfriend in self-defense.

Ponyboy and Johnny go on the lam, leading to a lengthy pastoral passage, as they hide in an abandoned church in the countryside, reading a paperback of *Gone with the Wind* and reciting the poetry of Robert Frost. When the church catches fire and the conflagration begins to spread, they are on hand to save a group of school children that happen to be picnicking nearby.

While Ponyboy and Johnny return to Tulsa as heroes, Hinton doesn't downplay the traumatic nature of these events. When Johnny dies from injuries sustained during the rescue, his death drives another greaser to commit suicide-by-cop, and Ponyboy drops into a deep depression. Formerly a good student and talented athlete, he finds himself unable to keep focus upon returning to his old activities.

The reader's sympathy stays firmly with the greasers throughout the novel; they're not criminals, they're just too emotional. Ponyboy lays out the differences between the gangs to Cherry: **"It's not money, it's feeling—you don't feel anything we feel too violently."** And the plot twists are shamelessly melodramatic, which is why teenage readers have made it into a classic. On the occasion of the 40th anniversary of the novel, even Hinton noted, "But its vices were its virtues."

Ultimately, the real conflict is the one raging within Ponyboy, as he's pulled in different directions, torn between the criminal that society wants to make him into, and the tiresome, thankless life represented by his brother Darry. Unsurprisingly, salvation is presented through writing: granted a second chance in school, he picks up a pen and begins writing the novel you just finished reading.

MOLLY GRATTAN

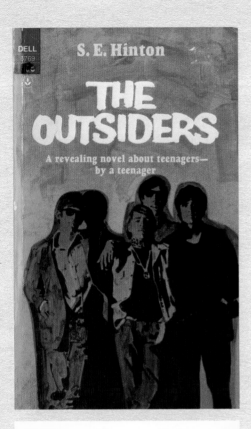

The Outsiders (Dell, 1968)
The Outsiders (Fontana, 1970)

"Ponyboy . . . I mean . . . if I see you in the hall at school or someplace and don't say hi, well, it's nothing personal or anything, but . . ."

"I know," I said.

"We couldn't let our parents see us with you all. You're a nice boy and everything . . ."

"It's okay," I said, wishing I was dead and buried somewhere. Or at least that I had on a decent shirt. "We aren't in the same class. Just don't forget that some of us watch the sunset too."

She looked at me quickly. "I could fall in love with Dallas Winston," she said.

"I hope I never see him again, or I will."

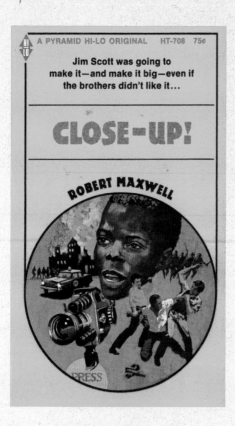

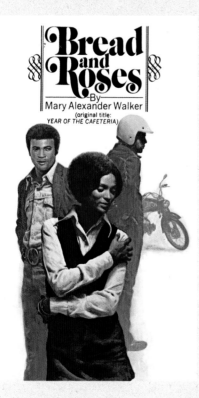

Close-Up! (Pyramid Hi-Lo, 1970)
Bread and Roses (Tempo, 1973)

A Hero Ain't Nothin' but a Sandwich—Alice Childress

(Coward, McCann and Geoghegan, 1973)

In the late 1960s and early 70s, authors and publishers finally realised there was a huge, largely untapped market for novels aimed at teenagers that incorporated aspects of actual teenage life. Today's Young Adult novels regularly include references to drugs, music, alcohol abuse, sex, racism, bullying and loneliness but the tendency in the 70s was to make such issues the point around which the whole plot revolved. As a result, many early 'problem' teen novels, while a huge step forward from their predecessors, wound up being rather worthy and humourless.

Addiction to hard drugs was an intractable problem by the early 70s. Most YA novels dealing with the issue were keen either to condemn what they saw as a product of the 'new permissiveness', or to situate such behaviour within a social context. A Hero Ain't Nothin' but a Sandwich falls into the latter category; it highlights the realities of heroin addiction in the African American community via the perspectives of various people involved with a 13-year-old junkie. The despair and confusion of many at the failure of civil rights and black power movements to bring about systemic change is well captured, and the author also explores other issues, such as the rise of a black middle class and the role of hard drugs in deflecting political resistance. The device of using a variety of first-person statements to relate its plot can become laboured at times, but the novel maintains its hold on the reader through a cleverly open-ended denouement and its fiercely political outlook.

One of the first—and most popular—YA novels to depict African American life from an African American perspective, A Hero Ain't Nothin' but a Sandwich earned its author, an established Harlem playwright, a number of awards. Its use of Black English and its graphic treatment of drugs and sex also drew controversy, and the book was removed from some school libraries. The novel then became part of a legal battle, resulting in a Supreme Court ruling that while school boards could determine the general curriculum, they could not ban or withhold books from their general libraries. Such notoriety, plus solid sales, ensured that the book was made into a film, for which Childress wrote the screenplay, in 1978.

IAIN MCINTYRE

AVON FLARE • 0-380-00132-2 • (CANADA $3.50) • U.S. $2.95

A HERO Ain't Nothin' BUT A Sandwich

Alice Childress
Author of RAINBOW JORDAN

Benjie is young, black, and well on his way
to being hooked on heroin.
"Brilliant...exciting...entertaining"
The New York Times

A Hero Ain't Nothing but a Sandwich (Avon, 1974)

C hildren got nothin to eat in the house . . . they livin offa Kool-Aid and crackers, plus what they can lift . . . while moms is waitin for the big "hit." Kids meanwhile comin down with ringworm and pellagra. Everybody lookin for a quick miracle . . . some kind of easy way to make it without buggin whitey too much.

Don'tcha know that if a fix could fix things I'd shoot skag myself? Nothin is for free . . . not even a feelin. Some-a these whiteys usin horse cause they feelin bad bout how good it's suppose to be for them but they seein how it ain't goin down that way. The parents done sent big brother's ass off to get murdered . . . smiled and waved "good-bye" to the boys. "Send him to the Army, that'll keep him outta trouble." They pushin war, dig it? Ain't no way to live without pushin somethin. They ain't stopped horse from ridin through the Army—or anywheres else.

Me, I say screw the weak and screw the power. If it's call free enterprise then let it be free. Nother thing, if I had my way bout it, I wouldn't be related to a Black-ass nigga on this earth. All them that wanta die let em put a five in my pocket, and I'll help em to slowly make it on outta here, with a smile on their face . . . and one on mine. Less of them makes more room for me! The hell with the junkie, the wino, the capitalist, the welfare checks, the world . . . yeah, and fuck you, too!

FRANK BONHAM'S DOGTOWN

The realistic teen novel that dealt with serious issues such as divorce, unwed pregnancies, suicide, sex and gang violence can be said to have truly begun in the 1950s. Its beginnings were much like those of rock-and-roll, boasting of rebellion, boredom, and youth with too much time on their hands. It was also a reflection of writers who grew up during the Depression and were no strangers to disappointment, hard times, and survival by any means possible.

As pulp magazines died out, they were quickly replaced by TV and mass-market paperbacks. A fiction subgenre categorized by juvenile delinquency heralded in the talents of writers such as Irving Shulman and Evan Hunter. The film *Rebel Without a Cause* helped popularize this sentiment, yet for a teenager to read JD books was still viewed as a somewhat delinquent activity in and of itself.

At the same time, books actually marketed to teens usually dealt with "safer" themes and were marked less by action than by strong character development. Two excellent writers in this field were John R. Tunis, a sports writer, and Beverly Cleary, a librarian; both also wrote for younger children. Thrown into this mix were more literary titles, such as J.D. Salinger's *The Catcher in the Rye* (1951), a model for YA fiction that set the standard for epiphanies in coming-of-age novels.

Frank Bonham was a pulp writer of this generation who in the late 60s turned his talents to writing edgy books for teenagers that dealt with social issues. His work helped bridge the gap between the grittiness of the pulp delinquent books and the humor and character development of less heavy-handed books by authors who focused on younger readers. His books received rave reviews and were even used by teachers in schools, heralding the era of psychologically focused YA novels aimed directly at teenagers.

Much of this had to do with Dell's Laurel-Leaf imprint, which brought together a range of such books originally issued by different publishers. These inexpensive pocket editions were edited by a professor of elementary education at New York University and another professor from Kean College. Their efforts helped usher in the breakout period for Young Adult books, including debuts by S.E. Hinton (*The Outsiders*, 1967) and Paul Zindel (*The Pigman*, 1968), to name just two authors whose debut books have become classics and remain in print to this day.

Bonham, born in 1914, had already established himself as a top-notch western writer with over 25 novels in print. He grew up in Los Angeles and began his writing career at 20, churning out short stories for pulp magazines and ghostwriting for sci-fi and adventure author Ed Repp, through which he learned how to fill his stories with action. He also tried his hand at television writing and sold a dozen scripts to Hollywood in the 50s. Bonham's writing was successful enough that he never held a 'real' job his entire life, and he remained prolific, publishing over 60 books in all. After his death in 1989, his western short stories had something of a revival in collections edited by mystery writer and pulp historian Bill Pronzini.

Durango Street (Dutton, 1965)

Durango Street is one of the first hard-edged novels dealing with gang violence that was marketed directly to teens. It also differs from its 50s predecessors in focusing exclusively on minority gangs; its protagonist is an African American. As an essayist in the *St. James Guide to Young Adult Writers* wrote: "Writing about a black teenager growing up and living in a ghetto was not the usual setting or model character that teenagers normally read about in the young adult books available in the early 60s. Frank Bonham was, in part, responsible for introducing social realism into young adult fiction."

Durango Street would be the first in a series of novels set in the fictionalized city of Dogtown, based on Watts and neighbouring, similarly impoverished communities in L.A. Published in 1965, its subject matter was so timely that it was published in the same week as the Watts riots. Bonham spent a year doing firsthand research into the area, gaining access to agencies in the area that worked directly with juvenile gangs. He visited camps, accompanied gang members at outings, spoke with gang members' families and met with both psychologists and social workers.

The end product of Bonham's research is far different from a book like David Wilkerson's *The Cross and the Switchblade* (1963), for example, which had a more heavy-handed objective. Instead of preachy reportage, Bonham created fiction from the facts he'd learned, in order to bring the reader into the complex personal life of one particular 'headman' and drew sympathy to social problems at large by focusing on this character. According to Bonham, in an essay for *Horn Book* magazine:

I became impressed with the tremendous challenge in rehabilitating a gang boy or girl. If rehabilitation means 'to restore to a former capacity,' then it is impossible. You cannot restore a capacity one has never possessed, and these young people never had a capacity for anything but hard luck and defeat. But with sufficient patience and skill, ideas of ambition, justice, and hope can be implanted.

Because Bonham's books addressed such issues directly, and fulfilled this need, they were well received by kids, as well as reviewers.

Durango Street begins as Rufus Henry is released from a juvenile detention camp. He has been sent there for stealing and wrecking a car. There is realism to the character for he appears both street-smart and skeptical of advice. When he goes back home to Dogtown, it is obvious from his family and surroundings that this is not the land of opportunity. His parole officer forbids Rufus to join a gang. Yet from the perspective of Rufus, joining a gang is a matter of survival.

After a quick attempt at going straight, by getting a job at a car repair shop, Rufus is quickly turned off when the owner talks down to him. It becomes apparent that Rufus's main characteristic is his pride. The reader gets glimpses of this through the manner with which he interacts with his siblings. Even more so, it is the way that Rufus interacts with other gang members. He is fearless.

This pride stems from Rufus being a fatherless child. As a kid, his mother told him a story that his birth father was Ernie Brown, a well-known halfback in the pro football leagues. While the reader never learns for sure whether or not this is fact or fiction, Brown becomes a hero for Rufus. Just the thought of big Ernie Brown as his protector gives Rufus the ability to escape from dangerous situations. Rufus has a scrapbook of Ernie's achievements, but keeps it hidden. The book is a record of his hopes and dreams and he dare not let anyone know of it, lest these aspirations get smashed.

When Rufus runs into trouble with a gang called the Gassers, he is literally backed into an alley. Using his wits and a broken milk bottle to escape, he realizes his troubles are not going to end there. He decides to meet up with the Moors, a rival gang he heard about through a friend he met while in the detention camp.

Joining the gang does not prove easy, though. Its leader, Bantu, and the other members induct Rufus by beating on him. After his parole officer finds out Rufus has been initiated, he assigns the gang a social

Durango Street (Scholastic, 1967)
Frank Bonham. Photo by Victor Avila

worker, Alex Robbins. The Moors, knowing that they are dealing with the law, reluctantly agree to meet with Robbins.

As the battle between the gangs grows more violent, Rufus overthrows Bantu in a fight, taking his place as headman. Angered after the Gasser's headman, Simon, threatens his sister, Rufus devises a plan to get revenge. He blows up the Gassers' car, attempts to get some of the other rival gangs to back him up, and subsequently gets hold of a rifle as part of his plan to remove Simon from the neighborhood.

The story takes a turn when Robbins is able to get both the Moors and the Gassers to attend a football training session with Ernie Brown. Rufus is thrilled to meet Ernie, yet manages to keep the father stuff a secret. But Simon manages to find out about his scrapbook and steals it. When he mockingly talks of the scrapbook to Ernie, Rufus's pride is hurt and he is filled with contempt.

Finally, Rufus devises a plan to rid himself of Simon. This involves organising a dance, a huge event with a band and paid admission, where he will either humiliate Simon or start World War Three. To his surprise, however the dance turns out to be a success, thanks to Robbins's help, and the encouragement of Rufus's new girlfriend Judy. At the end of the book, Rufus is still skeptical about his future, but it seems possible he may begin to see some good in Robbins's advice and start on the path back to school.

Perhaps the reason this book has stayed in print for over 30 years is that its story is so personal. In Bonham's own words: "To some extent I am a do-gooder in my books for young people, in that I often deal with a subject such as delinquency, in the hope that something I say in the book will have a positive effect on a young reader with personal problems."

After the publication of S.E. Hinton's *The Outsiders* two years later, *Durango Street* would get overlooked in discussions of the essential teenage gang novel. In fact, though the two books are very different, *The Outsiders* is a raw tale written by a teenager, while *Durango Street* is a well-researched book by a seasoned pro. The fact that Bonham is white takes nothing away from the fact that these characters are distinctly African American. Because of the author's skill in writing action he is as comfortable here as he is in the western genre. For example, he does not shy away from his characters using the N-word.

Parts of the material—the cultural references, for example—may be somewhat outdated, but for the most part the book remains relevant and retains an edge for modern teen audiences. In many ways it was the predecessor of films such as John Singleton's *Boyz n the Hood* (1991) or even Walter Dean Myers's Young Adult novel *Scorpions* (1988).

After the publication of *Durango Street*, Bonham wrote almost exclusively for young adults; he did not publish another western novel until the 1980s. And he was not the only writer to follow this trend: William Campbell Gault, a successful pulp fiction writer, also from Southern California, turned to writing juvenile fiction that dealt with social issues in the 60s when he saw the market changing and could no longer sell mysteries. Like Bonham, he would return to writing in his original genre in the 1980s.

The Nitty Gritty (Dutton, 1968)

In the three years following *Durango Street*, Bonham published five more novels for young adults—and he produced another 14 by 1984. Few of these books received multiple printings or had the longstanding renown of the first, but with each book Bonham continued to hone his skills. In *The Nitty Gritty*, his most well-known title after *Durango Street*, he loosens up a little, taking a step back from his research into gangs to show a lighter side to Dogtown.

This time the story is set on Ajax Street and focuses on Charlie Matthews, who has dropped out of school—not to steal cars, but to shine shoes. Like the famous play *A Raisin in the Sun* (1959) by Lorraine Hansberry, which is referenced in the book, this tale is set within a struggling black family unit and highlights the contrast between their poverty and their dreams.

The story begins as the Matthews family gathers over a dinner of 'soul food' in their decrepit apartment. Both parents are exhausted, stressed out by their jobs and the struggle to get by. Their son Charlie, lost in daydreams, pays little attention. He fantasizes about striking it rich, about a homeless man who tips him off about buried treasure, and about escaping Dogtown. He is a kid still filled with hope despite the grievances of his family. He is often quickly brought back down to earth by his jaded parents, who have no complaints about him missing school if he's able to make a contribution to the family's funds.

Luckily, there is an adult who believes in Charlie. Mr. Toia, his schoolteacher, recognizes his potential as a talented writer, and attempts to get his parents to ensure that he returns to school. For Charlie's parents, college and similar opportunities seem like a silly dream. Like the social worker, Robbins, in *Durango Street*, Mr. Toia insinuates himself into the family, but his voice, while that of conscience, is not always listened to.

Charlie seeks to replace his unsympathetic father with his own personal hero, his Uncle Baron. Baron is an uneducated drifter and gambler with an upbeat disposition. His adventurous stories, musical talent and freewheeling ways offer an alternative to Charlie. For Charlie, Baron symbolizes a ticket out of Dogtown with a more alluring pull than education.

When Uncle Baron unexpectedly arrives in a Volkswagen van he's been living in, Charlie is ecstatic. Baron tells him that he has plans to strike a deal in Dogtown. Once made, he boasts, this arrangement will help him make some big money. Charlie eagerly agrees to help. When he finds out that Uncle Baron needs $150 to set his plan in motion, Charlie is determined to make this impossibility a reality.

This is where the story gets truly interesting. Bonham introduces a slew of quirky, eccentric characters and comedic situations that set Charlie and Baron on a series of escapades. Such characters include Cowboy, a tough high school rival (and possibly a tongue-in-cheek reference to Bonham's western books), whose boots Charlie sets ablaze while working at the shoeshine parlor. Then, there is Breathing Man, one of Bonham's most fascinating characters, who appears in several of his books. Breathing Man sleeps sitting up and counts his breaths when awake, hasn't worked in 15 years, yet somehow manages to survive better than most in Dogtown. Charlie seeks out Breathing Man as a sort of ghetto sage and finds he is more than happy to impart advice.

Snapping out of his daydreams of healing the sick and being elected Mayor, Charlie decides it's time to hustle by salvaging bottles and bricks from a junk lot. He also finds some treasures, including $30 worth of antique coins that almost get stolen by Cowboy. The funniest part though, is when Charlie gets tipped off to a man who claims that he'll buy ladybugs, if he can manage to bag some from a canyon out East. Baron and Charlie take a road trip and discover a treasure trove of the tiny red and black insects. They gather a sack load, but the ladybugs escape in the van as they are driving back to the city, and their attempts to recapture them and drive at the same time lead to a hilarious scene.

Later in the story, Charlie and his friend Caesar become contenders in a ridiculous boxing match that includes animal blood and an oiled-up ring. They also make some extra dollars by visiting a blood bank. Surprisingly, Charlie is able to exceed his original goal of $150. He gladly hands over this hard-earned money to his great Uncle Baron while still enthusiastic about his hero's plans.

Charlie looks forward to seeing the machine that Baron has promised to purchase with his earnings, but is disappointed when he realizes the $150 has gone towards the purchase of a fighting rooster that Baron intends to enter and bet on in an illegal cockfight. When the cock is destroyed, so are Charlie's dreams, and the Baron takes off leaving the boy behind.

Back in Dogtown, Charlie comes to terms with his daydreams. Realizing that only he can choose the direction of his life and find a path out of the ghetto, he learns that he cannot follow the advice of his parents or his heroes and must take pride in himself.

Bonham's message is not your typical coming-of-age tale for it deals with a particular type of pride, black pride, as well as survival in a place of urban decay. Fortunately, the author infuses this story with enough energy and humor to balance out the hardship. The conclusion, as in *Durango Street*, remains open for the reader to decipher. The situations are so tight and fully realized, the characters so engaging, that reading *The Nitty Gritty* brings to mind images of a lost blaxploitation movie classic penned by a pulp giant while still maintaining a PG rating. It is also a book with rhythm, its language soulful yet unpretentious. In my opinion, it's an even greater work than *Durango Street, and* its clever chapter titles add an extra zing. One of these, 'Hey, Big Spender', Bonham would later use for another of his Dogtown books.

Mystery of the Fat Cat (Dutton, 1968)

This novel is also set in Dogtown but seems to be aimed at a younger audience. The story begins, when Buddy, a lifeguard at the Dogtown Boys Club, gets bitten by a rat in the swimming pool. When the club is then closed down, and the manager's liberal views on marijuana become widely known, its only chance of survival rests on a fortune a wealthy woman has left the institution with one stipulation: that it not be passed on until her cats have enjoyed it first. But is the money in fact being smuggled away by some real-life 'fat cats'? This novel is perhaps most notable for Bonham's depiction of Buddy's brother, Ralphie, a sensitive depiction of a child with autism most likely based on Bonham's own son.

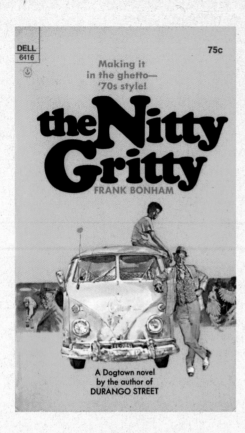

The Nitty Gritty (Dell, 1975)

Hey, Big Spender! (Dell, 1976)

Viva Chicano (Dutton, 1970)

Viva Chicano allowed Bonham to focus on a different group in his fictional Dogtown; it follows the story of Keeny, a Mexican-American. Unfairly blamed for his brother's death, the protagonist is on the run from both the law and the atmosphere of his home and neighborhood. He is helped by members of a gang, the Aztecs, when he hides out in an abandoned building. Through his subconscious, he converses with a cardboard dummy of Emiliano Zapata he stole from a theater, trying to find a solution to his dilemma. There is a lot happening in this book, including a gang fight and drug references, making it one of Bonham's stronger entries around the theme of youth being presumed guilty until proven innocent.

Hey, Big Spender! (Dutton, 1972)

Frank Bonham takes readers on their wildest ride yet through Dogtown in *Hey, Big Spender!* The book's main character is Cool Hankins, first introduced in *Mystery of the Fat Cat.* The 17-year-old Cool is just what his name suggests. He wears blue glasses and a floppy hat, and walks around with a confident bounce in his step. Cool seems freer than Bonham's other characters, driving a Buick and later a Harley; he recalls images from movies like *The Monkey Hu$tle* (1976) that have the same sort of funky rhythm (but minus the cheesiness). Despite the ease with which Cool gets around, though, life remains difficult for him; he lives in a foster home with several other children and his aunt. He acts as a big brother to the other kids, and gets by because of his familiarity with people and the hard times around him.

When the story begins, Cool is working a summer job doing gardening chores. He is approached by Monique, his female counterpart, who alerts him that Breathing Man has recently left the hospital and wants to see him. Breathing Man, who had an important role in *The Nitty Gritty*, is an even more interesting character here. He is still Dogtown's wise elder, doing just fine avoiding work and sitting outside all day in front of the Hob Nob Pool Parlor. In winter he lives under the Fourth Street Bridge; come summer he finds his home among a mass of underground storm drains.

When they meet outside the Hob Nob, Breathing Man offers Cool a job. At first Cool takes this as a put-on. Later, when he is handed a hundred-dollar bill, he begins to be swayed. He agrees to meet Breathing Man in his underground hideaway in order to discuss his secret plan. Breathing Man draws him a map while Cool remains skeptical.

On his trip through the storm drains, Cool encounters a community of subterranean hippies who avoid the hardships of Dogtown by staying out of the daylight. Then he finds Breathing Man, living alone in his neat, minimalist alcove. The older man explains that he is the inheritor of the Le Duke fortune, which pretty much makes him the richest black man that ever lived. Cool doesn't know what to believe, but when Breathing Man shows him a safe stacked with hundred-dollar bills, he is convinced. It turns out that the inheritance totals over $650,000.

Breathing Man believes any sort of excitement is bad for his health, and fears the prospect of inheriting this amount might kill him. He would prefer to 'do right' by giving the money to those in need. But he does not want to give the money to a charity, for he thinks it would go to waste on the salaries of those who work for such organizations. Instead, he wants to give the money—in cash—directly to the people in Dogtown who need it most; to the people the system has not been able to help. He has chosen Cool to act as middleman because he knows the boy, trusts him and believes he has a lot of heart.

Cool is wise to the fact that this is too big a job for just one kid to handle. Regardless, because of Breathing Man's trust, and because he can earn a hundred a week, Cool reluctantly agrees. He is also supplied with a brand-new custom chrome-plated Harley-Davidson motorcycle (with "HOPE" painted on the tank), so that he can deliver the goods in style. Cool quickly sets up shop by renting a store front and advertising "FREE Money" on a handmade sign taped to the window. Both the landlord and his friends are surprised when he attempts to explain the nature of his business, keeping Breathing Man's identity anonymous. Confused, one friend remarks, "If it's free, it isn't money. And if it's money, it isn't free . . ."

The ideas is to get people to line up outside, so Cool can let them in one by one, listen to their hard-luck stories, and take notes. At night he will then visit the Breathing Man to share the stories and allow the benefactor to pick a winner each day. The requested amount will then be given to Cool to deliver. On opening day there is only one visitor, a down-and-out white man named Snow who needs a set of tools to get his life back on track. Breathing Man agrees to help Snow, despite his race.

News spreads quickly and things begin to get out of hand. Monique acts as Cool's assistant and attempts to organize the crowds that begin to form outside the shop. Cool takes on the role of a social worker. He listens to the horrible tales of woe and tries to weigh in on who has it worst. It's never an easy decision. Nevertheless, money does get delivered, and Cool quickly picks up the nickname 'Big Spender'.

Not only do hard decisions follow; so does trouble. Cool has a run-in with a man who might be his estranged father. Then, he is threatened by Rat Ass, the chain-twirling leader of a motorcycle gang. Soon Cool is racing for his life, ducking into storm drains on his Harley. He keeps his wits about him and survives by creating an oil slick that wipes out both Rat-Ass and his bike. The trouble doesn't end there, though: the gang get their revenge by firebombing Cool's bike and nearly setting his foster home ablaze.

The final straw comes when Snow returns to the free-money office drunk, and asking for more help. This convinces Cool that while Breathing Man's intentions are good, his plan might not actually be helping at all. Disappointment sets in until Cool's aunt comes up with an alternative solution. And this is where Bonham's philosophy comes into play: it is agreed that if people in Dogtown need help, they need it early in life. A decision is made to help the hundreds of homeless children living in the slum by setting them up in foster homes. This is evidently a social cause close to Bonham's heart, but he makes it clear not by being didactic, but by being a pioneer in bringing such subjects to teen fiction.

The Golden Bees of Tulami (Dutton, 1974)

Cool Hankins was such a strong character that Bonham decided to write another Dogtown story featuring him and Breathing Man. This time, Cool is being pressured by his peers to join a gang. Violence is averted, however, when he meets an African stranger who has a solution in the form of a honey that seems to prevent crime. As word spreads about the positive effects of the Golden Bees, the government tries to destroy the stranger and co-opt his product. For those in power, could peace be economically disastrous? Again, Cool faces the quandary that easy solutions do not always solve difficult problems.

DAVID KIERSH

Go Ask Alice – Anonymous [Beatrice Sparks] (Prentice-Hall, 1971)

Thanks to long-running patterns of domestic violence, family breakdown, and plain boredom, the figure of the teen runaway is a familiar one in American society. During prolonged periods of economic hardship and social fracturing, such as the Great Depression of the 1930s, the numbers of young people fleeing their homes mushroomed into tens if not hundreds of thousands.

The intergenerational, cultural and political conflicts of the mid 60s and early 70s also sparked a massive exodus of youth out of small towns and suburbs and into hippie strongholds such as San Francisco's Haight-Ashbury and New York's Lower East Side. Despite the efforts of radical groups (like the Diggers and Up Against The Wall Motherfuckers) to feed, accommodate and protect runaways, their sheer numbers overwhelmed many fledgling alternative communities. Whilst some runaways enjoyed new-found freedoms, the neglect and desperation that ensued for many left them vulnerable to sexual and other predators.

As the issue became a national concern in the late 60s, it is unsurprising that writers associated with the emerging 'teen problem' genre turned their hand to tales involving runaways. 'Young Adult' mainstays, including Barbara Wersba, Jeanette Eyerly and Fran Arrick, produced novels on the topic, generally working in associated themes of drug use, premarital sex, sex work, and pregnancy, but often misunderstanding or ignoring the realities of communal life and youth culture.

The biggest seller in the field was without a doubt 1971's Go Ask Alice. Marketed as the genuine confessions of an anonymous 15-year-old victim of the streets, the unnamed diarist's descent into drug hell is rapid by anyone's measure. Despite being an ordinary kid with few problems at home, she goes from being dosed with acid to losing her virginity, gulping down sleeping pills and injecting speed within a week. Not much later we find her dealing LSD to nine-year-olds (who are in turn selling to their younger schoolmates), before she winds up strung-out and victimized by a series of older drug users. Despite the support of her concerned and loving parents, various attempts to restart her life come to naught. She soon winds up back on drugs, and then dead.

The over-the-top plot had some doubting its authenticity from the outset, but Go Ask Alice nevertheless proved a hit, selling over four million copies. A school reading list favourite, the book generated further controversy—and sales—because it was consistently targeted by conservative grassroots committees who were keen to ban anything mentioning sex and drugs from school and public libraries. To complete its iconic status, the novel was made into a TV movie in 1973, starring William Shatner and Andy Griffith.

The book's 'true story' status took a major hit with the release of Jay's Journal in 1979, which was promoted as the latest book from Beatrice Sparks, a middle-aged Mormon and volunteer youth counsellor, now revealed as the 'editor' of Go Ask Alice. If Alice had been on a wild ride, then Jay went even further, indulging in black masses, cattle mutilation and angel-dust binges, before following 'Alice' into the grave. When she was quizzed in interviews over the similarly stilted writing styles of the two books—and the two diarists' tendency to ignore contemporary music, movies, and events—Sparks modified her previous assertions. She now claimed that she had compiled various clients' diaries into a single narrative in Go Ask Alice and, while keeping the identity of 'Alice' a secret, she named the real Jay as a recently deceased teen called Alden Barrett. Unfortunately for Sparks, Barrett's family disowned the book, claiming the author had taken a few genuine diary entries and expanded them into a full-blown occult tale.

Further revelations, including a 1998 claim in the New York Times that teen/children's author Linda Glovach had co-written Go Ask Alice, have long seen the book reclassified as fiction. Despite this, many continue to consider it an authentic tale, a belief Sparks was happy to exploit with the publication of a further eight 'anonymous' diaries before her death in 2012.

IAIN McINTYRE

ANONYMOUS

'No one can read this book without crying for the young who find the world we have built too much to bear.' – *Sunday Mirror*

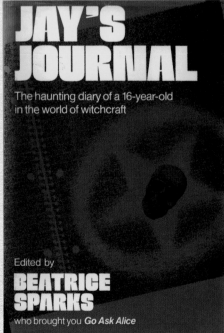

The haunting diary of a 16-year-old in the world of witchcraft

Edited by

BEATRICE SPARKS

who brought you *Go Ask Alice*

Go Ask Alice (Corgi, 1973)
Jay's Journal (Times, 1978)

Dear close, intimate, warm friend Diary,
     What a fantastic, unbelievable, expanding, thrilling week I've had. It's been like wow—the greatest thing that ever happened. Remember I told you I had a date with Bill? Well he introduced me to Torpedos on Friday and [the drug] Speed on Sunday. They are both like riding shooting stars through the Milky Way, only a million, trillion times better. The Speed was a little scary at first because Bill had to inject it right into my arm. I remembered how much I hated shots when I was in the hospital, but this is different, now I can't wait, I positively can't wait to try it again. No wonder it's called Speed! I could hardly control myself, in fact I couldn't have if I had wanted to, and I didn't want to. I danced like I have never dreamed possible for introverted, mousy little me. I felt great, free, abandoned, a different, improved, perfected specimen of a different, improved, perfected species. It was wild! It was beautiful! It really was.

High School Pusher—Jack W. Thomas (Bantam, 1977)

Jack W. Thomas's *High School Pusher* has exactly the same feel as the mid-day movies I used to watch on commercial television in the late 70s and 80s. A teen cautionary tale about hard drugs and fast sex, what sets it apart from the legion of similarly themed books is the superior writing and almost noir sensibility.

East Lake High is a school in a suburb that feels like it's come out of a kit, located in the great expanse of California suburbia. The sun always shines and the kids run riot. The teachers want to intervene but are powerless to do anything. The parents are gormless. They don't think their offspring are out of control, just misunderstood.

Joy is a drug pusher and the king of East Lake High. The book opens with Joy's two thugs, 'Battery' and 'Beak', beating up another kid, 'Pinch'. The violence brings Joy to the attention of Lee, the school counsellor and only black member of staff. Lee's a Vietnam vet, worked in ghetto schools in New York before moving to East Lake. He knows Joy is a bad apple and tries to get Pinch to incriminate him, but he won't. All Pinch wants is Joy's approval.

Meanwhile, 'good girl' Zane (short for Zandra) starts dating Joy. She finds him attractive in a sleazy sort of way. He's also got a great panel van, complete with shag-pile carpet and air conditioning. Zane has grown a bit of marijuana in the attic of her parent's house, nothing serious, but Joy introduces her to harder stuff, acid and speed. Soon she's having sex with him in the back of his panel van (which, in a prescient, much earlier form of sexting, he photographs with an instamatic camera), helping him do drug deals and hiding his stash of hard drugs in her parent's attic.

Joy continues to abuse gentle-natured Pinch, who eventually breaks down and in a graphic homage to Vietnam, sets himself on fire. This brings out Lee's latent post-traumatic stress and the counsellor becomes almost fanatical in his determination to get the dealer. Unbeknown to Zane, her younger sister is aware of her habit of hiding marijuana in the attic. Then the younger sister finds the stash of Joy's hard drugs that Zane hid there, and ODs.

Jack W. Thomas was a youth probation officer in Los Angeles Country for six years. He'd no doubt seen his share of teen tragedies and the experiences obviously went into *High School Pusher* and the ten similarly themed novels he wrote for Bantam in the 70s. He dealt with a drug-running biker in *The Bikers* (1972), a hellhole reform school for girls in *Girls Farm* (1974), and a sexually out-of-control teenage girl in *Turn Me On!* (1972).

Thomas's books have sold an estimated 1.5 million copies and been translated into several languages; sadly, they are all now out of print.

ANDREW NETTE

High School Pusher (Bantam, 1977)

D rugs were an integral part of high school, like cheerleaders and the dean's list. Occasional fights, busts or freakouts in the john surprised only Pollyanna staff or hopelessly naive students. To some, the irony of Pinch being thumped on just before the annual 'Back-to-School Drug-Horror Assembly' was amusing. East Lake's principal, Darrell Fisher, had decreed that sometime during the first few weeks of each new fall term all students would be re-alerted to the dangers of chemical euphoria. Summer was over; grass, pills, and booze time was at an end. Ordinarily, a narc, ex-addict, or Jesus Freak was engaged to run down the drugs scene the way it really was.

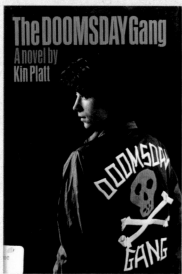

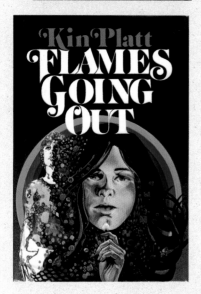

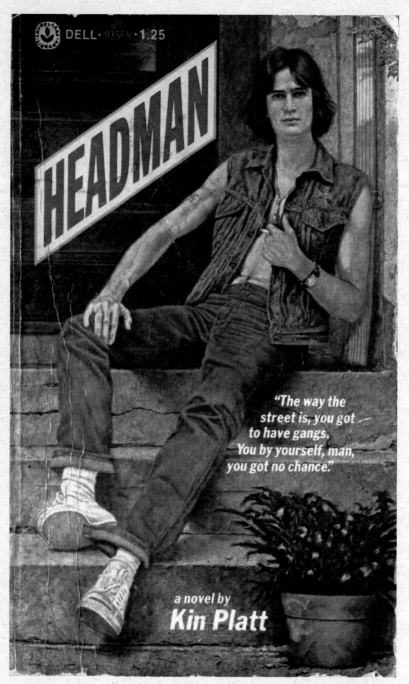

The Terrible Love Life of Dudley Cornflower (Bradbury Press, 1976)

Headman (Dell, 1977)

Flames Going Out (Routledge, 1980)

The Doomsday Gang (Greenwillow, 1978)

GIRL GANGS, BIKER BOYS, AND REAL COOL CATS

KIN PLATT'S YOUNG ADULT NOVELS

What makes a book or author controversial? Dealing with a current topic that the guardians consider too risky to discuss. All my good books were so categorized, and I've done a dozen since that were turned down for the same kind of attack on the injustices and frauds I see.

What makes Kin Platt's books distinctive in the Young Adult field is his sense of humor in dealing with serious subjects. He was probably the most controversial YA writer in the 70s. From 1968 to 1980 he tackled many topics that had previously been taboo in children's books. Nothing was off limits for Platt; he managed to create fiction on such subjects as adolescent male sexuality, divorce and parental neglect, schizophrenia, drug addiction, gang violence, and poverty.

To understand Platt's books it helps to know Platt's history as a caricaturist. In his stories for young adults, caricature sets the stage, setting a Kin Platt book apart from the many teenage dilemma novels of the 1970s that had a realistic or psychological bent. As one reviewer stated, "Platt takes the extreme, end of the line cases as his starting point, eschewing comfortable, typical, and familiar protagonists and situations for his fiction." *Headman* (1975) reads almost like a satire of Frank Bonham's 1965 novel *Durango Street*. *Flames Going Out* (1980), which concerns a schizophrenic adolescent, feels like a cartoonish version of Hannah Green's 1964 national bestseller, *I Never Promised You a Rose Garden*. Platt's talent as a writer lay in presenting true-to-life disturbing situations through the eyes of a humorist.

Platt's first children's book, *The Blue Man*, was published by Harper in 1961. It introduced the character Steve Forrester, who would appear in three more novels. The book was an underground hit with librarians, even though it was attacked at the time by some critics. One reviewer, from the *School Library Journal*, stated that the book "could not be recommended for purchase." Others found something special; comparisons were drawn with J.D. Salinger's *The Catcher in the Rye*, leading Scholastic to put it out in paperback. The story concerns a boy who takes the law into his own hands after he believes a blue-bodied alien has killed his uncle. The subject matter, while tame compared to some of Platt's later books, nevertheless set the standard for his distinctive style.

In the early 60s, Platt relocated to Santa Monica, California. During this time, he also performed in Las Vegas as 'the fastest draw in the West'. His act, learned in the army, consisted of him doing lightning-quick caricatures (in four to five seconds) that were projected onto a wall. From 1963 to 1965 Platt also contributed several stories to humorous comic books and a few war titles that were published by DC Comics. Platt's then wife, Ruth, also helped out by writing romance titles.

Platt's best-remembered contributions to popular entertainment were at the Hanna-Barbera studios, where he helped create the shows *Top Cat* and *The Jetsons* and also wrote for *The Flintstones* and *Jonny Quest*. Of these, *Top Cat*, with its cast of eccentric feline characters who hang out in an alley, best reflected his humor.

Platt's novel *Big Max*, his first mystery for beginning readers, was published by Harper in 1965. His second mystery, *Sinbad and Me*, was rejected by Harper but later bought by Chilton. It won an Edgar in 1967, was reprinted multiple times, and is still remembered and sought out by collectors. Though this book also featured Steve Forrester, it was very different to *The Blue Man*; its strengths relied not on Platt's 'edginess', but his skill as a mystery writer. Platt would go on to write two more Steve Forrester mysteries as well as ten mystery novels for adults, seven of which featured Max Roper, a karate expert private eye who sometimes killed with his hands. These mysteries usually had a sports theme.

In terms of material for teens, Platt's breakthrough book came in 1968, when he was 57. *The Boy Who Could Make Himself Disappear* would launch his career in a new direction. The story concerns Roger Baxter, a boy who is troubled as a result of a dysfunctional family. His mother abuses him and his absent father, who lives in L.A., is a comedy writer who completely ignores his son. As a result, Roger suffers from a severe speech impediment. His problems leave him lost in New York City and on the verge of a mental breakdown, until he finally learns to cope with the help of friends and the direction of a speech therapist.

The novel touched a nerve with readers and heralded a new form of psychologically based YA book. Authors such as Marjorie Kellogg and John Neufeld would later find success with similar material. *The Boy Who Could Make Himself Disappear* was translated

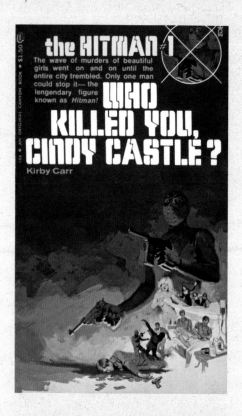

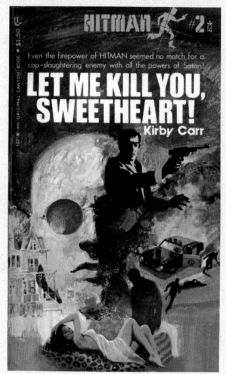

Who Killed You, Cindy Castle? (Canyon Books, 1974)
Let Me Kill You, Sweetheart! (Canyon Books, 1974)

into a number of languages, went through multiple Dell/Laurel-Leaf paperback printings, and was even adapted into a Hanna-Barbera-produced live-action film starring Scott Jacoby. *Hey, Dummy!* (1971) continued his interest in writing about psychologically complex young people. The story centers on the relationship between a boy similar in age to Roger Baxter, who becomes fascinated with an intellectually disabled boy who lives in his neighborhood.

Around this same time Platt also began writing under a number of pseudonyms. Beginning in the late 1960s, he published three 'Adults Only' paperbacks that included *Lovers & Exorcists* (1974, as Wesley Simon York) and *Sex Heel* (1970, as Guy West). The pseudonyms appear to derive from Kin's history of moving back and forth from New York to the West Coast ; he also used the name Nick West in the early 1970s to pen three books in the juvenile series *Alfred Hitchcock's Three Investigators*.

What's more, Platt wrote another eight paperback originals for California publisher Canyon Books from 1974 to 1976, under the name Kirby Carr. This lurid men's adventure series was entitled *The Hitman* and mixed Platt's trademark humor with all the elements you'd expect from a 70s action/exploitation movie. In the 1970s Platt also wrote the occasional comic book story as well as picture books for children based on animated characters.

Platt's final move to the Los Angeles area, where he remained until his death, shifted the settings of most of his titles from New York and New England to California. There is a quality in his late-70s books that resembles the drive-in films being produced in this area at the time; a sort of wildness and absurdist humor worthy of rediscovery. When I see such cult films such as Jack Hill's *The Swinging Cheerleaders* (1974) or *Switchblade Sisters* (1975), I wonder why Platt's out-of print books do not have the same legion of fans.

Platt's two gang novels, *Headman* (1975) and *The Doomsday Gang* (1978), differ greatly from the juvenile delinquency novels that flooded the market in the 1950s. Firstly, Platt's writing style is very direct and he avoids using rhythmic gang slang in favor of straightforward swear words. In addition, the chapters are unswerving and the books are brief, almost as if Platt imagined his audience as delinquents in a detention center with a short attention span. Neither of these titles ends with a moralizing tone. Instead it is anarchy and humor which seems to prevail, reflecting Platt's fondness for the underdog in society. *Headman* has something in common with Frank Bonham's *Durango Street*, a popular book from the 1960s that reflected, perhaps even predicted, the Watts riots. While *Headman* received positive reviews at the time and was later reprinted in paperback format, *The Doomsday Gang* did not impress critics. It is far more satirical, and the absurdist humor includes scenes of teens blowing up a high school and impersonating Hare Krishnas.

For me, Platt's wildest books are two more that were never reprinted in paperback. *The Terrible Love Life of Dudley Cornflower* was published by Bradbury Press in 1976 and may have completely missed the Young Adult audience it was intended for. Told in the first person, this book is an exaggerated view of a 15-year-old with a frustrated sex drive indulging in flights of fancy. Dudley Cornflower seems to be the only teenage virgin left in the entire L.A. area. His anxious, compulsive personality leads him to seek out every piece of advice that might help him achieve the goal of getting laid. His best friend Charley Dell, a self-proclaimed stud, gives him this simple yet torrid advice: **find 'em, feel 'em, fuck 'em.**

After eliminating over two hundred girls in his school as potential prey, Dudley is left with two options. First, there is Kelly Lake, a very sensible girl who also happens to be blind. Her only interest in Dudley seems to lie in trying to figure out why he is such a weirdo. Then there is Dolores Carter, an average-looking girl with a mustache who grabs Dudley's crotch and lets him feel her up in public; he does not have sex with her, though, for fear of catching the clap. Other encounters include sexual experiences in a decked-out 70s love van and nymphomaniacs who hang out amongst library stacks.

Dudley's single mother is portrayed as a swinger who only feeds Dudley's insecurities. Her bluntness is a major cause of his problems. She has been divorced three times and seems to think about sex as often as her son.

It is only through love that Dudley will be able to overcome his obsessions. However, the thin line between getting laid and having a relationship is distorted with hilarious cartoon precision. As in many of his other books, Platt places his character against a backdrop of failed parenting and a world gone mad.

In 1977, librarian and teacher Dorothy M. Broderick wrote to Kin Platt wanting to discuss his book in her new magazine *VOYA*, which was aimed at YA librarians. She asked Kin: "Because there are so many women in our profession, books that speak to the male

The Pushbutton Butterfly (Pyramid, 1973)
Kin Platt in 1980. Photo by Diane Wolfberg

experience are having a particular hard time. Some very nice men in our profession are being made to feel rotten for identifying with Dudley. I'd be interested in your observations."

Kin responded:

To begin with, I knew the subject was risky. The taboo was there but I decided to go against it. I had hoped that the highest level I could write it at might ward off the do-gooders who seek to protect those who might want to learn about life. I also thought Dudley's fantasizing might make it acceptable, and nobody would suffer from the idea and situations inherent in a real boy trying to make it with a real girl. It's funny, of course, that they won't allow this, but the puritan ethic is very strong, and almost everybody fears to come out and openly espouse Dudley, or any other boy in a determined sexual drive.

[However] nobody to my knowledge ever became pregnant from reading a book . . . Perhaps it might have been different if I had done Dudley seriously along the lines Judy Blume took with her most acceptable book *Forever* . . . (We're good friends and her kids love Dudley.) So the factors are that I dared to make fun of a serious situation, spoofed it, made motherhood common and spoiled everyone's notion of their own fantasy lives.

In a 1977 speech that Platt wrote for a talk at a workshop at Kern Library, he spoke about a new YA book he was working on:

I will go back to other forms of madness in our society and their effect on young people. I've started one of a brilliant, wonderful young girl going mad, called *Flames Going Out*—which I had to put aside, and hope now to get back to soon . . . It will be downbeat and depressing, and probably nobody will want it, and they will hope I had never written it. Just as before . . . But hopefully, my own interest and sympathy and understanding will communicate itself to others.

The protagonist of *Flames Going Out*, Tammy Darling, age 16, is a girl lost. She sees a psychologist named Dr. Greengold. He doesn't have any easy answers and has problems of his own—his son Jonathan is a drug addict. Tammy meets Jonathan in the waiting room one day and forms a relationship with the self-destructive boy. The three characters form a sort of triangle of support, as they all are struggling for survival. Tammy is searching for meaning in herself, Greengold is searching for purpose in others, and Jonathan is rebelling against his father while clinging on to Tammy.

The setting is Los Angeles and Platt paints an extremely fierce caricature of this area and time. In this world teenagers are having sex, getting stoned out of their mind, attending disco clubs and listening to punk rock. Tammy has created a double for herself in order to escape from the nightmare of her everyday life. By watching a match burn, she tries to reassure herself that she will not disappear, and that she will not become an object. Tammy is aware of psychology, understands poetry and is far from naive. Nevertheless, she is hiding from the world, and the reader can't blame her.

Platt's other teen books from this time period included a trilogy about an L.A. family struggling with issues of divorce: *Chloris and the Creeps* (1973), *Chloris and the Freaks* (1975) and *Chloris and the Weirdos* (1978). Platt also wrote several shorter books that had high interest for those with a low reading level. These included *Run for Your Life* (1977), *The Ape Inside Me* (1980), *Brogg's Brain* (1981) and *Crocker* (1983). Two others novels, *Dracula, Go Home* (1979) and *Frank and Stein and Me* (1982), were more in the spirit of the Steve Forrester books.

Kin Platt was a renaissance man. A prolific comic book artist, he also dabbled in painting and sculpture. Like the characters in his adult mystery novels, Platt was also athletic and fond of sports. Considering his output as whole, it is Platt's YA novels, written for teens, that remain the most surprising. He would usually start by researching a topic and filling a file with newspaper clippings and quotes. His oeuvre also included several unpublished short stories on youth-oriented topics, as well as two completed novels about sexual abuse that never found an audience. His teen novels were written in his most prolific period, when he balanced writing adult—sometimes even X-rated—material with stuff strictly for kids. They were written at a time when young adult books were a new genre, at least from a marketing perspective. His unique background and world view allowed him, for a short period, to break new ground.

DAVE KIERSH

CONTRIBUTORS

ROBERT BAKER writes about popular culture and is the man behind the Another Nickel in the Machine, a website examining the history of 20th-century London: nickelinthemachine.com.

Born in mid-Michigan and currently living in the Chicago area, **JOE BLEVINS** is a voracious chronicler of popular culture. His online base of operations is d2rights.blogspot.com, a journal whose contents include the heavily researched Ed Wood Wednesdays series. In addition to his day job in market research, he is a regular freelance contributor to the Onion AV Club. Joe's curriculum vitae also includes writing the musical spoof *The Rocky and Bullwinkle Horror Picture Show*, which was performed at the KC Fringe Festival in Kansas City in 2011, and appearing in the 2009 documentary *The Achievers*. Additionally, his work has appeared in such books as *First Time Dead 2* (2011) and *Lebowski 101* (2013).

JAMES COCKINGTON has been writing for *The Sydney Morning Herald* and *The Age* for the past 25 years. Along the way he has written several books on popular culture, including *Mondo Weirdo: Australia in the Sixties* (1992) and *Mondo Bizarro: Australia in the Seventies* (1994). His most recent books, *History Happened Here* (2003) and *Banned* (2005), were published by ABC Books. He has worked for the ABC as a writer/researcher on various TV projects including the 2001 music series *Long Way to the Top* and *Bodgie Dada*, a 1998 history of Australian jazz. He writes for several magazines, including *Australian Muscle Car*. As a teenager his ambition was to be either a stunt driver or greyhound trainer.

BRIAN COFFEY is a Melbourne-based collector of pulp fiction, with a particular interest in Australian pulp. He's been collecting for 15 years or so, after picking up a trashy secondhand novel to read while on a bushwalking trip. As it turned out, the author of the book was Carter Brown, and Brian's been hooked ever since. Rather than achieving great deeds on a sporting field, Brian's ideal Saturday would involve finding some pulp 'gold' in an op shop, and then browsing through his collection of books, while listening to DJ Emma Peel on Melbourne community radio station, 3PBS. His all-time favourite book is James Holledge's 'pulp faction' classic *The Flower People*, published in 1967 by the Horwitz offshoot, Scripts. He also collects secondhand Hawaiian records and loves the soundtrack to the documentary on Erich von Daniken's *Chariots of the Gods* by the Peter Thomas Sound Orchestra.

JAMES DOIG works at the National Archives of Australia in Canberra. He has a particular research interest in obscure and forgotten Australian writers of speculative fiction. He has edited several anthologies and single-author collections of early Australian supernatural and fantasy fiction and published numerous articles on Australian and British popular writers such as H.B. Marriott Watson, Reginald Hodder, H.T.W. Bousfield, and 'Keith Fleming'. He has a PhD in medieval history from Swansea University in Wales.

DAVID JAMES FOSTER writes under the pen name James Hopwood. He is the author of the retro-spy thrillers *The Librio Defection* (2012) and *The Danakil Deception* (2014). Writing as Jack Tunney in 2014, he also wrote *King of the Outback* and *Rumble in the Jungle*, two books in the popular Fight Card series. David can be found at permissiontokill.com.

MATTHEW ASPREY GEAR is an Australian writer and academic, and one of the founding editors of *Contrappasso*. His non-fiction has appeared in *The Los Angeles Review of Books*, *Senses of Cinema*, and *PopMatters*, his fiction in *Crime Factory*, *Island*, *Extempore*, and *Over My Dead Body!* He holds a PhD in media studies from Macquarie University in Sydney. He has lectured extensively on cinema and creative writing. His study of Orson Welles was published by Wallflower Books/Columbia University Press. His website is matthewasprey2.wordpress.com.

MOLLY GRATTAN has turned a longtime fascination with the minutiae of teenage social-problem novels into the long-running YA fiction and pop culture blog mondomolly.com. Growing up near Rochester, New York, she would often haunt the local public library until after closing time, although her attempts to get locked in overnight were always thwarted by the librarians. When she is not writing, she is a Girl Scout leader, a volunteer with a historical theatre and film society, and a vociferous filmgoer. She holds a degree in Media Studies from the City University of New York,

Hunter College and lives Queens, New York, not far from the old stomping grounds of the Amboy Dukes.

BRIAN GREENE's short stories and writing on books, music and film have appeared in over 20 publications since 2008. He is a longtime contributor to *Shindig!* music magazine in the UK and to Macmillan's blog, Criminal Element. His short story "The Notes" won a contest held by Jerry Jazz Musician in 2008. Greene lives in the Triangle Research area of North Carolina with his wife and their two daughters.

Melbourne-based freelance writer **JOHN HARRISON** grew up obsessed with the pop fantasies of Marvel Comics, creepy old amusement parks, glam rock and horror movies, all offset with a grim fascination for the seedier elements in life that came out of growing up in the suburb of St Kilda, at the time one of Australia's major hubs of crime. Aside from contributing to the true crime volumes *Death Cults*, *Bad Cop Bad Cop* and *Guns, Death, Terror*. Harrison has written for such publications as *Fatal Visions*, *Cult Movies*, *Is It Uncut?*, *Filmink*, *Crime Factory*, *Headpress Journal*, *Scary Monsters* and *Bachelor Pad*, as well as penning reviews and liner notes for many releases from Something Weird Video. His book on vintage adult paperbacks, *Hip Pocket Sleaze*, was published in 2012. In 2013, he self-published *Blood on the Windscreen*, a booklet which examined the notorious and violent driver's education films produced in America between 1959 and 1975. He is currently working on several fiction and non-fiction projects.

STEWART HOME is the most out-there writer on the planet—the only person on earth who is visible to the naked eye from outer space. He really does burn that brightly. The *London Review of Books* has praised Home by saying: "I really don't think anyone who is at all interested in literature has any business not knowing the work of Stewart Home." However, this notorious egg bagel eater prefers to liken himself to "a proletarian comedian with Tourette's spewing obscenities." He much prefers standing on his head and reciting sexually explicit passages from his work at public events to courting the literary establishment. More information and much of his writing can be found at stewarthomesociety.org.

DAVE KIERSH was born on Long Island, New York, in 1979. He is the author/illustrator of the self-published book *After School Special* (2012) and *Love is Strange* (2014). For the past ten years he has worked with young people as a public librarian in Boston, Arizona, and Maine.

IAIN McINTYRE is a Melbourne-based author, musician and community radio broadcaster who has written a variety of books on activism, history and music. Recent publications include *How To Make Trouble and Influence People: Pranks, Protest, Graffiti and Political Mischief-Making from across Australia* (2009/2013), *Wild About You: The Sixties Beat Explosion in Australia and New Zealand* (2010), and *Tomorrow Is Today: Australia in the Psychedelic Era, 1966–1970* (2006). He also helped compile the *Down Under Nuggets: Original Australian Artyfacts 1965–1967* CD compilation (2012).

AUSTIN MATTHEWS spends the majority of his time in the 'square' world, where he somehow earns a living by manipulating numbers on gigantic incomprehensible spreadsheets. When he's not doing that he's either listening to mind-bending psychedelic rock or collecting records and associated ephemera from the 60s and 70s. He lives in Reading, England, with his wife and two children, and despises writing about himself in the third person.

ANDREW NETTE is a writer and pulp scholar based in Melbourne, Australia. His first novel, *Ghost Money*, a crime story set in Cambodia in the mid-90s, was published in 2012. He is one of the founders of Crime Factory Publications, a small Melbourne-based press specialising in crime fiction, and co-edited *Hard Labour* (2012), an anthology of Australian short crime fiction, and *LEE* (2014), an anthology of fiction inspired by American cinema icon Lee Marvin. His short fiction, reviews and non-fiction writing has appeared in numerous print and online publications. His online home is pulpcurry.com.

J.F. NORRIS has spent the past 15 years as a bookseller, book collector and critic specializing in genre fiction of the late nineteenth and early 20th century. In collecting and writing about books, his focus is primarily on crime, supernatural, and adventure fiction. He has written numerous critical essays and features on forgotten books and writers for sites like Mystery*File, The Golden Age of Detective Fiction and his own blog, Pretty Sinister Books. He has also contributed essays to *CADS* (Crime and Detective Stories), and *The Weird Review*. Lately he has been supplying introductions and author biographical information for 2013 and 2014 special reprint editions of *The Incredible Adventures of Rowland Hern* (Ramble House), *The Starkenden Quest* and *Desert Town* (both from Raven's Head Press). He lives in Chicago surrounded by crowded bookcases and bookshelves that house nearly 15,000 volumes of unusual books by a myriad of forgotten authors and a handful of well-known ones, too.

BILL OSGERBY is professor of media, culture and communications at London Metropolitan University. His research focuses on 20th-century British and American cultural history, and his books include *Youth in Britain Since 1945* (1997), *Playboys in Paradise: Youth, Masculinity and Leisure-Style in Modern America* (2001), *Youth Media* (2004), and *Biker: Style and Subculture on Hell's Highway* (2007); along with the co-edited anthologies, *Action TV: Tough-Guys, Smooth Operators and Foxy Chicks* (2001), *Subcultures, Popular Music and Social Change* (2013), and *Fight Back: Punk, Politics and Resistance* (2014).

DAVID RIFE is professor emeritus in English at Lycoming College in Williamsport, Pennsylvania, where he taught courses in American literature and modern fiction for 35 years. He is the author of *Jazz Fiction: A History and Comprehensive Reader's Guide* (2007) and co-editor of *The Jazz Fiction Anthology* (2009). He has served as associate editor of the jazz and literature journal *Brilliant Corners* since its inception in 1996. His writings have appeared in such publications as *American Literary Realism*, *Dictionary of Literary Biography*, *Annual Review of Jazz Studies*, *Journal of Modern Fiction* and *The Oxford Companion to Crime and Mystery Writing*. He and his longtime spousal equivalent divide their time between Pennsylvania and Florida while he works—happily but desultorily—on a sequel to *Jazz Fiction* and listens endlessly to the endless recycling of jazz radio.

For the over 30 years, **MIKE STAX** has been the editor and publisher of *Ugly Things* magazine, a rock-and-roll fanzine focusing on the greatest overlooked bands and music of the 1960s and beyond. He has written and edited several rock-related books, and provided liner notes for dozens of reissues, including the track-by-track liners for Rhino's first two *Nuggets* box sets. He is also the lead singer of the San Diego–based rock-and-roll band the Loons. Born in England in 1962, he lives in La Mesa, California, with his wife Anja and their son Philip. ugly-things.com.

NICOLAS TREDELL has published 18 books and over 300 essays, articles and reviews on key topics in literary and film criticism and theory, and on authors from Shakespeare and Dickens to Scott Fitzgerald and Martin Amis. His books include *The Critical Decade* (1993), *Conversations with Critics* (1994), *Cinemas of the Mind: A Critical History of Film Theory* (2002), *Fighting Fictions: The Novels of B.S. Johnson* (2nd ed., 2010), *C.P. Snow: The Dynamics of Hope* (2012), *Shakespeare: The Tragedies* (2014). He is consultant editor of the Palgrave Readers' Guides to Essential Criticism series, which now numbers 71 volumes (7 of which he has himself produced). He formerly taught literature, drama, film and cultural studies at the University of Sussex, UK. One of his special interests is in British writers who emerged in the 'Angry Decade' of the 1950s, such as Laura Del-Rivo, Colin Wilson, Bill Hopkins, John Braine, John Wain and Alan Sillitoe. His website is nicolastredell.co.uk.

ALWYN W. TURNER lectures in cultural and political history at the University of Chichester, and is a widely published writer. Among his books are a critically acclaimed trilogy about modern Britain—*Crisis? What Crisis?* (2008), *Rejoice! Rejoice!* (2010) and *A Classless Society* (2013); his most recent work is *The Last Post: Music, Remembrance and the Great War* (2014). His website is AlwynWTurner.com.

CLINTON WALKER is a Sydney-based writer whom the *Sun-Herald* has called "our best chronicler of Australian grass-roots culture." Born in 1957 in Bendigo, Victoria, he is an art school dropout and recovering rock journalist, and has published nine books, including *Inner City Sound* (1981), *Highway to Hell* (1994), *Football Life* (1998), *Buried Country* (2000), *Golden Miles* (2005) and *History Is Made at Night* (2012). A tenth book, the graphic *Deadly Woman Blues*, is due in 2016. He has also worked extensively in television, most notably for the ABC on the 2001 Oz-rockumentary series *Long Way to the Top* and the late-night live music show *Studio 22*.

ACKNOWLEDGMENTS

This book would not have been possible with the assistance of many people.

Graeme Flanagan, Bill Crider, Lynn Monroe, David Rachels, Bernard Kiker, Trevor Block, Peter Lawrance, Tadhg Taylor, Rallou Lubitz, Bruce Milne, Adele Daniele, Kev Demant, Simon Cruise, David Hyman, Ross Bradshaw, Kevin Patrick, Simon Strong, Addam Duke, John Greco, Mark Young, Steve Holland, and Ellie Marney, as well as our contributors, assisted with sourcing and scanning many of the covers and images that appear in this book.

Special mention needs to be made of Justin Marriott, editor of *The Paperback Fanatic*, who provided a large number of scans for the section on New English Library biker novels. Randall Masteller, who helms the excellent site, Spy Guys & Gals (www.spyguysandgirls.com) provided crucial assistance to source a large number of spy-related pulp covers.

Jim Carroll from the San Francisco Book Company (www.sanfranciscobooksparis.com), kindly provided the ultra-hard-to-get cover of *Tripper* by Jocelyn. The scan of Jane Gallion's *Stoned* is courtesy of the National Archives of Australia. The covers for Terry Taylor's rare *Baron's Court, All Change* are courtesy of Amy Morrin.

The editors would also like to credit the following images:

The author image of Kin Platt by Diane Wolfberg originally appeared on the inside jacket of *Flames Going Out* (Routledge, 1980).

The author image of Frank Bonham appeared on the inside cover flap of his book *Gimme an H, Gimme an E, Gimme an L, Gimme a P* (Scribner, 1980).

The image of author Adam Diment that appears in this book is from the back cover of *The Dolly, Dolly Spy*, Dutton, 1967, and is uncredited.

The comic panels from *Dope Comix* #1 and *Wimmen's Comix* #1 and #5 appear courtesy of Sharon Rudahl.

The following material has been republished, with permission:

'Laura Del-Rivo's The Furnished Room' originally appeared on the site, London Fictions, http://www.londonfictions.com

'The Disappearance of Adam Diment' originally appeared on the site, Another Nickel In the Machine, http://www.nickelinthemachine.com/

'What My Love—Floyd Salas' originally appeared as a post on Andrew Nette's site, Pulp Curry, October 11, 2013

'The Power of the Word' originally appeared as a chapter in *Making Our Own Way: Rural West Virginia Women Artists*, 1990, an unpublished Master of Science in Journalism thesis by Harriet Emerson.

'Bike Boys, Skinheads & Drunken Hacks: Laurence James Interviewed by Stewart Home' and 'Gender, Sexuality and Control in New English Library Youthsploitation Novels of the 1970s', both originally appeared on the website of Stewart Home, http://www.stewarthomesociety.org/

'The Best of British Bovver' is an updated version of the piece '"Bovver" Books of the 1970s: Subcultures, Crisis and Youth-Sploitation Novels', which appeared in *Contemporary British History*, 2012, Volume 26 Issue 3, p299–p331

Earlier versions of 'Frank Bonham's Dogtown' and 'Kin Platt's Young Adult Novels' originally appeared on the Teenage Paperback blog, www.teenagepaperback-blogspot.com

Earlier versions of reviews of *The Amboy Dukes* and *The Grass Pipe* appeared on the blog Lost Classics of Teen Lit, www.mondomolly.wordpress.com

Earlier versions of reviews of *Sappho in Absence*, *Drummer*, and *The Leather Boys* appeared on the website Trash Fiction, www.trashfiction.co.uk

The review for *A Sad Song Singing* originally appeared on the blog Pretty Sinister Books, www.prettysinister.blogspot.com.au

Andrew would like to thank Angela Savage and Natasha for their support throughout the process of putting together this book, as well as for their patience while he checked out opportunity shops, book barns and garage sales to locate pulp paperbacks.

Iain would like to thank Naomi and Ruby for the same.

INDEX

ABOUT PM PRESS

PM Press was founded at the end of 2007 by a small collection of folks with decades of publishing, media, and organizing experience. PM Press co-conspirators have published and distributed hundreds of books, pamphlets, CDs, and DVDs. Members of PM have founded enduring book fairs, spearheaded victorious tenant organizing campaigns, and worked closely with bookstores, academic conferences, and even rock bands to deliver political and challenging ideas to all walks of life. We're old enough to know what we're doing and young enough to know what's at stake.

We seek to create radical and stimulating fiction and non-fiction books, pamphlets, T-shirts, visual and audio materials to entertain, educate, and inspire you. We aim to distribute these through every available channel with every available technology—whether that means you are seeing anarchist classics at our bookfair stalls; reading our latest vegan cookbook at the café; downloading geeky fiction e-books; or digging new music and timely videos from our website.

PM Press is always on the lookout for talented and skilled volunteers, artists, activists, and writers to work with. If you have a great idea for a project or can contribute in some way, please get in touch.

PM Press
PO Box 23912
Oakland CA 94623
510-658-3906
www.pmpress.org

FRIENDS OF PM

These are indisputably momentous times—the financial system is melting down globally and the Empire is stumbling. Now more than ever there is a vital need for radical ideas.

In the many years since its founding—and on a mere shoestring—PM Press has risen to the formidable challenge of publishing and distributing knowledge and entertainment for the struggles ahead. With hundreds of releases to date, we have published an impressive and stimulating array of literature, art, music, politics, and culture. Using every available medium, we've succeeded in connecting those hungry for ideas and information to those putting them into practice.

Friends of PM allows you to directly help impact, amplify, and revitalize the discourse and actions of radical writers, filmmakers, and artists. It provides us with a stable foundation from which we can build upon our early successes and provides a much-needed subsidy for the materials that can't necessarily pay their own way. You can help make that happen—and receive every new title automatically delivered to your door once a month—by joining as a Friend of PM Press. And, we'll throw in a free T-shirt when you sign up.

Here are your options (all receive a 50% discount on all webstore purchases):

- $30 a month: Get all books and pamphlets
- $40 a month: Get all PM Press releases (including CDs and DVDs)
- $100 a month: Superstar—Everything plus PM merchandise and free downloads

For those who can't afford $30 or more a month, we have Sustainer Rates at $15, $10, and $5. Sustainers get a free PM Press T-shirt and a 50% discount on all purchases from our website.

Your Visa or Mastercard will be billed once a month, until you tell us to stop. Or until our efforts succeed in bringing the revolution around. Or the financial meltdown of Capital makes plastic redundant. Whichever comes first.

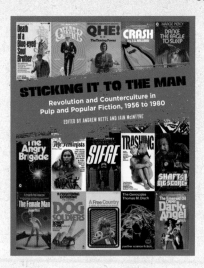

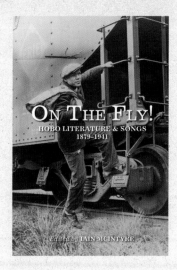

STICKING IT TO THE MAN
Revolution and Counterculture in Pulp and Popular Fiction, 1956 to 1980
Edited by Andrew Nette and Iain McIntyre
$29.95 • ISBN: 978-1-62963-524-8

From Civil Rights and Black Power to the New Left and Gay Liberation, the 1960s and 1970s saw a host of movements shake the status quo. The impact of feminism, anti-colonial struggles, wildcat industrial strikes, and anti-war agitation were all felt globally. With social strictures and political structures challenged at every level, pulp and popular fiction could hardly remain unaffected. Whilst an influx of New Wave nonconformists transformed science fiction, feminist, gay, and black authors broke into areas of crime, porn, and other paperback genres previously dominated by conservative, straight, white males. For their part pulp hacks struck back with bizarre takes on the revolutionary times creating vigilante driven fiction that echoed the Nixonian backlash and the coming conservatism of Thatcherism and Reaganism.

From the late 1950s onwards, *Sticking It to The Man* tracks the changing politics and culture of the period and how it was reflected in pulp and popular fiction in the US, UK, and Australia. Featuring more than 300 full-colour covers, the book includes in-depth author interviews, illustrated biographies, articles, and reviews from more than 30 popular culture critics and scholars. Works by science-fiction icons such as J.G. Ballard, Ursula Le Guin, Michael Moorcock, and Octavia Butler, street-level hustlers turned best-selling black writers Iceberg Slim and Donald Goines, crime heavyweights Chester Himes and Brian Garfield, and a myriad of lesser-known novelists ripe for rediscovery, are explored, celebrated, and analysed.

Contributors include Gary Phillips, Woody Haut, Emory Holmes, David Whish-Wilson, Susie Thomas, Bill Osgerby, Kinohi Nishikawa, Devin McKinney, Scott Aldeberg, Andrew Nette, Victor J. Banis, Cameron Ashley, Mike Dalke, Danae Bosler, Rjurik Davidson, Rob Latham, Michael Gonzales, Iain McIntyre, Donna Glee Williams, Nicolas Tredell, Brian Coffey, James Doig, Molly Grattan, Brian Green, Eric Beaumont, Bill Mohr, J. Kingston Smith, Steve Aldous, David Foster, Joe Weixlmann, and Cheryl Morgan.

ON THE FLY!
Hobo Literature and Songs, 1879–1941
Edited by Iain McIntyre
$27.95 • ISBN: 978-1-62963-518-7

From the 1870s until the Second World War, millions of Americans left their homes to board freight trains that would carry them vast distances, sometimes to waiting work, often to points unknown. Congregating in skid rows, socializing around campfires, and bringing in the nation's crops, these drifters were set apart from conformist America by a lifestyle possessing its own haunts, vocabulary, and cultural, sexual, and ethical standards. Alternatively derided and lionized for their footloose ways and nonconformity, hoboes played a crucial and largely neglected role in the creation of not only America's infrastructure, industry, and agriculture but also its culture, politics, and music.

The first anthology of its kind, *On the Fly!* brings forth the lost voices of Hobohemia. Dozens of stories, poems, songs, stories, and articles produced by hoboes are brought together to create an insider history of the subculture's rise and fall. Adrenaline-charged tales of train hopping, scams, and political agitation are combined with humorous and satirical songs, razor sharp reportage and unique insights into the lives of the women and men who crisscrossed America in search of survival and adventure.

From iconic figures such as labor martyr Joe Hill and socialist novelist Jack London through to pioneering blues and country musicians, and little known correspondents for the likes of the *Hobo News*, the authors and songwriters contained in *On the Fly!* run the full gamut of Hobohemia's wide cultural and geographical embrace. With little of the original memoirs, literature, and verse remaining in print, this collection, aided by a glossary of hobo vernacular and numerous illustrations and photos, provides a comprehensive and entertaining guide to the life and times of a uniquely American icon. Read on to enter a world where hoboes, tramps, radicals, and bums gather in jungles, flop houses, and boxcars; where gandy dancers, bindlestiffs, and timber beasts roam the rails once more.